THE WPA SLAVE NARRATIVES OF OKLAHOMA & TEXAS

A Folk History of Slavery in the United States
From Interviews with Former Slaves
An Original Compilation.

TYPEWRITTEN RECORDS PREPARED BY THE FEDERAL WRITERS' PROJECT 1936-1938. ASSEMBLED BY THE LIBRARY OF CONGRESS PROJECT.

WORK PROJECTS ADMINISTRATION FOR THE DISTRICT OF COLUMBIA SPONSORED BY THE LIBRARY OF CONGRESS

Illustrated with Photographs

VOLUME XIII OKLAHOMA NARRATIVES

Prepared by
the Federal Writers' Project of
the Works Progress Administration
for the State of Oklahoma

WASHINGTON 1941

HISTORIC PUBLISHING
San Antonio, Texas

PREPARED FOR PUBLICATION BY
HISTORIC PUBLISHING
San Antonio, Texas
All Rights Reserved
©2017

HISTORIC PUBLISHING
SLAVE NARRATIVE SERIES™

1) *The WPA Slave Narratives of Oklahoma: A Folk History of Slavery in the United States From Interviews With Former Slaves.* ISBN: 978-1-64227-020-4

2) *Anti-Slavery Leaders Of North Carolina & 75 WPA South Carolina Slave Narratives: A Folk History of Slavery in the United States From Interviews with Former Slaves & The Story of North Carolina's Leading Abolitionists.* ISBN: 978-1642270181

3) *Kansas Slave Narratives & Slave Songs. 136 Authentic Slave Songs With Sheet Music: A Folk History of Slavery in the United States From Interviews with Former Slaves Residing In The State of Kansas. An Original Compilation.* ISBN: 978-1642270174

4) *The WPA Arkansas Slave Narratives Collection. Part VII: A Folk History of Slavery in the United States from Interviews with Former Slaves.* ISBN: 978-1642270167

5) *Kentucky Slave Narratives & The Narrative of the Life of J. D. Green: A Runaway Slave From Kentucky, Containing an Account of His Three Escapes, in 1839, 1846, and 1848. An Original Compilation,* ISBN: 978-1642270150

6) *Alabama WPA Slave Narratives: From Interviews With Former Slaves* ISBN: 978-1642270259

7) Texas Slave Narratives & Photographs: A Traditional History of Slavery in the United States From Interviews with Former Slaves Illustrated with Photographs. Part 3. ISBN-13: 978-1642270129

8) *Texas Slave Narratives & Photographs: A Folk History of Slavery in the United States From Interviews with Former Slaves, Illustrated with Photographs. Part 4.* ISBN: 978-1642270228

9) *Former Slave Narratives & Interviews: From the States of Kentucky and Georgia* ISBN: 978-1642270112

10) *Recorded Audio Slave Narratives & Interviews Transcript Collection: Transcribed from Actual Recordings of Former Slaves.* ISBN-13: 978-1642270235

11) *Florida Slave Narratives: A Folk History of Slavery in the United States From Interviews with Former Slaves,* ISBN-13: 978-1642270013

12) *South Carolina Slave Narratives: A Folk History of Slavery in the United States From Interviews with Former Slaves.* ISBN-13: 978-1946640598

THE WPA SLAVE NARRATIVES OF OKLAHOMA

INFORMANTS

1. ISAAC ADAMS Age 87 yrs. Tulsa, Okla.

2. ALICE ALEXANDER Age 88 yrs. Oklahoma City, Okla.

3. PHOEBE BANKS Age 78 Muskogee, Oklahoma.

4. NANCY ROGERS BEAN Age about 82 Hulbert, Okla.

5. PRINCE BEE Age 85 yrs. Red Bird, Okla.

6. LEWIS BONNER Age 87 yrs. 507 N. Durland Oklahoma City, Oklahoma

7. FRANCIS BRIDGES Age 73 yrs. Oklahoma City, Okla.

8. JOHN BROWN Age (about) 87 yrs. West Tulsa, Okla.

9. SALLIE CARDER Age 83 yrs. Burwin, Okla.

10. BETTY FOREMAN CHESSIER Age 94 years Oklahoma City, Okla.

11. POLLY COLBERT Age 83 yrs. Colbert, Oklahoma

12. GEORGE CONRAD, JR., Age 77 yrs. Oklahoma City, Okla.

13. MARTHA CUNNINGHAM (white) Age 81 yrs. Oklahoma City, Oklahoma

14. WILLIAM CURTIS Age 93 yrs. McAlester, Oklahoma

15. LUCINDA DAVIS Age (about) 89 yrs. Tulsa, Okla.

16. ANTHONY DAWSON Age 105 yrs. 1008 E. Owen St., Tulsa, Okla.

17. ALICE DOUGLASS Age 77 yrs. Oklahoma City, Okla.

18. DOC DANIEL DOWDY Age 81 yrs. Oklahoma City, Oklahoma

19. JOANNA DRAPER Age 83 yrs. Tulsa, Okla.

20. MRS. ESTHER EASTER Age 85 yrs. Tulsa, Okla.

21. ELIZA EVANS Age 87 McAlester, Okla.

22. LIZZIE FARMER Age 80 years McAlester, Okla.

23. DELLA FOUNTAIN Age 69 years McAlester, Oklahoma

24. NANCY GARDNER Age 79 yrs. Oklahoma City, Oklahoma

25. OCTAVIA GEORGE Age 85 yrs. Oklahoma City, Okla.

26. MARY GRAYSON Age 83 yrs. Tulsa, Oklahoma

27. ROBERT R. GRINSTEAD Age 80 yrs. Oklahoma City, Okla.

28. MATTIE HARDMAN Age 78 yrs. Oklahoma City, Okla.

29. ANNIE HAWKINS Age 90 Colbert, Okla

30. IDA HENRY Age 83 Oklahoma City, Okla.

31. MORRIS HILLYER Age 84 yrs. Alderson, Okla.

32. HAL HUTSON Age 90 yrs. Oklahoma City, Okla.

33. WILLIAM HUTSON Age 98 yrs. Tulsa, Okla.

34. MRS. ISABELLA JACKSON Age 79 yrs. Tulsa, Okla.

35. NELLIE JOHNSON

36. MS. JOSIE JORDAN Age 75 yrs. 840 East King St., Tulsa, Oklahoma.

37. "UNCLE" GEORGE G. KING Age 83 yrs Tulsa, Oklahoma

38. MARTHA KING Age 85 yrs. McAlester, Oklahoma

39. GEORGE KYE Age 110 yrs. Fort Gibson, Okla.

40. BEN LAWSON Age 84 yrs. Oklahoma City, Okla.

41. MARY LINDSAY Age 91 yrs. Tulsa, Oklahoma.

42. MRS. MATTIE LOGAN Age 79 yrs. Route 5, West Tulsa, Oklahoma.

43. KIZIAH LOVE Age 93 Colbert, Okla.

44. DANIEL WILLIAM LUCAS Age 94 yrs. Red Bird, Okla.

45. BERT LUSTER Age 85 yrs. Oklahoma City, Oklahoma

46. STEPHEN McCRAY Age 88 yrs. Oklahoma City, Okla.

47. HANNAH McFARLAND Age 85 yrs. Oklahoma City, Okla.

48. MARSHALL MACK Age 83 yrs. Oklahoma City, Okla.

49. ALLEN V. MANNING Age 87 Tulsa, Okla.

50. BOB MAYNARD, AGE 79 23 East Choctaw Weleetka, Oklahoma.

51. JANE MONTGOMERY Age 80 yrs. Oklahoma City, Oklahoma

52. AMANDA OLIVER Age 80 yrs. Oklahoma City, Okla.

53. SALOMON OLIVER Age 78 yrs. Tulsa, Oklahoma.

54. PHYLLIS PETITE Age 83 yrs. Fort Gibson, Okla.

55. MATILDA POE Age 80 yrs. McAlester, Okla.

56. HENRY F. PYLES Age 81 yrs. Tulsa, Okla.

57. CHANEY RICHARDSON Age 90 years Fort Gibson, Okla.

58. RED RICHARDSON Age 75 yrs. Oklahoma City, Oklahoma

59. BETTY ROBERTSON Age 93 yrs. Fort Gibson, Oklahoma

60. HARRIET ROBINSON Age 95 yrs. 500 Block N. Fonshill Oklahoma City, Oklahoma.

61. KATIE ROWE Age 88 yrs. Tulsa, Oklahoma

62. MORRIS SHEPPARD Age 85 yrs. Fort Gibson, Okla.

63. ANDREW SIMMS Age 80 Sapulpa, Okla.

64. LIZA SMITH Age 91 Muskogee, Oklahoma

65. LOU SMITH Age 83 yrs. Platter, Okla.

66. JAMES SOUTHALL Age 82 years, Oklahoma City, Okla.

67. BEAUREGARD TENNEYSON Age 87 yrs. West Tulsa, Okla.

68. WILLIAM WALTERS Age 85 yrs. Tulsa, Oklahoma.

69. MARY FRANCES WEBB Grand daughter of Sarah Vest, aged 92, (deceased) McAlester, Okla.

70. EASTER WELLS Age 83 Colbert, Okla.

71. JOHN WHITE Age 121 years Sand Springs, Okla.

72. CHARLEY WILLIAMS Age 94 yrs. Tulsa, Okla.

73. SARAH WILSON Age 87 yrs. Fort Gibson, Okla.

74. TOM W. WOODS Age 83. Alderson, Okla.

75. ANNIE YOUNG Age 86 Oklahoma City, Okla.

[HW: ***] = Handwritten Note
[TR: ***] = Transcriber Note

OKLAHOMA ILLUSTRATIONS

Facing Page

Lucinda Davis

Anthony Dawson

Katie Rowe

Charley Williams and Granddaughter

Oklahoma Writers' Project
Ex-Slaves

ISAAC ADAMS
Age 87 yrs.
Tulsa, Okla.

I was born in Louisiana, way before the War. I think it was about ten years before, because I can remember everything so well about the start of the War, and I believe I was about ten years old.

My Mammy belonged to Mr. Sack P. Gee. I don't know what his real given name was, but it maybe was Saxon. Anyways we all called him Master Sack.

He was a kind of youngish man, and was mighty rich. I think he was born in England. Anyway his pappy was from England, and I think he went back before I was born.

Master Sack had a big plantation ten miles north of Arcadia, Louisiana, and his land run ten miles along both sides. He would leave in a buggy and be gone all day and still not get all over it.

There was all kinds of land on it, and he raised cane and oats and wheat and lots of corn and cotton. His cotton fields was the biggest anywheres in that part, and when chopping and picking times come he would get negroes from other people to help out. I never was no good at picking, but I was a terror with a hoe!

I was the only child my Mammy had. She was just a young girl, and my Master did not own her very long. He got her from Mr. Addison Hilliard, where my pappy belonged. I think she was going to have me when he got her; anyways I come along pretty soon, and my mammy never was very well afterwards. Maybe Master Sack sent her back over to my pappy. I don't know.

Mammy was the house girl at Mr. Sack's because she wasn't very strong, and when I was four or five years old she died. I was big enough to do little things for Mr. Sack and his daughter, so they kept me at the mansion, and I helped the house boys. Time I was nine or ten Mr. Sack's daughter was getting to be a young woman—fifteen or sixteen years old—and that was old enough to get married off in them days. They had a lot of company just before the War, and they had whole bunch of house negroes around all the time.

Old Mistress died when I was a baby, so I don't remember anything about her, but Young Mistress was a winder! She would ride horseback nearly all the time, and I had to go along with her when I got big enough. She never did go around the quarters, so I don't know nothing much about the negroes Mr. Sack had for the fields. They all looked pretty clean and healthy, though, when they would come up to the Big House. He fed them all good and they all liked him.

He had so much different kinds of land that they could raise anything they wanted, and he had more mules and horses and cattle than anybody around there. Some of the boys worked with his fillies all the time, and he went off to New Orleans ever once in a while with his race horses. He took his daughter but they never took me.

Some of his land was in pasture but most of it was all open fields, with just miles and miles of cotton rows. There was a pretty good strip along one side he called the "old" fields. That's what they called the land that was wore out and turned back. It was all growed up in young trees, and that's where he kept his horses most of the time.

The first I knowed about the War coming on was when Mr. Sack had a whole bunch of whitefolks at the Big House at a function. They didn't talk about anything else all evening and then the next time they come nearly all their menfolks wasn't there—just the womenfolks. It wasn't very long till Mr. Sack went off to Houma with some other men, and pretty soon we knew he was in the War. I don't remember ever seeing him come home. I don't think he did until it was nearly all over.

Next thing we knowed they was Confederate soldiers riding by pretty nearly every day in big droves. Sometimes they would come and buy corn and wheat and hogs, but they never did take any anyhow, like the Yankees done later on. They would pay with billets, Young Missy called them, and she didn't send them to git them cashed but saved them a long time, and then she got them cashed, but you couldn't buy anything with the money she got for them.

That Confederate money she got wasn't no good. I was in Arcadia with her at a store, and she had to pay seventy-five cents for a can of sardines for me to eat with some bread I had, and before the War you could get a can like that for two cents. Things was even higher then than later on, but that's the only time I saw her buy anything.

When the Yankees got down in that country the most of the big men paid for all the corn and meat and things they got, but some of the little bunches of them would ride up and take hogs and things like that and just ride off. They wasn't anybody at our place but the womenfolks and the negroes. Some of Mr. Sack's women kinfolks stayed there with Young Mistress.

Along at the last the negroes on our place didn't put in much stuff—jest what they would need, and could hide from the Yankees, because they would get it all took away from them if the Yankees found out they had plenty of corn and oats.

The Yankees was mighty nice about their manners, though. They camped all around our place for a while. There was three camps of them close by at one time, but they never did come and use any of our houses or cabins. There was lots of poor whites and Cajuns that lived down below us, between us and the Gulf, and the Yankees just moved into their houses and cabins and used them to camp in.

The negroes at our place and all of them around there didn't try to get away or leave when the Yankees come in. They wasn't no place to go, anyway, so they all stayed on. But they didn't do very much work. Just enough to take care of themselves and their whitefolks.

Master Sack come home before the War was quite over. I think he had been sick, because he looked thin and old and worried. All the negroes picked up and worked mighty hard after he come home, too.

One day he went into Arcadia and come home and told us the War was over and we was all free. The negroes didn't know what to make of it, and didn't know where to go, so he told all that wanted to stay on that they could just go on like they had been and pay him shares.

About half of his negroes stayed on, and he marked off land for them to farm and made arrangements with them to let them use their cabins, and let them have mules and tools. They paid him out of their shares, and some of them finally bought the mules and some of the land. But about half went on off and tried to do better somewheres else.

I didn't stay with him because I was jest a boy and he didn't need me at the house anyway.

Late in the War my Pappy belonged to a man named Sander or Zander. Might been Alexander, but the negroes called him Mr. Sander. When pappy got free he come and asked me to go with him, and I went along and lived with him. He had a share-cropper deal with Mr. Sander and I helped him work his patch. That place was just a little east of Houma, a few miles.

When my Pappy was born his parents belonged to a Mr. Adams, so he took Adams for his last name, and I did too, because I was his son. I don't know where Mr. Adams lived, but I don't think my Pappy was born in Louisiana. Alabama, maybe. I think his parents come off the boat, because he was very black—even blacker than I am.

I lived there with my Pappy until I was about eighteen and then I married and moved around all over Louisiana from time to time. My wife give me twelve boys and five girls, but all my children are dead now but five. My wife died in 1920 and I come up here to Tulsa to live. One of my daughters takes care and looks out for me now.

I seen the old Sack P. Gee place about twenty years ago, and it was all cut up in little places and all run down. Never would have known it was one time a big plantation ten miles long.

I seen places going to rack and ruin all around—all the places I lived at in Louisiana—but I'm glad I wasn't there to see Master Sack's place go down. He was a good man and done right by all his negroes.

Yes, Lord, my old feets have been in mighty nigh every parish in Louisiana, and I seen some mighty pretty places, but I'll never forget how that old Gee plantation looked when I was a boy.

ALICE ALEXANDER
Age 88 yrs.
Oklahoma City, Okla.

I was 88 years old the 15th of March. I was born in 1849, at Jackson Parish, Louisiana. My mother's name was Mary Marlow, and father's Henry Marlow.

I can't remember very much 'bout slavery 'cause I was awful small, but I can remember that my mother's master, Colonel Threff died, and my mother, her husband, and us three chillun was handed down to Colonel Threff's poor kin folks. Colonel Threff owned about two or three hundred head of niggers, and all of 'em was tributed to his poor kin. Ooh wee! he sho' had jest a lot of them too! Master Joe Threff, one of his poor kin, took my mother, her husband, and three of us chillun from Louisiana to the Mississippi Line.

Down there we lived in a one-room log hut, and slept on homemade rail bed steads with cotton, and sometimes straw, mostly straw summers and cotton winners. I worked round the house and looked after de smaller chillun—I mean my mother's chillun. Mostly we ate yeller meal corn bread and sorghum malasses. I ate possums when we could get 'em, but jest couldn't stand rabbit meat. Didn't know there was any Christmas or holidays in dem days.

I can't 'membuh nothing 'bout no churches in slavery. I was a sinner and loved to dance. I remembuh I was on the floor one night dancing and I had four daughters on the floor with me and my son was playing de music—that got me! I jest stopped and said I wouldn't cut another step and I haven't. I'm a member of the Baptist Church and been for 25 or 30 years. I jined 'cause I wanted to be good 'cause I was an awful sinner.

We had a overseer back on Colonel Threff's plantation and my mother said he was the meanest man on earth. He'd jest go out in de fields and beat dem niggers, and my mother told me one day he come out in de field beating her sister and she jumped on him and nearly beat him half to death and old Master come up jest in time to see it all and fired dat overseer. Said he didn't want no man working fer him dat a woman could whip.

After de war set us free my pappy moved us away and I stayed round down there till I got to be a grown woman and married. You know I had a pretty fine wedding 'cause my pappy had worked hard and commenced to be prosperous. He had cattle, hogs, chickens and all those things like that.

A college of dem niggers got together and packed up to leave Louisiana. Me and my husband went with them. We had covered wagons, and let me tell you I walked nearly all the way from Louisiana to Oklahoma. We left in March but didn't git here till May. We came in search of education. I got a pretty fair education down there but didn't take care of it. We come to Oklahoma looking for de same thing then that darkies go North looking fer now. But we got dissapointed. What little I learned I quit taking care of it and seeing after it and lost it all.

I love to fish. I've worked hard in my days. Washed and ironed for 30 years, and paid for dis home that way. Yes sir, dis is my home. My mother died right here in dis house. She was 111 yeahs old. She is been dead 'bout 20 yeahs.

I have three daughters here married, Sussie Pruitt, Bertie Shannon, and Irene Freeman. Irene lost her husband, and he's dead now.

Oklahoma Writers' Project
Ex-Slaves
10-19-1938
1,428 words

PHOEBE BANKS
Age 78
Muskogee, Oklahoma.

In 1860, there was a little Creek Indian town of Sodom on the north bank of the Arkansas River, in a section the Indians called Chocka Bottoms, where Mose Perryman had a big farm or ranch for a long time before the Civil War. That same year, on October 17, I was born on the Perryman place, which was northwest of where I live now in Muskogee; only in them days Fort Gibson and Okmulgee was the biggest towns around and Muskogee hadn't shaped up yet.

My mother belonged to Mose Perryman when I was born; he was one of the best known Creeks in the whole nation, and one of his younger brothers, Legus Perryman, was made the big chief of the Creeks (1887) a long time after the slaves was freed. Mother's name was Eldee; my father's name was William McIntosh, because he belonged to a Creek Indian family by that name. Everybody say the McIntoshes was leaders in the Creek doings away back there in Alabama long before they come out here.

With me, there was twelve children in our family; Daniel, Stroy, Scott, Segal, Neil, Joe, Phillip, Mollie, Harriett, Sally and Queenie.

The Perryman slave cabins was all alike—just two-room log cabins, with a fireplace where mother do the cooking for us children at night after she get through working in the Master's house.

Mother was the house girl—cooking, waiting on the table, cleaning the house, spinning the yarn, knitting some of the winter clothes, taking care of the mistress girl, washing the clothes—yes, she was always busy and worked mighty hard all the time, while them Indians wouldn't hardly do nothing for themselves.

On the McIntosh plantation, my daddy said there was a big number of slaves and lots of slave children. The slave men work in the fields, chopping cotton, raising corn, cutting rails for the fences, building log cabins and fireplaces. One time when father was cutting down a tree it fell on him and after that he was only strong enough to rub down the horses and do light work around the yard. He got to be a good horse trainer and long time after slavery he helped to train horses for the Free Fairs around the country, and I suppose the first money he ever earned was made that way.

Lots of the slave owners didn't want their slaves to learn reading and writing, but the Perrymans didn't care; they even helped the younger slaves with that stuff. Mother said her master didn't care much what the slaves do; he was so lazy he didn't care for nothing.

18

They tell me about the war times, and that's all I remember of it. Before the War is over some of the Perryman slaves and some from the McIntosh place fix up to run away from their masters.

My father and my uncle, Jacob Perryman, was some of the fixers. Some of the Creek Indians had already lost a few slaves who slip off to the North, and they take what was left down into Texas so's they couldn't get away. Some of the other Creeks was friendly to the North and was fixing to get away up there; that's the ones my daddy and uncle was fixing to join, for they was afraid their masters would take up and move to Texas before they could get away.

They call the old Creek, who was leaving for the North, "Old Gouge" (Opoethleyohola). All our family join up with him, and there was lots of Creek Indians and slaves in the outfit when they made a break for the North. The runaways was riding ponies stolen from their masters.

When they get into the hilly country farther north in the country that belong to the Cherokee Indians, they make camp on a big creek and there the Rebel Indian soldiers catch up, but they was fought back.

Then long before morning lighten the sky, the men hurry and sling the camp kettles across the pack horses, tie the littlest children to the horses backs and get on the move farther into the mountains. They kept moving fast as they could, but the wagons made it mighty slow in the brush and the lowland swamps, so just about the time they ready to ford another creek the Indian soldiers catch up and the fighting begin all over again.

The Creek Indians and the slaves with them try to fight off them soldiers like they did before, but they get scattered around and separated so's they lose the battle. Lost their horses and wagons, and the soldiers killed lots of the Creeks and Negroes, and some of the slaves was captured and took back to their masters.

Dead all over the hills when we get away; some of the Negroes shot and wounded so bad the blood run down the saddle skirts, and some fall off their horses miles from the battle ground, and lay still on the ground. Daddy and Uncle Jacob keep our family together somehow and head across the line into Kansas. We all get to Fort Scott where there was a big army camp; daddy work in the blacksmith shop and Uncle Jacob join with the Northern soldiers to fight against the South. He come through the war and live to tell me about the fighting he been in.

He went with the soldiers down around Fort Gibson where they fight the Indians who stayed with the South. Uncle Jacob say he killed many a man during the war, and showed me the musket and sword he used to fight with; said he didn't shoot the women and children—just whack their heads off with the sword, and almost could I see the blood dripping from the point! It made me scared at his stories.

The captain of this company want his men to be brave and not get scared, so before the fighting start he put out a tub of white liquor (corn whiskey) and steam them up so's they'd be mean enough to whip their grannie! The soldiers do lots of riding and the saddle-sores get so bad they grease their body every night with snake oil so's they could keep going on.

Uncle Jacob said the biggest battle was at Honey Springs (1863). That was down near Elk Creek, close by Checotah, below Rentiersville. He said it was the most terrible fighting he seen, but the Union soldiers whipped and went back into Fort Gibson. The Rebels was chased all over the country and couldn't find each other for a long time, the way he tell it.

After the war our family come back here and settle at Fort Gibson, but it ain't like the place my mother told me about. There was big houses and buildings of brick setting on the high land above the river when I first see it, not like she know it when the Perrymans come here years ago.

She heard the Indians talk about the old fort (1824), the one that rot down long before the Civil War. And she seen it herself when she go with the Master for trading with the stores. She said it was made by Matthew Arbuckle and his soldiers, and she talk about Companys B, C, D, K, and the Seventh Infantry who was there and made the Osage Indians stop fighting the Creeks and Cherokees. She talk of it, but that old place all gone when I first see the Fort.

Then I hear about how after the Arbuckle soldiers leave the old log fort, the Cherokee Indians take over the land and start up the town of Keetoowah. The folks who move in there make the place so wild and rascally the Cherokees give up trying to make a good town and it kinder blow away.

My husband was Tom Banks, but the boy I got ain't my own son, but I found him on my doorstep when he's about three weeks old and raise him like he is my own blood. He went to school at the manual training school at Tullahassee and the education he got get him a teacher job at Taft (Okla), where he is now.

Oklahoma Writers' Project
Ex-Slaves
10-19-38
520 Words

NANCY ROGERS BEAN
Age about 82
Hulbert, Okla.

I'm getting old and it's easy to forget most of the happenings of slave days; anyway I was too little to know much about them, for my mammy told me I was born about six years before the War. My folks was on their way to Fort Gibson, and on the trip I was born at Boggy Depot, down in southern Oklahoma.

There was a lot of us children; I got their names somewheres here. Yes, there was George, Sarah, Emma, Stella, Sylvia, Lucinda, Rose, Dan, Pamp, Jeff, Austin, Jessie, Isaac and Andrew; we all lived in a one-room log cabin on Master Rogers' place not far from the old military road near Choteau. Mammy was raised around the Cherokee town of Tahlequah.

I got my name from the Rogers', but I was loaned around to their relatives most of the time. I helped around the house for Bill McCracken, then I was with Cornelius and Carline Wright, and when I was freed my Mistress was a Mrs. O'Neal, wife of a officer at Fort Gibson. She treated me the best of all and gave me the first doll I ever had. It was a rag doll with charcoal eyes and red thread worked in for the mouth. She allowed me one hour every day to play with it. When the War ended Mistress O'Neal wanted to take me with her to Richmond, Virginia, but my people wouldn't let me go. I wanted to stay with her, she was so good, and she promised to come back for me when I get older, but she never did.

All the time I was at the fort I hear the bugles and see the soldiers marching around, but never did I see any battles. The fighting must have been too far away.

Master Rogers kept all our family together, but my folks have told me about how the slaves was sold. One of my aunts was a mean, fighting woman. She was to be sold and when the bidding started she grabbed a hatchet, laid her hand on a log and chopped it off. Then she throwed the bleeding hand right in her master's face. Not long ago I hear she is still living in the country around Nowata, Oklahoma.

Sometimes I would try to get mean, but always I got me a whipping for it. When I was a little girl, moving around from one family to another, I done housework, ironing, peeling potatoes and helping the main cook. I went barefoot most of my life, but the master would get his shoes from the Government at Fort Gibson.

I wore cotton dresses, and the Mistress wore long dresses, with different colors for Sunday clothes, but us slaves didn't know much about Sunday in a religious way. The Master had a brother who used to preach to the Negroes on the sly. One time he was caught and the Master whipped him something awful.

Years ago I married Joe Bean. Our children died as babies. Twenty year ago Joe Bean and I separated for good and all.

The good Lord knows I'm glad slavery is over. Now I can stay peaceful in one place—that's all I aim to do.

Oklahoma Writers' Project
Ex-Slaves
[Date stamp: AUG 16 1937]

PRINCE BEE
Age 85 yrs.
Red Bird, Okla.

I don't know how old I was when I found myself standing on the toppen part of a high stump with a lot of white folks walking around looking at the little scared boy that was me. Pretty soon the old master, (that's my first master) Saul Nudville, he say to me that I'm now belonging to Major Bee and for me to get down off the auction block.

I do that. Major Bee he comes over and right away I know I'm going to like him. Then when I get to the Major's plantation and see his oldest daughter Mary and all her brothers and sisters, and see how kind she is to all them and to all the colored children, why, I just keeps right on liking 'em more all the time.

They was about nine white children on the place and Mary had to watch out for them 'cause the mother was dead.

That Mary gal seen to it that we children got the best food on the place, the fattest possum and the hottest fish. When the possum was all browned, and the sweet 'taters swimming in the good mellow gravy, then she call us for to eat. Um-um-h! That was tasty eating!

And from the garden come the vegetables like okra and corn and onions that Mary would mix all up in the soup pot with lean meats. That would rest kinder easy on the stomach too, 'specially if they was a bit of red squirrel meats in with the stew!

Major Bee say it wasn't good for me to learn reading and writing. Reckoned it would ruin me. But they sent me to Sunday School. Sometimes. Wasn't many of the slaves knew how to read the Bible either, but they all got the religion anyhow. I believed in it then and I still do.

That religion I got in them way back days is still with me. And it ain't this pie crust religion such as the folks are getting these days. The old time religion had some filling between the crusts, wasn't so many empty words like they is today.

They was haunts in them way back days, too. How's I know? 'Cause I stayed right with the haunts one whole night when I get caught in a norther when the Major sends me to another plantation for to bring back some cows he's bargained for. That was a cold night and a frightful one.

The blizzard overtook me and it was dark on the way. I come to an old gin house that everybody said was the hauntinest place in all the county. But I went in account of the cold and then when the noises started I was just too scared to move, so there I stood in the corner, all the time 'til morning come.

There was nobody I could see, but I could hear peoples feet a-tromping and stomping around the room and they go up and down the stairway like they was running a race.

Sometimes the noises would be right by my side and I would feel like a hot wind passing around me, and lights would flash all over the room. Nobody could I see. When daylight come I went through that door without looking back and headed for the plantation, forgetting all about the cows that Major Bee sent me for to get.

When I tells them about the thing, Mary she won't let the old Major scold, and she fixes me up with some warm foods and I is all right again. But I stays me away from that gin place, even in the daylight, account of the haunts.

When the War come along the Major got kinder mean with some of the slaves, but not with me. I never did try to run off, but some of 'em did. One of my brothers tried and got caught.

The old Master whipped him 'til the blood spurted all over his body, the bull whip cutting in deeper all the time. He finish up the whipping with a wet coarse towel and the end got my brother in the eye. He was blinded in the one eye but the other eye is good enough he can see they ain't no use trying to run away no more.

After the War they was more whippings. This time it was the night riders—them Klan folks didn't fool with mean Negroes. The mean Negroes was whipped and some of them shot when they do something the Klan folks didn't like, and when they come a-riding up in the night, all covered with white spreads, they was something bound to happen.

Them way back days is gone and I is mighty glad. The Negroes of today needs another leader like Booker Washington. Get the young folks to working, that's what they need, and get some filling in their pie crust religion so's when they meet the Lord their soul won't be empty like is their pocketbooks today!

Oklahoma Writers' Project
Ex-Slaves

LEWIS BONNER
Age 87 yrs.
507 N. Durland
Oklahoma City, Oklahoma

I was born 7 miles north of Palestine, Texas, on Matt Swanson's place in 1850, but I kin not remember the date. My mistress was name Celia Swanson. My mistress was so good to me till I jest loved her.

My family and all slaves on our place was treated good. Mighty few floggings went on 'round and about. Master was the overseer over his darkies and didn't use no other'n. I waited table and churned in the Big House.

I ate at the table with my mistress and her family and nothing was evah said. We ate bacon, greens, Irish potatoes and such as we git now. Aunt Chaddy was the cook and nurse for all the chillun on the place.

We used to hear slaves on de other places hollering from whippings, but master never whipped his niggers 'less they lied. Sometimes slaves from other places would run off and come to our place. Master would take them back and tell the slave-holders how to treat them so dey wouldn't run off again.

Mistress had a little stool for me in the big house, and if I got sleepy, she put me on the foot of her bed and I stayed there til morning, got up washed my face and hands and got ready to wait on the table.

There was four or five hundred slaves on our place. One morning during slavery, my father killed 18 white men and ran away. They said he was lazy and whipped him, and he just killed all of 'em he could, which was 18 of 'em. He stayed away 3 years without being found. He come back and killed 7 before they could kill him. When he was on the place he jest made bluing.

My mother worked in the field and weaved cloth. Shirts dat she made lasted 12 months, even if wore and washed and ironed every day. Pants could not be ripped with two men pulling on dem with all their might. You talking 'bout clothes, them was some clothes then. Clothes made now jest don't come up to them near abouts.

Doing of slavery, we had the best church, lots better than today. I am a Baptist from head to foot, yes sir, yes sir. Jest couldn't be nothing else. In the first place, I wouldn't even try.

I knows when the war started and ceaseted. I tell you it was some war. When it was all over, the Yankees come thoo' singing, "You may die poor but you won't die a slave."

When the War was over, master told us that we could go out and take care of the crops already planted and plant the ones that need planting 'cause we knowed all 'bout the place and we would go halvers. We stayed on 3 years after slavery. We got a little money, but we got room and board and didn't have to work too hard. It was enough difference to tell you was no slaves any more.

After slavery and when I was old enough I got married. I married a gal that was a daughter of her master. He wanted to own her, but she sho' didn't return it. He kept up with her till he died and sent her money jest all the time. Before he died, he put her name in his will and told his oldest son to be sure and keep up with her. The son was sure true to his promise, for till she died, she was forever hearing from him or he would visit us, even after we moved to Oklahoma from Texas.

Our chillun and grandchillun will git her part since she is gone. She was sure a good wife and for no reason did I take the second look at no woman. That was love, which don't live no more in our hearts.

I make a few pennies selling fish worms and doing a little yard work and raising vegetables. Not much money in circulation. When I gets my old age pension, it will make things a little mite better. I guess the time will be soon.

Tain't nothing but bad treatment that makes people die young and I ain't had none.

Oklahoma Writers' Project
Ex-Slaves
[Date stamp: AUG 19 1937]

FRANCIS BRIDGES
Age 73 yrs.
Oklahoma City, Okla.

I was born in Red River County, Texas in 1864, and that makes me 73 years old. I had myself 75, and I went to my white folks and they counted it up and told me I was 73, but I always felt like I was older than that.

My husband's name is Henry Bridges. We was raised up children together and married. I had five sisters. My brother died here in Oklahoma about two years ago. He was a Fisher. Mary Russell, my sister, she lives in Parish, Texas; Willie Ann Poke, she lives in Greenville, Texas; Winnie Jackson, lives in Adonia, Texas, and Mattie White, my other sister, lives in Long Oak, Texas, White Hunt County.

Our Master was named Master Travis Wright, and we all ate nearly the same thing. Such things as barbecued rabbits, coon, possums baked with sweet potatoes and all such as that. I used to hang round the kitchen. The cook, Mama Winnie Long, used to feed all us little niggers on the flo', jest like little pigs, in tin cups and wooden spoons. We ate fish too, and I like to go fishing right this very day.

We lived right in old Master Wright's yard. His house sat way up on a high hill. It was jest a little old log hut we lived in a little old shack around the yard. They was a lot of little shacks in the yard, I can't tell jest how many, but it was quite a number of 'em. We slept in old-fashion beds that we called "corded beds", 'cause they had ropes crossed to hold the mattresses for slats. Some of 'em had beds nailed to the wall.

Master Travis Wright had one son named Sam Wright, and after old Master Travis Wright died, young Master Sam Wright come to be my mother's master. He jest died a few years ago.

My mother say dey had a nigger driver and he'd whip 'em all but his daughter. I never seen no slaves whipped, but my mother say dey had to whip her Uncle Charley Mills once for telling a story. She say he bored a hole in de wall of de store 'til he bored de hole in old Master's whiskey barrel, and he caught two jugs of whiskey and buried it in de banks of de river. When old Master found out de whiskey was gone, he tried to make Uncle Charley 'fess up, and Uncle Charley wouldn't so he brung him in and hung him and barely let his toes touch. After Uncle Charley thought he was going to kill him, he told where de whiskey was.

We didn't go to church before freedom, land no! 'cause the closest church was so far—it was 30 miles off. But I'm a member of the Baptist Church and I've been a member for some 40-odd years. I was past 40 when I heerd of a Methodist Church. My favorite song is "Companion." I didn't get to go to school 'til after slavery.

I 'member more after de War. I 'member my mother said dey had patrollers, and if de slaves would get passes from de Master to go to de dances and didn't git back before ten o'clock dey'd beat 'em half to death.

I used to hear 'em talking 'bout Ku Klux Klan coming to the well to get water. They'd draw up a bucket of water and pour the water in they false stomachs. They false stomachs was tied on 'em with a big leather buckle. They'd jest pour de water in there to scare 'em and say, "This is the first drink of water I've had since I left Hell." They'd say all sech things to scare the cullud folks.

I heerd my mother say they sold slaves on what they called an auction block. Jest like if a slave had any portly fine looking children they'd sell them chillun jest like selling cattle. I didn't see this, jest heerd it.

After freedom, when I was old enough then to work in the field, we lived on Mr. Martin's plantation. We worked awful hard in the fields. Lawd yes'm! I've heard 'bout shucking up de corn, but give me dem cotton pickings. Fry'd pick out all de crop of cotton in one day. The women would cook and de men'd pick the cotton, I mean on dem big cotton pickings. Some would work for they meals. Then after dey'd gather all de crops, dey'd give big dances, drink whiskey, and jest cut up sumpin terrible. We didn't know anything 'bout holidays.

I've heard my husband talk 'bout "Raw head an' bloody bones." Said whenever dey mothers wanted to scare 'em to make 'em be good dey'd tell 'em dat a man was outside de door and asked her if she'd hold his head while he fixed his back bone. I don't believe in voodooing, and I don't believe in hants. I used to believe in both of 'em when I was young.

I married Jake Bridges. We had a ordinary wedding. The preacher married us and we had a license. We have two sons grown living here. My husband told me that in slavery if your Master told you to live with your brother, you had to live with him. My father's mother and dad was first cousins.

I can 'member my husband telling me he was hauling lumber from Jefferson where the saw mill was and it was cold that night, and when they got halfway back it snowed, and he stopped with an old cullud family, and he said way in the night, a knock come at de door—woke 'em up, and it was an old cullud man, and he said dis old man commence inquiring, trying to find out who dey people was and dey told him best dey could remember, and bless de Lawd, 'fore dey finished talking de found out dis old cullud man and de other cullud woman an' man dat was married was all brothers and sisters, and he told his brother it was a shame he had married his sister and dey had nine chillun. My husband sho' told me dis.

I've heerd 'em say dey old master raised chillun by those cullud women. Why, there was one white man in Texas had a cullud woman, but didn't have no chillun by her, and he had this cullud woman and her old mistress there on the same place. So, when old Mistress died he wouldn't let this cullud woman leave, and he gave her a swell home right there on the place, and she is still there I guess. They say she say sometime, she didn't want no Negro man smutting her sheets up.

I think Abraham Lincoln was a good man, and I have read a whole lots 'bout him, but I don't know much 'bout Jeff Davis. I think Booker T. Washington is a fine man, but I aint heerd so much about him.

Oklahoma Writers' Project
Ex-Slaves
[Date stamp: AUG 16 1937]

JOHN BROWN
Age (about) 87 yrs.
West Tulsa, Okla.

Most of the folks have themselves a regular birthday but this old colored man just pick out any of the days during the year—one day just about as good as another.

I been around a long time but I don't know when I got here. That's the truth. Nearest I figures it the year was 1850—the month don't make no difference nohow.

But I know the borning was down in Taloga County, Alabama, near the county seat town. Miss Abby was with my Mammy that day. She was the wife of Master John Brown. She was with all the slave women every time a baby was born, or when a plague of misery hit the folks she knew what to do and what kind of medicine to chase off the aches and pains. God bless her! She sure loved us Negroes.

Most of the time there was more'n three hundred slaves on the plantation. The oldest ones come right from Africa. My Grandmother was one of them. A savage in Africa—a slave in America. Mammy told it to me. Over there all the natives dressed naked and lived on fruits and nuts. Never see many white mens.

One day a big ship stopped off the shore and the natives hid in the brush along the beach. Grandmother was there. The ship men sent a little boat to the shore and scattered bright things and trinkets on the beach. The natives were curious. Grandmother said everybody made a rush for them things soon as the boat left. The trinkets was fewer than the peoples. Next day the white folks scatter some more. There was another scramble. The natives was feeling less scared, and the next day some of them walked up the gangplank to get things off the plank and off the deck.

The deck was covered with things like they'd found on the beach. Two-three hundred natives on the ship when they feel it move. They rush to the side but the plank was gone. Just dropped in the water when the ship moved away.

Folks on the beach started to crying and shouting. The ones on the boat was wild with fear. Grandmother was one of them who got fooled, and she say the last thing seen of that place was the natives running up and down the beach waving their arms and shouting like they was mad. The boat men come up from below where they had been hiding and drive the slaves down in the bottom and keep them quiet with the whips and clubs.

The slaves was landed at Charleston. The town folks was mighty mad 'cause the blacks was driven through the streets without any clothes, and drove off the boat men after the slaves was sold on the market. Most of that load was sold to the Brown plantation in Alabama. Grandmother was one of the bunch.

The Browns taught them to work. Made clothes for them. For a long time the natives didn't like the clothes and try to shake them off. There was three Brown boys—John, Charley and Henry. Nephews of old Lady Hyatt who was the real owner of the plantation, but the boys run the place. The old lady she lived in the town. Come out in the spring and fall to see how is the plantation doing.

She was a fine woman. The Brown boys and their wives was just as good. Wouldn't let nobody mistreat the slaves. Whippings was few and nobody get the whip 'less he need it bad. They teach the young ones how to read and write; say it was good for the Negroes to know about such things.

Sunday was a great day around the plantation. The fields was forgotten, the light chores was hurried through and everybody got ready for the church meeting.

It was out of the doors, in the yard fronting the big log where the Browns all lived. Master John's wife would start the meeting with a prayer and then would come the singing. The old timey songs.

The white folks on the next plantation would lick their slaves for trying to do like we did. No praying there, and no singing.

The Master gave out the week's supply on Saturday. Plenty of hams, lean bacon, flour, corn meal, coffee and more'n enough for the week. Nobody go hungry on that place! During the growing season all the slaves have a garden spot all their own. Three thousand acres on that place—plenty of room for gardens and field crops.

Even during the war foods was plentiful. One time the Yankee soldiers visit the place. The white folks gone and I talks with them. Asks me lots of questions—got any meats—got any potatoes— got any this—some of that—but I just shake my head and they don't look around.

The old cook fixes them up though. She fry all the eggs on the place, skillet the ham and pan the biscuits! Them soldiers fill up and leave the house friendly as anybody I ever see!

The Browns wasn't bothered with the Ku Klux Klan either. The Negroes minded their own business just like before they was free.

I stayed on the plantation 'til the last Brown die. Then I come to Oklahoma and works on the railroad 'til I was too old to hustle the grips and packages. Now I just sits thinking how much better off would I be on the old plantation.

Homesick! Just homesick for that Alabama farm like it was in them good old times!

Oklahoma Writers' Project
Ex-Slaves

SALLIE CARDER
Age 83 yrs.
Burwin, Okla.

I was born in Jackson, Tennessee, and I'm going on 83 years. My mother was Harriett Neel and father Jeff Bills, both of them named after their masters. I has one brother, J. B. Bills, but all de rest of my brothers and sisters is dead.

No sir, we never had no money while I was a slave. We jest didn't have nothing a-tall! We ate greens, corn bread, and ash cake. De only time I ever got a biscuit would be when a misdemeanor was did, and my Mistress would give a buttered biscuit to de one who could tell her who done it.

In hot weather and cold weather dere was no difference as to what we wore. We wore dresses my mother wove for us and no shoes a-tall. I never wore any shoes till I was grown and den dey was old brogans wid only two holes to lace, one on each side. During my wedding I wore a blue calico dress, a man's shirt tail as a head rag, and a pair of brogan shoes.

My Master lived in a three-story frame house painted white. My Mistress was very mean. Sometimes she would make de overseer whip negroes for looking too hard at her when she was talking to dem. Dey had four children, three girls and one boy.

I was a servant to my Master, and as he had de palsy I had to care for him, feed him and push him around. I don't know how many slaves, but he had a good deal of 'em.

About four o' clock mornings de overseer or negro carriage driver who stayed at the Big House would ring de bell to git up and git to work. De slaves would pick a heap of cotton and work till late on moonshining nights.

Dere was a white post in front of my door with ropes to tie the slaves to whip dem. Dey used a plain strap, another one with holes in it, and one dey call de cat wid nine tails which was a number of straps plated and de ends unplated. Dey would whip de slaves wid a wide strap wid holes in it and de holes would make blisters. Den dey would take de cat wid nine tails and burst de blisters and den rub de sores wid turpentine and red pepper.

I never saw any slaves auctioned off but I seen dem pass our house chained together on de way to be sold, including both men and women wid babies all chained to each other. Dere was no churches for slaves, but at nights dey would slip off and git in ditches and sing and pray, and when dey would sometimes be caught at it dey would be whipped. Some of de slaves would turn down big pots and put dere heads in dem and pray. My Mistress would tell me to be a good obedient slave and I would go to heaven. When slaves would attempt to run off dey would catch dem and chain dem and fetch 'em back and whip dem before dey was turned loose again.

31

De patrollers would go about in de quarters at nights to see if any of de slaves was out or slipped off. As we sleep on de dirt floors on pallets, de patrollers would walk all over and on us and if we even grunt dey would whip us. De only trouble between de whites and blacks on our plantation was when de overseer tied my mother to whip her and my father untied her and de overseer shot and killed him.

Negroes never was allowed to git sick, and when dey would look somewhat sick, de overseer would give dem some blue-mass pills and oil of some sort and make dem continue to work.

During de War de Yankees would pass through and kill up de chickens, and hogs, and cattle, and eat up all dey could find. De day of freedom de overseer went into de field and told de slaves dat dey was free, and de slaves replied, "free how?" and he told dem: "free to work and live for demselves." And dey said dey didn't know what to do, and so some of dem stayed on. I married Josh Forch. I am mother of four children and 35 grand children.

I like Abraham Lincoln. I think he was a good man and president. I didn't know much who Jeff Davis was. What I heard 'bout Booker T. Washington, he was a good man.

Now dat slavery is over, I don't want to be in nary 'nother slavery, and if ever nary 'nothern come up I wouldn't stay here.

BETTY FOREMAN CHESSIER
Age 94 years
Oklahoma City, Okla.

I was born July 11, 1843 in Raleigh, N. C. My mother was named Melinda Manley, the slave of Governor Manley of North Carolina, and my father was named Arnold Foreman, slave of Bob and John Foreman, two young masters. They come over from Arkansas to visit my master and my pappy and mammy met and got married, 'though my pappy only seen my mammy in the summer when his masters come to visit our master and dey took him right back. I had three sisters and two brothers and none of dem was my whole brothers and sisters. I stayed in the Big House all the time, but my sisters and brothers was gived to the master's sons and daughters whey dey got married and dey was told to send back for some more when dem died. I didn't never stay with my mammy doing of slavery. I stayed in the Big House. I slept under the dining room table with three other darkies. The flo' was well carpeted. Don't remembah my grandmammy and grandpappy, but my master was they master.

I waited on the table, kept flies off'n my mistress and went for the mail. Never made no money, but dey did give the slaves money at Christmas time. I never had over two dresses. One was calico and one gingham. I had such underclothes as dey wore then.

Master Manley and Mistress had six sons an' six darters. Dey raised dem all till dey was grown too. Dey lived in a great big house 'cross from the mansion, right in town before Master was 'lected Governor, den dey all moved in dat mansion.

Plantation folks had barbecues and "lay crop feasts" and invited the city darkies out. When I first come here I couldn't understand the folks here, 'cause dey didn't quit work on Easter Monday. That is some day in North Carolina even today. I doesn't remember any play songs, 'cause I was almost in prison. I couldn't play with any of the darkies and I doesn't remember playing in my life when I was a little girl and when I got grown I didn't want to. I wasn't hongry, I wasn't naked and I got only five licks from the white folks in my life. Dey was for being such a big forgitful girl. I saw 'em sell niggers once. The only pusson I ever seen whipped at dat whipping post was a white man.

I never got no learning; dey kept us from dat, but you know some of dem darkies learnt anyhow. We had church in the heart of town or in the basement of some old building. I went to the 'piscopal church most all the time, till I got to be a Baptist.

The slaves run away to the North 'cause dey wanted to be free. Some of my family run away sometime and dey didn't catch 'em neither. The patrollers sho' watched the streets. But when dey caught any of master's niggers without passes, dey jest locked him up in the guard house and master come down in the mawnin' and git 'em out, but dem patrollers better not whip one.

I know when the War commenced and ended. Master Manley sent me from the Big House to the office about a mile away. Jest as I got to the office door, three men rid up in blue uniforms and said, "Dinah, do you have any milk in there?" I was sent down to the office for some beans for to cook dinner, but dem men most nigh scared me to death. They never did go in dat office, but jest rid off on horseback about a quarter a mile and seem lak right now, Yankees fell out of the very sky, 'cause hundeds and hundeds was everywhere you could look to save your life. Old Mistress sent one of her grandchillun to tell me to come on, and one of the Yankees told dat child, "You tell your grandmother she ain't coming now and never will come back there as a slave." Master was setting on the mansion porch. Dem Yankees come up on de porch, go down in cellar and didn't tech one blessed thing. Old Mistress took heart trouble, 'cause dem Yankees whipped white folks going and coming.

I laid in my bed a many night scared to death of Klu Klux Klan. Dey would come to your house and ask for a drink and no more want a drink than nothing.

After the War, I went to mammy and my step-pappy. She done married again, so I left and went to Warrington and Halifax, North Carolina, jest for a little while nursing some white chillun. I stayed in Raleigh, where I was born till 7 years ago, when I come to Oklahoma to live with my only living child. I am the mother of 4 chillun and 11 grandchillun.

When I got married I jumped a broomstick. To git unmarried, all you had to do was to jump backwards over the same broomstick.

Lincoln and Booker T. Washington was two of the finest men ever lived. Don't think nothing of Jeff Davis, 'cause he was a traitor. Freedom for us was the best thing ever happened. Prayer is best thing in the world. Everybody ought to pray, 'cause prayer got us out of slavery.

POLLY COLBERT
Age 83 yrs.
Colbert, Oklahoma

I am now living on de forty-acre farm dat de Government give me and it is just about three miles from my old home on Master Holmes Colbert's plantation where I lived when I was a slave.

Lawsy me, times sure has changed since slavery times! Maybe I notice it more since I been living here all de time, but dere's farms 'round here dat I've seen grown timber cleared off of twice during my lifetime. Dis land was first cleared up and worked by niggers when dey was slaves. After de War nobody worked it and it just naturally growed up again wid all sorts of trees. Later, white folks cleared it up again and took grown trees off'n it and now dey are still cultivating it but it is most wore out now. Some of it won't even sprout peas. Dis same land used to grow corn without hardly any work but it sure won't do it now.

I reckon it was on account of de rich land dat us niggers dat was owned by Indians didn't have to work so hard as dey did in de old states, but I think dat Indian masters was just naturally kinder any way, leastways mine was.

My mother, Liza, was owned by de Colbert family and my father, Tony, was owned by de Love family. When Master Holmes and Miss Betty Love was married dey fathers give my father and mother to dem for a wedding gift. I was born at Tishomingo and we moved to de farm on Red River soon after dat and I been here ever since. I had a sister and a brother, but I ain't seen dem since den.

My mother died when I was real small, and about a year after dat my father died. Master Holmes told us children not to cry, dat he and Miss Betsy would take good care of us. Dey did, too. Dey took us in de house wid dem and look after us jest as good as dey could colored children. We slept in a little room close to them and she allus seen dat we was covered up good before she went to bed. I guess she got a sight of satisfaction from taking care of us 'cause she didn't have no babies to care for.

Master Holmes and Miss Betsy was real young folks but dey was purty well fixed. He owned about 100 acres of land dat was cleared and ready for de plow and a lot dat was not in cultivation. He had de woods full of hogs and cows and he owned seven or eight grown slaves and several children. I remember Uncle Shed, Uncle Lige, Aunt Chaney, Aunt Lizzie, and Aunt Susy just as well as if it was yesterday. Master Holmes and Miss Betsy was both half-breed Choctaw Indians. Dey had both been away to school somewhere in de states and was well educated. Dey had two children but dey died when dey was little. Another little girl was born to dem after de War and she lived to be a grown woman.

Dey sure was fine young folks and provided well for us. He allus had a smokehouse full of meat, lard, sausage, dried beans, peas, corn, potatoes, turnips and collards banked up for winter. He had plenty of milk and butter for all of us, too.

Master Holmes allus say, "A hungry man caint work." And he allus saw to it that we had lots to eat.

We cooked all sorts of Indian dishes: Tom-fuller, pashofa, hickory-nut grot, Tom-budha, ash-cakes, and pound cakes besides vegetables and meat dishes. Corn or corn meal was used in all de Indian dishes. We made hominy out'n de whole grains. Tom-fuller was made from beaten corn and tasted sort of like hominy.

We would take corn and beat it like in a wooden mortar wid a wooden pestle. We would husk it by fanning it and we would den put it on to cook in a big pot. While it was cooking we'd pick out a lot of hickory-nuts, tie 'em up in a cloth and beat 'em a little and drop 'em in and cook for a long time. We called dis dish hickory-nut grot. When we made pashofa we beat de corn and cook for a little while and den we add fresh pork and cook until de meat was done. Tom-budha was green corn and fresh meat cooked together and seasoned wid tongue or pepper-grass.

We cooked on de fire place wid de pots hanging over de fire on racks and den we baked bread and cakes in a oven-skillet. We didn't use soda and baking powder. We'd put salt in de meal and scald it wid boiling water and make it into pones and bake it. We'd roll de ash cakes in wet cabbage leaves and put 'em in de hot ashes and bake 'em. We cooked potatoes, and roasting ears dat way also. We sweetened our cakes wid molasses, and dey was plenty sweet too.

Dey was lots of possums and coons and squirrels and we nearly always had some one of these to eat. We'd parboil de possum or coon and put it in a pan and bake him wid potatoes 'round him. We used de broth to baste him and for gravy. Hit sure was fine eating dem days.

I never had much work to do. I helped 'round de house when I wanted to and I run errands for Miss Betsy. I liked to do things for her. When I got a little bigger my brother and I toted cool water to de field for de hands.

Didn't none of Master Holmes' niggers work when dey was sick. He allus saw dat dey had medicine and a doctor iffen dey needed one. 'Bout de only sickness we had was chills and fever. In de old days we made lots of our own medicine and I still does it yet. We used polecat grease for croup and rheumatism. Dog-fennel, butterfly-root, and life-everlasting boiled and mixed and made into a syrup will cure pneumonia and pleurisy. Pursley-weed, called squirrel physic, boiled into a syrup will cure chills and fever. Snake-root steeped for a long time and mixed with whiskey will cure chills and fever also.

Our clothes was all made of homespun. De women done all de spinning and de weaving but Miss Betsy cut out all de clothes and helped wid de sewing. She learned to sew when she was away to school and she learnt all her women to sew. She done all the sewing for de children. Master Holmes bought our shoes and we all had 'em to wear in de winter. We all went barefoot in de summer.

He kept mighty good teams and he had two fine saddle horses. He and Miss Betsy rode 'em all de time. She would ride wid him all over de farm and dey would go hunting a lot, too. She could shoot a gun as good as any man.

Master Holmes sure did love his wife and children and he was so proud of her. It nearly killed 'em both to give up de little boy and girl. I never did hear of him taking a drink and he was kind to everybody, both black and white, and everybody liked him. Dey had lots of company and dey never turned anybody away. We lived about four miles from de ferry on Red River on de Texas Road and lots of travelers stopped at our house.

We was 'lowed to visit de colored folks on de Eastman and Carter plantations dat joined our farm. Eastman and Carter was both white men dat married Indian wives. Dey was good to dey slaves, too, and let 'em visit us.

Old Uncle Kellup (Caleb) Colbert, Uncle Billy Hogan, Rev. John Carr, Rev. Baker, Rev. Hogue, and old Father Murrow preached for de white folks all de time and us colored folks went to church wid dem. Dey had church under brush arbors and we set off to ourselves but we could take part in de singing and sometimes a colored person would get happy and pray and shout but nobody didn't think nothing 'bout dat.

De Patrollers was de law, kind of like de policeman now. Dey sure never did whip one of Master Holmes' niggers for he didn't allow it. He didn't whip 'em hisself and he sure didn't allow anybody else to either. I was afraid of de Ku Kluxers too, and I 'spects dat Master Holmes was one of de leaders iffen de truth was known. Dey sure was scary looking.

I was scared of de Yankee soldiers. Dey come by and killed some of our cattle for beef and took our meat and lard out'n de smokehouse and dey took some corn, too. Us niggers was awful mad. We didn't know anything 'bout dem fighting to free us. We didn't specially want to be free dat I knows of.

Right after de War I went over to Bloomfield Academy to take care of a little girl, but I went back to Master Holmes and Miss Betsy at de end of two years to take care of de little girl dat was born to dem and I stayed with her until I was about fifteen. Master Holmes went to Washington as a delegate, for something for de Indians, and he took sick and died and dey buried him dere. Poor Miss Betsy nearly grieved herself to death. She stayed on at de farm till her little girl was grown and married. Her nigger men stayed on with her and rented land from her and dey sure raised a sight of truck. Didn't none of her old slaves ever move very far from her and most of them worked for her till dey was too old to work.

I left Miss Betsy purty soon after Master Holmes died and went back to de Academy and stayed three years. I married a man dat belonged to Master Holmes' cousin. His name was Colbert, too. I had a big wedding. Miss Betsy and a lot of white folks come and stayed for dinner. We danced all evening and after supper we started again and danced all night and de next day and de next night. We'd eat awhile and den we'd dance awhile.

My husband and I had nine children and now I've got seven grandchildren. My husband has been dead a long time.

My sister, Chaney, lives here close to me but her mind has got feeble and she can't recollect as much as I can. I live with my son and he is mighty good to me. I know I ain't long for dis world but I don't mind for I has lived a long time and I'll have a lot of friends in de other world and I won't be lonesome.

Oklahoma Writers' Project
Ex-Slaves
[Date stamp: NOV 5 1937]

GEORGE CONRAD, JR.,
Age 77 yrs.
Oklahoma City, Okla.

I was born February 23, 1860 at Connersville, Harrison County, Kentucky. I was born and lived just 13 miles from Parish. My mother's name is Rachel Conrad, born at Bourbon County, Kentucky. My father, George Conrad, was born at Bourbon County Kentucky. My grandmother's name is Sallie Amos, and grandfather's name is Peter Amos. My grandfather, his old Master freed him and he bought my grandmother, Aunt Liza and Uncle Cy. He made the money by freighting groceries from Ohio to Maysville, Kentucky.

Our Master was named Master Joe Conrad. We sometimes called him "Mos" Joe Conrad. Master Joe Conrad stayed in a big log house with weather boarding on the outside.

I was born in a log cabin. We slept in wooden beds with rope cords for slats, and the beds had curtains around them. You see my mother was the cook for the Master, and she cooked everything—chicken, roasting ears. She cooked mostly everything we have now. They didn't have stoves; they cooked in big ovens. The skillets had three legs. I can remember the first stove that we had. I guess I was about six years old.

My old Master had 900 acres of land. My father was a stiller. He made three barrels of whisky a day. Before the War whisky sold for 12-1/2¢ and 13¢ a gallon. After the War it went up to $3 and $4 per gallon. When War broke out he had 300 barrels hid under old Master's barn.

There was 14 colored men working for old Master Joe and 7 women. I think it was on the 13th of May, all 14 of these colored men, and my father, went to the Army. When old Master Joe come to wake 'em up the next morning—I remember he called real loud, Miles, Esau, George, Frank, Arch, on down the line, and my mother told him they'd all gone to the army. Old Master went to Cynthia, Kentucky, where they had gone to enlist and begged the officer in charge to let him see all of his boys, but the officer said "No." Some way or 'nother he got a chance to see Arch, and Arch came back with him to help raise the crops.

My mother cooked and took care of the house. Aunt Sarah took care of the children. I had two little baby brothers, Charlie and John. The old Mistress would let my mother put them in her cradle and Aunt Sarah got jealous, and killed both of the babies. When they cut one of the babies open they took out two frogs. Some say she conjured the babies. Them niggers could conjure each other but they couldn't do nothing to the whitefolks, but I don't believe in it. There's an old woman living back there now (pointing around the corner of the house where he was sitting) they said her husband put a spell on her. They call 'em two-headed Negroes.

Old Master never whipped any of his slaves, except two of my uncles—Pete Conrad and Richard Sherman, now living at Falsmouth, Kentucky.

We raised corn, wheat, oats, rye and barley, in the spring. In January, February and March we'd go up to the Sugar Camp where he had a grove of maple trees. We'd make maple syrup and put up sugar in cakes. Sugar sold for $2.5O and $3 a cake. He had a regular sugar house. My old Master was rich I tell you.

Whenever a member of the white family die all the slaves would turn out, and whenever a slave would die, whitefolks and all the slaves would go. My Master had a big vault. My Mistress was buried in an iron coffin that they called a potanic coffin. I went back to see her after I was 21 years old and she look jest like she did when they buried her. All of the family was buried in them vaults, and I expect if you'd go there today they'd look the same. The slaves was buried in good handmade coffins.

I heard a lot of talk 'bout the patrollers. In them days if you went away from home and didn't have a pass they'd whip you. Sometimes they'd whip you with a long black cow whip, and then sometime they'd roast elm switches in the fire. This was called "cat-o-nine-tails", and they'd whip you with dat. We never had no jails; only punishment was just to whip you.

Now, the way the slaves travel. If a slave had been good sometimes old Master would let him ride his hoss; then, sometime they'd steal a hoss out and ride 'em and slip him back before old Master ever found it out. There was a man in them days by the name of John Brown. We called him an underground railroad man, 'cause he'd steal the slaves and carry 'em across the river in a boat. When you got on the other side you was free, 'cause you was in a free State, Ohio.

We used to sing, and I guess young folks today does too:

"John Brown's Body Lies A 'moulding In the Clay."

and

"They Hung John Brown On a Sour Apple Tree."

Our slaves all got very good attention when they got sick. They'd send and get a doctor for 'em. You see old Mistress Mary bought my mother, father and two children throwed in for $1,100 and she told Master Joe to always keep her slaves, not to sell 'em and always take good care of 'em.

When my father went to the army old Master told us he was gone to fight for us niggers freedom. My daddy was the only one that come back out of the 13 men that enlisted, and when my daddy come back old Master give him a buggy and hoss.

When the Yanks come, I never will forget one of 'em was named John Morgan. We carried old Master down to the barn and hid him in the hay. I felt so sorry for old Master they took all his hams, some of his whiskey, and all dey could find, hogs, chickens, and jest treated him something terrible.

The whitefolks learned my father how to read and write, but I didn't learn how to read and write 'til I enlisted in the U. S. Army in 1883.

They sent us here (Oklahoma Territory) to keep the immigrants from settling up Oklahoma. I went to Fort Riley the 1st day of October 1883, and stayed there three weeks. Left Fort Riley and went to Ft. Worth, Texas, and landed in Henryetta, Texas, on the 14th day of October 1883. Then, we had 65 miles to walk to Ft. Sill. We walked there in three days. I was assigned to my Company, Troop G. 9th Calvary, and we stayed and drilled in Ft. Sill six months, when we was assigned to duty. We got orders to come to Ft. Reno, Okla., on the 6th day of January 1885 where we was ordered to Stillwater, Okla., to move five hundred immigrants under Capt. Couch. We landed there on the 23rd day of January, Saturday evening, and Sunday was the 24th. We had general inspection Monday, January 25, 1885. We fell in line of battle, sixteen companies of soldiers, to move 500 immigrants to the Arkansas City, Kansas line.

We formed a line at 9:00 o'clock Monday morning and Captain Couch run up his white flag, and Colonel Hatch he sent the orderly up to see what he meant by putting up the flag, so Captain Couch sent word back, "If you don't fire on me, I'll leave tomorrow." Colonel Hatch turned around to the Major and told him to turn his troops back to the camp, and detailed three camps of soldiers of the 8th Cavalry to carry Captain Couch's troop of 500 immigrants to Arkansas City, Kansas. Troop L., Troop D., and Troop B. taken them back with 43 wagons and put them over the line of Kansas. Then we were ordered back to our supply camp at Camp Alice, 9 miles north of Guthrie in the Cimarron horseshoe bottom. We stayed there about three months, and Capt. Couch and his colony came back into the territory at Caldwell, Kansas June 1885.

I laid there 'til August 8, then we changed regiments with the 5th Calvary to go to Nebraska. There was a breakout with the Indians at Ft. Reno the 1st of July 1885. The Indian Agency tried to make the Indians wear citizens' clothes. They had to call General Sheridan from Washington, D. C., to quiet the Indians down. Now, we had to make a line in three divisions, fifteen miles a part, one non-commissioned officer to each squad, and these men was to go to Caldwell, Kansas and bring him to Ft. Reno that night. He came that night, so the next morning Colonel Brisbane and General Hatch reported to General Sheridan what the trouble was. General Sheridan called all the Indian Chiefs together and asked them why they rebelled against the agency, and they told them they weren't going to wear citizen's clothes. General Sheridan called his corporals and sergeants together and told them to go behind the guard house and dig a grave for this Indian agent in order to fool the Indian Chiefs. Then, he sent a detachment of soldiers to order the Indian Chiefs away from the guard house and to put this Indian agent in the ambulance that brought him to Ft. Reno and take him back to Washington, D. C., to remain there 'til he returned. The next morning he called all the Indian Chiefs to the guard house and pointed down to the grave and said that, "I have killed the agent and buried him there." The Indians tore the feathers out of their hats rejoicing that they killed the agent.

On the 12th of the same July, we had general inspection with General Foresides from Washington, then we was ordered back to our supply camp to stay there 'til we got orders of our change. On August 8, we got orders to change to go to Nebraska, to Ft. Robinson, Ft. Nibrary, and Ft. McKinney, and we left on the 8th of August.

This is my Oklahoma history. I gave this story to the Daily Oklahoman and Times at one time and they are supposed to publish it but they haven't.

Now you see that tree up there in front of my house? That tree is 50 years old. It is called the potopic tree. That was the only tree around here in 1882. This was a bald prairie. I enlisted over there where the City Market sets now. That was our starting camp under Capt. Payne, but he died.

I joined the A. M. E. Methodist Church in 1874. I love this song better than all the rest:

"Am I a Soldier of the Cross?"

Abraham Lincoln was a smart man, but he would have done more if he was not killed. I don't think his work was finished. I'll tell you the truth about Booker T. Washington. He argued our people to stay out of town and stay in the country. He was a Democrat. He was a smart man, but I think a man should live wherever he choose regardless. I never stopped work whenever I'd hear he was coming to town to speak. You know they wasn't fighting for freeing the slaves; they was fighting to keep Kansas from being a slave State; so when they had the North whipped, I mean the South had 'em whipped, they called for the Negroes to go out and fight for his freedom. Don't know nothing 'bout Jeff Davis. I've handled a lots of his money. It was counterfeited after the War.

I've been married four times. I had one wife and three women. I mean the three wasn't no good. My first wife's name: Amanda Nelson. 2nd: Pocahuntas Jackson. 3rd: Nannie Shumpard. We lived together 9 years. She tried to beat me out of my home.

Oklahoma Writers' Project
Ex-Slaves

MARTHA CUNNINGHAM
(white) Age 81 yrs.
Oklahoma City, Oklahoma

My father's name was A. J. Brown, and my mother's name was Hattie Brown. I was born in the East, in Saveer County, Tennessee. I had twelve sisters and brothers, all are dead but two. W. S. Brown lives at 327 W. California, and Maudie Reynolds, my sister lives at Minrovie, California.

We lived in different kinds of houses just like we do now. Some was of log, some frame and some rock. I remember when we didn't have stoves to cook on, no lamps, and not even any candles until I was about six years old. We would take a rag and sop it in lard to make lights.

All of our furniture was home made, but it was nice. We had just plenty of every thing. It wasn't like it is in these days where you have to pick and scrape for something to eat.

My grandfather and grandmother gave my mother and father two slaves, an old woman and man, when they married. My grandfather owned a large plantation, and had a large number of slaves, and my father and mother owned several farms at different places. Our mother and father treated our slaves good. They ate what we ate, and they stayed with us a long time after the War. I remember though all of the slave owners weren't good to their slaves. I have seen 'em take those young fine looking negroes, put them in a pen when they got ready to whip them, strip them and lay them face down, and beat them until white whelps arose on their bodies. Yes, some of them was treated awful mean.

I saw mothers sold from their babies, and babies sold from their mothers. They would strip them, put them on the auction block and sell them—bid them off just like you would cattle. Some would sell for lots of money.

They wouldn't take the slaves to church. I don't remember when the negroes had their first schools, but it was a long time after the War.

Why, I remember when they'd have those big corn shuckings, flax pullings, and quilting parties. They would sow acres after acres of flax, then they would meet at some house or plantation and pull flax until they had finished, then give a big party. There'd be the same thing at the next plantation and so on until they'd all in that neighborhood get their crops gathered. I remember they'd have all kinds of good eats—pies, cakes, chicken, fish, fresh pork, beef,—just plenty of good eats.

I went over the battlefield at Knoxville, Tennessee, two or three hours after the Yankees and the Rebels had a battle. It was about a mile from our house, and I walked over hundreds of dead men lying on the ground. Some were fatally wounded, and we carried about six or seven to our house. I saw the doctor pick the bullets out of their flesh.

When the Yankees came they treated the slave owners awful mean. They drew a gun on my mother, made her walk for several miles one real cold night and take them up on the top of a mountain and show them where a still was. They would make her cook for 'em. They took every thing we had. I was about twelve years old at that time.

I stayed there with my mother until after my father died, then we moved to Alabama. I was about 22 years old. I married a man named Kelley. He and my brothers were railroad graders. We traveled all over Texas.

I made the Run. Came here in '89 with my mother, husband and eight children. My husband and brothers graded the streets for the townsite of Oklahoma City and platted it off.

When we made the Run, we just stood on the property until it was surveyed, then we'd pay $1.00, and the lot was ours. I camped on the corner of Robinson and Pottawatomie Streets and Robinson and Chickasaw. I owned the Northwest corner. I later sold both lots.

I am a Christian, Baptist mostly, I guess, and I believe in the Great Beyond. I don't think you have to go to church all the time to be saved, but you have to be right with the Man up yonder before you can be saved.

I am a Republican, and it makes my blood boil whenever I hear a negro say he is a democrat. They should all be Republicans.

I have been married twice. I married William Cunningham here in 1922. He is dead; in fact, both my husbands are dead, so I don't see much need of talking about them.

Oklahoma Writers' Project
Ex-Slaves
[Date stamp: AUG 19 1937]

WILLIAM CURTIS
Age 93 yrs.
McAlester, Oklahoma

"Run Nigger, run,

De Patteroll git ye!

Run Nigger, run,

He's almost here!"

"Please Mr. Patteroll,

Don't ketch me!

Jest take dat nigger

What's behind dat tree."

Lawsy, I done heard dat song all my life and it warn't no joke neither. De Patrol would git ye too if he caught ye off the plantation without a pass from your Master, and he'd whup ye too. None of us dassn't leave without a pass.

We chillun sung lots of songs and we played marbles, mumble peg, and town ball. In de winter we would set around de fire and listen to our Mammy and Pappy tell ghost tales and witch tales. I don't guess dey was sho' nuff so, but we all thought dey was.

My Mammy was bought in Virginia by our Master, Hugh McKeown. He owned a big plantation in Georgia. Soon after she come to Georgia she married my pa. Old Master was good to us. We lived for a while in the quarters behind the Big House, and my mammy was de house woman.

Somehow, in a trade, or maybe my pa was mortgaged, but anyway old Master let a man in Virginia have him and we never see him no more 'till after the War. It nigh broke our hearts when he had to leave and old Master sho' done everything he could to make it up to us.

There was four of us chillun. I didn't do no work 'till I was about fifteen years old. Old Master bought a tavern and mammy worked as house woman and I went to work at the stables. I drove the carriage and took keer of the team and carriage. I kept 'em shining too. I'd curry the horses 'till they was slick and shiny. I'd polish the harness and the carriage. Old Master and Mistress was quality and I wanted everybody to know it. They had three girls and three boys and we boys played together and went swimming together. We loved each other, I tell ye.

Old Master built us a little house jest back of de tavern and mammy raised us jest like Old Mistress did her chillun. When I didn't have to work de boys and me would go hunting. We'd kill possum, coon, squirrels and wild hogs. Old Master killed a wild hog and he give mammy her ten tiny pigs. She raised 'em and my, at the meat we had when they was butchered.

They had lots of company at de Big House, and it was de only tavern too, so they was lots of cooking to do. They would go to church on Sunday and they would spread their dinners on the ground. My, but they was feasts. We'd allus git to go as I drive the carriage and mammy looked after the food. We had our own church too, with our own preacher.

We had a spinning house where all the old women would card and spin wool in de winter and cotton in de summer. Dey made all our clothes, what few we wore. Us boys just wore long tailed shirts 'till we was 12 or 13 years old, sometimes older. I was 15 when I started driving the fambly carriage and I got to put on pants then.

Our suits was made out of jeans. That cloth wore like buckskin. We'd wear 'em for a year before they had to be patched.

We made our own brogan shoes too. We'd kill a beef and skin it and spread the skin out and let it dry a while. We'd put the hide in lime water to get the hair off, then we'd oil it and work it 'till it was soft. Next we'd take it to the bench and scrape or 'plesh' it with knives. It was then put in a tight cabinet and smoked with oak wood for about 24 hours. Smoking loosened the skin. We'd then take it out and rub it to soften it. It was blacked and oiled and it was ready to be made into shoes. It took nearly a year to get a green hide made into shoes. Twan't no wonder we had to go barefooted.

Sometimes I'd work in the wood shop, dressing wagon spokes. We made spokes with a plane, by hand on a bench.

I didn't have much work to do before I was 15 except to run errands. One of my jobs was to take corn to the mill to be ground into meal. Some one would put my sack of corn on the mule's back and help me up and I'd ride to the mill and have it ground and they'd load me back on and I'd go back home.

I remember once my meal fell off and I waited and waited for somebody to come by and help me. I got tired waiting so I toted the sack to a big log and laid it acrost it. I led my mule up to the log and after working hard for a long time I managed to get it on his back. I climbed up and jest as we started off the mule jumped and I fell off and pulled the sack off with me. I couldn't do nothing but wait and finally old Master came after me. He knowed something was wrong.

Old Master was good to all of his slaves but his overseers had orders to make 'em work. He fed 'em good and took good keer of 'em and never made 'em work iffen they was sick or even felt bad. They was two things old Master jest wouldn't 'bide and dat was for a slave to be sassy or lazy. Sometimes if dey wouldn't work or slipped off de farm dey would whip 'em. He didn't whip often. Colored overseers was worse to whip than white ones, but Master allus said, "Hadn't you all rather have a nigger overseer than a white one? I don't want to white man over my niggers." I've seen the overseer whip some but I never did get no whipping. He would strip 'em to the waist and whip 'em with a long leather strop, about as wide as two fingers and fastened to a handle.

When de war broke out everthing was changed. My young Masters had to go. T. H. McKeown, the oldest was a Lieutenant and was one of the first to go. It nigh broke all of our hearts. Pretty soon he sent for me to come and keep him company. Old Master let me go and I stayed in his quarters. He was stationed at Atlanta and Griffin, Georgia. I'd stay with him a week or two and I'd go home for a few days and I'd take back food and fruit. I stayed with him and waited on him 'till he got used to being in the army and they moved him out to fighting. I wanted to go on with him but he wouldn't let me, he told me to go back and take care of Old Master and Old Mistress. They was getting old by then. Purty soon Young Master got wounded purty bad and they sent me home. I never went back. I got a "pass" to go home. Course, after the war nothing was right no more. Yes, we was free but we didn't know what to do. We didn't want to leave our old Master and our old home. We stayed on and after a while my pappy come home to us. Dat was de best thing about de war setting us free, he could come back to us.

We all lived on at the old plantation. Old Master and old Mistress died and young Master took charge of de farm. He couldn't a'done nothing without us niggers. He didn't know how to work. He was good to us and divided the crops with us.

I never went to school much but my white folks learned me to read and write. I could always have any of their books to read, and they had lots of 'em.

Times has changed a lot since that time. I don't know where the world is much better now, that it has everthing or then when we didn't have hardly nothing, but I believe there was more religion then. We always went to church and I've seen 'em baptize from in the early morning 'till afternoon in the Chatahooche river. Folks don't hardly know nowadays jest what to believe they's so many religions, but they's only one God.

I was eighteen when I married. I had eight chillun. My wife is 86, and she lives in St. Louis, Missouri.

Oklahoma Writers' Project
Ex-Slaves
[HW: (photo)]
[Date stamp: AUG 16 1937]

LUCINDA DAVIS
Age (about) 89 yrs.
Tulsa, Okla.

"What yo' gwine do when de meat give out?

What yo' gwine do when de meat give out?

    Set in de corner wid my lips pooched out!

Lawsy!

What yo' gwine do when de meat come in?

What yo' gwine do when de meat come in?

Set in de corner wid a greasy chin!

Lawsy!"

Dat's about de only little nigger song I know, less'n it be de one about:

"Great big nigger, laying 'hind de log—

Finger on de trigger and eye on the hawg!

Click go de trigger and bang go de gun!

Here come de owner and de buck nigger run!"

And I think I learn both of dem long after I been grown, 'cause I belong to a full-blood Creek Indian and I didn't know nothing but Creek talk long after de Civil War. My mistress was part white and knowed English talk, but she never did talk it because none of de people talked it. I heard it sometime, but it sound like whole lot of wild shoat in de cedar brake scared at something when I do hear it. Dat was when I was little girl in time of de War.

I don't know where I been born. Nobody never did tell me. But my mammy and pappy git me after de War and I know den whose child I is. De men at de Creek Agency help 'em git me, I reckon, maybe.

First thing I remember is when I was a little girl, and I belong to old Tuskaya-hiniha. He was big man in de Upper Creek, and we have a purty good size farm, jest a little bit to de north of de wagon depot houses on de old road at Honey Springs. Dat place was about twenty-five mile south of Fort Gibson, but I don't know nothing about whar de fort is when I was a little girl at dat time. I know de Elk River 'bout two mile north of whar we live, 'cause I been there many de time.

I don't know if old Master have a white name. Lots de Upper Creek didn't have no white name. Maybe he have another Indian name, too, because Tuskaya-hiniha mean "head man warrior" in Creek, but dat what everybody call him and dat what de family call him too.

My Mistress' name was Nancy, and she was a Lott before she marry old man Tuskaya-hiniha. Her pappy name was Lott and he was purty near white. Maybe so all white. Dey have two chillun, I think, but only one stayed on de place. She was name Luwina, and her husband was dead. His name was Walker, and Luwina bring Mr. Walker's little sister, Nancy, to live at de place too.

Luwina had a little baby boy and dat de reason old Master buy me, to look after de little baby boy. He didn't have no name cause he wasn't big enough when I was with dem, but he git a name later on, I reckon. We all call him "Istidji." Dat mean "little man."

When I first remember, before de War, old Master had 'bout as many slave as I got fingers, I reckon. I can think dem off on my fingers like dis, but I can't recollect de names.

47

Dey call all de slaves "Istilusti." Dat mean "Black man."

Old man Tuskaya-hiniha was near 'bout blind before de War, and 'bout time of de War he go plumb blind and have to set on de long seat under de bresh shelter of de house all de time. Sometime I lead him around de yard a little, but not very much. Dat about de time all de slave begin to slip out and run off.

My own pappy was name Stephany. I think he take dat name 'cause when he little his mammy call him "Istifani." Dat mean a skeleton, and he was a skinny man. He belong to de Grayson family and I think his master name George, but I don't know. Dey big people in de Creek, and with de white folks too. My mammy name was Serena and she belong to some of de Gouge family. Dey was big people in de Upper Creek, and one de biggest men of the Gouge was name Hopoethleyoholo for his Creek name. He was a big man and went to de North in de War and died up in Kansas, I think. Dey say when he was a little boy he was called Hopoethli, which mean "good little boy", and when he git grown he make big speeches and dey stick on de "yoholo." Dat mean "loud whooper."

Dat de way de Creek made de name for young boys when I was a little girl. When de boy git old enough de big men in de town give him a name, and sometime later on when he git to going round wid de grown men dey stick on some more name. If he a good talker dey sometime stick on "yoholo", and iffen he make lots of jokes dey call him "Hadjo." If he is a good leader dey call him "Imala" and if he kind of mean dey sometime call him "fixigo."

My mammy and pappy belong to two masters, but dey live together on a place. Dat de way de Creek slaves do lots of times. Dey work patches and give de masters most all dey make, but dey have some for demselves. Dey didn't have to stay on de master's place and work like I hear de slaves of de white people and de Cherokee and Choctaw people say dey had to do.

Maybe my pappy and mammy run off and git free, or maybeso dey buy demselves out, but anyway dey move away some time and my mammy's master sell me to old man Tuskaya-hiniha when I was jest a little gal. All I have to do is stay at de house and mind de baby.

Master had a good log house and a bresh shelter out in front like all de houses had. Like a gallery, only it had de dirt for de flo' and bresh for de roof. Dey cook everything out in de yard in big pots, and dey eat out in de yard too.

Dat was sho' good stuff to eat, and it make you fat too! Roast de green corn on de ears in de ashes, and scrape off some and fry it! Grind de dry corn or pound it up and make ash cake. Den bile de greens—all kinds of greens from out in de woods—and chop up de pork and de deer meat, or de wild turkey meat; maybe all of dem, in de big pot at de same time! Fish too, and de big turtle dat lay out on de bank!

Dey always have a pot full of sofki settin right inside de house, and anybody eat when dey feel hungry. Anybody come on a visit, always give 'em some of de sofki. Ef dey don't take none de old man git mad, too!

When you make de sofki you pound up de corn real fine, den pour in de water an dreen it off to git all de little skin from off'n de grain. Den you let de grits soak and den bile it and let it stand. Sometime you put in some pounded hickory nut meats. Dat make it real good.

I don't know whar old Master git de cloth for de clothes, less'n he buy it. Befo' I can remember I think he had some slaves dat weave de cloth, but when I was dar he git it at de wagon depot at Honey Springs, I think. He go dar all de time to sell his corn, and he raise lots of corn, too.

Dat place was on de big road, what we called de road to Texas, but it go all de way up to de North, too. De traders stop at Honey Springs and old Master trade corn for what he want. He git some purty checkedy cloth one time, and everybody git a dress or a shirt made off'n it. I have dat dress 'till I git too big for it.

Everybody dress up fine when dey is a funeral. Dey take me along to mind de baby at two-three funerals, but I don't know who it is dat die. De Creek sho' take on when somebody die!

Long in de night you wake up and hear a gun go off, way off yonder somewhar. Den it go again, and den again, jest as fast as dey can ram de load in. Dat mean somebody dead. When somebody die de men go out in de yard and let de people know dat way. Den dey jest go back in de house and let de fire go out, and don't even tech de dead person till somebody git dar what has de right to tech de dead.

When somebody bad sick dey build a fire in de house, even in de summer, and don't let it die down till dat person git well or die. When dey die dey let de fire go out.

In de morning everybody dress up fine and go to de house whar de dead is and stand around in de yard outside de house and don't go in. Pretty soon along come somebody what got a right to tech and handle de dead and dey go in. I don't know what give dem de right, but I think dey has to go through some kind of medicine to git de right, and I know dey has to drink de red root and purge good before dey tech de body. When dey git de body ready dey come out and all go to de graveyard, mostly de family graveyard, right on de place or at some of the kinfolkses.

When dey git to de grave somebody shoots a gun at de north, den de west, den de south, and den de east. Iffen dey had four guns dey used 'em.

Den dey put de body down in de grave and put some extra clothes in with it and some food and a cup of coffee, maybe. Den dey takes strips of elm bark and lays over de body till it all covered up, and den throw in de dirt.

When de last dirt throwed on, everybody must clap dey hands and smile, but you sho hadn't better step on any of de new dirt around de grave, because it bring sickness right along wid you back to your own house. Dat what dey said, anyways.

Jest soon as de grave filled up dey built a little shelter over it wid poles like a pig pen and kiver it over wid elm bark to keep de rain from soaking down in de new dirt.

Den everybody go back to de house and de family go in and scatter some kind of medicine 'round de place and build a new fire. Sometime dey feed everybody befo' dey all leave for home.

Every time dey have a funeral dey always a lot of de people say, "Didn't you hear de stikini squalling in de night?" "I hear dat stikini all de night!" De "stikini" is de screech owl, and he suppose to tell when anybody going to die right soon. I hear lots of Creek people say dey hear de screech owl close to de house, and sho' nuff somebody in de family die soon.

When de big battle come at our place at Honey Springs dey jest git through having de green corn "busk." De green corn was just ripened enough to eat. It must of been along in July.

Dat busk was jest a little busk. Dey wasn't enough men around to have a good one. But I seen lots of big ones. Ones whar dey had all de different kinds of "banga." Dey call all de dances some kind of banga. De chicken dance is de "Tolosabanga", and de "Istifanibanga" is de one whar dey make lak dey is skeletons and raw heads coming to git you.

De "Hadjobanga" is de crazy dance, and dat is a funny one. Dey all dance crazy and make up funny songs to go wid de dance. Everybody think up funny songs to sing and everybody whoop and laugh all de time.

But de worse one was de drunk dance. Dey jest dance ever whichaway, de men and de women together, and dey wrassle and hug and carry on awful! De good people don't dance dat one. Everybody sing about going to somebody elses house and sleeping wid dem, and shout, "We is all drunk and we don't know what we doing and we ain't doing wrong 'cause we is all drunk" and things like dat. Sometime de bad ones leave and go to de woods, too!

Dat kind of doing make de good people mad, and sometime dey have killings about it. When a man catch one his women—maybeso his wife or one of his daughters—been to de woods he catch her and beat her and cut off de rim of her ears!

People think maybeso dat ain't so, but I know it is!

I was combing somebody's hair one time—I ain't going tell who—and when I lift it up off'n her ears I nearly drap dead! Dar de rims cut right off'n 'em! But she was a married woman, and I think maybeso it happen when she was a young gal and got into it at one of dem drunk dances.

Dem Upper Creek took de marrying kind of light anyways. Iffen de younguns wanted to be man and wife and de old ones didn't care dey jest went ahead and dat was about all, 'cepting some presents maybe. But de Baptists changed dat a lot amongst de young ones.

I never forgit de day dat battle of de Civil War happen at Honey Springs! Old Master jest had de green corn all in, and us had been having a time gitting it in, too. Jest de women was all dat was left, 'cause de men slaves had all slipped off and left out. My uncle Abe done got up a bunch and gone to de North wid dem to fight, but I didn't know den whar he went. He was in dat same battle, and after de War dey called him Abe Colonel. Most all de slaves 'round dat place done gone off a long time before dat wid dey masters when dey go wid old man Gouge and a man named McDaniel.

We had a big tree in de yard, and a grape vine swing in it for de little baby "Istidji", and I was swinging him real early in de morning befo' de sun up. De house set in a little patch of woods wid de field in de back, but all out on de north side was a little open space, like a kind of prairie. I was swinging de baby, and all at once I seen somebody riding dis way 'cross dat prairie—jest coming a-kiting and a-laying flat out on his hoss. When he see de house he begin to give de war whoop, "Eya-a-a-he-ah!" When he git close to de house he holler to git out de way 'cause dey gwine be a big fight, and old Master start rapping wid his cane and yelling to git some grub and blankets in de wagon right now!

We jest leave everything setting right whar it is, 'cepting putting out de fire and grabbing all de pots and kettles. Some de nigger women run to git de mules and de wagon and some start gitting meat and corn out of de place whar we done hid it to keep de scouters from finding it befo' now. All de time we gitting ready to travel we hear dat boy on dat horse going on down de big Texas road hollering. "Eya-a-a-he-he-hah!"

Den jest as we starting to leave here come something across dat little prairie sho' nuff! We know dey is Indians de way dey is riding, and de way dey is all strung out. Dey had a flag, and it was all red and had a big criss-cross on it dat look lak a saw horse. De man carry it and rear back on it when de wind whip it, but it flap all 'round de horse's head and de horse pitch and rear lak he know something going happen, sho!

'Bout dat time it turn kind of dark and begin to rain a little, and we git out to de big road and de rain come down hard. It rain so hard for a little while dat we jest have to stop de wagon and set dar, and den long come more soldiers dan I ever see befo'. Dey all white men, I think, and dey have on dat brown clothes dyed wid walnut and butternut, and old Master say dey de Confederate soldiers. Dey dragging some big guns on wheels and most de men slopping 'long in de rain on foot.

Den we hear de fighting up to de north 'long about what de river is, and de guns sound lak hosses loping 'cross a plank bridge way off somewhar. De head men start hollering and some de hosses start rearing and de soldiers start trotting faster up de road. We can't git out on de road so we jest strike off through de prairie and make for a creek dat got high banks and a place on it we call Rocky Cliff.

We git in a big cave in dat cliff, and spend de whole day and dat night in dar, and listen to de battle going on.

Dat place was about half-a-mile from de wagon depot at Honey Springs, and a little east of it. We can hear de guns going all day, and along in de evening here come de South side making for a getaway. Dey come riding and running by whar we is, and it don't make no difference how much de head men hollers at 'em dey can't make dat bunch slow up and stop.

After while here come de Yankees, right after 'em, and dey goes on into Honey Springs and pretty soon we see de blaze whar dey is burning de wagon depot and de houses.

De next morning we goes back to de house and find de soldiers ain't hurt nothing much. De hogs is whar dey is in de pen and de chickens come cackling 'round too. Dem soldiers going so fast dey didn't have no time to stop and take nothing, I reckon.

Den long come lots of de Yankee soldiers going back to de North, and dey looks purty wore out, but dey is laughing and joshing and going on.

Old Master pack up de wagon wid everything he can carry den, and we strike out down de big road to git out de way of any more war, is dey going be any.

Dat old Texas road jest crowded wid wagons! Everybody doing de same thing we is, and de rains done made de road so muddy and de soldiers done tromp up de mud so bad dat de wagons git stuck all de time.

De people all moving along in bunches, and every little while one bunch of wagons come up wid another bunch all stuck in de mud, and dey put all de hosses and mules on together and pull em out, and den dey go on together awhile.

At night dey camp, and de women and what few niggers dey is have to git de supper in de big pots, and de men so tired dey eat everything up from de women and de niggers, purty nigh.

After while we come to de Canadian town. Dat whar old man Gouge been and took a whole lot de folks up north wid him, and de South soldiers got in dar ahead of us and took up all de houses to sleep in.

Dey was some of de white soldiers camped dar, and dey was singing at de camp. I couldn't understand what dey sing, and I asked a Creek man what dey say and he tell me dey sing, "I wish I was in Dixie, look away—look away."

I ask him whar dat is, and he laugh and talk to de soldiers and dey all laugh, and make me mad.

De next morning we leave dat town and git to de big river. De rain make de river rise, and I never see so much water! Jest look out dar and dar all dat water!

Dey got some boats we put de stuff on, and float de wagons and swim de mules and finally git across, but it look lak we gwine all drown.

Most de folks say dey going to Boggy Depot and around Fort Washita, but old Master strike off by hisself and go way down in de bottom somewhar to live.

I don't know whar it was, but dey been some kind of fighting all around dar, 'cause we camp in houses and cabins all de time and nobody live in any of 'em.

Look like de people all git away quick, 'cause all de stuff was in de houses, but you better scout up around de house before you go up to it. Liable to be some scouters already in it!

Dem Indian soldiers jest quit de army and lots went scouting in little bunches and took everything dey find. Iffen somebody try to stop dem dey git killed.

Sometime we find graves in de yard whar somebody jest been buried fresh, and one house had some dead people in it when old Mistress poke her head in it. We git away from dar, and no mistake!

By and by we find a little cabin and stop and stay all de time. I was de only slave by dat time. All de others done slip out and run off. We stay dar two year I reckon, 'cause we make two little crop of corn. For meat a man name Mr. Walker wid us jest went out in de woods and shoot de wild hogs. De woods was full of dem wild hogs, and lots of fish in de holes whar he could sicken 'em wid buck root and catch 'em wid his hands, all we wanted.

I don't know when de War quit off, and when I git free, but I stayed wid old man Tuskaya-hiniha long time after I was free, I reckon. I was jest a little girl, and he didn't know whar to send me to, anyways.

One day three men rid up and talk to de old man awhile in English talk. Den he called me and tell me to go wid dem to find my own family. He jest laugh and slap my behind and set me up on de hoss in front of one de men and dey take me off and leave my good checkedy dress at de house!

Before long we git to dat Canadian river again, and de men tie me on de hoss so I can't fall off. Dar was all dat water, and dey ain't no boat, and dey ain't no bridge, and we jest swim de hosses. I knowed sho' I was going to be gone dat time, but we git across.

When we come to de Creek Agency dar is my pappy and my mammy to claim me, and I live wid dem in de Verdigris bottom above Fort Gibson till I was grown and dey is both dead. Den I marries Anderson Davis at Gibson Station, and we git our allotments on de Verdigris east of Tulsa—kind of south too, close to de Broken Arrow town.

I knowed old man Jim McHenry at dat Broken Arrow town. He done some preaching and was a good old man, I think.

I knowed when dey started dat Wealaka school across de river from de Broken Arrow town. Dey name it for de Wilaki town, but dat town was way down in de Upper Creek country close to whar I lived when I was a girl.

I had lots of children, but only two is alive now. My boy Anderson got in a mess and went to dat McAlester prison, but he got to be a trusty and dey let him marry a good woman dat got lots of property dar, and dey living all right now.

When my old man die I come to live here wid Josephine, but I'se blind and can't see nothing and all de noises pesters me a lot in de town. And de children is all so ill mannered, too. Dey jest holler at you all de time! Dey don't mind you neither!

When I could see and had my own younguns I could jest set in de corner and tell 'em what to do, and iffen dey didn't do it right I could whack 'em on de head, 'cause dey was raised de old Creek way, and dey know de old folks know de best!

Oklahoma Writers' Project
 Ex-Slaves
 [HR: (photo)]
 [Date stamp: AUG 16 1937]

ANTHONY DAWSON
Age 105 yrs.
1008 E. Owen St.,
Tulsa, Okla.

"Run nigger, run,

De Patteroll git you!

Run nigger, run,

De Patteroll come!

"Watch nigger, watch—

De Patteroll trick you!

Watch nigger, watch,

He got a big gun!"

Dat one of the songs de slaves all knowed, and de children down on de "twenty acres" used to sing it when dey playing in de moonlight 'round de cabins in de quarters. Sometime I wonder iffen de white folks didn't make dat song up so us niggers would keep in line.

None of my old Master's boys tried to git away 'cepting two, and dey met up wid evil, both of 'em.

One of dem niggers was fotching a bull-tongue from a piece of new ground way at de back of de plantation, and bringing it to my pappy to git it sharped. My pappy was de blacksmith.

Dis boy got out in de big road to walk in de soft sand, and long come a wagon wid a white overseer and five, six, niggers going somewhar. Dey stopped and told dat boy to git in and ride. Dat was de last anybody seen him.

Dat overseer and another one was cotched after awhile, and showed up to be underground railroaders. Dey would take a bunch of niggers into town for some excuse, and on de way jest pick up a extra nigger and show him whar to go to git on de "railroad system." When de runaway niggers got to de North dey had to go in de army, and dat boy from our place got killed. He was a good boy, but dey jest talked him into it. Dem railroaders was honest, and dey didn't take no presents, but de patrollers was low white trash!

We all knowed dat if a patroller jest rode right by and didn't say nothing dat he was doing his honest job, but iffen he stopped his hoss and talked to a nigger he was after some kind of trade.

Dat other black boy was hoeing cotton way in de back of de field and de patroller rid up and down de big road, saying nothing to nobody.

De next day another white man was on de job, and long in de evening a man come by and axed de niggers about de fishing and hunting! Dat black boy seen he was de same man what was riding de day befo' and he knowed it was a underground trick. But he didn't see all de trick, bless God!

We found out afterwards dat he told his mammy about it. She worked at de big house and she stole something for him to give dat low white trash I reckon, 'cause de next day he played sick along in de evening and de black overlooker—he was my uncle—sent him back to de quarters.

He never did git there, but when dey started de hunt dey found him about a mile away in de woods wid his head shot off, and old Master sold his mammy to a trader right away. He never whipped his grown niggers.

Dat was de way it worked. Dey was all kinds of white folks jest like dey is now. One man in Sesesh clothes would shoot you if you tried to run away. Maybe another Sesesh would help slip you out to the underground and say "God bless you poor black devil", and some of dem dat was poor would help you if you could bring 'em sumpin you stole, lak a silver dish or spoons or a couple big hams. I couldn't blame them poor white folks, wid the men in the War and the women and children hongry. The niggers didn't belong to them nohow, and they had to live somehow. But now and then they was a devil on earth, walking in the sight of God and spreading iniquity before him. He was de low-down Sesesh dat would take what a poor runaway nigger had to give for his chance to git away, and den give him 'structions dat would lead him right into de hands of de patrollers and git him caught or shot!

Yes, dat's de way it was. Devils and good people walking in de road at de same time, and nobody could tell one from t'other.

I remember about de trickery so good 'cause I was "grown and out" at that time. When I was a little boy I was a house boy, 'cause my mammy was the house woman, but when the war broke I already been sent to the fields and mammy was still at de house.

I was born on July 25, 1832. I know, 'cause old Master keep de book on his slaves jest like on his own family. He was a good man, and old Mistress was de best woman in de world!

De plantation had more than 500 acres and most was in cotton and tobacco. But we raised corn and oats, and lots of cattle and horses, and plenty of sheep for wool.

I was born on the plantation, soon after my pappy and mammy was brought to it. I don't remember whether they was bought or come from my Mistress's father. He was mighty rich and had several hundred niggers. When she was married he give her 40 niggers. One of them was my pappy's brother. His name was John, and he was my master's overlooker.

We called a white man boss the "overseer", but a nigger was a overlooker. John could read and write and figger, and old Master didn't have no white overseer.

Master's name was Levi Dawson, and his plantation was 18 miles east of Greenville, North Carolina. It was a beautiful place, with all the fences around the Big House and along the front made out of barked poles, rider style, and all whitewashed.

The Big House set back from the big road about a quarter of a mile. It was only one story, but it had lots of rooms.

There was four rooms in a bunch on one side and four in a bunch on the other, with a wide hall in between. They was made of square adzed logs, all weatherboarded on the outside and planked up and plastered on the inside. Then they was a long gallery clean across the front with big pillars made out of bricks and plastered over. They called it the passage 'cause it din't have no floor excepting bricks, and a buggy could drive right under it. Mostly it was used to set under and talk and play cards and drink the best whiskey old Master could buy.

Back in behind the big house was the kitchen, and the smokehouse in another place made of plank, and all was whitewashed and painted white all the time.

Old Mistress was named Miss Susie and she was born an Isley. She brought 40 niggers from her pappy as a present, and Master Levi jest had 4 or 5, but he had got all his land from his pappy.

She had the niggers and he had the land. That's the way it was, and that's the way it stayed! She never let him punish one of her niggers and he never asked her about buying or selling land. Her pappy was richer than his pappy, and she was sure quality!

My pappy's name was Anthony, and mammy's name was Chanie. He was the blacksmith and fixed the wagons, but he couldn't read and figger like uncle John. Mammy was the head house woman but didn't know any letters either.

They was both black like me. Old man Isley, where they come from, had lots of niggers, but I don't think they was off the boat.

You can set the letters up and I can't tell them, but you can't fool me with the figgers, 'less they are mighty big numbers.

Master Levi had three sons and no daughters. The oldest son was Simeon. He was in the Sesesh army. The other two boys was too young. I can't remember their names. They was a lot younger and I was grown and out befo' they got big.

Old Master was a fine Christian but he like his juleps anyways. He let us niggers have preachings and prayers, and would give us a parole to go 10 or 15 miles to a camp meeting and stay two or three days with nobody but Uncle John to stand for us. Mostly we had white preachers, but when we had a black preacher that was Heaven.

We didn't have no voodoo women nor conjure folks at our 20 acres. We all knowed about the Word and the unseen Son of God and we didn't put no stock in conjure.

Course we had luck charms and good and bad signs, but everybody got dem things even nowadays. My boy had a white officer in the Big War and he tells me that man had a li'l old doll tied around his wrist on a gold chain.

We used herbs and roots for common ailments, like sassafras and boneset and peach tree poultices and coon root tea, but when a nigger got bad sick Old Master sent for a white doctor. I remember that old doctor. He lived in Greenville and he had to come 18 miles in a buggy.

When he give some nigger medicine he would be afraid the nigger was like lots of them that believed in conjure, and he would say, "If you don't take that medicine like I tell you and I have to come back here to see you I going to break your dam black neck next time I come out here!"

When it was bad weather sometime the black boy sent after him had to carry a lantern to show him the way back. If that nigger on his mule got too fur ahead so old doctor couldn't see de light he sho' catch de devil from that old doctor and from old Master, too, less'n he was one of old Missy's house niggers, and then old Master jest grumble to satisfy the doctor.

Down in the quarters we had the spinning house, where the old woman card the wool and run the loom. They made double weave for the winter time, and all the white folks and slaves had good clothes and good food.

Master made us all eat all we could hold. He would come to the smokehouse and look in and say, "You niggers ain't cutting down that smoke side and that souse lak you ought to! You made dat meat and you got to help eat it up!"

Never no work on Sunday 'cepting the regular chores. The overlooker made everybody clean up and wash de children up and after the praying we had games. Antny over and marbles and "I Spy" and de likes of that. Some times de boys would go down in de woods and git a possum. I love possum and sweet taters, but de coon meat more delicate and de har don't stink up de meat.

I wasn't at the quarters much as a boy. I was at the big house with my mammy, and I had to swing the fly bresh over my old Mistress when she was sewing or eating or taking her nap. Sometime I would keep the flies off'n old Master, and when I would get tired and let the bresh slap his neck he would kick at me and cuss me, but he never did reach me. He had a way of keeping us little niggers scared to death and never hurting nobody.

I was down in the field burning bresh when I first heard the guns in the War. De fighting was de battle at Kingston, North Carolina, and it lasted four days and nights. After while bunches of Sesesh come riding by hauling wounded people in wagons, and then pretty soon big bunches of Yankees come by, but dey didn't ack like dey was trying very hard to ketch up.

Dey had de country in charge quite some time, and they had forages coming round all the time. By dat time old Master done buried his money and all de silver and de big clock, but the Yankees didn't pear to search out dat kind of stuff. All dey ask about was did anybody find a bottle of brandy!

When de War ended up most all de niggers stay with old Master and work on de shares, until de land git divided up and sold off and the young niggers git scattered to town.

I never did have no truck wid de Ku Kluckers, but I had to step mighty high to keep out'n it! De sho' nuff Kluxes never did bother around us 'cause we minded our own business and never give no trouble.

We wouldn't let no niggers come 'round our place talking 'bout delegates and voting, and we jest all stayed on the place. But dey was some low white trash and some devilish niggers made out like dey was Ku Klux ranging 'round de country stealing hosses and taking things. Old Master said dey wasn't shore enough, so I reckon he knowed who the regular ones was.

These bunches that come around robbing got into our neighborhood and old Master told me I better not have my old horse at the house, 'cause if I had him they would know nobody had been there stealing and it wouldn't do no good to hide anything 'cause they would tear up the place hunting what I had and maybe whip or kill me.

"Your old hoss aint no good, Tony, and you better kill him to make them think you already been raided on," old Master told me, so I led him out and knocked him in the head with an axe, and then we hid all our grub and waited for the Kluckers to come most any night, but they never did come. I borried a hoss to use in the day and took him back home every night for about a year.

The niggers kept talking about being free, but they wasn't free then and they ain't now.

Putting them free jest like putting goat hair on a sheep. When it rain de goat come a running and git in de shelter, 'cause his hair won't shed the rain and he git cold, but de sheep ain't got sense enough to git in the shelter but jest stand out and let it rain on him all day.

But the good Lord fix the sheep up wid a woolly jacket that turn the water off, and he don't git cold, so he don't have to have no brains.

De nigger during slavery was like de sheep. He couldn't take care of hisself but his Master looked out for him and he didn't have to use his brains. De master's protection was like de wooly coat.

But de 'mancipation come and take off de woolly coat and leave de nigger wid no protection and he cain't take care of hisself either.

When de niggers was sot free lots of them got mighty uppity, and everybody wanted to be a delegate to something or other. The Yankees told us we could go down and vote in the 'lections and our color was good enough to run for anything. Heaps of niggers believed them. You cain't fault them for that, 'cause they didn't have no better sense, but I knowed the black folks didn't have no business mixing in until they knowed more.

It was a long time after the War before I went down to vote and everything quiet by that time, but I heard people talk about the fights at the schoolhouse when they had the first election.

I jest stayed on around the old place a long time, and then I got on another piece of ground and farmed, not far from Greenville until 1900. Then I moved to Hearn, Texas, and stayed with my son Ed until 1903 when we moved to Sapulpa in the Creek Nation. We come to Tulsa several years ago, and I been living with him ever since.

I can't move off my bed now, but one time I was strong as a young bull. I raised seven boys and seven girls. My boys was named Edward, Joseph, Furney, Julius, James, and William, and my girls was Luvenia, Olivia, Chanie Mamie, Rebecca and Susie.

I always been a deep Christian and depend on God and know his unseen Son, the King of Glory. I learned about Him when I was a little boy. Old Master was a good man, but on some of the plantations the masters wasn't good men and the niggers didn't get the Word.

I never did get no reading and writing 'cause I never did go to the schools. I thought I was too big, but they had schools and the young ones went.

But I could figger, and I was a good farmer, and now I bless the Lord for all his good works. Everybody don't know it I reckon, but we all needed each other. The blacks needed the whites, and still do.

There's a difference in the color of the skin, but the souls is all white, or all black, 'pending on the man's life and not on his skin. The old fashioned meetings is busted up into a thousand different kinds of churches and only one God to look after them. All is confusion, but I ain't going to worry my old head about 'em.

Oklahoma Writers' Project
Ex-Slaves
[Date stamp AUG 19 1937]

ALICE DOUGLASS
Age 77 yrs.
Oklahoma City, Okla.

I was born December 22, 1860 in Sumner County, Tennessee. My mother—I mean mammy, 'cause what did we know 'bout mother and mamma. Master and Mistress made dey chillun call all nigger women, "Black Mammy." Jest as I was saying my mammy was named Millie Elkins and my pappy was named Isaac Garrett. My sisters and brothers was Frank, Susie and Mollie. They is all in Nashville, Tennessee right now. They lived in log houses. I 'member my grandpappy and when he died. I allus slept in the Big House in a cradle wid white babies.

We all the time wore cotton dresses and we weaved our own cloth. The boys jest wore shirts. Some wore shoes, and I sho' did. I kin see 'em now as they measured my feets to git my shoes. We had doctors to wait on us iffen we got sick and ailing. We wore asafedida to keep all diseases offen us.

When a nigger man got ready to marry, he go and tell his master that they was a woman on sech and sech a farm that he'd lak to have. Iffen master give his resent, then he go and ask her master and iffen he say yes, well, they jest jump the broomstick. Mens could jest see their wives on Sadday nite.

They laid peoples 'cross barrels and whupped 'em wid bull whups till the blood come. They'd half feed 'em and niggers'd steal food and cook all night. The things we was forced to do then the whites is doing of their own free will now. You gotta reap jest what you sow 'cause the Good Book says it.

They used to bid niggers off and then load 'em on wagons and take 'em to cotton farms to work. I never seen no cotton till I come heah. Peoples make big miration 'bout girls having babies at 11 years old. And you better have them whitefolks some babies iffen you didn't wanta be sold. Though a funny thing to me is, iffen a nigger woman had a baby on the boat on the way to the cotton farms, they throwed it in the river. Taking 'em to them cotton farms is jest the reason niggers is so plentiful in the South today.

I ain't got no education a'tall. In dem days you better not be caught with a newspaper, else you got a beating and your back almost cut off. When niggers got free, whitefolks killed 'em by the carload, 'cause they said it was a nigger uprising. I used to lay on the flo' with the whitefolks and hear 'em pass. Them patrollers roved trying to ketch niggers without passes to whup 'em. They was sometimes called bush whackers.

We went to white folks' church. I was a great big girl before we went to cullud church. We'd stay out and play while they worshipped. We jest played marbles—girls, white chillun and all.

The Yankees come thoo' and took all the meat and everything they could find. They took horses, food and all. Mammy cooked their vittles. One come in our cabin and took a sack of dried fruit with my mammy's shoes on the top. I tried to make 'em leave mammy's shoes too but he didn't.

I stayed in the house with the whitefolks till I was 19. They lak to kept me in there too long. That's why I'm selfish as I am. Within three weeks after I was out of the house, I married William Douglass. Whitefolks now don't want you to tech 'em, and I slept with white chillun till I was 19. You kin cook for 'em and put your hands in they vittles and they don't say nothing, but jest you tech one!

We stayed on, on the place, three or four years and it was right then mammy give us our pappy's name. We moved from the place to one three or four miles from our master's place, and mammy cooked there a long time.

Abraham Lincoln gits too much praise. I say, shucks, give God the praise. Lincoln come thoo' Gallitan, Tennessee and stopped at Hotel Tavern with his wife. They was dressed jest lak tramps and nobody knowed it was him and his wife till he got to the White House and writ back and told 'em to look 'twixt the leaves in the table where he had set and they sho' nuff found out it was him.

I never mentions Jeff Davis. He ain't wuff it.

Booker T. Washington was all right in his place. He come here and told these whitefolks jest what he thought. Course he wouldn't have done that way down South. I declare to God he sho' told 'em enough. They toted him 'round on their hands. No Jim Crow here then.

I jined the church 'cause I had religion round 60 years ago. People oughta be religious sho'; what for they wanta live in sin and die and go to the Bad Man. To git to Heaven, you sho' ought to work some. I want a resting place somewhar, 'cause I ain't got none here. I am a member of Tabernacle Baptist Church, and I help build the first church in Oklahoma City.

I got three boys and three girls. I don't know none's age. I give 'em the best education I could.

Oklahoma Writers' Project
Ex-Slaves
[Date stamp: AUG 13 1937]

DOC DANIEL DOWDY
Age 81 yrs.
Oklahoma City, Oklahoma

I was born June 6, 1856 in Madison County, Georgia. Father was named Joe Dowdy and mother was named Mary Dowdy. There was 9 of us boys, George, Smith, Lewis, Henry, William, myself, Newt, James and Jeff. There was one girl and she was my twin, and her name was Sarah. My mother and father come from Richmond, Va., to Georgia. Father lived on one side of the river and my mother on the other side. My father would come over ever week to visit us. Noah Meadows bought my father and Elizabeth Davis, daughter of the old master took my mother. They married in Noah Meadows' house.

My mother was the cook in the Big House. They'd give us pot likker with bread crumbs in it. Sometimes meat, jest sometimes, very seldom. I liked black-eyed peas and still do till now. We lived in weatherboard house. Our parents had corded-up beds with ropes and us chillun slept on the floor for most part or in a hole bored in a log. Our house had one window jest big enough to stick your head out of, and one door, and this one door faced the Big House which was your master's house. This was so that you couldn't git out 'less somebody seen you.

My job was picking up chips and keeping the calves and cows separate so that the calves wouldn't suck the cows dry. Mostly, we had Saturday afternoons off to wash. I was show boy doing [HW: during] the war, me and my sister, 'cause we was twins. My mother couldn't be bought 'cause she done had 9 boys for one farm and neither my father, 'cause he was the father of 'em. I was religious and didn't play much, but I sho' did like to listen to preachings. I did used to play marbles sometimes.

We jest wore shirts and nothing else both winter and summer. They was a little heavier in winter and that's all. No shoes ever. I had none till after I was set free. I guess I was almost 12 years old then.

The overseer on our place was a large tall, black man. We had plenty poor white neighbors. They was one of our biggest troubles. They'd allus look in our window and door all the time.

I saw slaves sold. I can see that old block now. My cousin Eliza was a pretty girl, really good looking. Her master was her father. When the girls in the big house had beaux coming to see 'em, they'd ask, "Who is that pretty gal?" So they decided to git rid of her right away. The day they sold her will allus be remembered. They stripped her to be bid off and looked at. I wasn't allowed to stand in the crowd. I was laying down under a fig brush. The man that bought Eliza was from New York. The Negroes had made up nuff money to buy her off theyself, but they wouldn't let that happen. There was a man bidding for her who was a Swedeland. He allus bid for the good looking cullud gals and bought 'em for his own use. He ask the man from New York, "Whut you gonna do with her when you git 'er?" The man from New York said, "None of your damn business, but you ain't got money nuff to buy 'er." When the man from New York had done bought her, he said, "Eliza, you are free from now on." She left and went to New York with him. Mama and Eliza both cried when she was being showed off, and master told 'em to shet up before he knocked they brains out.

Iffen you didn't do nothing wrong, they whipped you now and then anyhow. I called a boy Johnny once and he took me 'hind the garden and poured it on me and made me call him master. It was from then on I started to fear the white man. I come to think of him as a bear. Sometimes fellows would be a little late making it in and they got whipped with a cow-hide. The same man whut whipped me to make me call him master, well, he whipped my mamma. He tied her to a tree and beat her unmerciful and cut her tender parts. I don't know why he tied her to that tree.

The first time you was caught trying to read or write, you was whipped with a cow-hide, the next time with a cat-o-nine tails and the third time they cut the first jint offen your forefinger. They was very severe. You most allus got 30 and 9 lashes.

They carried news from one plantation by whut they call relay. Iffen you was caught, they whipped you till you said, "Oh, pray Master!" One day a man gitting whipped was saying "Oh pray master, Lord have mercy!" They'd say "Keep whipping that nigger Goddamn him." He was whipped till he said, "Oh pray Master, I gotta nuff." Then they said, "Let him up now, 'cause he's praying to the right man."

My father was the preacher and an educated man. You know the sermon they give him to preach?—Servant, Obey Your Master. Our favorite baptizing hymn was On Jordan's Stormy Bank I Stand. My favorite song is Nobody Knows the Trouble I've Seen.

Oh, them patrollers! They had a chief and he git'em together and iffen they caught you without a pass and sometimes with a pass, they'd beat you. But iffen you had a pass, they had to answer to the law. One old master had two slaves, brothers, on his place. They was both preachers. Mitchell was a hardshell Baptist and Andrew was a Missionary Baptist. One day the patroller chief was rambling thoo' the place and found some letters writ to Mitchell and Andrew. He went to the master and said, "Did you know you had some niggers that could read and write?" Master said, "No, but I might have, who do you 'spect?" The patroller answered, "Mitchell and Andrew." The old master said, "I never knowed Andrew to tell me a lie 'bout nothing!"

Mitchell was called first and asked could he read and write. He was scared stiff. He said, "Naw-sir." Andrew was called and asked. He said, "Yes-sir." He was asked iffen Mitchell could. He said, "Sho', better'n me." The master told John Arnold, the patroller chief, not to bother 'em. He gloried in they spunk. When the old master died, he left all of his niggers a home apiece. We had Ku Klux Klans till the government sent Federal officers out and put a stop to their ravaging and sent 'em to Sing Sing.

Doing the war my father was carpenter. His young master come to him 'cause he was a preacher and asked him must he go to the front and my father told him not to go 'cause he wouldn't make it. He went on jest the same and when he come back my father had to tote him in the house 'cause he had one leg tore off. The Yankees come thoo', ramshacked houses, leave poor horses and take fat ones and turn the poor ones in the corn they left. They took everthing they could. They cussed niggers who dodged 'em for being fools and make 'em show 'em everything they knowed whar was.

Our old master was mighty old and him and the women folks cried when we was freed. He told us we was free as he was.

I come to Oklahoma in 1906. I come out of that riot in 1906. Some fellow knocked up a colored woman or something and we waded right in and believe me we made Atlanta a fit place to live in. It is one of the best cities in America.

I married Miss Emmaline Witt. I carried her to the preacher one of the coldest nights I ever rid. I have three chillun and don't know how many grandchillun. My chillun is one a nurse, one in Arizona for his health and the other doing first one thing and another.

I think Abraham Lincoln was the greatest human being ever been on earth 'cepting the Apostle Paul. Who any better'n a man who liberated 4,000,000 Negroes? Some said he wasn't a Christian, but he told some friends once, "I'm going to leave you and may never see you again (and he didn't) so I'm going to take the Divine Spirit with me and leave it with you."

Jeff Davis was as bloody as he could be. I don't lak him a'tall. But you know good things come from enemies. I don't even admire George Washington. White men from the south that will help the Negro is far and few between. Booker T. Washington was a great man. He made some blunders and mistakes, but he was a great man. He is the father of industrial education and you know that sho' is a great thing.

The white folks was ignorant. You know the better you prepare yourself the better you act. Iffen they had put some sense in our heads 'stead of sticks on our heads, we'ud been better off and more benefit to 'em.

I had something from within that made me fear God and taught me how to pray. People say God don't hear sinners pray, but he do. Everybody ought to be Christians so not to be lost.

I work in real estate and can do a lot of work. I don't use no crutches and no cane and walk all the time, never hardly ride. I come in at 1 and 2 o'clock a. m. and get up between 8 and 9 a. m. 'cept Sundays, I get up at 7 or 8 a. m. so I can be ready to go to Sunday School. I cook for my own self all the time too. I am a Baptist and a member of Tabernacle Baptist Church. I am a trustee in my church too.

Oklahoma Writers' Project
Ex-Slaves
[Date stamp: AUG 19 1937]

JOANNA DRAPER
Age 83 yrs.
Tulsa, Okla.

Most folks can't remember many things happened to 'em when they only eight years old, but one of my biggest tribulations come about dat time and I never will forget it! That was when I was took away from my own mammy and pappy and sent off and bound out to another man, way off two-three hundred miles away from whar I live. And dat's the last time I ever see either one of them, or any my own kinfolks!

Whar I was born was at Hazelhurst, Mississippi. Jest a little piece east of Hazelhurst, close to the Pearl River, and that place was a kind of new plantation what my Master, Dr. Alexander, bought when he moved into Mississippi from up in Virginia awhile before the War.

They said my mammy brings me down to Mississippi, and I was born jest right after she got there. My mammy's name was Margaret, and she was born under the Ramson's, back in Tennessee. She belonged to Dave Ramson, and his pappy had come to Tennessee to settle on war land, and he had knowed Dr. Alexander's people back in Virginia too. My pappy's name was Addison, and he always belonged to Dr. Alexander. Old doctor bought my mammy 'cause my pappy liked her. Old doctor live in Tennessee a little while before he go on down in Mississippi.

Old doctor's wife named Dinah, and she sho' was a good woman, but I don't remember about old doctor much. He was away all the time, it seem like.

When I is about six year old they take me into the Big House to learn to be a house woman, and they show me how to cook and clean up and take care of babies. That Big House wasn't very fine, but it was mighty big and cool, and made out of logs with a big hall, but it didn't have no long gallery like most the houses around there had.

They was lots of big trees in the yard, and most the ground was new ground 'round that place, 'cause the old Doctor jest started to done farming on it when I was took away, but he had some more places not so far away, over towards the river that was old ground and made big crops for him. I went to one of the places one time, but they wasn't nobody on 'em but niggers and a white overseer. I don't know how many niggers old Doctor had, but Master John Deeson say he had about a hundred.

At old Doctor's house I didn't have to work very hard. Jest had to help the cooks and peel the potatoes and pick the guineas and chickens and do things like that. Sometime I had to watch the baby. He was a little boy, and they would bring him into the kitchen for me to watch. I had to git up way before daylight and make the fire in the kitchen fireplace and bring in some fresh water, and go get the milk what been down in the spring all night, and do things like that until breakfast ready. Old Master and old Mistress come in the big hall to eat in the summer, and I stand behind them and shoo off the flies.

Old doctor didn't have no spinning and weaving niggers 'cause he say they don't do enough work and he buy all the cloth he use for everybody's clothes. He can do that 'cause he had lots of money. He was big rich, and he keep a whole lot of hard money in the house all the time, but none of the slaves know it but me. Sometimes I would have the baby in the Mistress' room and she would go git three or four big wood boxes full of hard money for us to play with. I would make fences out of the money all across the floor, to keep the baby satisfied, and when he go to sleep I would put the money back in the boxes. I never did know how much they is, but a whole lot.

Even after the War start old Doctor have that money, and he would exchange money for people. Sometimes he would go out and be gone a long time, and come back with a lot more money he got from somewhar.

Right at the first they made him a high officer in the War and he done doctoring somewhar at a hospital most of the time. But he could go on both sides of the War, and sometime he would come in at night and bring old Mistress pretty little things, and I heard him tell her he got them in the North.

One day I was fanning him and I asked him is he been to the North and he kick out at me and tell to shut up my black mouth, and it nearly scared me to death the way he look at me! Nearly every time he been gone and come in and tell Mistress he been in the North he have a lot more hard money to put away in them boxes, too!

One evening long come a man and eat supper at the house and stay all night. He was a nice mannered man, and I like to wait on him. The next morning I hear him ask old Doctor what is my name, and old Doctor start in to try to sell me to that man. The man say he can't buy me 'cause old Doctor say he want a thousand dollars, and then old Doctor say he will bind me out to him.

I run away from the house and went out to the cabin whar my mammy and pappy was, but they tell me to go on back to the Big House 'cause maybe I am just scared. But about that time old Doctor and the man come and old Doctor make me go with the man. We go in his buggy a long ways off to the South, and after he stop two or three night at peoples houses and put me out to stay with the niggers he come to his own house. I ask him how far it is back home and he say about a hundred miles or more, and laugh, and ask me if I know how far that is.

I wants to know if I can go back to my mammy some time, and he say "Sho', of course you can, some of these times. You don't belong to me, Jo, I'se jest your boss and not your master."

He live in a big old rottendy house, but he aint farming none of the land. Jest as soon as he git home he go off again, and sometimes he only come in at night for a little while.

His wife's name was Kate and his name was Mr. John. I was there about a week before I found out they name was Deeson. They had two children, a girl about my size name Joanna like me, and a little baby boy name Johnny. One day Mistress Kate tell me I the only nigger they got. I been thinking maybe they had some somewhar on a plantation, but she say they aint got no plantation and they aint been at that place very long either.

That little girl Joanna and me kind of take up together, and she was a mighty nice mannered little girl, too. Her mammy raised her good. Her mammy was mighty sickly all the time, and that's the reason they bind me to do the work.

Mr. John was in some kind of business in the War too, but I never see him with no soldier clothes on but one time. One night he come in with them on, but the next morning he come to breakfast in jest his plain clothes again. Then he go off again.

I sho' had a hard row at that house. It was old and rackady, and I had to scrub off the staircase and the floors all the time, and git the breakfast for Mistress Kate and the two children. Then I could have my own breakfast in the kitchen. Mistress Kate always get the supper, though.

Some days she go off with the two children and leave me at the house all day by myself, and I think maybe I run off, but I didn't know whar to go.

After I been at that place two years Mr. John come home and stay. He done some kind of trading in Jackson, Mississippi, and he would be gone three or four days at a time, but I never did know what kind of trading it was.

About the time he come home to stay I seen the first Ku Klux I ever seen one night. I was going down the road in the moonlight and I heard a hog grunting out in the bushes at the side of the road. I jest walk right on and in a little ways I hear another hog in some more bushes. This time I stop and listen, and they's another hog grunts across the road, and about that time two mens dressed up in long white skirts steps out into the road in front of me! I was so scared the goose bumps jump up all over me 'cause I didn't know what they is! They didn't say a word to me, but jest walked on past me and went on back the way I had come. Then I see two more mens step out of the woods and I run from that as fast as I can go!

I ast Miss Kate what they is and she say they Ku Klux, and I better not go walking off down the road any more. I seen them two, three times after that, though, but they was riding hosses them times.

I stayed at Mr. John's place two more years, and he got so grumpy and his wife got so mean I make up my mind to run off. I bundle up my clothes in a little bundle and hide them, and then I wait until Miss Kate take the children and go off somewhere, and I light out on foot. I had me a piece of that hard money what Master Dr. Alexander had give me one time at Christmas. I had kept it all that time and nobody knowed I had it, not even Joanna. Old Doctor told me it was fifty dollars, and I thought I could live on it for a while.

I never had been away from that place, not even to another plantation in all the four years I was with the Deesons, and I didn't know which-a-way to go, so I jest started west.

I been walking about all evening it seem like, and I come to a little town with jest a few houses. I see a nigger man and ask him whar I can git something to eat, and I say I got fifty dollars.

"What you doing wid fifty dollars, child? Where you belong at, anyhow?" He ask me, and I tell him I belong to Master John Deeson, but I is running away. I explain that I jest bound out to Mr. John, but Dr. Alexander my real master, and then that man tell me the first time I knowed it that I aint a slave no more!

That man Deeson never did tell me, and his wife never did!

Well, dat man asked me about the fifty dollars, and then I found out that it was jest fifty cents!

I can't begin to tell about all the hard times I had working for something to eat and roaming around after that. I don't know why I never did try to git back up around Hazelhurst and hunt up my pappy and mammy, but I reckon I was jest ignorant and didn't know how to go about it. Anyways I never did see them no more.

In about three years or a little over I met Bryce Draper on a farm in Mississippi and we was married. His mammy had had a harder time than I had. She had five children by a man that belong to her master, Mr. Bryce and already named one of the boys—that my husband—Bryce after him, and then he take her in and sell her off away from all her children!

One was jest a little baby, and the master give it laudanum, but it didn't die, and he sold her off and lied and said she was a young girl and didn't have no husband, 'cause the man what bought her said he didn't want to buy no woman and take her away from a family. That new master name was Draper.

The last year of the War Mr. Draper die, and his wife already dead, and he give all his farm to his two slaves and set them free. One of them slaves was my husband's mammy.

Then right away the whites come and robbed the place of every thing they could haul off, and run his mammy and the other niggers off! Then she went and found her boy, that was my husband, and he live with her until she died, jest before we is married.

We lived in Mississippi a long time, and then we hear about how they better to the Negroes up in the North, and we go up to Kansas, but they ain't no better there, and we come down to Indian Territory in the Creek Nation in 1898, jest as they getting in that Spanish War.

We leased a little farm from the Creek Nation for $15 an acre, but when they give out the allotments we had to give it up. Then we rent 100 acres from some Indians close to Wagoner, and we farm it all with my family. We had enough to do it too!

For children we had John and Joe, and Henry, and Jim and Robert and Will that was big enough to work, and then the girls big enough was Mary, Nellie, Izora, Dora, and the baby. Dora married Max Colbert. His people belonged to the Colberts that had Colbert's Crossin' on the Red River way before the War, and he was a freedman and got allotment.

I lives with Dora now, and we is all happy, and I don't like to talk about the days of the slavery times, 'cause they never did mean nothing to me but misery, from the time I was eight years old.

I never will forgive that white man for not telling me I was free, and not helping me to git back to my mammy and pappy! Lots of white people done that.

Oklahoma Writers' Project
Ex-Slaves

MRS. ESTHER EASTER
Age 85 yrs.
Tulsa, Okla.

I was born near Memphis, Tenn., on the old Ben Moore plantation, but I don't know anything about the Old South because Master Ben moves us all up into Missouri (about 14-miles east of Westport, now Kansas City), long before they started fighting about slavery.

Mary Collier was my mother's name before she was a Moore. About my father, I dunno. Mammy was sickly most of the time when I was a baby, and she was so thin and poorly when they move to Missouri the white folks afraid she going die on the way.

But she fool 'em, and she live two-three year after that. That's what good Old Master Ben tells me when I gets older.

I stay with Master Ben's married daughter, Mary, till the coming of the War. Times was good before the War, and I wasn't suffering none from slavery, except once in a while the Mistress would fan me with the stick—bet I needed it, too.

When the War come along Master he say to leave Mistress Mary and get ready to go to Texas. Jim Moore, one of the meanest men I ever see, was the son of Master Ben; he's going take us there.

Demon Jim, that's what I call him when he ain't round the place, but when he's home it was always Master Jim 'cause he was reckless with the whip. He was a Rebel officer fighting round the country and didn't take us slaves to Texas right away. So I stayed on at his place not far from Master Ben's plantation.

Master Jim's wife was a demon, just like her husband. Used the whip all the time, and every time Master Jim come home he whip me 'cause the Mistress say I been mean.

One time I tell him, you better put me in your pocket (sell me), Master Jim, else I'se going run away'. He don't pay no mind, and I don't try to run away 'cause of the whips.

I done see one whipping and that enough. They wasn't no fooling about it. A runaway slave from the Jenkin's plantation was brought back, and there was a public whipping, so's the slaves could see what happens when they tries to get away.

The runaway was chained to the whipping post, and I was full of misery when I see the lash cutting deep into that boy's skin. He swell up like a dead horse, but he gets over it, only he was never no count for work no more.

While Master Jim is out fighting the Yanks, the Mistress is fiddling round with a neighbor man, Mister Headsmith. I is young then, but I knows enough that Master Jim's going be mighty mad when he hears about it.

The Mistress didn't know I knows her secret, and I'm fixing to even up for some of them whippings she put off on me. That's why I tell Master Jim next time he come home.

See that crack in the wall? Master Jim say yes, and I say, it's just like the open door when the eyes are close to the wall. He peek and see into the bedroom.

That's how I find out about the Mistress and Mister Headsmith, I tells him, and I see he's getting mad.

What you mean? And Master Jim grabs me hard by the arm like I was trying to get away.

I see them in the bed.

That's all I say. The Demon's got him and Master Jim tears out of the room looking for the Mistress.

Then I hears loud talking and pretty soon the Mistress is screaming and calling for help, and if old Master Ben hadn't drop in just then and stop the fight, why, I guess she be beat almost to death, that how mad the Master was.

Then Master Ben gets mad 'cause his boy Jim ain't got us down in Texas yet. Then we stay up all the night packing for the trip. Master Jim takes us, but the Mistress stay at home, and I wonder if Master Jim beat her again when he gets back.

We rides the wagons all the way, how many days, I dunno. The country was wild most of the way, and I know now that we come through the same country where I lives now, only it was to the east. (The trip was evidently made over the "Texas Road.") And we keeps on riding and comes to the big river that's all brown and red looking, (Red River) and the next thing I was sold to Mrs. Vaughn at Bonham, Texas, and there I stays till after the slaves is free.

The new Mistress was a widow, no children round the place, and she treat me mighty good. She was good white folks—like old Master Ben, powerful good.

When the word get to us that the slaves is free, the Mistress says I is free to go anywheres I want. And I tell her this talk about being free sounds like foolishment to me—anyway, where can I go? She just pat me on the shoulder and say I better stay right there with her, and that's what I do for a long time. Then I hears about how the white folks down at Dallas pays big money for house girls and there I goes.

That's all I ever do after that—work at the houses till I gets too old to hobble on these tired old feets and legs, then I just sits down.

Just sits down and wishes for old Master Ben to come and get me, and take care of this old woman like he use to do when she is just a little black child on the plantation in Missouri!

God Bless old Master Ben—he was good white folks!

Oklahoma Writers' Project
Ex-Slaves

ELIZA EVANS
Age 87
McAlester, Okla.

I sho' remember de days when I was a slave and belonged to de best old Master what ever was, Mr. John Mixon. We lived in Selma, Dallas County, Alabama.

My grandma was a refugee from Africa. You know dey was white men who went slipping 'round and would capture or entice black folks onto their boats and fetch them over here and sell 'em for slaves. Well, grandma was a little girl 'bout eight or nine years old and her parents had sent her out to get wood. Dey was going to have a feast. Dey was going to roast a baby. Wasn't that awful? Well, they captured her and put a stick in her mouth. The stick held her mouth wide open so she wouldn't cry out. When she got to de boat she was so tired out she didn't do nothing.

They was a lot of more colored folks on de boat. It took about four months to get across on de boat and Mr. John Mixon met the boat and bought her. I think he gave five hundred dollars for her. She was named Gigi, but Master John called her Gracie. She was so good and they thought so much of her dat they gave her a grand wedding when she was married. Master John told her he'd never sell none of her chillun. He kept dat promise and he never did sell any of her grandchillun either. He thought it was wrong to separate famblys. She was one hundred and three years old when she died. I guess her mind got kind of feeble 'cause she wandered off and fell into a mill race and was drowned.

Master John Mixon had two big plantations. I believe he owned about four hundred slaves, chillun and all. He allowed us to have church one time a month with de white folks and we had prayer meeting every Sunday. Sometimes when de men would do something like being sassy or lazy and dey knowed dey was gonna be whipped, dey'd slip off and hide in de woods. When dey'd slip back to get some food dey would all pray for 'em dat Master wouldn't have 'em whipped too hard, and for fear the Patroller would hear 'em they'd put their faces down in a dinner pot. I'd sit out and watch for the Patroller. He was a white man who was appointed to catch runaway niggers. We all knew him. His name was Howard Campbell. He had a big pack of dogs. The lead hound was named Venus. There was five or six in the pack, and they was vicious too.

My father was a carriage driver and he allus took the family to church. My mother went along to take care of the little chilluns. She'd take me too. They was Methodist and after they would take the sacrament we would allus go up and take it. The niggers could use the whitefolks church in the afternoon.

De Big House was a grand place. It was a two-story house made out of logs dat had been peeled and smoothed off. There was five big rooms and a big open hall wid a wide front porch clean across de front. De porch had big posts and pretty banisters. It was painted white and had green shutters on de windows. De kitchen was back of de Big House.

De slaves quarters was about a quarter of a mile from de Big House. Their houses was made of logs and the cracks was daubed with mud. They would have two rooms. Our bedsteads was made of poplar wood and we kept them scrubbed white with sand. We used roped woven together for slats. Our mattresses were made of cotton, grass, or even shucks. My mother had a feather bed. The chairs was made from cedar with split white oak bottoms.

Each family kept their own home and cooked and served their own meals. We used wooden trays and wooden spoons. Once a week all the cullud chillun went to the Big House to eat dinner. The table was out in de yard. My nickname was "Speck". I didn't like to eat bread and milk when I went up there and I'd just sit there. Finally they'd let me go in de house and my mother would feed me. She was the house woman and my Auntie was cook. I don't know why they had us up there unless it was so they could laugh at us.

None of old Master's young niggers never did much work. He say he want 'em to grow up strong. He gave us lots to eat. He had a store of bacon, milk, bread, beans and molasses. In summer we had vegetables. My mother could make awful good corn pone. She would take meal and put salt in it and pour boiling water over it and make into pones. She'd wrap these pones in wet cabbage or collard leaves and roll dem into hot ashes and bake dem. They sho' was good. We'd have possum and coon and fish too.

The boys never wore no britches in de summer time. Boys fifteen years old would wear long shirts with no sleeves and they went barefooted. De girls dressed in shimmys. They was a sort of dress with two seams in it and no sleeves.

Old Master had his slaves to get up about five o'clock. Dey did an ordinary day's work. He never whipped them unless they was lazy or sassy or had a fight. Sometimes his slaves would run away but they allus come back. We didn't have no truck with railroaders 'cause we like our home.

A woman cussed my mother and it made her mad and they had a fight. Old Master had them both whipped. My mother got ten licks and de other woman got twenty-five. Old Mistress sho' was mad 'cause mother got whipped. Said he wouldn't have done it if she had known it. Old Mistress taught mother how to read and write and mother taught my father. I went to school jest one day so I can't read and write now.

Weddings was big days. We'd have big dinners and dances once in a while [HW: and] when somebody died they'd hold a wake. They'd sit up all night and sing and pray and talk. At midnight they'd serve sandwiches and coffee. Sometimes we'd all get together and play ring plays and dance.

Once the Yankee soldiers come. I was big enough to tote pails and piggins then. These soldiers made us chillun tote water to fill their canteens and water their horses. We toted the water on our heads. Another time we heard the Yankee's was coming and old Master had about fifteen hundred pounds of meat. They was hauling it off to bury it and hide it when the Yankees caught them. The soldiers ate and wasted every bit of that good meat. We didn't like them a bit.

One time some Yankee soldiers stopped and started talking to me—they asked me what my name was. "I say Liza," and they say, "Liza who?" I thought a minute and I shook my head, "Jest Liza, I ain't got no other name."

He say, "Who live up yonder in dat Big House?" I say, "Mr. John Mixon." He say, "You are Liza Mixon." He say, "Do anybody ever call you nigger?" And I say, "Yes Sir." He say, "Next time anybody call you nigger you tell 'em dat you is a Negro and your name is Miss Liza Mixon." The more I thought of that the more I liked it and I made up my mind to do jest what he told me to.

My job was minding the calves back while the cows was being milked. One evening I was minding the calves and old Master come along. He say, "What you doin' nigger?" I say real pert like, "I ain't no nigger, I'se a Negro and I'm Miss Liza Mixon." Old Master sho' was surprised and he picks up a switch and starts at me.

Law, but I was skeered! I hadn't never had no whipping so I run fast as I can to Grandma Gracie. I hid behind her and she say, "What's the matter of you child?" And I say, "Master John gwine whip me." And she say, "What you done?" And I say, "Nothing." She say she know better and 'bout that time Master John got there. He say, "Gracie, dat little nigger sassed me." She say, "Lawsie child, what does ail you?" I told them what the Yankee soldier told me to say and Grandma Gracie took my dress and lift it over my head and pins my hands inside, and Lawsie, how she whipped me and I dassent holler loud either. I jest said dat [HW: to] de wrong person. [TR: "didn't I?" at end was crossed out.]

I'se getting old now and can't work no more. I jest sits here and thinks about old times. They was good times. We didn't want to be freed. We hated the Yankee soldiers. Abe Lincoln was a good man though, wasn't he? I tries to be a good Christian 'cause I wants to go to Heaven when I die.

Oklahoma Writers' Project
Ex-Slaves

LIZZIE FARMER
Age 80 years
McAlester, Okla.

"Cousin Lizzie!"

"What."

"I'se seventy years old."

And I say, "Whut's you telling me for. I ain't got nothing to do with your age!"

I knowed I was one year older than she was and it sorta riled me for her to talk about it. I never would tell folks my age for I knowed white folks didn't want no old woman working for 'em and I just wouldn't tell 'em how old I really was. Dat was nine years ago and I guess I'm seventy five now. I can't work much now.

I was born four years before de War.—"The one what set the cullud folks free." We lived on a big plantation in Texas. Old Master's name was John Booker and he was good to us all. My mammy died just at de close of de War and de young mistress took me and kept me and I growed up with her chillun. I thought I was quality sure nuff and I never would go to school 'cause I couldn't go 'long to de same school with de white chillun. Young mistress taught me how to knit, spin, weave, crochet, sew and embroider. I couldn't recollect my age and young Mistress told me to say, "I'se born de second year of de War dat set de cullud folks free," and the only time she ever git mad at me was when I forgot to say it jest as she told me to. She take hold of me and shook me. I recollects all it, all de time.

Young mistress' name was Elizabeth Booker McNew. I'se named after her. She finally gave me to my aunt when I was a big girl and I never lived wid white folks any more. I never saw my pappy till I was grown.

In the cullud quarters, we cooked on a fireplace in big iron pots. Our bread was baked in iron skillets with lids and we would set the skillet on de fire and put coals of fire on de lid. Bread was mighty good cooked like dat. We made our own candles. We had a candle mold and we would put a string in the center of the mold and pour melted tallow in it and let it harden. We would make eight at one time. Quality folks had brass lamps.

When we went to cook our vegetables we would put a big piece of hog jowl in de pot. We'd put in a lot of snap beans and when dey was about half done we'd put in a mess of cabbage and when it was about half done we'd put in some squash and when it was about half done we'd put in some okra. Then when it was done we would take it out a layer at a time. Go 'way! It makes me hungry to talk about it.

When we cooked possum dat was a feast. We would skin him and dress him and put him on top de house and let him freeze for two days or nights. Then we'd boil him with red pepper, and take him out and put him in a pan and slice sweet 'taters and put round him and roast him. My, dat was good eating.

It was a long time after de War 'fore all de niggers knowed dey was really free. My grandpappy was Master Booker's overseer. He wouldn't have a white man over his niggers. I saw grandpappy whip one man with a long whip. Master Booker was good and wouldn't whip 'em less'n he had to. De niggers dassent leave de farm without a pass for fear of de Ku Kluxers and patrolers.

We would have dances and play parties and have sho' nuff good times. We had "ring plays." We'd all catch hands and march round, den we'd drop all hands 'cept our pardners and we'd swing round and sing:

"You steal my pardner, and I steal yours,

Miss Mary Jane.

My true lover's gone away,

Miss Mary Jane!

"Steal all round and don't slight none,

Miss Mary Jane.

He's lost out but I'se got one,

Miss Mary Jane!"

We always played at log rollin's an' cotton pickin's.

Sometimes we would have a wedding and my what a good time we'd have. Old Master's daughter, Miss Janie, got married and it took us more'n three weeks to get ready for it. De house was cleaned from top to bottom and us chillun had to run errands. Seemed like we was allers under foot, at least dat was what mammy said. I never will fergit all the good things they cooked up. Rows of pies and cakes, baked chicken and ham, my, it makes my mouth water jest thinking of it. After de wedding and de feast de white folks danced all night and us cullud folks ate all night.

When one of de cullud folks die we would allers hold a "wake." We would set up with de corpse and sing and pray and at midnight we'd all eat and den we'd sing and pray some more.

In de evening after work was done we'd sit round and de older folks would sing songs. One of de favorites was:

"Miss Ca'line gal,

Yes Ma'am

Did you see dem buzzards?

Yes Ma'am,

Did you see dem floppin',

How did ye' like 'em?

Mighty well.

"Miss Ca'line gal,

Yes Ma'am,

Did you see dem buzzards?

Yes Ma'am,

Did you see dem sailin',

Yes Ma'am.

How did you like 'em?

Mighty well."

I've heered folks talk about conjures and hoodoo charms. I have a hoss shoe over de door dat will bring good luck. I sho' do believe certain things bring bad luck. I hate to hear a scrinch (screech) owl holler at night. Whenever a scrinch owl git in dat tree at night and start to holler I gits me a stick and I say, "Confound you, I'll make yet set up dar and say 'Umph huh'," so I goes out and time I gits dar he is gone. If you tie a knot in de corner of de bed sheet he will leave, or turn your hat wrong side out too. Dey's all good and will make a scrinch owl leave every time.

I believes in dreams and visions too. I dreamed one night dat I had tall palings all 'round my house and I went out in de yard and dere was a big black hoss and I say, "How come you is in my yard? I'll jest put you out jest lak you got in." I opened de gate but he wouldn't go out and finally he run in de door and through the house and went towards de East. Right after dat my son died. I saw dat hoss again de other night. A black hoss allus means death. Seeing it de other night might mean I'se gwineter die.

I know one time a woman named May Runnels wanted to go to church about a mile away and her old man wouldn't go with her. It made her mad and she say, "I'll be dammed if I don't go." She had to go through a grave yard and when she was about half way across it a icy hand jest slap her and her mouth was twisted way 'round fer about three months. Dat was a lesson to her fer cussing.

One time there was a nigger what belonged on a adjoining farm to Master John Bookers and dey told us dis story:

"Dis nigger went down to de spring and found a terrapin and he say, 'What brung you here?' Jest imagine how he felt when it say to him, 'Teeth and tongue brung me here, and teeth and tongue will bring you here.' He run to de house and told his Master dat he found a terrapin dat could talk. Dey went back and he asked de terrapin what bring him here and it wouldn't say a word. Old Master didn't like it 'cause he went down there jest to see a common ordinary terrapin and he told de nigger he was going to git into trouble fer telling him a lie. Next day the nigger seen de terrapin and it say de same thing again. Soon after dat dis nigger was lynched right close to de place he saw de terrapin."

Master John Booker had two niggers what had a habit of slipping across de river and killing old Master's hogs and hiding de meat in de loft of de house. Master had a big blue hog and one day he missed him and he sent Ned to look fer him. Ned knowed all de time dat he had killed it and had it hid in his loft. He hunted and called "Pig-ooie, Pig." Somebody done stole old Master's big blue hog. Dey couldn't find it but old Master thought Ned knowed something 'bout it. One night he found out Ned was gonna kill another hog and had asked John to go with him. He borrowed John's clothes and blacked his face and met Ned at de river. Soon dey find a nice big one and Ned say, "John, I'll drive him round and you kill him." So he drove him past old Master but he didn't want to kill his own hog so he made lak he'd like to kill him but he missed him. Finally Ned got tired and said. "I'll kill him, you drive him by me." So Master John drove him by him and Ned knock de hog on de head and cut his throat and dey load him on de canoe. When dey was nearly 'cross de river Old Master dip up some water and wash his face a little, then he look at Ned and he say, "Ned you look sick, I believe you've got lepersy." Ned row on little more and he jump in de river and Master had a hard time finding him again. He had the overseer whip Ned for that.

I think Lincoln was a wonderful man. Everybody was sorry when he died, but I never heerd of Jeff Davis.

Oklahoma Writers' Project
Ex-Slaves
10-19-38
1,876-words

DELLA FOUNTAIN
Age 69 years
McAlester, Oklahoma

I was born after de War of de Rebellion but I 'member lots o' things dat my parents told me 'bout slavery.

My grandmother was captured in Africa. Traders come dere in a big boat and dey had all sorts of purty gew-gaws—red handkerchiefs, dress goods, beads, bells, and trinkets in bright colors. Dey would pull up at de shore and entice de colored folks onto de boat to see de purty things. Befo' de darkies realized it dey would be out from shore. Dat's de way she was captured. Fifteen to twenty-five would pay dem for de trip as dey all brought good prices.

I was born and raised in Louisiana, near Winfield. My mother's Master was John Rogers and his wife was Miss Millie. Dey was awful good to deir slaves and he never whupped his grown niggers.

I 'member when I was a child dat we didn't have hardly anything to keep house wid, but we got along purty well I guess. Our furniture was home-made and we cooked on de fireplace.

We saved all our oak-wood ashes, and would put a barrel on a slanting scaffold and put sticks and shucks in de bottom of de barrel and den fill it wid de ashes. We'd pour water in it and let it drip. Dese drippings made pure lye. We used dis wid cracklings and meat scraps to make our soap.

Father took a good-sized pine long and split it open, planed it down smooth and bored holes in de bottom and drove pegs in dem for legs; dis was our battling bench. We'd spread our wet clothes on dis and rub soap on 'em and take a paddle and beat de dirt out. We got 'em clean but had to be careful not to wear 'em out wid de paddle.

We had no tubs either, so father took a hollow log and split it open and put partitions in it. He bored a hole in each section and drove a peg in it. He next cut two forked poles and drove 'em in de ground and rested de ends of de hollow log in dese forks. We'd fill de log trough wid water and rinse our clothes. We could pull out de pegs and let de water out. We had no brooms either, so we made brush brooms to sweep our floors.

Dere was lots of wild game near our home. I 'member father and two more men going out and killing six deer in jest a little while. Dey was plentiful, and so was squirrels, coon, possums and quail. Dere was lots of bears, too. We'd be in de field working and hear de dogs, and father and de boys would go to 'em and maybe dey'd have a bear. We liked bear meat. It was dark, but awful good and sweet.

De grown folks used to have big times at log-rollings, corn-shuckings and quiltings. Dey'd have a big supper and a big dance at night. Us children would play ring plays, play with home-made rag dolls, or we'd take big leaves and pin 'em together wid thorns and make hats and dresses. We'd ride saplings, too. All of us would pull a sapling down and one would climb up in it near de top and git a good hold on it, and dey would turn it loose. It took a purty good holding to stay wid it, I can tell you.

All de ladies rode horseback, and dey rode side-saddles. I had a purty side-saddle when I growed up. De saddle seat was flowered plush. I had a purty riding habit, too. De skirt was so long dat it almost touched de ground.

We spun and wove all our clothes. I had to spin three broaches ever night before bedtime. Mother would take bark and make dye to give us different colored dresses.

Red oak and sweet gum made purple. Bois d'arc made yellow or orange. Walnut made a purty brown. We knitted our socks and stockings, too.

We celebrated Christmas by having a big dance and egg-nog for ever' body.

During slavery young colored boys and girls didn't do much work but just growed up, care-free and happy. De first work boys done was to learn to hitch up de team to Master's carriage and take de young folks for a drive.

My older brothers and sisters told me lots of things dey done during slave days. My brother Joe felt mighty big after freedom and strutted about. One day he took his younger brother, Ol wid him to where father was building a house. Dey played 'bout de house and come up to where a white man and father was talking. De white man was rolling a little ball of mud in his hands and he just pitched it over on Ol's foot. It didn't hurt him a mite, but Joe bridled up and he started to git smart, and father told him he'd break his neck if he didn't go on home and keep his mouth shet. Father finally had to whup Joe to make him know he was black. He give father and mother lots of concern, for dey was afraid the Ku Kluxers would git him. One day he was playing wid a axe and chopped off brother Ol's finger. Mother told him she was going to kill him when she caught him. He took to de woods. His three sisters and two neighbor girls run him nearly all day but couldn't catch him. Late in de evening, he come up to a white neighbor's house and she told him to go in and git under de bed and dey couldn't find him. Curtains come down to de floor and as he was tired he decided to risk it. He hadn't much more dan got hid when he heard de girls coming. He heard de woman say, "He's under de bed." He knowed he was caught, and he put up a fight, but dey took him to mother. He got a whupping, but he was shocked dat mother didn't kill him like she said she was. He didn't mind de whupping. He growed up to be a good man, and was de apple of my mother's eye.

Father knowed a man that stole his Master's horse out and rode him to a dance. For some reason de horse died. De poor man knowed he was up against it, and he let in to begging de men to help him git de horse on his back so he could put him back in his stable and his Master would think he died dere. Poor fellow, he really did think he could tote dat horse on his back. He couldn't git anybody to help him, so he went to the woods. He was shot by a patroller 'cause he wouldn't surrender. Dey captured him but he died.

Paul Castleberry was a white preacher. De colored would go to church de same as de whites. He give de colored instructions on obeying Masters. He say, "while your Master is going fom pillar to post, looking after your intrusts, you is always doing some devilment." I 'spect dat was jest about de truth.

My sister played wid Miss Millie's little girl, Mollie. De big house was on a high hill and at de foot of de hill. Nearly a half-mile away was a big creek wid a big wooden bridge across it. Soldiers come by ever' few days, and you could hear deir horses when dey struck de bridge. Sister and Mollie would run upstairs and look down de hill, and if it was Confederate soldiers dey would run back and tell Miss Millie and dey would start putting out de best food dey had. If dey saw Yankee soldiers, dey would run down and tell 'em and dey'd start hiding things.

De Yankees come through dere and took ever' body's horses. Lots of people took deir horses and cows and hid 'em in some low place in de deep wood.

Miss Millie had a young horse and she had 'em take him to de wheat field and hide him. De wheat was as high as he was. De Yankees come by, and a man had stopped dere just before dey come. He was riding an old horse, and he was wearing a long linen-duster—a duster was a long coat dat was worn over de suit to protect it from de dust.

Dis smart-aleck hid behind de house and as de soldiers rode up he shot at 'em. Dey started shooting at him and he started running, and his coat was sticking straight out behind him. De soldiers surely wasn't trying to hit him, but dey sure did scare him plenty. Miss Millie was certain dey was going to find her horse but dey didn't.

Master John Rogers was good to all his slaves, and they all loved him and would a'died for him. One day he was sitting in his yard and Mollie come running down stairs and told him de Yankees was coming. He never say nothing, but kept sitting dere. Dat morning he had a big sack of money and he give it to my mother to hide for him. She ripped her mattress, and put it in de middle of it and sewed it up. She den made up de bed and put de covers on it. De Yankees searched de house and took de jewelry and silverware and old Master's gold mug, but dey didn't find his money.

My parents lived close to de old plantation dat they lived on when dey was slaves. De big house was still dere, but it was sure dilapidated. Ever'body was poor after de War, whites and blacks alike. I really think de colored was de best off, for they knowed all 'bout hardships and hard work and de white folks didn't.

At first some of 'em was too proud to do drudgery work, but most of 'em went right to work and build up deir homes again. Food, clothes, and in fact everything needed, was scarce.

Mother always say, "If you visit on New Years, you'll visit all de year." We always had black-eyed peas and hog jowl for New Year's dinner, for it brought good luck.

The Nineteenth of June was Emancipation Day, and we always had a big picnic and speeches.

I knowed one woman who was a conjur woman. Lots of people went to her to git her to break a evil spell dat some one had over them. She'd brew a tea from herbs and give to 'em to drink, and it always cured 'em.

I've seen people use all kinds o' roots and herbs for medicine, and I also seen 'em use all kind of things for cures. I've knowed 'em to put wood lice in a bag and tie 'em 'round a baby's neck so it'd teeth easy.

Black-haw root, sour dock, bear grass, grape root, bull nettle, sweet-gum bark and red-oak bark boiled separately and mixed, makes a good blood medicine.

Oklahoma Writers' Project
Ex-Slaves

NANCY GARDNER
Age 79 yrs.
Oklahoma City, Oklahoma

Well, to tell you de truth I don't know my age, but I was born in 1858, in Franklin, Tennessee. Now, you can figger for yourself and tell how old I is. I is de daughter of Prophet and Callie Isaiah, and dey was natives of Tennessee. Dere was three of us children, two boys and myself. I'm de only girl. My brothers names was Prophet and Billie Isaiah. I don't 'member much about dem as we was separated when I was seven years old. I'll never forget when me, my ma and my auntie had to leave my pa and brothers. It is jest as clear in my mind now as it was den, and dat's been about seventy years ago.

Oh God! I tell you it was awful dat day when old Jeff Davis had a bunch of us sent to Memphis to be sold. I can see old Major Clifton now. He was a big nigger trader you know. Well, dey took us on up dere to Memphis and we was sold jest like cattle. Dey sold me and ma together and dey sold pa and de boys together. Dey was sent to Mississippi and we was sent to Alabama. My pa, O how my ma was grieved to death about him! She didn't live long after dat. She didn't live long enough to be set free. Poor ma, she died a slave, but she is saved though. I know she is, and I'll be wid her some day.

It was thirty years before my pa knew if we was still living. Finally in some way he heard dat I was still alive, and he began writing me. Course I was grown and married den and me and my husband had moved to Missouri. Well, my pa started out to see me and on his way he was drowned in de Missouri River, and I never saw him alive after we was sold in Memphis.

I can't tell you much 'bout work during de slave days 'cause you see I was jest a baby you might say when de War broke out. I do remember our Master's name though, it was Dr. Perkins, and he was a good Master. Ma and pa sure hated to have to leave him, he was so good to dem. He was a rich man, and had a big fine house and thousands of acres of land. He was good to his niggers too. We had a good house too, better dan some of dese houses I see folks living in now. Course Dr. Perkins niggers had to work, but dey didn't mind 'cause he would let dem have little patches of dey own such as 'tatoes, corn, cotton and garden. Jest a little, you know. He couldn't let dem have much, there was so many on Dr. Perkins plantation.

I don't remember seeing anybody sick in slavery time. You see I was jest a kid and dere's a lot of things I can't remember.

I am a Christian. I jined de church nigh on seventy years ago and when I say dat, I don't mean I jest jined de church. I mean I gave myself up to de Heavenly Father, and I've been gwine straight down de line for Him ever since. You know in dem days, we didn't get religion like young folks do now. Young folks today jest find de church and den call theyselves Christians, but they aint.

I remember jest as well when I was converted. One day I was thinking 'bout a sermon de preacher had preached and a voice spoke to me and said, "De Holy Ghost is over your head. Accept it!" Right den I got down on my knees and prayed to God dat I might understand dat voice, and God Almighty in a vision told me dat I should find de church. I could hardly wait for de next service so I could find it, and when I was in de water getting my baptisement, dat same voice spoke and said, "Now you have accepted don't turn back 'cause I will be wid you always!" O you don't know nothing 'bout dat kind of religion!

I 'member one night shortly after I jined de church I was laying in bed and dere was a vine tied 'round my waist and dat vine extended into de elements. O my God! I can see it now! I looked up dat vine and away in de elements I could see my Divine Master and he spoke to me and said, "When you get in trouble shake dis vine; I'm your Master and I will hear your cry."

I knowed old Jeff Davis good. Why I was jest as close to him as I am to dat table. I've talked wid him too. I reckon I do know dat scoundrel! Why, he didn't want de niggers to be free! He was known as a mean old rascal all over de South.

Abraham Lincoln? Now you is talking 'bout de niggers friend! Why dat was de best man God ever let tramp de earth! Everybody was mighty sad when poor old Abraham was 'sassinated, 'cause he did a mighty good deed for de colored race before he left dis world.

I wasn't here long during slavery, but I saw enough of it to know it was mighty hard going for most of de niggers den, and young folks wouldn't stand for dat kind of treatment now. I know most of the young folks would be killed, but they jest wouldn't stand for it. I would hate to have to go through wid my little share of it again.

Oklahoma Writers' Project
Ex-Slaves

OCTAVIA GEORGE
Age 85 yrs.
Oklahoma City, Okla.

I was born in Mansieur, Louisiana, 1852, Avoir Parish. I am the daughter of Alfred and Clementine Joseph. I don't know much about my grandparents other than my mother told me my grandfather's name was Fransuai, and was one time a king in Africa.

Most of the slaves lived in log cabins, and the beds were home-made. The mattresses were made out of moss gathered from trees, and we used to have lots of fun gathering that moss to make those mattresses.

My job was taking care of the white children up at the Big House (that is what they called the house where our master lived), and I also had to feed the little Negro children. I remember quite well how those poor little children used to have to eat. They were fed in boxes and troughs, under the house. They were fed corn meal mush and beans. When this was poured into their box they would gather around it the same as we see pigs, horses and cattle gather around troughs today.

We were never given any money, but were able to get a little money this way: our Master would let us have two or three acres of land each year to plant for ourselves, and we could have what we raised on it. We could not allow our work on these two or three acres to interfere with Master's work, but we had to work our little crops on Sundays. Now remind you, all the Negroes didn't get these two or three acres, only good masters allowed their slaves to have a little crop of their own. We would take the money from our little crops and buy a few clothes and something for Christmas. The men would save enough money out of the crops to buy their Christmas whiskey. It was all right for the slaves to get drunk on Christmas and New Years Day; no one was whipped for getting drunk on those days. We were allowed to have a garden and from this we gathered vegetables to eat; on Sundays we could have duck, fish, and pork.

We didn't know anything about any clothes other than cotton; everything we wore was made of cotton, except our shoes, they were made from pieces of leather cut out of a raw cowhide.

Our Master and Mistress was good, they let us go to church with them, have our little two- or three-acre crops and any other thing that the good masters would let their slaves do. They lived in a big fine house and had a fine barn. Their barn was much better than the house we lived in. Master Depriest (our master) was a Frenchman, and had eight or nine children, and they were sure mean. They would fight us, but we were not allowed to fight our little Master or Mistress as we had to call them.

The overseer on Master's plantation was a mean old fellow, he carried his gun all the time and would ride a big fine horse and go from one bunch of slaves to the other. Some poor white folks lived close to us. They could not own slaves and they had to work for the rich plantation owners. I believe that those poor white folk are to blame for the Negroes stealing because they would get the Negroes to steal their master's corn, hogs, chickens and many other things and sell it to them for practically nothing.

We had to work plenty hard, because our Master had a large plantation. Don't know just how many acres it was, but we had to be up at 5 o'clock in the morning and would work until dark than we would have to go home and do our night work, that is cook, milk, and feed the stock.

The slaves were punished for stealing, running off, not doing what their master told them and for talking back to their master. If any of these rules were disobeyed their feet and hands were chained together and they were put across a log or a barrel and whipped until the blood came from them.

There were no jails; the white man was the slaves' jail. If whipping didn't settle the crime the Negro committed—the next thing would be to hang him or burn him at stake.

I've seen them sell slaves. The whites would auction them off just as we do cattle and horses today. The big fine healthy slaves were worth more than those that were not quite so good. I have seen men sold from their wives and I thought that was such a crime. I knew that God would settle thing someday.

Slaves would run away but most of the time they were caught. The Master would put blood hounds on their trail, and sometimes the slave would kill the blood hound and make his escape. If a slave once tried to run away and was caught, he would be whipped almost to death, and from then on if he was sent any place they would chain their meanest blood hound to him.

Funerals were very simple for slaves, they could not carry the body to the church they would just take it to the grave yard and bury it. They were not even allowed to sing a song at the cemetery. Old Mistress used to tell us ghost stories after funerals and they would nearly scare me to death. She would tell of seeing men with no head, and see cattle that would suddenly turn to cats, and she made us believe if a fire was close to a cemetery it was coming from a ghost.

I used to hear quite a bit about voodoo, but that some thing I never believed in, therefore, I didn't pay any attention to it.

When a slave was sick, the master would get a good doctor for him if he was a good slave, but if he wasn't considered a good slave he would be given cheap medical care. Some of the doctors would not go to the cabin where the slaves were, and the slave would have to be carried on his bed to his master's back porch and the doctor would see him there.

When the news came that we were free, all of us were hid on the Mississippi River. We had been there for several days, and we had to catch fish with our hands and roast them for food. I remember quite well when old Master came down to there and hollered, Come on out niggers; you are free now and you can do as you please! We all went to the Big House and there we found old Miss crying and talking about how she hated to lose her good niggers.

Abraham Lincoln! Why we mourned three months for that man when he died! I wouldn't miss a morning getting my black arm band and placing it on in remembrance of Abraham, who was the best friend the Negroes ever had. Now old Jeff Davis, I didn't care a thing about him. He was a Democrat and none of them mean anything to the Negro. And if these young Negroes don't quit messing with the democratic bunch they are going to be right back where we started from. If they only knew as I know they would struggle to keep such from happening, because although I had a good master I wouldn't want to go through it again.

Oklahoma Writers' Project
Ex-Slaves

MARY GRAYSON
Age 83 yrs.
Tulsa, Oklahoma

I am what we colored people call a "native." That means that I didn't come into the Indian country from somewhere in the Old South, after the War, like so many negroes did, but I was born here in the old Creek Nation, and my master was a Creek Indian. That was eighty three years ago, so I am told.

My mammy belonged to white people back in Alabama when she was born—down in the southern part I think, for she told me that after she was a sizeable girl her white people moved into the eastern part of Alabama where there was a lot of Creeks. Some of them Creeks was mixed up with the whites, and some of the big men in the Creeks who come to talk to her master was almost white, it looked like. "My white folks moved around a lot when I was a little girl", she told me.

When mammy was about 10 or 13 years old some of the Creeks begun to come out to the Territory in little bunches. They wasn't the ones who was taken out here by the soldiers and contractor men—they come on ahead by themselves and most of them had plenty of money, too. A Creek come to my mammy's master and bought her to bring out here, but she heard she was being sold and run off into the woods. There was an old clay pit, dug way back into a high bank, where the slaves had been getting clay to mix with hog hair scrapings to make chinking for the big log houses that they built for the master and the cabins they made for themselves. Well, my mammy run and hid way back in that old clay pit, and it was way after dark before the master and the other man found her.

The Creek man that bought her was a kind sort of a man, mammy said, and wouldn't let the master punish her. He took her away and was kind to her, but he decided she was too young to breed and he sold her to another Creek who had several slaves already, and he brought her out to the Territory.

The McIntosh men was the leaders in the bunch that come out at that time, and one of the bunch, named Jim Perryman, bought my mammy and married her to one of his "boys", but after he waited a while and she didn't have a baby he decided she was no good breeder and he sold her to Mose Perryman.

Mose Perryman was my master, and he was a cousin to Legus Perryman, who was a big man in the Tribe. He was a lot younger than Mose, and laughed at Mose for buying my mammy, but he got fooled, because my mammy got married to Mose's slave boy Jacob, the way the slaves was married them days, and went ahead and had ten children for Mr. Mose.

Mose Perryman owned my pappy and his older brother, Hector, and one of the McIntosh men, Oona, I think his name was, owned my pappy's brother William. I can remember when I first heard about there was going to be a war. The older children would talk about it, but they didn't say it was a war all over the country. They would talk about a war going to be "back in Alabama", and I guess they had heard the Creeks talking about it that way.

When I was born we lived in the Choska bottoms, and Mr. Mose Perryman had a lot of land broke in all up and down the Arkansas river along there. After the War, when I had got to be a young woman, there was quite a settlement grew up at Choska (pronounced Choe-skey) right across the river east of where Haskell now is, but when I was a child before the War all the whole bottoms was marshy kind of wilderness except where farms had been cleared out. The land was very rich, and the Creeks who got to settle there were lucky. They always had big crops. All west of us was high ground, toward Gibson station and Fort Gibson, and the land was sandy. Some of the McIntoshes lived over that way, and my Uncle William belonged to one of them.

We slaves didn't have a hard time at all before the War. I have had people who were slaves of white folks back in the old states tell me that they had to work awfully hard and their masters were cruel to them sometimes, but all the Negroes I knew who belonged to Creeks always had plenty of clothes and lots to eat and we all lived in good log cabins we built. We worked the farm and tended to the horses and cattle and hogs, and some of the older women worked around the owner's house, but each Negro family looked after a part of the fields and worked the crops like they belonged to us.

When I first heard talk about the War the slaves were allowed to go and see one another sometimes and often they were sent on errands several miles with a wagon or on a horse, but pretty soon we were all kept at home, and nobody was allowed to come around and talk to us. But we heard what was going on.

The McIntosh men got nearly everybody to side with them about the War, but we Negroes got word somehow that the Cherokees over back of Ft. Gibson was not going to be in the War, and that there were some Union people over there who would help slaves to get away, but we children didn't know anything about what we heard our parents whispering about, and they would stop if they heard us listening. Most of the Creeks who lived in our part of the country, between the Arkansas and the Verdigris, and some even south of the Arkansas, belonged to the Lower Creeks and sided with the South, but down below us along the Canadian River they were Upper Creeks and there was a good deal of talk about them going with the North. Some of the Negroes tried to get away and go down to them, but I don't know of any from our neighborhood that went to them.

Some Upper Creeks came up into the Choska bottoms talking around among the folks there about siding with the North. They were talking, they said, for old man Gouge, who was a big man among the Upper Creeks. His Indian name was Opoeth-le-ya-hola, and he got away into Kansas with a big bunch of Creeks and Seminoles during the War.

Before that time, I remember one night my uncle William brought another Negro man to our cabin and talked a long time with my pappy, but pretty soon some of the Perryman Negroes told them that Mr. Mose was coming down and they went off into the woods to talk. But Mr. Mose didn't come down. When pappy came back Mammy cried quite a while, and we children could hear them arguing late at night. Then my uncle Hector slipped over to our cabin several times and talked to pappy, and mammy began to fix up grub, but she didn't give us children but a little bit of it, and told us to stay around with her at the cabin and not go playing with the other children.

Then early one morning, about daylight, old Mr. Mose came down to the cabin in his buggy, waving a shot gun and hollering at the top of his voice. I never saw a man so mad in all my life, before nor since!

He yelled in at mammy to "git them children together and git up to my house before I beat you and all of them to death!" Mammy began to cry and plead that she didn't know anything, but he acted like he was going to shoot sure enough, so we all ran to mammy and started for Mr. Mose's house as fast as we could trot.

We had to pass all the other Negro cabins on the way, and we could see that they were all empty, and it looked like everything in them had been tore up. Straw and corn shucks all over the place, where somebody had tore up the mattresses, and all the pans and kettles gone off the outside walls where they used to hang them.

At one place we saw two Negro boys loading some iron kettles on a wagon, and a little further on was some boys catching chickens in a yard, but we could see all the Negroes had left in a big hurry.

I asked mammy where everybody had gone and she said, "Up to Mr. Mose's house, where we are going. He's calling us all in."

"Will pappy be up there too?" I asked her.

"No. Your pappy and your Uncle Hector and your Uncle William and a lot of other menfolks won't be here any more. They went away. That's why Mr. Mose is so mad, so if any of you younguns say anything about any strange men coming to our place I'll break your necks!" Mammy was sure scared!

We all thought sure she was going to get a big whipping, but Mr. Mose just looked at her a minute and then told her to get back to the cabin and bring all the clothes, and bed ticks and all kinds of cloth we had and come back ready to travel.

"We're going to take all you black devils to a place where there won't no more of you run away!" he yelled after us. So we got ready to leave as quick as we could. I kept crying about my pappy, but mammy would say, "Don't you worry about your pappy, he's free now. Better be worrying about us. No telling where we all will end up!" There was four or five Creek families and their Negroes all got together to leave, with all their stuff packed in buggies and wagons, and being toted by the Negroes or carried tied on horses, jack asses, mules and milk cattle. I reckon it was a funny looking sight, or it would be to a person now; the way we was all loaded down with all manner of baggage when we met at the old ford across the Arkansas that lead to the Creek Agency. The Agency stood on a high hill a few miles across the river from where we lived, but we couldn't see it from our place down in the Choska bottoms. But as soon as we got up on the upland east of the bottoms we could look across and see the hill.

When we got to a grove at the foot of the hill near the agency Mr. Mose and the other masters went up to the Agency for a while. I suppose they found out up there what everybody was supposed to do and where they was supposed to go, for when we started on it wasn't long until several more families and their slaves had joined the party and we made quite a big crowd.

The little Negro boys had to carry a little bundle apiece, but Mr. Mose didn't make the little girls carry anything and let us ride if we could find anything to ride on. My mammy had to help lead the cows part of the time, but a lot of the time she got to ride an old horse, and she would put me up behind her. It nearly scared me to death, because I had never been on a horse before, and she had to hold on to me all the time to keep me from falling off.

Of course I was too small to know what was going on then, but I could tell that all the masters and the Negroes seemed to be mighty worried and careful all the time. Of course I know now that the Creeks were all split up over the War, and nobody was able to tell who would be friendly to us or who would try to poison us or kill us, or at least rob us. There was a lot of bushwhacking all through that country by little groups of men who was just out to get all they could. They would appear like they was the enemy of anybody they run across, just to have an excuse to rob them or burn up their stuff. If you said you was with the South they would be with the North and if you claimed to be with the Yankees they would be with the South, so our party was kind of upset all the time we was passing through the country along the Canadian. That was where old Gouge had been talking against the South. I've heard my folks say that he was a wonderful speaker, too.

We all had to move along mighty slow, on account of the ones on foot, and we wouldn't get very far in one day, then we Negroes had to fix up a place to camp and get wood and cook supper for everybody. Sometimes we would come to a place to camp that somebody knew about and we would find it all tromped down by horses and the spring all filled in and ruined. I reckon old Gouge's people would tear up things when they left, or maybe some Southern bushwhackers would do it. I don't know which.

When we got down to where the North Fork runs into the Canadian we went around the place where the Creek town was. There was lots of Creeks down there who was on the other side, so we passed around that place and forded across west of there. The ford was a bad one, and it took us a long time to get across. Everybody got wet and a lot of the stuff on the wagons got wet. Pretty soon we got down into the Chickasaw country, and everybody was friendly to us, but the Chickasaw people didn't treat their slaves like the Creeks did. They was more strict, like the people in Texas and other places. The Chickasaws seemed lighter color than the Creeks but they talked more in Indian among themselves and to their slaves. Our masters talked English nearly all the time except when they were talking to Creeks who didn't talk good English, and we Negroes never did learn very good Creek. I could always understand it, and can yet, a little, but I never did try to talk it much. Mammy and pappy used English to us all the time.

Mr. Mose found a place for us to stop close to Fort Washita, and got us places to stay and work. I don't know which direction we were from Fort Washita, but I know we were not very far. I don't know how many years we were down in there, but I know it was over two for we worked on crops at two different places, I remember. Then one day Mr. Mose came and told us that the War was over and that we would have to root for ourselves after that. Then he just rode away and I never saw him after that until after we had got back up into the Choska country. Mammy heard that the Negroes were going to get equal rights with the Creeks, and that she should go to the Creek Agency to draw for us, so we set out to try to get back.

We started out on foot, and would go a little ways each day, and mammy would try to get a little something to do to get us some food. Two or three times she got paid in money, so she had some money when we got back. After three or four days of walking we came across some more Negroes who had a horse, and mammy paid them to let us children ride and tie with their children for a day or two. They had their children on the horse, so two or three little ones would get on with a larger one to guide the horse and we would ride a while and get off and tie the horse and start walking on down the road. Then when the others caught up with the horse they would ride until they caught up with us. Pretty soon the old people got afraid to have us do that, so we just led the horse and some of the little ones rode it.

We had our hardest times when we would get to a river or big creek. If the water was swift the horse didn't do any good, for it would shy at the water and the little ones couldn't stay on, so we would have to just wait until someone came along in a wagon and maybe have to pay them with some of our money or some of our goods we were bringing back to haul us across. Sometimes we had to wait all day before anyone would come along in a wagon.

We were coming north all this time, up through the Seminole Nation, but when we got to Weeleetka we met a Creek family of freedmen who were going to the Agency too, and mammy paid them to take us along in their wagon. When we got to the Agency mammy met a Negro who had seen pappy and knew where he was, so we sent word to him and he came and found us. He had been through most of the War in the Union army.

When we got away into the Cherokee country some of them called the "Pins" helped to smuggle him on up into Missouri and over into Kansas, but he soon found that he couldn't get along and stay safe unless he went with the Army. He went with them until the War was over, and was around Gibson quite a lot. When he was there he tried to find out where we had gone but said he never could find out. He was in the battle of Honey Springs, he said, but never was hurt or sick. When we got back together we cleared a selection of land a little east of the Choska bottoms, near where Clarksville now is, and farmed until I was a great big girl.

I went to school at a little school called Blackjack school. I think it was a kind of mission school and not one of the Creek nation schools, because my first teacher was Miss Betty Weaver and she was not a Creek but a Cherokee. Then we had two white teachers, Miss King and John Kernan, and another Cherokee was in charge. His name was Ross, and he was killed one day when his horse fell off a bridge across the Verdigris, on the way from Tullahassee to Gibson Station.

When I got to be a young woman I went to Okmulgee and worked for some people near there for several years, then I married Tate Grayson. We got our freedmen's allotments on Mingo Creek, east of Tulsa, and lived there until our children were grown and Tate died, then I came to live with my daughter in Tulsa.

Oklahoma Writers' Project
Ex-Slaves

ROBERT R. GRINSTEAD
Age 80 yrs.
Oklahoma City, Okla.

I was born in Lawrence County, Mississippi, February 17, 1857. My father's name is Elias Grinstead, a German, and my mother's name is Ann Greenstead after that of her master. I am a son by my mother and her Master. I have four other half brothers William (Bill) oldest, Albert, Silas, and John.

I was only eight years of age at freedom and for that reason I was too young to work and on account of being the son of my Master's I received no hard treatment and did little or no work. Yet, I wore the same clothing as did the rest of the slaves: a shirt of lowell for summer and shirt and trousers for winter and no shoes. I could walk through a briar patch in my bare feet without sticking one in the bottom of my feet as they were so hard and resistant.

I was the only child of my Master as he had no wife. When the War broke out he went to the War and left the plantation in charge of his overseer and his two sisters. As the overseers were hard for them to get along with they were oftener without an overseer as with one, and therefore they used one of the Negroes as overseer for the most of the time.

Across the river was another large plantation and slave owner by the name of Master Wilson. We called him Master too, for he was a close friend and neighbor to our Mistresses. There was one Negro man slave who decided to not work after Master went to the War and the white overseer was fired and the Negro overseer was acting as overseer, so my Mistress gave him a note to take across the river to Master Wilson. The note was an order to whip this Negro and as he couldn't read he didn't know what the note contained until after Master Wilson read it and gave orders to his men to tie him for his whipping. After this, the whipping was so severe that they never had any more trouble in making this Negro slave work and they never had to send him back again to Master Wilson to be whipped. The fun part of this above incidence was the Negro carried his own note and went alone to be whipped and didn't know it 'til the lashes was being put on him.

My Master's plantation was about 2 miles long and 1-1/2 mile wide and he owned between 30 or 40 slaves. The Negro overseer would wake up the slaves and have them in the field before they could see how to work each morning and as they would go to work so soon their breakfast was carried to the field to them. One morning the breakfast was taken to the field and the slaves were hoeing cotton and among them was a lad about 15 years of age who could not hoe as fast as the older slaves and the breakfast was sat at the end of the rows and as they would hoe out to the end they would eat, and if you would be late hoeing to the end the first to go to the end would began eating and eat everything. So, this 15 year old lad in order to get out to eat before everything was gone did not hoe his row good and the overseer, who was white at this time, whipped him so severely that he could not eat nor work, that day.

The Negroes went to church with the white people and joined their church. The church was Baptist in denomination, and they built a pen in the church in which the Negroes sat, and when they would take sacrament the Negroes would be served after the whites were through and one of the Negro group would pass it around to the others within the pen.

As there were no dances held on the plantation the Negroes would oftimes slip off and go at nights to a nearby dance or peanut parching or rice suppers at nights after work. Some of the slaves would be allowed to make for themselves rice patches which they would gather and save for the dances. To prepare this rice for cooking after harvested they would burn a trough into a log, they called mortar and with a large wooden mallet they called pessel, and which they would pound upon the rice until hulled and ready for cooking. This rice would be boiled with just salt and water and eaten as a great feast with delight.

During slavery some of the Negro slaves would kill snakes and skin them and wear these snake skins to prevent being voodooed they said. When some of the slaves would take sick and the home remedies would fail to cure them our Mistress would allow one of the Negro men slaves to go to the white doctor and get some medicine for the patient. The doctor would ask questions as to the actions of the patient and from said description would send medicine without ever going to see the patient and his medicine would always cure the patient of his disease if consulted in time.

After the news came that brought our freedom a white union officer with 20 trained Negro soldiers visited the plantations and saw that the Negroes received their freedom. He would put on a demonstration with his Negro soldiers by having them line up and then at a command they would all rush forward and stand their guns up together on the stock end without a one falling and get back into line and upon another command they would rush forward and each get his gun again without allowing one to fall and again reline up.

When I was large enough to pay attention to my color and to that of the other slaves I wondered to myself why I was not black like the rest of the slaves and concluded to myself that I would when I got grown like they were as I knew not then that I was the son of my Master.

During the War and as the men and our Master all went to the War the Negroes or a Negro would have to go to the Mistress' homes each morning and start fires and never, did I ever hear of a rape case under such close conditions as Negroes going into the bed rooms each morning of the white mistress to start fires.

My first wife was name Tracy Smith. As I had been free for over 12 years. We had ordinary marriage ceremony. I have 11 grown children, 15 or 20 grandchildren and 3 great grandchildren.

I think Abraham Lincoln was a fine old gentlemen and as to Jeff Davis I don't think he was what he should have been, and as to Booker T. Washington I think his idea of educating or training Negroes as servants to serve the white race appealed more to the white race than the Negroes.

My viewpoint as to slavery is that it was as much detrimental to the white race as it was to the Negroes, as one elevated ones minds too highly, and the other degraded ones mind too lowly.

Oklahoma Writers' Project
Ex-Slaves
[Date stamp: NOV 5 1937]

MATTIE HARDMAN
Age 78 yrs.
Oklahoma City, Okla.

I was born January 2, 1859, at Gunalis, Texas. My father's name was William Tensley and my mother's name Mildred Howard. They was brought from Virginia. I did have 8 brothers and sisters but all of them are dead.

My Master was name William Henry Howard. Since I was too young to work I nursed my sisters' children while they worked. The cooking was done all up to the general kitchen at Masters house and when slaves come from work they would send their children up to the kitchen to bring their meals to their homes in the quarters. Our Mistress would have one of the cooks to dish up vegetables and she herself would slice or serve the meat to see that it wasn't wasted, as seemingly it was thought so precious.

As my mother worked 'round the Big House quite a deal I would go up to the Big House with her and play with the white children who seemed to like for me to come to play with them. One day in anger while playing I called one of the white girls, "old black dog" and they pretended they would tell their mother (my Mistress) about it. I was scared, as they saw, and they promised me they would not tell if I'd promise to not do it again, and which I was so glad to do and be let off so lightly.

For summer I wore a cotton slip and for winter my mother knitted at nights after her days work was done so I wore red flannels for underwear and thick linsey for an over-dress, and had knitted stockings and bought shoes. As my Master was a doctor he made his slaves wear suitable clothes in accordance to the weather. We also wore gloves my mother knitted in winter.

My Mistress was good to all of the slaves. On Sunday morning she would make all the Negro children come to the Big House and she would stand on the front steps and read the Catechism to us who sat or stood in front on the ground.

My Master was also good. On Wednesdays and Friday nights he would make the slaves come up to the Big House and he would read the Bible to them and he would pray. He was a doctor and very fractious and exact. He didn't allow the slaves to claim they forgot to do thus and so nor did he allow them to make the expression, "I thought so and so." He would say to them if they did: "Who told you, you could think!"

They had 10 children, 7 boys and 3 girls. Their house was a large 2-story log house painted white. My father was overseer on the plantation.

The plantation consisted of 400 acres and about 40 slaves including children. The slaves were so seldom punished until they never'd worry about being punished. They treated their slaves as though they loved them. The poor white neighbors were also good and treated the slaves good, for my Master would warn them to not bother his Negroes. My Mistress always told the slaves she wanted all of them to visit her and come to her funeral and burial when she died and named the men slaves she wanted to be her pallbearers, all of which was carried out as she planned even though it was after freedom.

The slaves even who lived adjoining our plantation would have church at our Big House. They would hold church on Sundays and Sunday nights.

As my mother worked a deal for her Mistress she had an inkling or overheard that they was going to be set free long before the day they were. She called all the slaves on the plantation together and broke to them this news after they had promised her they would not spread the news so that it would get back to our Master. So, everybody kept the news until Saturday night June 19th, when Master called all the slaves to the big gate and told them they were all free, but could stay right on in their homes if they had no places to go and which all of them did. They went right out and gathered the crop just like they'd always done, and some of them remained there several years.

My first husband was name, S. W. Warnley. We had 4 children, 1 girl and three boys and 3 grandchildren. I now have two grandchildren.

Now that slavery is over I sometime wish 'twas still existing for some of our lazy folks, so that so many of them wouldn't or couldn't loaf around so much lowering our race, walking the streets day by day and running from house to house living corruptible lives which is keeping the race down as though there be no good ones among us.

Oklahoma Writers' Project
Ex-Slaves
[Date stamp: AUG 16 1937]

ANNIE HAWKINS
Age 90
Colbert, Okla

I calls myself 90, but I don't know jest how old I really am but I was a good sized gal when we moved from Georgia to Texas. We come on a big boat and one night the stars fell. Talk about being scared! We all run and hid and hollered and prayed. We thought the end of the world had come.

I never had no whitefolks that was good to me. We all worked jest like dogs and had about half enough to eat and got whupped for everything. Our days was a constant misery to us. I know lots of niggers that was slaves had a good time but we never did. Seems hard that I can't say anything good for any of 'em but I sho' can't. When I was small my job was to tote cool water to the field to the hands. It kept me busy going back and forth and I had to be sho' my old Mistress had a cool drink when she wanted it, too. Mother and my sister and me worked in the field all day and come in time to clear away the things and cook supper. When we was through in the kitchen we would spin fer a long time. Mother would spin and we would card.

My old Master was Dave Giles, the meanest man that ever lived. He didn't have many slaves, my mammy, and me, and my sister, Uncle Bill, and Truman. He had owned my grandma but he give her a bad whupping and she never did git over it and died. We all done as much work as a dozen niggers—we knowed we had to.

I seen old Master git mad at Truman and he buckled him down across a barrel and whupped him till he cut the blood out of him and then he rubbed salt and pepper in the raw places. It looked like Truman would die it hurt so bad. I know that don't sound reasonable that a white man in a Christian community would do such a thing but you can't realize how heartless he was. People didn't know about it and we dassent tell for we knowed he'd kill us if we did. You must remember he owned us body and soul and they wasn't anything we could do about it. Old Mistress and her three girls was mean to us too.

One time me and my sister was spinning and old Mistress went to the well-house and she found a chicken snake and killed it. She brought it back and she throwed it around my sister's neck. She jest laughed and laughed about it. She thought it was a big joke.

Old Master stayed drunk all the time. I reckon that is the reason he was so fetched mean. My, how we hated him! He finally killed hisself drinking and I remember Old Mistress called us in to look at him in his coffin. We all marched by him slow like and I jest happened to look up and caught my sister's eye and we both jest natchelly laughed—Why shouldn't we? We was glad he was dead. It's a good thing we had our laugh fer old Mistress took us out and whupped us with a broomstick. She didn't make us sorry though.

Old Master and Mistress lived in a nice big house on top of a hill and us darkies lived in log cabins with log floors. Our dresses was made out of coarse cloth like cotton sacking and and [TR: sic] it sho' lasted a long time. It ort to been called mule-hide for it was about that tough.

We went to church sometimes. They had to let us do that or folks would have found out how mean they was to us. Old Master'd give us a pass to show the patroller. We was glad to git the chance to git away and we always went to church.

During the War we seen lots of soldiers. Some of them was Yankees and some were Sesesh soldiers. My job every day was to take a big tray of food and set it on a stump about a quarter of a mile from our house. I done this twice a day and ever time I went back the dishes would be empty. I never did see nobody and didn't nobody tell me why I was to take the food up there but of course it was either for soliders [TR: sic] that was scouting 'round or it may been for some lowdown dirty bushwhacker, and again it might a been for some of old Master's folks scouting 'round to keep out of the army.

We was the happiest folks in the world when we knowed we was free. We couldn't realize it at first but how we did shout and cry for joy when we did realize it. We was afraid to leave the place at first for fear old Mistress would bring us back or the pateroller would git us. Old Mistress died soon after the War and we didn't care either. She didn't never do nothing to make us love her. We was jest as glad as when old Master died. I don't know what become of the three gals. They was about grown.

We moved away jest as far away as we could and I married soon after. My husband died and I married again. I been married four times and all my husbands died. The last time I married it was to a man that belonged to a Indian man, Sam Love. He was a good owner and was one of the best men that ever lived. My husband never did move far away from him and he loved him like a father. He always looked after him till he died. My husband has been dead five years.

I have had fifteen children. Four pairs of twins, and only four of them are living. The good Lawd wouldn't let me keep them. I'se lived through three wars so you see I'se no baby.

Oklahoma Writers' Project
Ex-Slaves
[Date stamp: NOV 5 1937]

IDA HENRY
Age 83
Oklahoma City, Okla.

I was born in Marshall, Texas, in 1854. Me mother was named Millie Henderson and me father Silas Hall. Me mother was sold in South Carolina to Mister Hall, who brought her to Texas. Me father was born and raised by Master John Hall. Me mother's and father's family consisted of five girls and one boy. My sisters' names were: Margrette, Chalette, Lottie, Gracy and Loyo, and me brother's name was Dock Howard. I lived with me mother and father in a log house on Master Hall's plantation. We would be sorry when dark, as de patrollers would walk through de quarters and homes of de slaves all times of night wid pine torch lights to whip de niggers found away from deir home.

At nights when me mother would slip away for a visit to some of de neighbors homes, she would raise up the old plank floor to de log cabin and make pallets on de ground and put us to bed and put the floor back down so dat we couldn't be seen or found by the patrollers on their stroll around at nights.

My grandmother Lottie would always tell us to not let Master catch you in a lie, and to always tell him de truth.

I was a house girl to me Mistress and nursed, cooked, and carried de children to and from school. In summer we girls wore cotton slips and yarn dresses for winter. When I got married I was dress in blue serge and was de third person to marry in it. Wedding dresses was not worn after de wedding in dem days by niggers as we was taught by our Mistress dat it was bad luck to wear de wedding dress after marriage. Therefore, 'twas handed down from one generation to the other one.

Me Mistress was sometimes good and sometimes mean. One day de cook was waiting de table and when passing around de potatoes, old Mistress felt of one and as hit wasn't soft done, she exclaimed to de cook, "What you bring these raw potatoes out here for?" and grab a fork and stuck it in her eye and put hit out. She, de cook, lived about 10 years and died.

Me Mistress was de mother of five children, Crock, Jim, Boss and two girls name, Lea and Annie.

Dere home was a large two-story white house wid de large white posts.

As me Master went to de War de old overseer tried himself in meanness over de slaves as seemingly he tried to be important. One day de slaves caught him and one held him whilst another knocked him in de head and killed him.

Master's plantation was about 300 acres and he had 'bout 160 slaves. Before de slaves killed our overseer, he would work 'em night and day. De slaves was punished when dey didn't do as much work as de overseer wanted 'em to do.

He would lock 'em in jail some nights without food and kept 'em dere all night, and after whipping 'em de next morning would only give 'em bread and water to work on till noon.

When a slave was hard to catch for punishment dey would make 'em wear ball and chains. De ball was 'bout de size of de head and made of lead.

On Sunday mornings before breakfast our Mistress would call us together, read de Bible and show us pictures of de Devil in de Bible and tell us dat if we was not good and if we would steal and tell lies dat old Satan would git us.

Close to our Master's plantation lived several families of old "poor white trash" who would steal me Master's hogs and chickens and come and tell me Mistress dat dey seen some of de slaves knock one of dere hogs in de head. Dis continued up till Master returned from de War and caught de old white trash stealing his hogs. De niggers did at times steal Master's hogs and chickens, and I would put biscuits and pieces of chicken in a sack under me dress dat hung from me waist, as I waited de table for me Mistress, and later would slip off and eat it as dey never gave de slaves none of dis sort of food.

We had church Sundays and our preacher Rev. Pat Williams would preach and our Master and family and other nearby white neighbors would ofttime attend our services. De patrollers wouldn't allow de slaves to hold night services, and one night dey caught me mother out praying. Dey stripped her naked and tied her hands together and wid a rope tied to de hand cuffs and threw one end of de rope over a limb and tied de other end to de pommel of a saddle on a horse. As me mother weighed 'bout 200, dey pulled her up so dat her toes could barely touch de ground and whipped her. Dat same night she ran away and stayed over a day and returned.

During de fall months dey would have corn shucking and cotton pickings and would give a prize to de one who would pick de highest amount of cotton or shuck de largest pile of corn. De prize would usually be a suit of clothes or something to wear and which would be given at some later date.

We could only have dances during holidays, but dances was held on other plantations. One night a traveler visiting me Master and wanted his boots shined. So Master gave de boots to one of de slaves to shine and de slave put de boots on and went to a dance and danced so much dat his feet swelled so dat when he returned he could not pull 'em off.

De next morning as de slave did not show up with de boots dey went to look for him and found him lying down trying to pull de boots off. He told his Master dat he had put de boots on to shine 'em and could not pull 'em off. So Master had to go to town and buy de traveler another pair of boots. Before he could run away de slave was beaten wid 500 lashes.

De War dat brought our freedom lasted about two years. Me Master went and carried one of de slaves for a servant. He was kind and good and from dat day on he never whipped another slave nor did he allow any of his slaves whipped. Dis time lasted from January to June de 19th when we was set free in de State of Texas.

Lincoln and Davis both died short of promise. I means dat dey both died before dey carried out dere plans and promises for freeing de slaves.

Oklahoma Writers' Project
Ex-Slaves

MORRIS HILLYER
Age 84 yrs.
Alderson, Okla.

My father was Gabe Hillyer and my mother was Clarisay Hillyer, and our home was in Rome, Georgia. Our owner was Judge Hillyer. He was de last United States senator to Washington, D. C., before de War.

My mother died when I was only a few days old and the only mother I ever knew was Judge Hillyer's wife, Miss Jane. Her nine children were all older than I was and when mother died Miss Jane said mother had raised her children and she would raise hers. So she took us into her house and we never lived at de quarters any more. I had two sisters, Sally and Sylvia, and we had a room in de Big House and sister Sally didn't do nothing else but look after me. I used to stand with my thumb in my mouth and hold to Miss Jane's apron while she knitted.

When Judge Hillyer was elected he sold out his farm and gave his slaves to his children. He owned about twelve or fourteen slaves at this time. He gave me and my sister Sylvia to his son, Dr. Hillyer, and my father to another one of his sons who was studying law. Father stayed with him and took care of him until he graduated. Father learned to be a good carpenter while he lived with George Hillyer. George never married until after de War.

Dr. Hillyer lived on a big plantation but he practiced medicine all de time. He didn't have much time to look after de farm but he had good overseers and they sure didn't beat his slaves or mistreat 'em in any way. Dr. Hillyer married a rich girl, Miss Mary Cooley, and her father gave her fifteen slaves when she married and Judge Hillyer gave him five so he had a purty good start from de first and he knowed how to make money so he was a wealthy man when de Rebellion started.

My sister and I didn't know how to act when we was sent out there among strangers. We had to live in de quarters just like de other niggers, and we didn't especially like it. I guess I was a sort of bad boy.

There was several more boys about my age and we didn't have any work to do but just busy ourselves by getting into mischief. We'd ride de calves, chase de pigs, kill de chickens, break up hens nests, and in fact do most everything we hadn't ought to do. Finally they put us to toting water to de field hands, minding de gaps, taking de cows to pasture and as dat kept us purty busy we wasn't so bad after dat.

My happiest days was when I was with de old Judge and Miss Jane. I can sit here and think of them old times and it seems like it was just yesterday dat it all happened. He was a great hand to go to town every day and lounge around wid his cronies. I used to go with him, and my how they would argue. Sometimes they would get mad and shake their canes in each other's faces. I guess they was talking politics.

Our old Master liked cats better than any man I ever saw, and he always had five or six that followed him about de place like dogs. When he went to eat they was always close to him and just as soon as he finished he would always feed them. When he was gone us boys used to throw at his cats or set de dogs on 'em. We was always careful dat no one saw us for if he had known about it he would a-whipped us and no mistake. I wouldn't a-blamed him either, for I like cats now. I think they are lots of company.

He was a typical Southern gentleman, medium sized, and wore a Van Dyke beard. He never whipped his slaves, and he didn't have a one dat wouldn't a-died for him.

Judge Hillyer had one son, William, dat wouldn't go to college. He made fun of his brothers for going to school so long, and said that he would be ashamed to go and stay five or six years. After de War he settled down and studied law in Judge Akin's office and opened a office in Athens, Georgia, and he made de best lawyer of them all.

Us boys used to go hunting with Master William. He hunted rabbits, quails, squirrels, and sometimes he would kill a deer. He hunted mostly with dogs. He never used a gun but very little. Lead was so scarce and cost so much dat he couldn't afford to waste a bullet on rabbits or snakes. He made his own bullets. The dogs would chase a rabbit into a hollow tree and we'd take a stick and twist him out. Sometimes we'd have nearly all de hide twisted off him when we'd git him out.

Old Judge Hillyer smoked a pipe with a long stem. He used to give me ten cents a day to fill it for him. He told me I had to have $36 at the end of the year, but I never made it. There was a store right close to us and I'd go down there and spend my money for lemon stick candy, ginger cakes, peanuts, and firecrackers. Old Master knowed I wouldn't save it, and he didn't care if I did spent it for it was mine to do with just as I pleased.

Every time a circus come to town I'd run off and they wouldn't see me again all day. Seemed like I just couldn't help it. I wouldn't take time to git permission to go. One time to punish me for running off he tied me up by my thumbs, and I had to stay home while de rest went. I didn't dare try to git loose and run off for I knowed I'd git my jacket tanned if I did. Old Master never laid his hand on me, but I knowed he would if I didn't do as he told me. He never told us twice to do anything either.

Coins had curious names in them days. A dime was called a thrip. Fourpen was about the same value as three cents or maybe a little more. It took three of 'em to make a thrip. There was all sorts of paper money.

Every first Tuesday slaves were brought in from Virginia and sold on de block. De auctioneer was Cap'n Dorsey. E. M. Cobb was de slave bringer. They would stand de slaves up on de block and talk about what a fine looking specimen of black manhood or womanhood dey was, tell how healthy dey was, look in their mouth and examine their teeth just like they was a horse, and talk about de kind of work they would be fit for and could do. Young healthy boys and girls brought the best prices. I guess they figured dat they would grow to be valuable. I used to stand around and watch de sales take place but it never entered my mind to be afraid for I knowed old Judge wasn't going to sell me. I thought I was an important member of his family.

Old Judge bought every roguish nigger in the country. He'd take him home and give him the key to everything on de place and say to help hisself. Soon as he got all he wanted to eat he'd quit being a rogue. Old Judge said that was what made niggers steal—they was hungry.

They used to scare us kids by telling us dat a runaway nigger would git us. De timber was awful heavy in de river bottoms, and dey was one nigger dat run off from his master and lived for years in these bottoms. He was there all during de War and come out after de surrender. Every man in dat country owned him at some time or other. His owner sold him to a man who was sure he could catch him—he never did, so he sold him to another slave owner and so on till nearly everybody had him. He changed hands about six or seven times. They would come in droves with blood hounds and hunt for him but dey couldn't catch him for he knowed them woods too well. He'd feed de dogs and make friends with 'em and they wouldn't bother him. He lived on nuts, fruit, and wild game, and niggers would slip food to him. He'd slip into town and get whiskey and trade it to de niggers for food.

Judge Hillyer never 'lowanced his niggers and dey could always have anything on de place to eat. We had so much freedom dat other slave owners in our neighborhood didn't like for us to come among their slaves for they said we was free niggers and would make their slaves discontented.

After I went to live with Judge Hillyer's son, Dr. Hillyer, one of my jobs was to tote the girls books to school every morning. All the plantation owners had a colored boy dat did that. After we had toted de books to de school house we'd go back down de road a piece and line up and have the "gone-bying-est" fight you ever see. We'd have regular battles. If I got licked in de morning I'd go home and rest up and I'd give somebody a good licking dat evening. I reckon I caught up with my fighting for in all my working life I have always worked with gangs of men of from one to two-hundred and I never struck a man and no man ever struck me.

Jim Williams was a patroller, and how he did like to catch a nigger off de farm without a permit so he could whip him. Jim thought he was de best man in de country and could whip de best of 'em. One night John Hardin, a big husky feller, was out late. He met Jim and knowed he was in for it. Jim said, "John I'm gonna give you a white man's chance. I'm gonna let you fight me and if you are de best man, well and good."

John say, "Master Jim, I can't fight wid you. Come on and give me my licking, and let me go on home."

But Jim wouldn't do it, and he slapped John and called him some names and told him he is a coward to fight him. All dis made John awful mad and he flew into him and give him the terriblest licking a man ever toted. He went on home but knew he would git into trouble over it.

Jim talked around over the country about what he was going to do to John but everybody told him dat he brought it all on hisself. He never did try to git another nigger to fight with him.

Yes, I guess charms keep off bad luck. I have wore 'em but money always was my best lucky piece. I've made lots of money but I never made good use of it.

I was always afraid of ghosts but I never saw one. There was a graveyard beside de road from our house to town and I always was afraid to go by it. I'd shut my eyes and run for dear life till I was past de grave yard. I had heard dat there was a headless man dat stayed there on cold rainy days or foggy nights he'd hide by de fence and throw his head at you. Once a man got hit and he fell right down dead. I believed dat tale and you can imagine how I felt whenever I had to go past there by myself and on foot.

I saw lots of Ku Kluxers but I wasn't afraid of them. I knowed I hadn't done nothing and they wasn't after me. One time I met a bunch of 'em and one of 'em said, "Who is dis feller?" Another one said, "Oh, dat's Gabe's foolish boy, come on, don't bother him." I always did think dat voice sounded natural but I never did say anything about it. It sounded powerful like one of old Judge's boys. Dey rode on and didn't bother me and I never was a bit afraid of 'em any more.

I went to school one month after de War. I never learned much but I learned to read some where along de road dat I come over. My father come from Athens, Georgia, and took us away with him. I learned the carpenter's trade from him. He was so mean to me dat I run away when I was nineteen. I went back to Rome, Georgia, and got a job with a bridge gang and spent two years with 'em. I went then to Henderson, Kentucky, and worked for ten years. There was hundreds of colored people coming to de mines at Krebs and Alderson and I decided to come along, too. I never worked in de mines but I did all sorts of carpentering for them.

I married in Atoka, Oklahoma, thirty-three years ago. I never had no children.

I've made lots of money but somehow it always got away from me. But me and my wife have our little home here and we are both still able to work a little, so I guess we are making it all right.

Oklahoma Writers' Project
Ex-Slaves

HAL HUTSON
Age 90 yrs.
Oklahoma City, Okla.

I was born at Galveston, Tennessee, October 12, 1847. There were 11 children: 7 brothers; Andrew, George, Clent, Gilbert, Frank, Mack and Horace; and 3 girls: Rosie, Marie and Nancy. We were all Hutsons. Together with my mother and father we worked for the same man whose name was Mr. Barton Brown, but who we all call Master Brown, and sometimes Mr. Brown.

Master Brown had a good weather-board house, two story, with five or six rooms. They lived pretty well. He had eight children. We lived in one-room log huts. There were a long string of them huts. We slept on the floor like hogs. Girls and boys slept together—jest everybody slept every whar. We never knew what biscuits were! We ate "seconds and shorts" (wheat ground once) for bread. Ate rabbits, possums baked with taters, beans, and bean soup. No chicken, fish and the like. My favorite dish now is beans.

Master Brown owned about 36 or 40 slaves, I can't recall jest now, and about 200 acres of ground. There was very little cotton raised in Galveston—I mean jest some corn. Sometimes we would shuck corn all night. He would not let us raise gardens of our own, but didn't mind us raising corn and a few other truck vegetables to sell for a little spending change.

I learned to read, write and figger at an early age. Master Brown's boy and I were the same age you see (14 years old) and he would send me to school to protect his kids, and I would have to sit up there until school was out. So while sitting there I listened to what the white teacher was telling the kids, and caught on how to read, write and figger—but I never let on, 'cause if I was caught trying to read or figger dey would whip me something terrible. After I caught on how to figger the white kids would ask me to teach them. Master Brown would often say: "My God O'mighty, never do for that nigger to learn to figger."

We weren't allowed to count change. If we borrowed a fifty-cent piece, we would have to pay back a fifty-cent piece—not five dimes or fifty pennies or ten nickels.

We went barefooted the year round and wore long shirts split on each side. All of us niggers called all the whites "poor white trash." The overseer was nothing but poor white trash and the meanest man that ever walked on earth. He never did whip me much 'cause I was kind of a pet. I worked up to the Big House, but he sho' did whip them others. Why, one day he was beating my mother, and I was too small to say anything, so my big brother heard her crying and came running, picked up a chunk and that overseer stopped a'beating her. The white boy was holding her on the ground and he was whipping her with a long leather whip. They said they couldn't teach her no sense and she said "I don't wanna learn no sense." The overseer's name was Charlie

104

Clark. One day he whipped a man until he was bloody as a pig 'cause he went to the mill and stayed too long.

The patroller rode all night and iffen we were caught out later than 10:00 o'clock they would beat us, but we would git each other word by sending a man round way late at night. Always take news by night. Of course the Ku Klux Klan didn't come 'til after the war. They was something like the patrollers. Never heard of no trouble between the black and whites 'cause them niggers were afraid to resist them.

My biggest job was keeping flies off'n the table up at the Big House. When time come to go in for the day we would cut up and dance. I can't remember any of the songs jest now, but we had some that we sung. We danced a whole lots and jest sung "made up" songs.

Old Master would stay up to hear us come in. Of course Saturday afternoon was a holiday. We didn't work no holidays. Master gave us one week off for Christmas, and never worked us on Sunday, unless the "ox was in the ditch." When the slaves got sick we had white doctors, and we would wait on each other. Drink dock root tea, mullin tea, and flaxweed tea, but we never wore charms.

I think it's a good thing that slavery's over. It ought to been over a good while ago. But its going to be slavery all over again if things don't git better. But I thank God I've been a Christian for 70 years, and now is a member of Tabernacle Baptist Church and deacon of the church, and a Christian 'cause the Bible teaches me to be.

That war was a awful thing. I used to pack them soldiers water on my head, and then I worked at Fort Sill and Fort Dawson in Tennessee. Those Yankees came by nights—got behind those rebels, and took their hams, drove horses in the houses, killed their chickens and ate up the rebels food, but the Yanks didn't bother us niggers.

When freedom come old Master called us all in from the fields and told us, "All of you niggers are free as frogs now to go wherever you choose. You are your own man now." We all continued working for him at $5.00 a month. After the crops were gathered the niggers scattered out. Some went North—and we would say when they went North that they had "crossed the water."

I never married 'till after the War. Married at my mother's house 'cause my wife's mother didn't let us marry at her house, so I sent Jack Perry after her on a hoss and we had a big dinner—and jest got married.

I am the father of nine children, but jest three is living. One is a dentist in Muskogge, Dr. Andrew Hutson. All of the children are pretty well read. We never had schools for niggers until after slavery.

I think Abraham Lincoln was a great man, but I don't know much about Jeff Davis. Booker T. Washington was a fine man.

Oklahoma Writers' Project
Ex-Slaves
[Date stamp: AUG 16 1937]

WILLIAM HUTSON
Age 98 yrs.
Tulsa, Okla.

When a feller gets as old as me it's a heap easier to forget things than it is to remember, but I ain't never forgot that old plantation where good old Doctor Allison lived back there in Georgia long before the War that brought us slaves the freedom.

I hear the slaves talking about mean masters when I was a boy. They wasn't talking about Master Allison though, 'cause he was a good man and took part for the slaves when any trouble come up with the overseer.

The Mistress' name was Louisa (the same name as the gal I was married to later after the War), and she was just about as mean as was the old Master good. I was the house boy when I gets old enough to understand what the Master wants done and I does it just like he says, so I reckon that's why we always get along together.

The Master helped to raise my mammy. When I was born he says to her (my mammy tells me when I gets older): "Cheney", the old Master say, "that boy is going be different from these other children. I aims to see that he is. He's going be in the house all the time, he ain't going work in the fields; he's going to stay right with me all the time."

They was about twenty slaves on the plantation but I was the one old Master called for when he wanted something special for himself. I was the one he took with him on the trips to town, I was the one who fetch him the cooling drink after he look about the fields and sometimes I carry the little black bag when he goes a-doctoring folks with the misery away off some other farm.

The Master hear about there going be an auction one day and he figgered maybe he needed some more slaves if they was good ones, so he took me and started out early in the morning. It wasn't very far and we got there early before the auction started. Rockon that was the first time I ever see any slaves sold.

They was a long platform made of heavy planks and all the slaves was lined up on the platform, and they was stripped to the waist, men, women, and children. One or two of the women folks was bare naked. They wasn't young women neither, just middle age ones, but they was built good. Some of them was well greased and that grease covered up many a scar they'd earned for some foolishment or other.

The Master don't buy none and pretty soon we starts home. The Master was riding horseback,—he didn't ever use no buggy 'cause he said that was the way for folks to travel who was too feeble to sit in the saddle—and I rode back of him on another horse, but that horse I rides is just horse while the Master's was a real thoroughbred like maybe you see on race tracks down in the South.

That auction kept bothering me all the way back to the plantation. I kept seeing them little children standing on the flatform (platform), their mammy and pappy crying hard 'cause their young'uns is being sold. They was a lot of heartaches even they was slaves and it gets me worried.

I asked the Master is he going to have an auction and he jest laugh. I ain't never sold no slaves yet and I ain't going to, he says. And I gets easier right then. I kind of hates to think about standing up on one of them platforms, kinder sorry to leave my old mammy and the Master, so I was easy in the heart when he talked like that.

The plantation house was a big frame and the yard was shaded with trees all around. The Master's children—four boys and two girls—would play in the yard with me just like I was one of the family. And we'd go hunting and fishing. There was a creek not far away and they was good fishing in the stream and squirrels in the trees. Mighty lot of fun to catch them fishes but more fun when they is all fried brown and ready for to eat with a piece of hot pone. Ain't no fish ever taste that good since!

One thing I sort of ponders about. The old Master don't let us have no religion meetings and reading and writing is something I learn after the War. Some of the slaves talk about meeting 'round the country and wants to have preaching on the plantation. Master says NO. No preacher around here to tell about the Bible and religion will be just a puzzlement, the Master say, and we let it go at that. I reckon that was the only thing he was set against.

That and the Yankees. The Master went to the War and stayed 'til it was most over. He was a mighty sick man when he come back to the old place, but I was there waiting for him just like always. All the time he was away I take care around the house. That's what he say for me to do when he rides away to fight the Yankees. Lot's of talk about the War but the slaves goes right on working just the same, raising cotton and tobacco.

The slaves talk a heap about Lincoln and some trys to run away to the North. Don't hear much about Jeff Davis, mostly Lincoln. He give us slaves the freedom but we was better off as we was.

The day of freedom come around just [HW: like] any other day, except the Master say for me to bring up the horses, we is going to town. That's when he hears about the slaves being free. We gets to the town and the Master goes into the store. It's pretty early but the streets was filled with folks talking and I wonder what makes the Master in such a hurry when he comes out of the store.

He gets on his horse and tells me to follow fast. When we gets back to the plantation he sounds the horn calling the slaves. They come in from the fields and meet 'round back of the kitchen building that stood separate from the Master's house. They all keeps quiet while the Master talks: "You-all is free now, and all the rest of the slaves is free too. Nobody owns you now and nobody going to own you anymore!" That was good news, I reckon, but nobody know what to do about it.

The crops was mostly in and the Master wants the folks to stay 'til the crop is finished. They talk about it the rest of that day. They wasn't no celebration 'round the place, but they wasn't no work after the Master tells us we is free. Nobody leave the place though. Not 'til in the fall when the work is through. Then some of us go into the town and gets work 'cause everybody knows the Allison slaves was the right kind of folks to have around.

That was the first money I earn and then I have to learn how to spend it. That was the hardest part 'cause the prices was high and the wages was low.

Then I moves on and meets the gal that maybe I been looking for, Louisa Baker, and right away she takes to me and we is married. Ain't been no other woman but her and she's waiting for me wherever the dead waits for the living.

I reckon she won't have so long to wait now, even if I is feeling pretty spry and got good use of the feets and hands. Ninety-eight years brings a heap of wear and some of these days the old body'll need a long time rest and then I'll join her for all the time.

I is ready for the New Day a-coming!

Oklahoma Writers' Project
Ex-Slaves
[Date stamp: AUG 16 1937]

MRS. ISABELLA JACKSON
Age 79 yrs.
Tulsa, Okla.

"Boom ... Boom! Boom ... Boom!" That's the way the old weaver go all day long when my sister, Margaret, is making cloth for the slaves down on old Doc Joe Jackson's plantation in Louisiana.

That was near the little place of Bunker, and its my birthplace, and I guess where all Mammy's children were born because she was never sold but once and nobody but the old Doc ever did own her after she come to his place.

He always say couldn't nobody get work out of Mammy but him. I guess that's just his foolery 'cause if she ain't no good the Old Doc most likely sell her to some of them white folks in Texas.

That's what they done to them mean, no account slaves—just send them to Texas. Them folks sure knew how for to handle 'em!

But I was talking about my sister, Margaret. I can still see her weaving the cloth—Boom!... Boom!—and she hear that all the day and get mighty tired. Sometimes she drop her head and go to sleep. The Mistress get her then sure. Rap her on the head with almost anything handy, but she hit pretty easy, just trying to scare her that's all.

The old Master though, he ain't so easy as that. The whippings was done by the master and the overseer just tell the old Doc about the troubles, like the old Doc say:

"You just watch the slaves and see they works and works hard, but don't lay on with the whip, because I is the only one who knows how to do it right!"

Maybe the old Master was sickened of whippings from the stories the slaves told about the plantation that joined ours on the north.

If they ever was a living Devil that plantation was his home and the owner was It! That's what the old slaves say, and when I tell you about it see if I is right.

That man got so mean even the white folks was scared of him, 'specially if he was filled with drink. That's the way he was most of the time, just before the slaves was freed.

All the time we hear about slaves on that place getting whipped or being locked in the stock—that one of them things where your head and hands is fastened through holes in a wide board, and you stands there all the day and all the night—and sometimes we hears of them staying in the stock for three-four weeks if they trys to run away to the north.

Sometimes we hears about some slave who is shot by that man while he is wild with the drink. That's what I'm telling about now.

Don't nobody know what made the master mad at the old slave—one of the oldest on the place. Anyway, the master didn't whip him; instead of that he kills him with the gun and scares the others so bad most of 'em runs off and hides in the woods.

The drunk master just drags the old dead slave to the graveyard which is down in the corner away from the growing crops, and hunts up two of the young boys who was hiding in the barn. He takes them to dig the grave.

The master stands watching every move they make, the dead man lays there with his face to the sky, and the boys is so scared they could hardly dig. The master keeps telling them to hurry with the digging.

After while he tells them to stop and put the body in the grave. They wasn't no coffin, no box, for him. Just the old clothes that he wears in the fields.

But the grave was too short and they start to digging some more, but the master stop them. He says to put back the body in the grave, and then he jumps into the grave hisself. Right on the dead he jumps and stomps 'til the body is mashed and twisted to fit the hole. Then the old nigger is buried.

That's the way my Mammy hears it and told it to us children. She was a Christian and I know she told the truth.

Like I said, Mammy was never sold only to Master Jackson. But she's seen them slave auctions where the men, women and children was stripped naked and lined up so's the buyers could see what kind of animals they was getting for their money.

My pappy's name was Jacob Keller and my mother was Maria. They's both dead long ago, and I'm waiting for the old ship Zion that took my Mammy away, like we use to sing of in the woods:

"It has landed my old Mammy,

It has landed my old Mammy,

Get on board, Get on board,

'Tis the Old Ship of Zion—

Get on board!"

Oklahoma Writers' Project
Ex-Slaves
[Date stamp: AUG 16 1937]

NELLIE JOHNSON

I don't know how old I is, but I is a great big half grown gal when the time of the War come, and I can remember how everything look at that time, and what all the people do, too.

I'm pretty nigh to blind right now, and all I can do is set on this little old front porch and maybe try to keep the things picked up behing my grandchild and his wife, because she has to work and he is out selling wood most of the time.

But I didn't have to live in any such a house during the time I was young like they is, because I belonged to old Chief Rolley McIntosh, and my pappy and mammy have a big, nice, clean log house to live in, and everything round it look better than most renters got these days.

We never did call old Master anything but the Chief or the General for that's what everybody called him in them days, and he never did act towards us like we was slaves, much anyways. He was the mikko of the Kawita town long before the War and long before I was borned, and he was the chief of the Lower Creeks even before he got to be the chief of all the Creeks.

But just at the time of the War the Lower Creeks stayed with him and the Upper Creeks, at least them that lived along to the south of where we live, all go off after that old man Gouge, and he take most of the Seminole too. I hear old Tuskenugge, the big man with the Seminoles, but I never did see him, nor mighty few of the Seminoles.

My mammy tells me old General ain't been living in that Kawita town very many years when I was borned. He come up there from down in the fork of the river where the Arkansas and the Verdigris run together a little while after all the last of the Creeks come out to the Territory. His brother old Chili McIntosh, live down in that forks of the rivers too, but I don't think he ever move up into that Kawita town. It was in the narrow stretch where the Verdigris come close to the Arkansas. They got a pretty good sized white folks town there now they call Coweta, but the old Creek town was different from that. The folks lived all around in that stretch between the rivers, and my old Master was the boss of all of them.

For a long time after the Civil War they had a court at the new town called Coweta court, and a school house too, but before I was born they had a mission school down the Kawita Creek from where the town now is.

Earliest I can remember about my master was when he come to the slave settlement where we live and get out of the buggy and show a preacher all around the place. That preacher named Mr. Loughridge, and he was the man had the mission down on Kawita Creek before I was born, but at that time he had a school off at some other place. He git down out the buggy and talk to all us children, and ask us how we getting along.

I didn't even know at that time that old Chief was my master, until my pappy tell me after he was gone. I think all the time he was another preacher.

My pappy's name was Jackson McInotsh, and my mammy name was Hagar. I think old Chief bring them out to the Territory when he come out with his brother Chili and the rest of the Creek people. My pappy tell me that old Master's pappy was killed by the Creeks because he signed up a treaty to bring his folks out here, and old Master always hated that bunch of Creeks that done that.

I think old man Gouge was one of the big men in that bunch, and he fit in the War on the Government side, after he done holler and go on so about the Government making him come out here.

Old Master have lots of land took up all around that Kawita place, and I don't know how much, but a lot more than anybody else. He have it all fenced in with good rail fence, and all the Negroes have all the horses and mules and tools they need to work it with. They all live in good log houses they built themselves, and everything they need.

Old Master's land wasn't all in one big field, but a lot of little fields scattered all over the place. He just take up land what already was a kind of prairie, and the niggers don't have to clear up much woods.

We all live around on them little farms, and we didn't have to be under any overseer like the Cherokee Negroes had lots of times. We didn't have to work if they wasn't no work to do that day.

Everybody could have a little patch of his own, too, and work it between times, on Saturdays and Sundays if he wanted to. What he made on that patch belong to him, and the old Chief never bothered the slaves about anything.

Every slave can fix up his own cabin any way he want to, and pick out a good place with a spring if he can find one. Mostly the slave houses had just one big room with a stick-and-mud chimney, just like the poor people among the Creeks had. Then they had a brush shelter built out of four poles with a roof made out of brush, set out to one side of the house where they do the cooking and eating, and sometimes the sleeping too. They set there when they is done working, and lay around on corn shuck beds, because they never did use the log house much only in cold and rainy weather.

Old Chief just treat all the Negroes like they was just hired hands, and I was a big girl before I knowed very much about belonging to him.

I was one of the youngest children in my family; only Sammy and Millie was younger than I was. My big brothers was Adam, August and Nero, and my big sisters was Flora, Nancy and Rhoda. We could work a mighty big patch for our own selves when we was all at home together, and put in all the work we had to for the old Master too, but after the War the big children all get married off and took up land of they own.

Old Chief lived in a big log house made double with a hall in between, and a lot of white folks was always coming there to see him about something. He was gone off somewhere a lot of the time, too, and he just trusted the Negroes to look after his farms and stuff. We would just go on out in the fields and work the crops just like they was our own, and he never come around excepting when we had harvest time, or to tell us what he wanted planted.

Sometimes he would send a Negro to tell us to gather up some chickens or turkeys or shoats he wanted to sell off, and sometimes he would send after loads of corn and wheat to sell. I heard my pappy say old Chief and Mr. Chili McIntosh was the first ones to have any wheat in the Territory, but I don't know about that.

Along during the War the Negro men got pretty lazy and shiftless, but my pappy and my big brothers just go right on and work like they always did. My pappy always said we better off to stay on the place and work good and behave ourselves because old Master take care of us that way. But on lots of other places the men slipped off.

I never did see many soldiers during the War, and there wasn't any fighting close to where we live. It was kind of down in the bottoms, not far from the Verdigris and that Gar Creek, and the soldiers would have bad crossings if the come by our place.

We did see some whackers riding around sometimes, in little bunches of about a dozen, but they never did bother us and never did stop. Some of the Negro girls that I knowed of mixed up with the poor Creeks and Seminoles, and some got married to them after the War, but none of my family ever did mix up with them that I knows of.

Along towards the last of the War I never did see old Chief come around any more, and somebody say he went down into Texas. He never did come back that I knows of, and I think he died down there.

One day my pappy come home and tell us all that the Creek done sign up to quit the War, and that old Master send word that we all free now and can take up some land for our own selves or just stay where we is if we want to. Pappy stayed on that place where he was at until he died.

I got to be a big girl and went down to work for a Creek family close to where they got that Checotah town now. At that time it was just all a scattered settlement of Creeks and they call it Eufaula town. After while I marry a man name Joe Johnson, at a little settlement they call Rentesville. He have his freedmen's allotment close to that place, but mine is up on the Verdigris, and we move up there to live.

We just had one child, named Louisa, and she married Tom Armstrong. They had three-four children, but one was named Ton, and it is him I live with now. My husband's been dead a long, long time now.

Oklahoma Writers' Project
Ex-Slaves
[Date stamp: AUG 16 1937]

MS. JOSIE JORDAN
Age 75 yrs.
840 East King St.,
Tulsa, Oklahoma.

I was born right in the middle of the War on the Mark Lowery plantation at Sparta, in White County, Tennessee, so I don't know anything much about them slave days except what my mammy told me long years ago. 'Course I mean the Civil War, for to us colored folks they just wasn't no other war as meanful as that one.

My mother she come from Virginia when a little girl, but never nobody tells me where at my pappy is from. His name was David Lowery when I was born, but I guess he had plenty other names, for like my mammy he was sold lots of times.

Salina was my mammy's name, and she belonged to a Mister Clark, who sold her and pappy to Mark Lowery 'cause she was a fighting, mule-headed woman.

It wasn't her fault 'cause she was a fighter. The master who owned her before Mister Clark was one of them white mens who was always whipping and beating his slaves and mammy couldn't stand it no more.

That's the way she tells me about it. She just figgured she would be better off dead and out of her misery as to be whipped all the time, so one day the master claimed they was something wrong with her work and started to raise his whip, but mammy fought back and when the ruckus was over the Master was laying still on the ground and folks thought he was dead, he got such a heavy beating.

Mammy says he don't die and right after that she was sold to Mister Clark I been telling you about. And mammy was full of misery for a long time after she was carried to Mark Lowery's plantation where at I was born during of the War.

She had two children while belonging to Mister Clark and he wouldn't let them go with mammy and pappy. That's what caused her misery. Pappy tried to ease her mind but she jest kept a'crying for her babies, Ann and Reuban, till Mister Lowery got Clark to leave them visit with her once a month.

Mammy always says that Mark Lowery was a good master. But he'd heard things about mammy before he got her and I reckon was curious to know if they was all true. Mammy says he found out mighty quick they was.

114

It was mammy's second day on the plantation and Mark Lowery acted like he was going to whip her for something she'd done or hadn't, but mammy knocked him plumb through the open cellar door. He wasn't hurt, not even mad for mammy says he climbed out the cellar a'laughing, saying he was only fooling to see if she would fight.

But mammy's troubles wasn't over then, for Mark Lowery he got himself a new young wife (his first wife was dead), and mammy was round of the house most of the time after that.

Right away they had trouble. The Mistress was trying to make mammy hurry up with the work and she hit mammy with the broom stick. Mammy's mule temper boiled up all over the kitchen and the Master had to stop the fighting.

He wouldn't whip mammy for her part in the trouble, so the Mistress she sent word to her father and brothers and they come to Mister Lowery's place.

They was going to whip mammy, they was good and mad. Master was good and mad, too, and he warned 'em home.

"Whip your own slaves." He told them. "Mine have to work and if they're beat up they can't do a days work. Get on home—I'll take care of this." And they left.

My folks didn't have no food troubles at Mark Lowery's like they did somewheres else. I remember mammy told me about one master who almost starved his slaves. Mighty stingy I reckon he was.

Some of them slaves was so poorly thin they ribs would kinder rustle against each other like corn stalks a-drying in the hot winds. But they gets even one hog-killing time, and it was funny too, mammy said.

They was seven hogs, fat and ready for fall hog-killing time. Just the day before old master told off they was to be killed something happened to all them porkers. One of the field boys found them and come a-telling the master: "The hogs is all died, now they won't be any meats for the winter."

When the master gets to where at the hogs is laying, they's a lot of Negroes standing round looking sorrow-eyed at the wasted meat. The master asks: "What's the illness with 'em?"

"Malitis." They tell him, and they acts like they don't want to touch the hogs. Master says to dress them anyway for they ain't no more meat on the place.

He says to keep all the meat for the slave families, but that's because he's afraid to eat it hisself account of the hogs' got malitis.

"Don't you-all know what is malitis?" Mammy would ask the children when she was telling of the seven fat hogs and seventy lean slaves. And she would laugh, remembering how they fooled the old master so's to get all them good meats.

"One of the strongest Negroes got up early in the morning," Mammy would explain, "long 'fore the rising horn called the slaves from their cabins. He skitted to the hog pen with a heavy mallet in his hand. When he tapped Mister Hog 'tween the eyes with that mallet 'malitis' set in mighty quick, but it was a uncommon 'disease', even with hungry Negroes around all the time."

Mammy had me three sisters and a brother while on the Lowery plantation. They was Lisa, Addie, Alice and Lincoln. It was a long time after the War and we was all freed before we left old Master Lowery.

Stayed right there where we was at home, working in the fields, living in the same old cabins, just like before the War. Never did have no big troubles after the War, except one time the Ku Klux Klan broke up a church meeting and whipped some of the Negroes.

The preacher was telling about the Bible days when the Klan rode up. They was all masked up and everybody crawled under the benches when they shouted: "We'll make you damn niggers wish you wasn't free!"

And they just about did. The preacher got the worst whipping, blood was running from his nose and mouth and ears, and they left him laying on the floor.

They whipped the women just like the men, but Mammy and the girls wasn't touched none and we run all the way back to the cabin. Layed down with all our clothes on and tried to sleep, but we's too scairt to close our eyes.

Mammy reckoned old Master Lowery was a-riding with the Klan that night, else we'd got a flogging too.

We first moved about a mile from Master Lowery's place and ever week we'd ask mammy if we children could go see old Master and she'd say: "Yes, if you-all are good niggers."

The old Master was always glad to see us children and he would give us candy and apples and treat us mighty fine.

The old plantations gone, the old Masters gone, the old slaves is gone, and I'll be a going some of these days, too, for I been here a mighty long time and they ain't nobody needs me now 'cause I is too old for any good.

Oklahoma Writers' Project
Ex-Slaves

"UNCLE" GEORGE G. KING
Age 83 yrs
Tulsa, Oklahoma

"Prayers for sale.... Prayers for sale...." Uncle George chants in sing-song fashion as he roams around Tulsa's Greenwood Negro district—pockets filled with prayer papers that are soiled and dirty with constant handling.

But they are potent, Uncle George tells those who fear the coming of some trouble, disaster or just ordinary misery, and there's a special prayer for each and every trouble—including one to keep away the bill collector when the young folks forget to make payments on the radio, the furniture, the car, or the Spring outfit purchased months ago from the credit clothier.

Its all in the Bible and the Bible is his workshop—'cause folks don't know how to pray.

He's mighty old, is Uncle George King, and he'll tell you that he was born on two-hundred acres of Hell, but the whitefolks called it Samuel Roll's plantation (six miles N.E. of Lexington, South Carolina).

Kinder small for a plantation, Uncle George explains, but plenty room for that devil overseer to lay on the lash, and plenty room for the old she-devil Mistress to whip his mammy til' she was just a piece of living raw meat!

The old Master talked hard words, but the Mistress whipped. Lot's of difference, and Uncle George ought to know, 'cause he's felt the lash layed on pretty heavy when he was no older than kindergarten children of today.

The Mistress owned the slaves and they couldn't be sold without her say-so. That's the reason George was never sold, but the Master once tried to sell him 'cause the beatings was breaking him down. Old Mistress said "No", and used it for an excuse to whip his Mammy. Uncle George remembers that, too.

They crossed her wrists and tied them with a stout cord. They made her bend over so that her arms was sticking back between her legs and fastened the arms with a stick so's she couldn't straighten up.

He saw the Mistress pull his Mammy's clothes over her head so's the lash would reach the skin. He saw the overseer lay on the whip with hide busting blows that left her laying, all a shiver, on the ground, like a wounded animal dying from the chase.

He saw the Mistress walk away, laughing, while his Mammy screamed and groaned—the old Master standing there looking sad and wretched, like he could feel the blows on Mammy's bared back and legs as much as she.

The Mistress was a great believer in the power of punishment, and Uncle George remembers the old log cabin jail built before the War, right on the plantation, where runaway slaves were stowed away 'till they would promise to behave themselves.

The old jail was full up during most of the War. Three runaway slaves were still chained to its floor when the Master gave word the Negroes were free.

They were Prince, Sanovey (his wife), and Henry, who were caught and whipped by the patrollers, and then brought back to the plantation for another beating before being locked in jail.

The Mistress ordered them chained, and the overseer would come every morning with the same question: "Will you niggers promise not to runaway no more?"

But they wouldn't promise. One at a time the overseer would loosen the chains, and lead them from the jail to cut them with powerful blows from the lash, then drag them back to be chained until the next day when more lickings were given 'cause they wouldn't promise.

The jail was emptied on the day Master Roll called together all the men, women and children to tell them they wasn't slaves no more. Uncle George tells it this way:

"The Master he says we are all free, but it don't mean we is white. And it don't mean we is equal. Just equal for to work and earn our own living and not depend on him for no more meats and clother." [TR: clothes?]

Food was scarce before the War; it was worse after the shooting and killing was over, and Uncle George says: "There wasn't no corn bread, no bacon—just trash eating trash, like when General Sherman marched down through the country taking everything the soldiers could lug away, and burning all along the way.

"Wasn't nothing to eat after he march by. Darkies search 'round the barns, maybe find some grains of corn in the manure, and they'd parch the grains—nothing else to eat, except sometimes at night Mammy would skit out and steal scraps from the Master's house for the children.

"She had lots of hungry mouths, too. They was seven of us then, six boys and a girl, Eliza. The boys was Wesley, Simeon, Moses, Peter, William and me, George. This pappy's name was Griffin.

"But they was other pappys (Mammy told him) when Eva was born long before any of us, and Laura come next, but from a white daddy. Mammy lost them when she was sold around on the markets.

"The Klan they done lots of riding round the country. One night the come down to the old slave quarters where the cabins is all squared round each other, and called everybody outdoors. They's looking for two women.

"They picks 'em out of the crowd right quick and say they been with white men. Says their children is by white men, and they're going to get whipped so's they'll remember to stay with their own kind. The women kick and scream, but the mens grab them and roll them over a barrel and let fly with the whip."

It was a long time after the Civil War that Uncle George got his first schooling or attended regular church meetings. Like he says:

"Getting up at four o'clock in the morning, hoeing in the fields all day, doing chores when they come in from the fields, and then piddling with the weaver 'til nine or ten every night—it just didn't leave no time for reading and such, even if we was allowed to."

And religion, that came later too, for during the old plantation days Uncle George's white folks didn't think a Negro needed religion—there wasn't a Heaven for Negroes anyhow.

Finally, though, the Master gave them right to hold meetings on the plantation, and old Peter Coon was the preacher. The overseer was there with guards to keep the Negroes from getting too much riled up when old Peter started talking about Paul or some of the things in the Old Testament. That's all he would talk about; nothing 'bout Jesus, just Paul and the Old Testament.

His Mammy went to every meeting. Like he says: "She knew them good things was good for her children and she told us about the Bible."

Like his old Mammy, Uncle George is a firm believer in the power of the word. "Prayers are saving!" Uncle George says, "But they's lots of folks' don't know how to pray."

That's why he has prayers for sale—and he knows they are never failing, "If you tack 'em up on the wall and say 'em over and over every day they's sure to be answered."

Oklahoma Writers' Project
Ex-Slaves
[Date stamp: AUG 19 1937]

MARTHA KING
Age 85 yrs.
McAlester, Oklahoma

"They hung Jeff Davis to a sour apple tree!

They hung Jeff Davis to a sour apple tree!

They hung Jeff Davis to a sour apple tree!

While we go marching on!"

Dat was de song de Yankees sang when they marched by our house. They didn't harm us in any way. I guess de War was over then 'cause a few days after dat old Master say, "Matt", and I say, "Suh?" He say, "Come here. You go tell Henry I say come out here and to bring the rest of the niggers with him." I went to the north door and I say, "Henry, Master Willis say ever one of you come out here." We all went outside and line up in front of old Master. He say, "Henry". Henry say, "Yes sah". Old Master say, "Every one of you is free—as free as I am. You all can leave or stay 'round here if you want to."

We all stayed on for a long time 'cause we didn't have no other home and didn't know how to take keer of ourselves. We was kind of scared I reckon. Finally I heard my mother was in Walker County, Alabama, and I left and went to live with her.

My mother was Harriet Davis and she was born in Virginia. I don't know who my father was. My grandmother was captured in Africa when she was a little girl. A big boat was down at the edge of a bay an' the people was all excited about it an' some of the bravest went up purty close to look at it. The men on the boat told them to come on board and they could have the pretty red handkerchiefs, red and blue beads and big rings. A lot of them went on board and the ship sailed away with them. My grandmother never saw any of her folks again.

When I was about five years old they brought my grandmother, my mother and my two aunts and two uncles to Tuskaloosa from Fayettesville, Alabama. We crossed a big river on a ferry boat. They put us on the "block" and sold us. I can remember it well. A white man "cried" me off just like I was a animal or varmint or something. He said, "Here's a little nigger, who will give me a bid on her. She will make a good house gal someday." Old man Davis give him $300.00 for me. I don't know whether I was afraid or not; I don't think I cared just so I had something to eat. I was allus hungry. Miss Davis' grandmother and one of my aunts and uncles. Old man Davis bought the rest of us. Uncle Henry looked after me when he could. I could see my mother once in awhile but not often.

I had a purty easy time. I didn't have to work very hard 'till I was about ten years old. I started working in the field and I had to work in the weaving room too. We made all our own clothes. I spun and wove cotton and wool. Old Master bought our shoes. We made fancy cloth. We could stripe the cloth or check it or leave it plain. We also wove coverlids and jeans to make mens suits out of. I could still do that if I had to.

We all went to church with the white folks. We didn't have no colored preachers. The niggers would get happy and shout all over the place. Sometimes they'd fall out doors.

The Big House was a double log, two story house, not very fine but awful comfortable. They was four big fireplace rooms downstairs and two upstairs. Then they was two sort of shed rooms. There was a big piazza across the front. The kitchen was a way off from the house, seems like it was 200 feet at least. Our quarters were close by at the back. He didn't have many slaves and they was nearly all my kinfolks. There was Aunt Emmy and Phillis, Uncles Henry, Mitchell, Louis and Andy, and the others were Uncle Logan and Uncle Nathan. They was old Mistress' slaves when she done married.

Old Master and old Mistress had three boys, Eli, Billy and Dock. They had to go to war and old Mistress sho' did cry. She say they might get killed and she might not see 'em any more. I wonder why all dem white folks didn't think of that when they sold mothers away from they chillun. I had to be sold away from my mother. Two of her boys was badly wounded but they all come back.

Abe Lincoln done everything he could for the niggers. We lost our best friend when he got killed.

Oklahoma Writers' Project
Ex-Slaves

GEORGE KYE
Age 110 yrs.
Fort Gibson, Okla.

I was born in Arkansas under Mr. Abraham Stover, on a big farm about twenty miles north of Van Buren. I was plumb grown when the Civil War come along, but I can remember back when the Cherokee Indians was in all that part of the country.

Joe Kye was my pappy's name what he was born under back in Garrison County, Virginia, and I took that name when I was freed, but I don't know whether he took it or not because he was sold off by old Master Stover when I was a child. I never have seen him since. I think he wouldn't mind good, leastways that what my mammy say.

My mammy was named Jennie and I don't think I had any brothers or sisters, but they was a whole lot of children at the quarters that I played and lived with. I didn't live with mammy because she worked all the time, and us children all stayed in one house.

It was a little one room log cabin, chinked and daubed, and you couldn't stir us with a stick. When we went to eat we had a big pan and all ate out of it. One what ate the fastest got the most.

Us children wore homespun shirts and britches and little slips, and nobody but the big boys wore any britches. I wore just a shirt until I was about 12 years old, but it had a long tall down to my calves. Four or five of us boys slept in one bed, and it was made of hewed logs with rope laced acrost it and a shuck mattress. We had stew made out of pork and potatoes, and sometimes greens and pot liquor, and we had ash cake mostly, but biscuits about once a month.

In the winter time I had brass toed shoes made on the place, and a cloth cap with ear flaps.

The work I done was hoeing and plowing, and I rid a horse a lot for old Master because I was a good rider. He would send me to run chores for him, like going to the mill. He never beat his negroes but he talked mighty cross and glared at us until he would nearly scare us to death sometimes.

He told us the rules and we lived by them and didn't make trouble, but they was a neighbor man that had some mean negroes and he nearly beat them to death. We could hear them hollering in the field sometimes. They would sleep in the cotton rows, and run off, and then they would catch the cat-o-nine tails sure nuff. He would chain them up, too, and keep them tied out to trees, and when they went to the field they would be chained together in bunches sometimes after they had been cutting up.

We didn't have no place to go to church, but old Master didn't care if we had singing and praying, and we would tie our shoes on our backs and go down the road close to the white church and all set down and put our shoes on and go up close and listen to the service.

Old Master was baptized almost every Sunday and cussed us all out on Monday. I didn't join the church until after freedom, and I always was a scoundrel for dancing. My favorite preacher was old Pete Conway. He was the only ordained colored preacher we had after freedom, and he married me.

Old Master wouldn't let us take herb medicine, and he got all our medicine in Van Buren when we was sick. But I wore a buckeye on my neck just the same.

When the War come along I was a grown man, and I went off to serve because old Master was too old to go, but he had to send somebody anyways. I served as George Stover, but every time the sergeant would call out "Abe Stover", I would answer "Here".

They had me driving a mule team wagon that Old Master furnished, and I went with the Sesesh soldiers from Van Buren to Texarkana and back a dozen times or more. I was in the War two years, right up to the day of freedom. We had a battle close to Texarkana and another big one near Van Buren, but I never left Arkansas and never got a scratch.

One time in the Texarkana battle I was behind some pine trees and the bullets cut the limbs down all over me. I dug a big hole with my bare hands before I hardly knowed how I done it.

One time two white soldiers named Levy and Briggs come to the wagon train and said they was hunting slaves for some purpose. Some of us black boys got scared because we heard they was going to Squire Mack and get a reward for catching runaways, so me and two more lit out of there.

They took out after us and we got to a big mound in the woods and hid. Somebody shot at me and I rolled into some bushes. He rid up and got down to look for me but I was on t'other side of his horse and he never did see me. When they was gone we went back to the wagons just as the regiment was pulling out and the officer didn't say nothing.

They was eleven negro boys served in my regiment for their masters. The first year was mighty hard because we couldn't get enough to eat. Some ate poke greens without no grease and took down and died.

How I knowed I was free, we was bad licked, I reckon. Anyways, we quit fighting and a Federal soldier come up to my wagon and say: "Whose mules?" "Abe Stover's mules," I says, and he tells me then, "Let me tell you, black boy, you are as free now as old Abe Stover his own self!" When he said that I jumped on top of one of them mules' back before I knowed anything!

I married Sarah Richardson, February 10, 1870, and had only eleven children. One son is a deacon and one grandson is a preacher. I am a good Baptist. Before I was married I said to the gal's old man, "I'll go to the mourners bench if you'll let me have Sal," and sure nuff I joined up just a month after I got her. I am head of the Sunday School and deacon in the St. Paul Baptist church in Muskogee now.

I lived about five miles from Van Buren until about twelve years ago when they found oil and then they run all the negroes out and leased up the land. They never did treat the negroes good around there anyways.

I never had a hard time as a slave, but I'm glad we was set free. Sometimes we can't figger out the best thing to do, but anyways we can lead our own life now, and I'm glad the young ones can learn and get somewhere these days.

Oklahoma Writers' Project
Ex-Slaves
[Date stamp: NOV 5 1937]

BEN LAWSON
Age 84 yrs.
Oklahoma City, Okla.

I was born in Danville, Illinois. De best I can get at my age I is 84 years old. My father dey tell me was name Dennis Lawson and died before I was born. My mother's name was Ann Lawson, who I saw once. I was given by her to my Mistress, Mrs. Jane Brazier, when a kid and she was too. My mother raised me, she and her son to manhood. I got no brothers or sisters to my knowledge. I was de only slave dey had and dey raised me to be humble and fear dem as a slave and servant. As I was de only slave I slept in de same room wid my Mistress and her son who was grown, her husband and father being dead.

I worked on the farm doing general farm work, hoeing, plowing, harvesting the crop of wheat, corn, barley, oats, rice, peas, etc. To make and harvest the crops dey would hire poor white help and as dey was grown and I was a lad, dey kept me in a strain in order to keep up wid dem for if I didn't it was just too bad for my back. So's dere would be work for me to do during the bad days of winter dey built a pen under a shed and dey would lay a cloth on de ground covering the ground in the pen and wid small mesh wire on top of de pen on which de wheat was laid and wid a wooden maul I would pounder out wheat all day long, even though dey could have thrashed it as dey did de biggest part of it.

At meal time dey would give me what was left of de scraps off dey table in a plate, which I would eat most de time on de back porch in warm weather and in de kitchen in winter.

For summer I wore a lowell shirt and for winter I wore de same old lowell shirt only wid outing slips and a pair of brogan shoes or a pair of old shoes dat was thrown away by my Mistress' son.

Their house was a 3-room log house unpainted, wid only one bed room and a dining room and kitchen.

The plantation had 'bout 160 acres and was worked by my Mistress' son and myself plus poor white hired help, my being de only slave.

I was treated most harshly 'mongst a group of just white people and who seemed to think me de old work ox for all de hardest work. De nearest other Negro slaves were 'bout 15 or 20 miles from me.

When I was grown I ran away one night and walked and rode de rods under stage coaches to Paducah, Kentucky. I got me a job and worked as a roustabout on a boat where I learned to gamble wid dice. I fought and gambled all up and down de Mississippi River, and in de course of time I had 'bout $3,000, but I lost it.

I don't know de month or de year I was born in but I can 'member de sinking of de biggest circus show in de Mississippi River at Mobile, Alabama when I was 10 to 14 years old, I ain't sure which.

There wasn't no children for me to play with and it seem like I never was a child but was just always a man. I wasn't never told dat I was free, and I didn't know nothing 'bout de War much dat brought my freedom. Dey kept all of dat away from me and I couldn't read or write so I didn't know.

I've been married only once. My wife is 54 years old, and her name is Hattie Lawson. We have no children. Since we married after freedom there wasn't nothing unusual at our wedding.

Oklahoma Writers' Project
Ex-Slaves
[Date stamp: AUG 16 1937]

MARY LINDSAY
Age 91 yrs.
Tulsa, Oklahoma.

My slavery days wasn't like most people tell you about, 'cause I was give to my young Mistress and sent away to Texas when I was jest a little girl, and I didn't live on a big plantation a very long tine.

I got an old family Bible what say I was born on September 20, in 1846, but I don't know who put de writing in it unless it was my mammy's mistress. My mammy had de book when she die.

My mammy come out to the Indian country from Mississippi two years before I was born. She was the slave of a Chickasaw part-breed name Sobe Love. He was the kinsfolks of Mr. Benjamin Love, and Mr. Henry Love what bring two big bunches of the Chickasaws out from Mississippi to the Choctaw country when the Chickasaws sign up de treaty to leave Mississippi, and the whole Love family settle 'round on the Red River below Fort Washita. There whar I was born.

My mammy say dey have a terrible hard time again the sickness when they first come out into that country, because it was low and swampy and all full of cane brakes, and everybody have the smallpox and the malaria and fever all the time. Lots of the Chickasaw families nearly died off.

Old Sobe Love marry her off to a slave named William, what belong to a full-blood Chickasaw man name Chick-a-lathe, and I was one of de children.

De children belong to the owner of the mother, and me and my brother Franklin, what we called "Bruner", was born under the name of Love and then old Master Sobe bought my pappy William, and we was all Love slaves then. My mammy had two more girls, name Hatty and Rena.

My mammy name was Mary, and I was named after her. Old Mistress name was Lottie, and they had a daughter name Mary. Old Master Sobe was powerful rich, and he had about a hundred slaves and four or five big pieces of that bottom land broke out for farms. He had niggers on all the places, but didn't have no overseers, jest hisself and he went around and seen that everybody behave and do they work right.

Old Master Sobe was a mighty big man in the tribe, and so was all his kinfolks, and they went to Fort Washita and to Boggy Depot all the time on business, and leave the Negroes to look after old Mistress and the young daughter. She was almost grown along about that time, when I can first remember about things.

125

'Cause my name was Mary, and so was my mammy's and my young Mistress' too. Old Master Sobe called me Mary-Ka-Chubbe to show which Mary he was talking about.

Miss Mary have a black woman name Vici what wait on her all the time, and do the carding and spinning and cooking 'round the house, and Vici belong to Miss Mary. I never did go 'round the Big House, but jest stayed in the quarters with my mammy and pappy and helped in the field a little.

Then one day Miss Mary run off with a man and married him, and old Master Sobe nearly went crazy! The man was name Bill Merrick, and he was a poor blacksmith and didn't have two pair of britches to his name, and old Master Sobe said he jest stole Miss Mary 'cause she was rich, and no other reason. 'Cause he was a white man and she was mostly Chickasaw Indian.

Anyways old Master Sobe wouldn't even speak to Mr. Bill, and wouldn't let him set foot on the place. He jest reared and pitched around, and threatened to shoot him if he set eyes on him, and Mr. Bill took Miss Mary and left out for Texas. He set up a blacksmith shop on the big road between Bonham and Honey Grove, and lived there until he died.

Miss Mary done took Vici along with her, and pretty soon she come back home and stay a while, and old Master Sobe kind of soften up a little bit and give her some money to git started on, and he give her me too.

Dat jest nearly broke my old mammy's and pappy's heart, to have me took away off from them, but they couldn't say nothing and I had to go along with Miss Mary back to Texas. When we git away from the Big House I jest cried and cried until I couldn't hardly see, my eyes was so swole up, but Miss Mary said she gwine to be good to me.

I ask her how come Master Sobe didn't give her some of the grown boys and she say she reckon it because he didn't want to help her husband out none, but jest wanted to help her. If he give her a man her husband have him working in the blacksmith shop, she reckon.

Master Bill Merrick was a hard worker, and he was more sober than most the men in them days, and he never tell me to do nothing. He jest let Miss Mary tell me what to do. They have a log house close to the shop, and a little patch of a field at first, but after awhile he git more land, and then Miss Mary tell me and Vici we got to help in the field too.

That sho' was hard living then! I have to git up at three o'clock sometimes so I have time to water the hosses and slop the hogs and feed the chickens and milk the cows, and then git back to the house and git the breakfast. That was during the times when Miss Mary was having and nursing her two children, and old Vici had to stay with her all the time. Master Bill never did do none of that kind of work, but he had to be in the shop sometimes until way late in the night, and sometimes before daylight, to shoe peoples hosses and oxen and fix wagons.

He never did tell me to do that work, but he never done it his own self and I had to do it if anybody do it.

He was the slowest one white man I ever did see. He jest move 'round like de dead lice falling off'n him all the time, and everytime he go to say anything he talk so slow that when he say one word you could walk from here to way over there before he say de next word. He don't look sick, and he was powerful strong in his arms, but he act like he don't feel good jest the same.

I remember when the War come. Mostly by the people passing 'long the big road, we heard about it. First they was a lot of wagons hauling farm stuff into town to sell, and then purty soon they was soldiers on the wagons, and they was coming out into the country to git the stuff and buying it right at the place they find it.

Then purty soon they commence to be little bunches of mens in soldier clothes riding up and down the road going somewhar. They seem like they was mostly young boys like, and they jest laughing and jollying and going on like they was on a picnic.

Then the soldiers come 'round and got a lot of the white men and took them off to the War even iffen they didn't want to go. Master Bill never did want to go, 'cause he had his wife and two little children, and anyways he was gitting all the work he could do fixing wagons and shoeing hosses, with all the traffic on de road at that time. Master Bill had jest two hosses, for him and his wife to ride and to work to the buggy, and he had one old yoke of oxen and some more cattle. He got some kind of a paper in town and he kept it with him all the time, and when the soldiers would come to git his hosses or his cattle he would jest draw that paper on 'em and they let 'em alone.

By and by the people got so thick on the big road that they was somebody in sight all the time. They jest keep a dust kicked up all day and all night 'cepting when it rain, and they git all bogged down and be strung all up and down the road camping. They kept Master Bill in the shop all the time, fixing the things they bust trying to git the wagons out'n the mud. They was whole families of them, with they children and they slaves along, and they was coming in from every place because the Yankees was gitting in their part of the country, they say.

We all git mighty scared about the Yankees coming but I don't reckon they ever git thar, 'cause I never seen none, and we was right on the big road and we would of seen them. They was a whole lot more soldiers in them brown looking jeans, round-about jackets and cotton britches a-faunching up and down the road on their hosses, though. Them hoss soldiers would come b'iling by, going east, all day and night, and the two-three days later on they would all come tearing by going west! Dey acted like dey didn't know whar dey gwine, but I reckon dey did.

Den Master Bill git sick. I reckon he more wore out and worried than anything else, but he go down with de fever one day and it raining so hard Mistress and me and Vici can't neither one go nowhar to git no help.

We puts peach tree poultices on his head and wash him off all the time, until it quit raining so Mistress can go out on de road, and then a doctor man come from one of the bunches of soldiers and see Master Bill. He say he going be all right and jest keep him quiet, and go on.

Mistress have to tend de children and Vici have to take care of Master Bill and look after the house, and dat leave me all by myself wid all the rest of everything around the place.

I got to feed all the stock and milk the cows and work in the field too. Dat the first time I ever try to plow, and I nearly git killed, too! I got me a young yoke of oxens I broke to pull the wagon, 'cause Vici have to use the old oxens to work the field. I had to take the wagon and go 'bout ten miles west to a patch of woods Master Bill owned to git fire wood, 'cause we lived right on a flat patch of prairie, and I had to chop and haul the wood by myself. I had to git postoak to burn in the kitchen fireplace and willow for Master Bill to make charcoal out of to burn in his blacksmith fire.

Well, I hitch up them young oxen to the plow and they won't follow the row, and so I go git the old oxens. One of them old oxens didn't know me and took in after me, and I couldn't hitch 'em up. And then it begins to rain again.

After the rain was quit I git the bucket and go milk the cows, and it is time to water the hosses too, so I starts to the house with the milk and leading one of the hosses. When I gits to the gate I drops the halter across my arm and hooks the bucket of milk on my arm too, and starts to open the gate. The wind blow the gate wide open, and it slap the hoss on the flank. That was when I nearly git killed!

Out the hoss go through the gate to the yard, and down the big road, and my arm all tangled up in the halter rope and me dragging on the ground!

The first jump knock the wind out of me and I can't git loose, and that hoss drag me down the road on the run until he meet up with a passel of soldiers and they stop him.

The next thing I knowed I was laying on the back kitchen gallery, and some soldiers was pouring water on me with a bucket. My arm was broke, and I was stove up so bad that I have to lay down for a whole week, and Mistress and Vici have to do all the work.

Jest as I gitting able to walk 'round here come some soldiers and say they come to git Master Bill for the War. He still in the bed sick, and so they leave a parole paper for him to stay until he git well, and then he got to go into Bonham and go with the soldiers to blacksmith for them that got the cannons, the man said.

Mistress take on and cry and hold onto the man's coat and beg, but it don't do no good. She say they don't belong in Texas but they belong in the Chickasaw Nation, but he say that don't do no good, 'cause they living in Texas now.

Master Bill jest stew and fret so, one night he fever git way up and he go off into a kind of a sleep and about morning he died.

My broke arm begin to swell up and hurt me, and I git sick with it again, and Mistress git another doctor to come look at it.

He say I got bad blood from it how come I git so sick, and he git out his knife out'n his satchel and bleed me in the other arm. The next day he come back and bleed me again two times, and the next day one more time, and then I git so sick I puke and he quit bleeding me.

While I still sick Mistress pick up and go off to the Territory to her pappy and leave the children thar for Vici and me to look after. After while she come home for a day or two and go off again somewhere else. Then the next time she come home she say they been having big battles in the Territory and her pappy moved all his stuff down on the river, and she home to stay now.

We git along the best we can for a whole winter, but we nearly starve to death, and then the next spring when we getting a little patch planted Mistress go into Bonham and come back and say we all free and the War over.

She say, "You and Vici jest as free as I am, and a lot freer, I reckon, and they say I got to pay you if you work for me, but I ain't got no money to pay you. If you stay on with me and help me I will feed and home you and I can weave you some good dresses if you card and spin the cotton and wool."

Well, I stayed on, 'cause I didn't have no place to go, and I carded and spinned the cotton and wool and she make me just one dress. Vici didn't do nothing but jest wait on the children and Mistress.

Mistress go off again about a week, and when she come back I see she got some money, but she didn't give us any of it.

After while I asked her ain't she got some money for me, and she say no, ain't she giving me a good home? Den I starts to feeling like I aint treated right.

Every evening I git done with the work and go out in the back yard and jest stand and look off to the west towards Bonham, and wish I was at that place or some other place.

Den along come a nigger boy and say he working for a family in Bonham and he git a dollar every week. He say Mistress got some kinfolks in Bonham and some of Master Sobe Love's niggers living close to there.

So one night I jest put that new dress in a bundle and set foot right down the big road a-walking west, and don't say nothing to nobody!

Its ten miles into Bonham, and I gits in town about daylight. I keeps on being afraid, 'cause I con't git it out'n my mind I still belong to Mistress.

Purty soon some niggers tells me a nigger name Bruner Love living down west of Greenville, and I know that my brother Franklin, 'cause we all called him Bruner. I don't remember how all I gits down to Greenville, but I know I walks most the way, and I finds Bruner. Him and his wife working on a farm, and they say my sister Hetty and my sister Rena what was little is living with my mammy way back up on the Red River. My pappy done died in time of the War and I didn't know it.

129

Bruner taken me in a wagon and we went to my mammy, and I lived with her until she died and Hetty was married. Then I married a boy name Henry Lindsay. His people was from Georgia and he live with them way west at Cedar Mills, Texas. That was right close to Gordonville, on the Red River.

We live at Cedar Mills until three my children was born and then we come to the Creek Nation in 1887. My last one was born here.

My oldest is named Georgia on account of her pappy. He was born in Georgia and that was in 1838, so his whitefolks got a book that say. My next child was Henry. We called him William Henry, after my pappy and his pappy. Then come Donie, and after we come here we had Madison, my youngest boy.

I lives with Henry here on this little place we got in Tulsa.

When we first come here we got some land for $15 an acre from the Creek Nation, but our papers said we can only stay as long as it is the Creek Nation. Then in 1901 comes the allotments, and we found out our land belong to a Creek Indian, and we have to pay him to let us stay on it. After while he makes us move off and we lose out all around.

But my daughter Donie git a little lot, and we trade it for this place about thirty year ago, when this town was a little place.

Oklahoma Writers' Project
Ex-Slaves

MRS. MATTIE LOGAN
Age 79 yrs.
Route 5, West Tulsa, Oklahoma.

This is a mighty fitting time to be telling about the slave days, for I'm just finished up celebrating my seventy-nine years of being around and the first part of my life was spent on the old John B. Lewis plantation down in old Mississippi.

Yes, sir! my birthday is just over. September 1 it was and the year was 1858. Borned on the John B. Lewis plantation just ten mile south of Jackson in the Mississippi country. Rankin County it was.

My mother's name was Lucinda, and father's name was Levi Miles. My mother was part Indian, for her mother was a half-blood Cherokee Indian from Virginia.

There was children a-plenty besides me. There was Sally, Julia, Hubbard, Ada, Ira, Anthony, Henry, Amanda, Mary, John, Lucinda, Daniel and me, Mattie. That was my family.

The master's family was a large one, too. Six children was born to the Master and Mistress. Her name, his first wife, was Jennie, the second and last was named, Louise. The children was, Rebecca, Mollie, Jennie, Susie, Silas, and Begerlan. They kind of leaned to females.

My mother belonged to Mistress Jennie who thought a heap of her, and why shouldn't she? Mother nursed all Miss Jennie's children because all of her young ones and my mammy's was born so close together it wasn't no trouble at all for mammy to raise the whole kaboodle of them. I was born about the same time as the baby Jennie. They say I nursed on one breast while that white child, Jennie, pulled away at the other!

That was a pretty good idea for the Mistress, for it didn't keep her tied to the place and she could visit around with her friends most any time she wanted 'thout having to worry if the babies would be fed or not.

Mammy was the house girl and account of that and because her family was so large, the Mistress fixed up a two room cabin right back of the Big House and that's where we lived. The cabin had a fireplace in one of the rooms, just like the rest of the slave cabins which was set in a row away from the Big House. In one room was bunk beds, just plain old two-by-fours with holes bored through the plank so's ropes could be fastened in and across for to hold the corn-shuck mattress.

My brothers and sisters was allowed to play with the Master's children, but not with the children who belonged to the field Negroes. We just played yard games like marbles and tossing a ball. I don't rightly remember much about games, for there wasn't too much fun in them days even if we did get raised with the Master's family. We wasn't allowed to learn any reading or writing. They say if they catched a slave learning them things they'd pull his finger nails off! I never saw that done, though.

Each slave cabin had a stone fireplace in the end, just like ours, and over the flames at daybreak was prepared the morning meal. That was the only meal the field negroes had to cook.

All the other meals was fixed up by an old man and woman who was too old for field trucking. The peas, the beans, the turnips, the potatoes, all seasoned up with fat meats and sometimes a ham bone, was cooked in a big iron kettle and when meal time come they all gathered around the pot for a-plenty of helpings! Corn bread and buttermilk made up the rest of the meal.

Ten or fifteen hogs was butchered every fall and the slaves would get the skins and maybe a ham bone. That was all, except what was mixed in with the stews. Flour was given out every Sunday morning and if a family run out of that before the next week, well, they was just out that's all!

The slaves got small amounts of vegetables from the plantation garden, but they didn't have any gardens of their own. Everybody took what old Master rationed out.

Once in a while we had rabbits and fish, but the best dish of all was the 'possum and sweet potatoes—baked together over red-hot coals in the fireplace. Now, that was something to eat!

The Lewis plantation was about three hundred acres, with usually fifty slaves working on the place. Master Lewis was a trader. He couldn't sell of our family, for we belonged to Mistress Jennie. Negro girls, the fat ones who was kinder pretty, was the most sold. Folks wanted them pretty bad but the Mistress said there wasn't going to be any selling of the girls who was mammy's children.

There was no overseer on our place, just the old Master who did all the bossing. He wasn't too mean, but I've seen him whip Old John. I'd run in the house to get away from the sight, but I could still hear Old John yelling, 'Pray, Master! Oh! Pray, Master!', but I guess that there was more howling than there was hurting at that.

My uncle Ed Miles run away to the North and joined with Yankees during the War. He was lucky to get away, for lots of them who tried it was ketched up by the patrollers. I seen some of them once. They had chains fastened around their legs, fastened short, too, just long enough to take a short step. No more running away with them chains anchoring the feets!

There wasn't any negro churches close by our plantation. All the slaves who wanted religion was allowed to join the Methodist church because that was the Mistress' church.

A doctor was called in when the slaves would get sick. He'd give pills for most all the ailments, but once in a while, like when the children would get the whooping cough, some old negro would try to cure them with home made remedies.

The whooping cough cure was by using a land turtle. Cut off his head and drain the blood into a cup. Then take a lump of sugar and dip in the blood, eat the sugar and the coughing was supposed to stop. If it did or not I don't know.

And that makes me think about another cure they use to tell about. A cure for mean overseers. And I don't mean kill, just scare him, that's all. They say the cure was tried on an overseer who worked for Silas Stien, who was a slave owner living close by the Lewis plantation.

It seems like this overseer was of the meanest kind, always whipping the slaves for no reason at all, and the slaves tried to figure out a way to even up with him by chasing him off the place.

One of the slaves told how to cure him. Get a King snake and put the snake in the overseer's cabin. Slip the snake in about, no, not about, but just exactly nine o'clock at night. Seems like the time was important, why so, I don't remember now.

That's what the slaves did. Put in the snake and out went the overseer. Never no more did he whip the slaves on that plantation because he wasn't working there no more! When he went, when he went, or how he went nobody knows, but they all say he went. That's what counted—he was gone!

The Yankees didn't come around our plantation during the war. All we heard was, 'They'll kill all the slaves,' and such hearing was a-plenty!

After the war some man come to the plantation and told the field negroes they was free. But he didn't know about the cabin we lived in and didn't tell my folks nothing about it. They learned about the freedom from the old Master.

That was some days after the man left the place. The Master called my mother and father into the Big House and told them they was free. Free like him. But he didn't want my folks to leave and they stayed, stayed there three year after they was free to go anywhere they wanted.

The master paid them $200 a month to work for him and that wasn't so much if you stop to figure there was two grown folks and thirteen children who could do plenty of work around the place.

But that money paid for an 80-acre farm my folks bought not far from the old plantation and they moved onto it three year after the freedom come.

I think Lincoln was a mighty good man, and I think Roosevelt is trying to carry some of the good ideas Lincoln had. Lincoln would have done a heap more if he had lived.

The young negroes who are living now are selfish and shiftless. They're not worth two cents and don't have the respect for other folks to get along right. That's what I think.

I been married three times, but no children did I have. The first man was Frank Morris, the next was Jim White, and the last was John Logan. All gone. Dead.

From Mississippi I come to Idabel, Oklahoma, in 1909, two year after statehood. I moved to Muskogee in 1910, staying there while the times was good and coming to Tulsa some years ago.

I'm pretty old and can't work hard anymore, but I manage to get along. I'm glad to be free and I don't believe I could stand them slavery days now at all.

I'm my own boss, get up when I want, go to bed the same way. Nobody to say this or that about what I do.

Yes, I'm glad to be free!

Oklahoma Writers' Project
Ex-Slaves
[Date stamp: AUG 16 1937]

KIZIAH LOVE
Age 93
Colbert, Okla.

Lawd help us, I sho' remembers all about slavery times for I was a grown woman, married and had one baby when de War done broke out. That was a sorry time for some poor black folks but I guess Master Frank Colbert's niggers was about as well off as the best of 'em. I can recollect things that happened way back better than I can things that happen now. Funny ain't it?

Frank Colbert, a full blood Choctaw Indian, was my owner. He owned my mother but I don't remember much about my father. He died when I was a little youngun. My Mistress' name was Julie Colbert. She and Master Frank was de best folks that ever lived. All the niggers loved Master Frank and knowed jest what he wanted done and they tried their best to do it, too.

I married Isom Love, a slave of Sam Love, another full-blood Indian that lived on a jining farm. We lived on Master Frank's farm and Isom went back and forth to work fer his master and I worked ever day fer mine. I don't 'spect we could of done that way iffen we hadn't of had Indian masters. They let us do a lot like we pleased jest so we got our work done and didn't run off.

Old Master Frank never worked us hard and we had plenty of good food to eat. He never did like to put us under white overseers and never tried it but once. A white man come through here and stopped overnight. He looked 'round the farm and told Master Frank that he wasn't gitting half what he ought to out of his rich land. He said he could take his bunch of hands and double his amount of corn and cotton.

Master Frank told him that he never used white overseers, that he had one nigger that bossed around some when he didn't do it hisself. He also told the white man that he had one nigger named Bill that was kind of bad, that he was a good worker but he didn't like to be bothered as he liked to do his own work in his own way. The white boss told him he wouldn't have any trouble and that he could handle him all right.

Old Master hired him and things went very well for a few days. He hadn't said anything to Bill and they had got along fine. I guess the new boss got to thinking it was time for him to take Bill in hand so one morning he told him to hitch up another team before he caught his own team to go to work.

Uncle Bill told him that he didn't have time, that he had a lot of plowing to git done that morning and besides it was customary for every man to catch his own team. Of course this made the overseer mad and he grabbed a stick and started cussing and run at Uncle Bill. Old Bill grabbed a single-tree and went meeting him. Dat white man all on a sudden turned 'round and run fer dear life and I tell you, he fairly bust old Red River wide open gitting away from there and nobody never did see hide nor hair of him 'round to this day.

Master Colbert run a stage stand and a ferry on Red River and he didn't have much time to look after his farm and his niggers. He had lots of land and lots of slaves. His house was a big log house, three rooms on one side and three on the other, and there was a big open hall between them. There was a big gallery clean across the front of the house. Behind the house was the kitchen and the smokehouse. The smokehouse was always filled with plenty of good meat and lard. They would kill the polecat and dress it and take a sharp stick and run it up their back jest under the flesh. They would also run one up each leg and then turn him on his back and put him on top of the house and let him freeze all night. The next morning they'd pull the sticks out and all the scent would be on them sticks and the cat wouldn't smell at all. They'd cook it like they did possum, bake it with taters or make dumplings.

We had plenty of salt. We got that from Grand Saline. Our coffee was made from parched meal or wheat bran. We made it from dried sweet potatoes that had been parched, too.

One of our choicest dishes was "Tom Pashofa", an Indian dish. We'd take corn and beat it in a mortar with a pestle. They took out the husks with a riddle and a fanner. The riddle was a kind of a sifter. When it was beat fine enough to go through the riddle we'd put it in a pot and cook it with fresh pork or beef. We cooked our bread in a Dutch oven or in the ashes.

When we got sick we would take butterfly root and life-everlasting and boil it and made a syrup and take it for colds. Balmony and queen's delight boiled and mixed would make good blood medicine.

The slaves lived in log cabins scattered back of the house. He wasn't afraid they'd run off. They didn't know as much as the slaves in the states, I reckon. But Master Frank had a half brother that was as mean as he was good. I believe he was the meanest man the sun ever shined on. His name was Buck Colbert and he claimed he was a patroller. He was sho' bad to whup niggers. He'd stop a nigger and ask him if he had a pass and even if they did he'd read it and tell them they had stayed over time and he'd beat 'em most to death. He'd say they didn't have any business off the farm and to git back there and stay there.

One time he got mad at his baby's nurse because she couldn't git the baby to stop crying and he hit her on the head with some fire-tongs and she died. His wife got sick and she sent for me to come and take care of her baby. I sho' didn't want to go and I begged so hard for them not to make me that they sent an older woman who had a baby of her own so she could nurse the baby if necessary.

In the night the baby woke up and got to crying and Master Buck called the woman and told her to git him quiet. She was sleepy and was sort of slow and this made Buck mad and he made her strip her clothes off to her waist and he began to whip her. His wife tried to git him to quit and he told her he'd beat her iffen she didn't shut up. Sick as as she was she slipped off and went to Master Frank's and woke him up and got him to go and make Buck quit whipping her. He had beat her so that she was cut up so bad she couldn't nurse her own baby any more.

Master Buck kept on being bad till one day he got mad at one of his own brothers and killed him. This made another one of his brothers mad and he went to his house and killed him. Everybody was glad that Buck was dead.

We had lots of visitors. They'd stop at the stage inn that we kept. One morning I was cleaning the rooms and I found a piece of money in the bed where two men had slept. I thought it was a dime and I showed it to my mammy and she told me it was a five dollar piece. I sho' was happy fer I had been wanting some hoops fer my skirts like Misstress had so Mammy said she would keep my money 'til I could send fer the hoops. My brother got my money from my mammy and I didn't git my hoops fer a long time. Miss Julie give me some later.

When me and my husband got married we built us a log cabin about half-way from Master Frank's house and Master Sam Love's house. I would go to work at Master Frank's and Isom would go to work at Mister Sam's. One day I was at home with jest my baby and a runner come by and said the Yankee soldiers was coming. I looked 'round and I knowed they would git my chickens. I had 'em in a pen right close to the house to keep the varmints from gitting 'em so I decided to take up the boards in the floor and put 'em in there as the wall logs come to the ground and they couldn't git out. By the time I got my chickens under the floor and the house locked tight the soldiers had got so close I could hear their bugles blowing so I jest fairly flew over to old Master's house. Them Yankees clumb down the chimbley and got every one of my chickens and they killed about fifteen of Master Frank's hogs. He went down to their camp and told the captain about it and he paid him for his hogs and sent me some money for my chickens.

We went to church all the time. We had both white and colored preachers. Master Frank wasn't a Christian but he would help build brush-arbors fer us to have church under and we sho' would have big meetings I'll tell you.

One day Master Frank was going through the woods close to where niggers was having church. All on a sudden he started running and beating hisself and hollering and the niggers all went to shouting and saying "Thank the Lawd, Master Frank has done come through!" Master Frank after a minute say, "Yes, through the worst of 'em." He had run into a yellow jacket's nest.

One night my old man's master sent him to Sherman, Texas. He aimed to come back that night so I stayed at home with jest my baby. It went to sleep so I set down on the steps to wait and ever minute I thought I could hear Isom coming through the woods. All a sudden I heard a scream that fairly made my hair stand up. My dog that was laying out in the yard give a low growl and come and set down right by me. He kept growling real low.

Directly, right close to the house I heard that scream again. It sounded like a woman in mortal misery. I run into the house and made the dog stay outside. I locked the door and then thought what must I do. Supposing Isom did come home now and should meet that awful thing? I heard it again. It wasn't more'n a hundred yards from the house. The dog scratched on the door but I dassent open it to let him in. I knowed by this time that it was a panther screaming. I turned my table over and put it against the opening of the fireplace. I didn't aim fer that thing to come down the chimbley and git us.

Purty soon I heard it again a little mite further away—it was going on by. I heard a gun fire. Thank God, I said, somebody else heard it and was shooting at it. I set there on the side of my bed fer the rest of the night with my baby in my arms and praying that Isom wouldn't come home. He didn't come till about nine o'clock the next morning and I was that glad to see him that I jest cried and cried.

I ain't never seen many sperits but I've seen a few. One day I was laying on my bed her myself. My son Ed was cutting wood. I'd been awful sick and I was powerful weak. I I somebody walking real light like they was barefooted. I said, "Who's dat?"

He catch hold of my hand and he has the littlest hand I ever seen, and he say, "You bee.. .... sick and I want you to come and go with me to Sherman to see a doctor."

I say, "I ain't got nobody at Sherman what knows me."

He say, "You'd better come and go with me anyway."

I jest lay there fer a minute and didn't say nothing and purty soon he say, "Have you got any water?"

I told him the water was on the porch and he got up and went outside and I set in to calling Ed. He come hurrying and I asked him why he didn't lock the door when he went out and I told him to go see if he could see the little man and find out what he wanted. He went out and looked everywhere but he couldn't find him nor he couldn't even find his tracks.

I always keep a butcher-knife near me but it was between the mattress and the feather bed and I couldn't get to it. I don't guess it would have done any good though fer I guess it was jest a sperit.

The funniest thing that ever happened to me was when I was a real young gal. Master and Miss Julie was going to see one of his sisters that was sick. I went along to take care of the baby fer Miss Julie. The baby was about a year old. I had a bag of clothes and the baby to carry. I was riding a pacing mule and it was plumb gentle. I was riding along behind Master Frank and Miss Julie and I went to sleep. I lost the bag of clothes and never missed it. Purty soon I let the baby slip out of my lap and I don't know how far I went before I nearly fell off myself and jest think how I felt when I missed that baby! I turned around and went back and found the baby setting in the trail sort of crying. He wasn't hurt a mite as he fell in the grass. I got off the mule and picked him up and had to look fer a log so I could get back on again.

Jest as I got back on Master Frank rode up. He had missed me and come back to see what was wrong. I told him that I had lost the bag of clothes but I didn't say anything about losing the baby. We never did find the clothes and I sho' kept awake the rest of the way. I wasn't going to risk losing that precious baby again! I guess the reason he didn't cry much was because he was a Indian baby. He was sho' a sweet baby though.

Jest before the War people would come through the Territory stealing niggers and selling 'em in the states. Us women dassent git fur from the house. We wouldn't even go to the spring if we happened to see a strange wagon or horsebacker. One of Master Sam Love's women was stole and sold down in Texas. After freedom she made her way back to her fambly. Master Frank sent one of my brothers to Sherman on an errand. After several days the mule come back but we never did see my brother again. We didn't know whether he run off or was stole and sold.

I was glad to be free. What did I do and say? Well, I jest clapped my hands together and said, "Thank God Almighty, I'se free at last!"

I live on the forty acres that the government give me. I have been blind for nine years and don't git off my bed much. I live here with my son, Ed. Isom has been dead for over forty years. I had fifteen children, but only ten of them are living.

Oklahoma Writers' Project
Ex-Slaves

DANIEL WILLIAM LUCAS
Age 94 yrs.
Red Bird, Okla.

I remember them slave days well as it was yesterday, and when I get to remembering the very first thing comes back to me is the little log cabin where at I lived when I was a slave boy back 'fore the War.

Just like yesterday—I see that little old cabin standing on a bit of hill about a quarter-mile from the Master's brick mansion, and I see into the cabin and there's the old home-made bed with rope cords a-holding up the corn shuck bedding where on I use to sleep after putting in the day at hoeing cotton or following a slow time mule team down the corn rows 'till it got so dark the old overseer just naturally had to call it a day.

And then I see the old baker swinging in the fireplace. That cooked up the corn pone to go with the fat side meats the Master Doctor (didn't I tell you the Master was a doctor?) give us for the meals of the week day. But on a Sunday morning we always had flour bread, excepting after the War is over and then we is lucky do we get anything.

Just like yesterday—I hear the old overseer making round of the cabins every day at four, and I means in the morning, too, when the night sleep is the best, and the folkses tumbling out of the door getting ready for the fields.

All the mens dressed about the same. Just like me. Wearing the grey jeans with the blue shirt stuck in loose around the belt, brogan shoes that feels like brakes on the feet about the hot time of day when the old sun's a-grinning down like he was saying: "work, niggers, work!" And the overseer is saying the same thing, only we pays more attention to him 'cause of the whip he shakes around when the going gets kinder slow down the row.

Now I sees them getting ready for the slave auction. Many of 'em there was. The Master Doctor done owned about two hundred slaves and sometimes he sell some for to beat the bad crops.

There they'd stand on the wooden blocks, their faces greased and shiny, their arms and bodies pretty well greased too; seemed like they looked better and stronger that way, maybe some other reason, I dunno. And when the auction was over lots of the slaves would try to figger out when would the next one be and worry some afraid they'd be standing up there waiting for the buyers to punch and slap to see is they sound of limb and able to do the days work without loafing down the rows.

There's the old white preacher who tried to tell the slaves about the Lord. He had a mighty hard job sometimes, 'cause of the teaching was hard to understand. And then—then he'd just seem to be riled with anger and lay down the law of the Lord between cuss-words that all the slaves could understand. So finally I guess everybody was religionized even it was cussed into 'em right from the pulpit!

That old preacher always makes me think of haunts, 'cause every evening when I drive up the cows for milking, there's a old, old log cabin right on the way that I pass every night—and it's so haunted won't nobody pass it after the darkness covers in the daylight.

I didn't always get by 'fore then, and the sounds I hear! Like they was people inside jumping and knocking on the floor, maybe they was dancing, I dunno. But they was a light in the big room. Wasn't the moon a-shining through the windows either, 'cause sometimes I would stop at the gate and say HELLO, then out go the light and the noises would stop quick, like them haunts was a-scairt as me—and then, then I run like the old preacher's Devil is after me with all his forks.

Then along come the War. The slaves would go around from cabin to cabin telling each other about how mean and cruel was the master or the overseer, and maybe some of them would make for the North. They was the unlucky ones, 'cause lots of times they was caught.

And when the patrollers get 'em caught, they was due for a heavy licking that would last for a long time.

The slaves didn't know how to travel. The way would be marked when they'd start North, but somehow they'd get lost, 'cause they didn't know one direction from another, they was so scairt.

Just like yesterday—I remember the close of the War. Nothing exciting about it down on the plantation. Just the old overseer come around and say:

"The Yankees has whipped the Rebels and the War is over. But the Old Master don't want you to leave. He just wants you to stay right on here where at is your home. That's what the Master say is best for you to do."

That's what I do, but some of them other slaves is kinder filled up with the idea of freedom and wants to find out is it good or bad, so they leave and scatter round.

But I stays, and the Master Doctor he pays me ten dollars every month, gives me board and my sleeping place just like always, and when I gets sick there he is with the herb medicine for my ailment and I is well again.

It's long after the War before I leaves the old place. And that's when I gets married in 1885. That was my first licensed wife and we is married in Holly Springs. Her name was Josephine and we has maybe eight-ten children, I dunno.

And I is thankful they ain't none of my children born slaves and have to remember all them terrible days when we was ruled by the whip—like I remember it, just like it was yesterday.

Oklahoma Writers' Project
Ex-Slaves
[Date stamp: AUG 19 1937]

BERT LUSTER
Age 85 yrs.
Oklahoma City, Oklahoma

I'll be jest frank, I'm not for sho' when I was born, but it was in 1853. Don't know the month, but I was sho' born in 1853 in Watson County, Tennessee. You see my father was owned by Master Luster and my mother was owned by Masters Joe and Bill Asterns (father and son). I can remember when Master Astern moved from Watson County, Tennessee he brought me and my mother with him to Barnum County Seat, Texas. Master Astern owned about twelve slaves, and dey was all Astern 'cept Miriah Elmore's son Jim. He owned 'bout five or six hundred acres of ground, and de slaves raised and shucked all de corn and picked all de cotton. De whites folks lived in a big double log house and we slaves lived in log cabins. Our white folks fed us darkies! We ate nearly ever'thing dey ate. Dey ate turkey, chickens, ducks, geese, fish and we killed beef, pork, rabbits and deer. Yes, and possums too. And whenever we killed beef we tanned the hide and dere was a white man who made shoes for de white folks and us darkies. I tell you I'm not gonna lie, dem white folks was good to us darkies. We didn't have no mean overseer. Master Astern and his son jest told us niggers what to do and we did it, but 50 miles away dem niggers had a mean overseer, and dey called him "poor white trash", "old whooser", and sometime "old red neck", and he would sho' beat 'em turrible iffen dey didn't do jest like he wanted 'em to.

Seem like I can hear dem "nigger hounds" barking now. You see whenever a darky would get a permit to go off and wouldn't come back dey would put de "nigger hounds" on his trail and run dat nigger down.

De white women wove and spin our clothes. You know dey had looms, spins, and weavers. Us darkies would stay up all night sometime sep'rating cotton from the seed. When dem old darkies got sleepy dey would prop their eyes open wid straws.

Sho', we wore very fine clothes for dem days. You know dey dyed the cloth with poke berries.

We cradled de wheat on pins, caught the grain, carried it to de mill and had it ground. Sho', I ate biscuits and cornbread too. Keep telling you dat we ate.

We got de very best of care when we got sick. Don't you let nobody tell you dem white folks tried to kill out dem darkies 'cause when a darkey took sick dey would send and git de very best doctors round dat country. Dey would give us ice water when we got sick. You see we put up ice in saw dust in winter and when a slave got sick dey give him ice water, sometimes sage tea and chicken gruel. Dey wanted to keep dem darkies fat so dey could git top price for 'em. I never saw a slave sold, but my half brother's white folks let him work and buy hisself.

I was about 14, and I milked the cows, packed water, seeded cotton, churned milk up at de Big House and jest first one chore and den another. My mother cooked up at de Big House.

Dey was a lot of talk 'bout conjure but I didn't believe in it. Course dem darkies could do everything to one another, and have one another scared, but dey couldn't conjure dat overseer and stop him from beating 'em near to death. Course he didn't flog 'em till dey done sumping.

I married my woman, Nannie Wilkerson, 58 years ago. Dat was after slavery, and I love her, honest to God I does. Course in dem days we didn't buy no license, we jest got permits from old Master and jumped over a broom stick and jest got married.

I sho' did hate when de Yanks come 'cause our white folks was good to us, and jest take us right along to church with 'em. We didn't work on Sad'days or Christmas.

We raised gardens, truck patches and such for spending change.

I sho' caught hell after dem Yanks come. Befo' de war, you see de patroller rode all nite but wouldn't bother a darkey iffen he wouldn't run off. Why dem darkeys would run off I jest couldn't see.

Dose Yanks treated old master and mistress so mean. Dey took all his hams, chickens, and drove his cattle out of the pasture, but didn't bother us niggers honest. Dey drove old master Aster off'n his own plantation and we all hid in de corn field.

My mother took me to Greenville, Texas, 'cause my step-pappy was one of dem half smart niggers round dere trying to preach and de Ku Klux Klan beat him half to death.

Dere was some white folks who would take us to church wid 'em—dis dis [TR: sic] was aftah the war now—and one night we was all sitting up thar and one old woman with one leg was dah and when dem Klans shot in amongst us niggers and white folks aunt Mandy beat all of us home. Yes suh.

My first two teachers was two white men, and dem Klans shot in de hotel what dey lived in, but dey had school for us niggers jest de same. After dat, dose Klans got so bad Uncle Sam sent soljers down dere to keep peace.

After de soljers come and run de Klans out we worked hard dat fall and made good crops. 'Bout three years later I came to Indian Territory in search of educating my kids.

I landed here 46 years ago on a farm not far from now Oklahoma City. I got to be a prosperous farmer. My bale of cotton amongst 5,000 bales won the blue ribbon at Guthrie, Oklahoma, and dat bale of cotton and being a good democrat won for me a good job as a clerk on the Agriculture Board at the State Capitol. All de white folks liked me and still like me and called me "cotton king."

I have jest three chillun living. Walter is parcel post clerk here at de post office downtown. Delia Jenkins, my daughter is a housewife and Cleo Luckett, my other daughter, a common laborer.

142

Have been a christian 20 years. Jest got sorry for my wicked ways. I am a member of the Church of God. My wife is a member of the Church of Christ. I'm a good democrat and she is a good republican.

My fav'rite songs is: "Dark Was the Nite, and Cold the Ground" and "Couldn't Hear Nobody Pray."

I'm glad slavery is over, but I don't think dem white folks was fighting to free us niggers. God freed us. Of course, Abraham Lincoln was a pretty fine man. Don't know much about Jeff Davis. Never seen him. Yes, and Booker T. Washington. He was one of the Negro leaders. The first Negro to represent the Negroes in Washington. He was a great leader.

During slavery time never heerd of a cullud man committing 'sault on a white woman. The white and cullud all went to church together too. Niggers and white shouted alike.

I remember some of the little games we played now: "Fox in the wall", "Mollie, Mollie Bride", and "Hide and go seek."

Oklahoma Writers' Project
Ex-Slaves
[Date stamp: AUG 19 1937]

STEPHEN McCRAY
Age 88 yrs.
Oklahoma City, Okla.

I was born in Huntsville County, Alabama, right where the Scottsboro boys was in jail, in 1850.

My parents was Wash and Winnie McCray. They was the mother and father of 22 chillun. Jest five lived to be grown and the rest died at baby age. My father's mother and father was named Mandy and Peter McCray, and my mother's mother and father was Ruthie and Charlie McCray. They all had the same Master, Mister McCray, all the way thoo'.

We live in log huts and when I left home grown, I left my folks living in the same log huts. Beds was put together with ropes and called rope beds. No springs was ever heard of by white or cullud as I knows of.

All the work I ever done was pick up chips for my grandma to cook with. I was kept busy doing this all day.

The big boys went out and got rabbits, possums and fish. I would sho' lak to be in old Alabama fishing, 'cause I am a fisherman. There is sho' some pretty water in Alabama and as swift as cars run here. Water so clear and blue you can see the fish way down, and dey wouldn't bite to save your life.

Slaves had their own gardens. All got Friday and Sadday to work in garden during garden time. I liked cornbread best and I'd give a dollar to git some of the bread we had on those good old days and I ain't joking. I went in shirt tail all the time. Never had on no pants 'til I was 15 years old. No shoes, 'cept two or three winters. Never had a hat 'til I was a great big boy.

Marriage was performed by getting permission from Master and go where the woman of your choice had prepared the bed, undress and flat-footed jump a broom-stick together into the bed.

Master had a brick house for hisself and the overseer. They was the only ones on the place. The overseer woke up the slaves all the way from 2 o'clock till 4 o'clock of mornings. He wasn't nothing but white trash. Nothing else in the world but that. They worked till they couldn't see how to work. I jest couldn't jedge the size of that big place, and there was a mess of slaves, not less'n three hundred.

I doesn't have no eggycation, edgecation, or ejecation, and about all I can do is spell. I jest spell till I get the pronouncements.

We had church, but iffen the white folks caught you at it, you was beat most nigh to death. We used a big pot turned down to keep our voices down. When we went to hear white preachers, he would say, "Obey your master and mistress." I am a hard shell-flint Baptist. I was baptised in Pine Bluff, Arkansas. Our baptizing song was mostly "On Jordan's Stormy Banks I Stand" and our funeral song was "Hark From The Tomb."

We had some slaves who would try to run off to the North but the white folks would catch 'em with blood hounds and beat 'em to death. Them patrollers done their work mostly at night. One night I was sleeping on cotton and the patrollers come to our house and ask for water. Happen we had plenty. They drunk a whole lot and got warm and told my father to be a good nigger and they wouldn't bother him at all. They raided till General Grant come thoo'. He sent troops out looking for Klu Klux Klanners and killed 'em jest lak killing black birds. General Grant was one of the men that caused us to set heah free today and able to talk together without being killed.

I didn't and don't believe in no conjure. No sensible person do either. We had a doctor on the place. Ever master had a doctor who waited on his slaves, but we wore asafetida or onion 'round our necks to keep off diseases. A dime was put 'round a teething baby's neck to make it tooth easy, and it sho' helped too. But today all folks done got 'bove that.

The old folks talked very little of freedom and the chillun knew nothing at all of it, and that they heard they was daresome to mention it.

Bushwhacker, nothing but poor white trash, come thoo' and killed all the little nigger chillun they could lay hands on. I was hid under the house with a big rag on my mouf many a time. Them Klu Klux after slavery sho' got enough from them soldiers to last 'em.

144

I was married to Kan Pry in 1884. Two chillun was born. The girl is living and the boy but I don't know. My daughter works out in service.

I wish Lincoln was here now. He done more for the black face than any one in that seat Davis kept slavery up till General Grant met him at the battle. Lincoln sho' snowed him under. General Grant put fire under him jest lak I'm fixing to do my pipe. Booker T. Washington was jest all right.

Every time I think of slavery and if it done the race any good, I think of the story of the coon and dog who met. The coon said to the dog "Why is it you're so fat and I am so poor, and we is both animals?" The dog said: "I lay round Master's house and let him kick me and he gives me a piece of bread right on." Said the coon to the dog: "Better then that I stay poor." Them's my sentiment. I'm lak the coon, I don't believe in 'buse.

I used to be the most wicked man in the world but a voice converted me by saying, "Friend, friend, why is you better to everybody else than you is to your self? You are sending your soul to hell." And from that day I lived like a Christian. People here don't live right and I don't lak to 'tend church. I base my Christian life on: "Believe in me, trust my work and you shall be saved, for I am God and beside me there is no other."

Oklahoma Writers' Project
Ex-Slaves

HANNAH McFARLAND
Age 85 yrs.
Oklahoma City, Okla.

I was born in Georgetown, South Carolina, February 29, 1853. My father was name James Gainey and my mother was name Katie Gainey. There was three chillun born to my folks doing slavery. My father was a free man, but my mother was de slave of the Sampsons, some Jews. My father was de richest Negro in South Carolina doing this time. He bought all three of we chillun for $1,000 apiece, but dem Jews jest wouldn't sell mamma. Dey was mighty sweet to her. She come home ever night and stayed with us. Doing the day a Virginian nigger woman stayed with us and she sho' was mean to we chillun. She used to beat us sumpin' terrible. You know Virginia people is mean to cullud people. My father bought her from some white folks too.

We lived in town and in a good house.

It was a good deal of confusion doing de War. I waited on the Yankees. Dey captured mamma's white people's house. Dey tried to git mamma to tell dem jest whut de white folks done done to her and all she could say was dey was good to her. Shucks, dey wouldn't sell her. She jest told them she had a free husband.

My father was a blockader. He run rafts from one place to another and sho' made a lot of money. He was drowned while doing this while I was a good size child.

Dem patrollers tied you to a whipping post iffen dey caught you out after 10 o'clock. They 'tempted to do my mother that way, but my papa sho' stopped dat. I can't say I lak white people even now, 'cause dey done done so much agin us.

I was free, but I couldn't go to school, 'cause we didn't had none. I been in Oklahoma over 40 years. Have done some traveling and could go some whar else, but I jest stays here 'cause I ain't got no desire to travel.

All we ever wore to keep off diseases was asafetida, nothing else.

I done heard more 'bout conjure in Oklahoma than I ever heerd in South Carolina. All dat stuff is in Louisiana. I didn't heah nothing 'bout the Klu Klux Klan till I come to Oklahoma neither. More devilment in Oklahoma than any place I know. South got more religion too. I jest as soon be back with the Rebels.

Bushwhackers whipped you iffen you stayed out late, and sho' nuff if dey didn't lak you.

I felt sorry for Jeff Davis when the Yankees drilled him through the streets. I saw it all. I said, "Mama, Mama, look, dey got old Jeff Davis." She said, "Be quiet, dey'll lynch you." She didn't know no better! She was a old slave nigger. I showed the Yankees where the white folks hid their silver and money and jewelry, and Mamma sho' whipped me about it too. She was no fool 'bout slavery. Slavery sho' didn't he'p us none to my belief.

I didn't care much 'bout Lincoln. It was nice of him to free us, but 'course he didn't want to.

The overseer was sho' nothing but poor white trash, the kind who didn't lak niggers and dey still don't, old devils. Don't let 'em fool you, dey don't lak a nigger a'tall.

I'm a Methodist. People ought to praise God 'cause he done done so much for dese sinners. Dey was heap more religious in my early days. I jined church in 1863. I jined the Holiness so I could git baptized and the Methodist wouldn't baptize you. After my baptism, I went back to the Methodist Church. You know my pastor, Reverend Miller, is the first Methodist preacher I ever knowed that was baptized, and that baptizes everybody.

I was married in Akin, South Carolina to Andrew Pew. We had 12 chillun. Jest one boy is my only living child today.

Oklahoma Writers' Project
Ex-Slaves

MARSHALL MACK
Age 83 yrs.
Oklahoma City, Okla.

I was born September 10, 1854. I am the second child of five. My mother was named Sylvestus Mack and my father Booker Huddleston. I do not remember my mother's master, 'cause he died before I was born. My Mistress was named Nancy Mack. She was the mother of six children, four boys and two girls. Three of dem boys went to the War and one packed and went off somewhar and nobody heard from him doing of the whole War. But soon as the War was over he come home and he never told whar he had been.

I never saw but one grown person flogged during slavery and dat was my mother. The younger son of my mistress whipped her one morning in de kitchen. His name was Jack. De slaves on Mistress' place was treated so good, all de people round and 'bout called us "Mack's Free Niggers." Dis was 14 miles northwest of Liberty, county seat of Bedford County, Virginia.

One day while de War was going on, my Mistress got a letter from her son Jim wid jest one line. Dat was "Mother: Jack's brains spattered on my gun this morning." That was all he written.

Jack Huddleston owned my father, who was his half-brother, and he was the meanest man I ever seen. He flogged my father with tobacco sticks and my mother after these floggings (which I never seen) had to pick splinters out of his back. My father had to slip off a night to come and visit us. He lived a mile and a half from our house on the south side of the Blue Ridge Mountains, and it sho' is a rocky country. He'd oversleep hisself and git up running. We would stand in our door and hear him running over them rocks til he got home. He was trying to git dere before his master called him.

It was a law among the slave-holders that if you left your master's place, you had to have a pass, for if the patroller caught you without one, he would give you 9 and 30 lashes and carry you to your master, and if he was mean, you got the same again!

On the 3-foot fireplace my mother and father cooked ash cakes and my father having to run to work, had to wash his cakes off in a spring betwixt our house and his. My mother was the cook in the Big House.

All the time we would see "nigger traders" coming through the country. I have seen men and women cuffed to 60-foot chains being took to Lynchburg, Va., to the block to be sold. Now I am talking 'bout what I know, for it would not mean one thing for me to lie. I ain't jest heard dis. My uncle John was a carpenter and always took Mistress' chillun to school in a two-horse surrey. On sech trips, the chillun learned my uncle to read and write. Dey slipped and done this, for it was a law among slave-holders that a slave not be caught wid a book.

One morning when I was on my way to de mill with a sack of corn, I had to go down de main pike. I saw sech a fog 'til I rid close enough to see what was gwine on. I heard someone say "close up." I was told since dat it was Hood's Raid. They took every slave that could carry a gun. It was at dis time, Negroes went into de service. Lee was whipping Grant two battles to one 'til them raids, and den Grant whipped Lee two battles to one, 'cause he had Negroes in the Union Army. Dey took Negroes and all de white people's food. Dey killed chickens and picked dem on horseback. I never will forgit that time long as I live.

Ever day I had to get the mail for three families. I carried it around in a bag and each family took his'n out. I guess I was one of the first Negro mailmen.

We had church on the place and had right good meetings. Everybody went and took part in the service. We had to have passes to go off the place to the meetings.

The children wore just one garment from this time of year (spring) till the frost fell. Mistress' daughters made dese. We sure kept healthy and fat.

I will be 83 years of age September 10, 1937 and am enjoying my second eyesight. I could not see a thing hardly for some few years, but now I can read sometimes without glasses. I keep my lawn in first class shape and work all the time. I think this is 'cause I never was treated bad during slavery.

Oklahoma Writers' Project
Ex-Slaves
[Date stamp: AUG 19 1937]

ALLEN V. MANNING
Age 87
Tulsa, Okla.

I always been somewhar in the South, mostly in Texas when I was a young man, and of course us Negroes never got much of a show in court matters, but I reckon if I had of had the chance to set on a jury I would of made a mighty poor out at it.

No sir, I jest can't set in judgement on nobody, 'cause I learned when I was jest a little boy that good people and bad people—makes no difference which—jest keep on living and doing like they been taught, and I jest can't seem to blame them none for what they do iffen they been taught that way.

I was born in slavery, and I belonged to a Baptist preacher. Until I was fifteen years old I was taught that I was his own chattel-property, and he could do with me like he wanted to, but he had been taught that way too, and we both believed it. I never did hold nothing against him for being hard on Negroes sometimes, and I don't think I ever would of had any trouble even if I had of growed up and died in slavery.

The young Negroes don't know nothing 'bout that today, and lots of them are rising up and amounting to something, and all us Negroes is proud of them. You see, it's because they been taught that they got as good a show to be something as anybody, if they tries hard.

Well, this old Negro knows one thing: they getting somewheres 'cause the young whitefolks is letting them and helping them to do it, 'cause the whitefolks has been taught the same way, and I praise God its getting to be that way, too. But it all go to show, people do like they been taught to do.

Like I say, my master was a preacher and a kind man, but he treated the Negroes jest like they treated him. He been taught that they was jest like his work hosses, and if they act like they his work hosses they git along all right. But if they don't—Oh, oh!

Like the Dixie song say, I was born "on a frosty mornin'" at the plantation in Clarke County, Mississippi, in the fall of 1850 they tell me. The old place looked the same all the time I was a child, clean up to when we pull out and leave the second year of the War.

I can shet my eyes and think about it and it seem to come right up in front of me jest like it looked. From my Pappy's cabin the Big House was off to the west, close to the big road, and most of the fields stretched off to the north. They was a big patch of woods off to the east, and no much open land between us and the Chickasawhay River. Off to the southwest a few miles was the Bucatunna Creek, and the plantation was kind of in the forks between them, a little ways east of Quitman, Mississippi.

Old Master's people been living at that place a mighty long time, and most the houses and barns was old and been repaired time and time again, but it was a mighty pretty place. The Big House was built long, with a lot of rooms all in a row and a long porch, but it wasn't fine like a lot of the houses we seen as we passed by when we left that place to go to Louisiana.

Old Master didn't have any overseer hired, but him and his boys looked after the place and had a Negro we called the driver. We-all shore hated that old black man, but I forget his name now. That driver never was allowed to think up nothing for the slaves to do, but jest was told to make them work hard at what the master and his boys told them to do. Whitefolks had to set them at a job and then old driver would whoopity and whoopity around, and egg them and egg them until they finish up, so they can go at something else. He worked hard hisself, though, and set a mighty hard pattern for the rest to keep up with. Like I say, he been taught he didn't know how to think, so he didn't try.

Old Mistress name was Mary, and they had two daughters, Levia and Betty. Then they had three sons. The oldest was named Bill Junior, and he was plumb grown when I was a boy, but the other two, Jedson and Jim, was jest a little older then me.

Old Master didn't have but two or three single Negroes, but he had several families, and most of them was big ones. My own family was pretty good size, but three of the children was born free. Pappy's name was William and Mammy's was Lucy. My brother Joe was the oldest child and then come Adeline, Harriet, and Texana and Betty before the surrender, and then Henry, Mattie and Louisa after it.

When the War come along old Master jest didn't know what to do. He always been taught not to raise his hand up and kill nobody—no matter how come—and he jest kept holding out against all them that was talking about fighting, and he wouldn't go and fight. He been taught that it was all right to have slaves and treat them like he want to, but he been taught it was sinful to go fight and kill to keep them, and he lived up to what he been taught.

They was some Choctaw people lived 'round there, and they flew up and went right off to the War, and Mr. Trot Hand and Mr. Joe Brown that had plantations on the big road towards Quitman both went off with their grown boys right at the start, but old Master was a preacher and he jest stayed out of it. I remember one day I was sent up to the Big House and I heard old Master and some men out at the gate 'xpounding about the War. Some of the men had on soldier clothes, and they acted like they was mad. Somebody tell me later on that they was getting up a home guard because the yankees done got down in Alabama not far away, but old Master wouldn't go in with them.

Two, three days after that, it seems like, old Master come down to the quarters and say git everything bundled up and in the wagons for a long trip. The Negroes all come in and everybody pitch in to help pack up the wagons. Then old Master look around and he can't find Andy. Andy was one Negro that never did act like he been taught, and old Master's patience about wore out with him anyways.

We all know that Andy done run off again, but we didn't know where to. Leastwise all the Negroes tell old Master that. But old Master soon show us we done the work and he done the thinking! He jest goes ahead and keeps all the Negroes busy fixing up the wagons and bundling up the stuff to travel, and keeps us all in his sight all the time, and says nothing about Andy being gone.

Then that night he sends for a white man name Clements that got some blood hounds, and him and Mr. Clements takes time about staying awake and watching all the cabins to see nobody slips out of them. Everybody was afraid to stick their head out.

Early next morning we has all the wagons ready to drive right off, and old Master call Andy's brother up to him. He say, "You go down to that spring and wait, and when Andy come down to the spring to fill that cedar bucket you stole out'n the smokehouse for him to git water in you tell him to come on in here. Tell him I know he is hiding out way down the branch whar he can come up wading the water clean up to the cornfield and the melon patch, so the hounds won't git his scent, but I'm going to send the hounds down there if he don't come on in right now." Then we all knowed we was for the work and old Master was for the thinking, 'cause pretty soon Andy come on in. He'd been right whar old Master think he is.

About that time Mr. Sears come riding down the big road. He was a deacon in old Master's church, and he see us all packed up to leave and so he light at the big gate and walk up to whar we is. He ask old Master where we all lighting out for, and old Master say for Louisiana. We Negroes don't know where that is. Then old deacon say what old Master going to do with Andy, 'cause there stood Mr. Clements holding his bloodhounds and old Master had his cat-o-nine-tails in his hand.

Old Master say just watch him, and he tell Andy if he can make it to that big black gum tree down at the gate before the hounds git him he can stay right up in that tree and watch us all drive off. Then he tell Andy to git!

Poor Andy jest git hold of the bottom limbs when the blood hounds grab him and pull him down onto the ground. Time old Master and Mr. Clements git down there the hounds done tore off all Andy's clothes and bit him all over bad. He was rolling on the ground and holding his shirt up 'round his throat when Mr. Clements git there and pull the hounds off of him.

Then old Master light in on him with that cat-o-nine-tails, and I don't know how many lashes he give him, but he jest bloody all over and done fainted pretty soon. Old Deacon Sears stand it as long as he can and then he step up and grab old Master's arm and say, "Time to stop, Brother! I'm speaking in the name of Jesus!" Old Master quit then, but he still powerful mad. I don't think he believe Andy going to make that tree when he tell him that.

Then he turn on Andy's brother and give him a good beating too, and we all drive off and leave Andy setting on the ground under a tree and old Deacon standing by him. I don't know what ever become of Andy, but I reckon maybe he went and live with old Deacon Sears until he was free.

When I think back and remember it, it all seems kind of strange, but it seem like old Master and old Deacon both think the same way. They kind of understand that old Master had a right to beat his Negro all he wanted to for running off, and he had a right to set the hounds on him if he did, but he shouldn't of beat him so hard after he told him he was going let him off if he made the tree, and he ought to keep his word even if Andy was his own slave. That's the way both them white men had been taught, and that was the way they both lived.

Old Master had about five wagons on that trip down into Louisiana, but they was all full of stuff and only the old slaves and children could ride in them. I was big enough to walk most of the time, but one time I walked in the sun so long that I got sick and they put me in the wagon for most the rest of the way.

We would come to places where the people said the Yankees had been and gone, but we didn't run into any Yankees. They was most to the north of us I reckon, because we went on down to the south part of Mississippi and ferried across the big river at Baton Rouge. Then we went on to Lafayette, Louisiana, before we settled down anywhere.

All us Negroes thought that was a mighty strange place. We would hear white folks talking and we couldn't understand what they said, and lots of the Negroes talked the same way, too. It was all full of French people around Lafayette, but they had all their menfolks in the Confederate

Army just the same. I seen lots of men in butternut clothes coming and going hither and yon, but they wasn't in bunches. They was mostly coming home to see their folks.

Everybody was scared all the time, and two—three times when old Master hired his Negroes out to work the man that hired them quit his place and went on west before they got the crop in. But old Master got a place and we put in a cotton crop, and I think he got some money by selling his place in Mississippi. Anyway, pretty soon after the cotton was all in he moves again and goes to a place on Simonette Lake for the winter. It aint a bit cold in that place, and we didn't have no fire 'cepting to cook, and sometimes a little charcoal fire in some crock pots that the people left on the place when they went on out to Texas.

The next spring old Master loaded up again and we struck out for Texas, when the Yankees got too close again. But Master Bill didn't go to Texas, because the Confederates done come that winter and made him go to the army. I think they took him to New Orleans, and old Master was hopping mad, but he couldn't do anything or they would make him go too, even if he was a preacher.

I think he left out of there partly because he didn't like the people at that place. They wasn't no Baptists around anywheres, they was all Catholics, and old Master didn't like them.

About that time it look like everybody in the world was going to Texas. When we would be going down the road we would have to walk along the side all the time to let the wagons go past, all loaded with folks going to Texas.

Pretty soon old Master say git the wagons loaded again, and this time we start out with some other people, going north. We go north a while and then turn west, and cross the Sabine River and go to Nachedoches, Texas. Me and my brother Joe and my sister Adeline walked nearly all the way, but my little sister Harriet and my mammy rid in a wagon. Mammy was mighty poorly, and jest when we got to the Sabine bottoms she had another baby. Old Master didn't like it 'cause it was a girl, but he named her Texana on account of where she was born and told us children to wait on Mammy good and maybe we would get a little brother next time.

But we didn't. Old Master went with a whole bunch of wagons on out to the prairie country in Coryell County and set up a farm where we just had to break the sod and didn't have to clear off much. And the next baby Mammy had the next year was a girl. We named her Betty because Mistress jest have a baby a little while before and its name was Betty.

Old Master's place was right at the corner where Coryell and McLennan and Bosque Counties come together, and we raised mostly cotton and jest a little corn for feed. He seem like he changed a lot since we left Mississippi, and seem like he paid more attention to us and looked after us better. But most the people that already live there when we git there was mighty hard on their Negroes. They was mostly hard drinkers and hard talkers, and they work and fight jest as hard as they talk, too!

One day Old Master come out from town and tell us that we all been set free, and we can go or stay jest as we wish. All of my family stay on the place and he pay us half as shares on all we make. Pretty soon the whitefolks begin to cut down on the shares, and the renters git only a third and some less, and the Negroes begin to drift out to other places, but old Master stick to the halves a year or so after that. Then he come down to a third too.

It seem like the white people can't git over us being free, and they do everything to hold us down all the time. We don't git no schools for a long time, and I never see the inside of a school. I jest grow up on hard work. And we can't go 'round where they have the voting, unless we want to ketch a whipping some night, and we have to jest keep on bowing and scraping when we are 'round white folks like we did when we was slaves. They had us down and they kept us down. But that was the way they been taught, and I don't blame them for it none, I reckon.

When I git about thirty years old I marry Betty Sadler close to Waco, and we come up to the Creek Nation forty years ago. We come to Muskogee first, and then to Tulsa about thirty seven years ago.

We had ten children but only seven are alive. Three girls and a boy live here in Tulsa and we got one boy in Muskogee and one at Frederick, Oklahoma.

I sells milk and makes my living, and I keeps so busy I don't think back on the old days much, but if anybody ask me why the Texas Negroes been kept down so much I can tell them. If they set like I did on the bank at that ferry across the Sabine, and see all that long line of covered wagons, miles and miles of them, crossing that river and going west with all they got left out of the War, it aint hard to understand.

Them whitefolks done had everything they had tore up, or had to run away from the places they lived, and they brung their Negroes out to Texas and then right away they lost them too. They always had them Negroes, and lots of them had mighty fine places back in the old states, and then they had to go out and live in sod houses and little old boxed shotguns and turn their Negroes loose. They didn't see no justice in it then, and most of them never did until they died. The folks that stayed at home and didn't straggle all over the country had their old places to live on and their old friends around them, but them Texans was different.

So I says, when they done us the way they did they was jest doing the way they was taught. I don't blame them, because anybody will do that.

Whitefolks mighty decent to me now, and I always tried to teach my children to be respectful and act like they think the whitefolks they dealing with expects them to act. That the way to git along, because some folks been taught one way and some been taught another, and folks always thinks the way they been taught.

Oklahoma Writers' Project
Ex-Slaves

BOB MAYNARD, AGE 79
23 East Choctaw
Weleetka, Oklahoma.

I was born near what is now Marlin, Texas, Falls County. My father was Robert Maynard and my mother was Chanie Maynard, both born slaves. Our Master, Gerard Branum, was a very old man and wore long white whiskers. He sho' was a fine built man, and walked straight and tall like a young man.

I was too little to do much work so my job was to carry the key basket for old Mistress. I sho' was proud of that job. The basket held the keys to the pantry, the kitchen, the linen closet, and extra keys to the rooms and smokehouse. When old Mistress started out on her rounds every morning she'd call to me to get de basket and away we'd go. I'd run errands for all the house help too, so I was kept purty busy.

The "big house" was a fine one. It was a big two-story white house made of pine lumber. There was a big porch or veranda across the front and wings on the east and west. The house faced south. There was big round white posts that went clean up to the roof and there was a big porch upstairs too. I believe the house was what you'd call colonial style. There was twelve or fifteen rooms and a big wide stairway. It was a purty place, with a yard and big trees and the house that set in a walnut and pecan grove. They was graveled walks and driveways and all along by the driveway was cedars. There was a hedge close to the house and a flower garden with purty roses, holly hocks and a lot of others I don't know the name of.

Back to the right of the house was the smokehouse, kept full of meat, and further back was the big barns. Old Master kept a spanking pair of carriage horses and several fine riding horses. He kept several pairs of mules, too, to pull the plow. He had some ox teams too.

To the left and back of the "big house" was the quarters. He owned about two thousand acres of land and three hundred slaves. He kept a white overseer and the colored overlooker was my uncle. He sho' saw that the gang worked. He saw to it that the cotton was took to the gin. They used oxen to pull the wagons full of cotton. There was two gins on the plantation. Had to have two for it was slow work to gin a bale of cotton as it was run by horse power.

Old Master raised hundreds of hogs; he raised practically all the food we et. He gave the food out to each family and they done their own cooking except during harvest. The farm hands was fed at the "big house." They was called in from the farm by a big bell.

Sunday was our only day for recreation. We went to church at our own church, and we could sing and shout jest as loud as we pleased and it didn't disturb nobody.

During the week after supper we would all set round the doors outside and sing or play music. The only musical instruments we had was a jug or big bottle, a skillet lid or frying pan that they'd hit with a stick or a bone. We had a flute too, made out of reed cane and it'd make good music. Sometimes we'd sing and dance so long and loud old Master'd have to make us stop and go to bed.

The Patrollers, Ku Kluxers or night riders come by sometimes at night to scare the niggers and make 'em behave. Sometimes the slaves would run off and the Patroller would catch 'em and have 'em whipped. I've seen that done lots of times. They was some wooden stocks (a sort of trough) and they'd put the darky in this and strap him down, take off his clothers and give him 25 to 50 licks, 'cording to what he had done.

I reckon old Master had everything his heart could wish for at this time. Old Mistress was a fine lady and she always went dressed up. She wore long trains on her skirts and I'd walk behind her and hold her train up when she made de rounds. She was awful good to me. I slept on the floor in her little boy's room, and she give me apples and candy just like she did him. Old Master gave ever chick and child good warm clothes for winter. We had store boughten shoes but the women made our clothes. For underwear we all wore 'lowers' but no shirts.

After the war started old Master took a lot of his slaves and went to Natchez, Mississippi. He thought he'd have a better chance of keeping us there I guess, and he was afraid we'd be greed [TR: freed?] and he started running with us. I remember when General Grant blowed up Vicksburg. I had a free born Uncle and Aunt who sometimes visited in the North and they'd till us how easy it was up there and it sho' made us all want to be free.

I think Abe Lincoln was next to de Lawd. He done all he could for de slaves; he set 'em free. People in the South knowed they'd lose their slaves when he was elected president. 'Fore the election he traveled all over the South and he come to our house and slept in old Mistress' bed. Didn't nobody know who he was. It was a custom to take strangers in and put them up for one night or longer, so he come to our house and he watched close. He seen how the niggers come in on Saturday and drawed four pounds of meat and a peck of meal for a week's rations. He also saw 'em whipped and sold. When he got back up north he writ old Master a letter and told him he was going to have to free his slaves, that everybody was going to have to, that the North was going to see to it. He also told him that he had visited at his house and if he doubted it to go in the room he slept in and look on the bedstead at the head and he'd see where he'd writ his name. Sho' nuff, there was his name: A. Lincoln.

Didn't none of us like Jeff Davis. We all liked Robert E. Lee, but we was glad that Grant whipped him.

When the War was over, old Master called all the darkies in and lined 'em up in a row. He told 'em they was free to go and do as they pleased. It was six months before any of us left him.

Darkies could vote in Mississippi. Fred Douglas, a colored man, came to Natchez and made political speeches for General Grant.

155

After the war they was a big steam boat line on the Mississippi River known as the Robert E. Lee Line. They sho' was fine boats too.

We used to have lots of Confederate money. Five cent pieces, two bit pieces, half dollar bills and half dimes. During the war old Master dug a long trench and buried all de silver ware, fine clothes, jewelry and a lot of money. I guess he dug it up, but I don't remember.

Master died three years after the War. He took it purty good, losing his niggers and all. Lots of men killed theirselves. Old Master was a good old man.

I'm getting old, I reckon. I've been married twice and am the father of 19 chillun. The oldest if 57 and my youngest is two boys, ten and twelve. I has great grandchillun older than them two boys.

Oklahoma Writers' Project
Ex-Slaves
[Date stamp: AUG 19 1937]

JANE MONTGOMERY
Age 80 yrs.
Oklahoma City, Oklahoma

I was born March 15, 1857, in Homer, Louisiana. I claim to be 75 years old, but that's jest my way of counting. My mother was Sarah Strong and my father was Edmond Beavers. We lived in a log cabin that had jest one door. I had two sisters named Peggy and Katie. Mammy was bought from the Strong family and my pappy was bought from Beavers by Mister Eason.

We slept on wooden slabs which was jest make-shift beds. I didn't do no work in slave times 'cause I was too little. You jest had to be good and husky to work on that place. I listened and told mammy everything I heerd. I ate right side dat old white woman on the flo'. I was a little busy-body. I don't recollect eating in our quarters on Sunday and no other time.

I don't remember no possums and rabbits being on our place, 'cause when white folks killed a chicken for their selves, dey killed one for the niggers. My pappy never ate no cornbread in all his put-together. Meat was my favorite food. I never ate no dry bread without no meat.

We wore homespun clothes. My first pair of shoes was squirrel skin. Mammy had 'em made. We wore clothes called linsey that was wool and cotton mixed.

My father was the onliest overseer. It was sho' a great big old place. My master jest seen the place on Sundays. They was jest seven Niggers on our plantation. No working late at night but we had to git up at daylight. When our day's work was done, we went to bed, but sometimes they sung. Sadday was a holiday from working on the plantation. You had Sadday to wash for yourself. We didn't do nothing on Christmas and all holidays.

Mistress never whip us and iffen master would start, mistress would git a gun and make him stop. She said, "Let ever bitch whip her own chillun." I never seen no patrollers, I jest heerd of 'em. They never come on our place. I guess they was scared to. The Klu Klux whipped niggers when so never they could catch 'em. They rid at night mostly.

I am a Baptist. I belong to Calvary Baptist Church. I was baptized in a creek. Our favorite hymn was "Dark Was the Night an' Cold the Ground." Our favorite revival hymn was "Lord I'd Come to Thee, a Sinner Undefiled." Our favorite funeral song was "Hark From the Tomb."

My family didn't believe in conjure an' all that stuff, 'though they's a heap of it was going on and still is for that matter. They had "hands" that was made up of all kinds of junk. You used 'em to make folks love you more'n they did. We used asafetida to keep off smallpox and measles. Put mole foots round a baby's neck to make him teethe easy. We used to use nine red ants tied in a sack round they neck to make 'em teethe easy and never had no trouble with 'em neither.

I think I seen a haunt once, 'cause when I looked the second time, what I seen the first time was gone.

When the War was over, mistress' son come home and he cleaned his guns on my dress tail. It sho' stunk up my dress and made me sick too. He told old mistress that niggers was free now. I went and told mammy that old Betsy's son told her the niggers was free and what did he mean. She said, "Shhhhhh!" They never did jest come out and tell us we was free. We was free in July and mammy left in September. We lived in Jordan Saline, out from Smith County. Then my mother give me to my father 'cause she was married to another man. Her and my step-father moved to Gilmore, Texas. They sent for me round 'bout Christmas and we lived on Sampers' farm.

We lived so far out, we couldn't go to school, 'though they was for us. We didn't own no land. Didn't nobody learn me to read and write.

Abe Lincoln was a good man. It was through Mr. Lincoln that God fit to free us. I don't know much 'bout Jeff Davis and don't care nothing 'bout him. Booker T. Washington built that school through God. He used to live in a cabin jest lak I done. He was sho' a great man.

I married Trole Kemp in 1883. I 'mind you they didn't marry in slavery, they jest took up. Master jest give a permit. I am the mother of 10 chillun and 5 grandchillun. Four of my chillun died young. Them what's living is doing different things sech as: writing policy, working on made work, housework, government clerk and hotel maid. One is in the pen.

Oklahoma Writers' Project
Ex-Slaves
[Date stamp: AUG 13 1937]

AMANDA OLIVER
Age 80 yrs.
Oklahoma City, Okla.

I 'membuh what my mother say—I was born November 9, 1857, in Missouri. I was 'bout eight years old, when she was sold to a master named Harrison Davis. They said he had two farms in Missouri, but when he moved to northern Texas he brought me, my mother, Uncle George, Uncle Dick and a cullud girl they said was 15 with 'im. He owned 'bout 6 acres on de edge of town near Sherman, Texas, and my mother and 'em was all de slaves he had. They said he sold off some of de folks.

We didn't have no overseers in northern Texas, but in southern Texas dey did. Dey didn't raise cotton either; but dey raised a whole lots of corn. Sometime de men would shuck corn all night long. Whenever dey was going to shuck all night de women would piece quilts while de men shuck de corn and you could hear 'em singing and shucking corn. After de cornshucking, de cullud folks would have big dances.

Master Davis lived in a big white frame house. My mother lived in the yard in a big one-room log hut with a brick chimney. De logs was "pinted" (what dey call plastered now with lime). I don't know whether young folks know much 'bout dat sort of thing now.

I slept on de floor up at de "Big House" in de white woman's room on a quilt. I'd git up in de mornings, make fires, put on de coffee, and tend to my little brother. Jest do little odd jobs sech as that.

We ate vegetables from de garden, sech as that. My favorite dish is vegetables now.

I don't remember seeing any slaves sold. My mother said dey sold 'em on de block in Kentucky where she was raised.

I don't remembuh when de War broke out, but I remembuh seeing the soldiers with de blue uniforms on. I was afraid of 'em.

Old mistress didn't tell us when he was free, but another white woman told my mother and I remembuh. One day old mistress told my mother to git to that wheel and git to work, and my mother said, "I ain't gwineter, I'm jest as free as you air." So dat very day my mother packed up all our belongings and moved us to town, Sherman, Texas. She worked awful hard, doing day work for 50¢ a day, and sometimes she'd work for food, clothes or whatever she could git.

I don't believe in conjuring though I heard lotta talk 'bout it. Sometimes I have pains and aches in my hands, feel like sometime dat somebody puts dey hands on me, but I think jest de way my nerves is.

I can't say much 'bout Abe Lincoln. He was a republican in favor of de cullud folk being free. Jeff Davis? Yeah, the boys usta sing a song 'bout 'im:

Lincoln rides a fine hoss,

Jeff Davis rides a mule,

Lincoln is de President,

Jeff Davis is de fool.

Booker T. Washington—I guess he is a right good man. He's for the cullud people I guess.

I been a Christian thirty some odd years. I've been here some thirty odd years. Had to come when my husband did. He died in 1902. We married in 18—I've forgot, but we went to de preacher and got married. We did more than jump over de broom stick.

In those days we went to church with de white folks. Dey had church at eleven and the cullud folks at three, but all of us had white preachers. Our church is standing right there now, at least it was de last time I was there.

I don't have a favorite song, theys so many good ones, but I like, "Bound for the Promised Land." I'm a Baptist, my mother was a Baptist, and her white folks was Baptist.

I have two daughters, Julia Goodwin and Bertha Frazier, and four grandchildren, both of 'ems been separated. Dey do housework.

Oklahoma Writers' Project
Ex-Slaves

SALOMON OLIVER
Age 78 yrs.
Tulsa, Oklahoma.

John A. Miller owned the finest plantation in Washington County, Mississippi, about 12-mile east of Greenville. I was born on this 20,000-acre plantation November 17, 1859, being one of about four hundred slave children on the place.

About three hundred negro families living in box-type cabins made it seem like a small town. Built in rows, the cabins were kept whitewashed, neat and orderly, for the Master was strict about such things. Several large barns and storage buildings were scattered around the plantation. Also, two cotton gins and two old fashioned presses, operated by horses and mules, made Miller's plantation one of the best equipped in Mississippi.

Master John was quite a character. The big plantation didn't occupy all his time. He owned a bank in Vicksburg and another in New Orleans, and only came to the plantation two or three times a year for a week or two visit.

Things happened around there mighty quick when the Master showed up. If the slaves were not being treated right—out go the white overseer. Fired! The Master was a good man and tried to hire good boss men. Master John was bad after the slave women. A yellow child show up every once in a while. Those kind always got special privileges because the Master said he didn't want his children whipped like the rest of them slaves.

My own Mammy, Mary, was the Master's own daughter! She married Salomon Oliver (who took the name of Oliver after the War), and the Master told all the slave drivers to leave her alone and not whip her. This made the overseers jealous of her and caused trouble. John Santhers was one of the white overseers who treated her bad, and after I was born and got strong enough (I was a weakling for three-four years after birth), to do light chores he would whip me just for the fun of it. It was fun for him but not for me. I hoped to whip him when I grew up. That is the one thing I won't ever forget. He died about the end of the War so that's one thing I won't ever get to do.

My mother was high-tempered and she knew about the Master's orders not to whip her. I guess sometimes she took advantage and tried to do things that maybe wasn't right. But it did her no good and one of the white men flogged her to death. She died with scars on her back!

Father use to preach to the slaves when a crowd of them could slip off into the woods. I don't remember much about the religious things, only just what Daddy told me when I was older. He was caught several times slipping off to the woods and because he was the preacher I guess they layed on the lash a little harder trying to make him give up preaching.

Ration day was Saturday. Each person was given a peck of corn meal, four pounds of wheat flour, four pounds of pork meat, quart of molasses, one pound of sugar, the same of coffee and a plug of tobacco. Potatoes and vegetables came from the family garden and each slave family was required to cultivate a separate garden.

During the Civil War a battle was fought near the Miller plantation. The Yankees under General Grant came through the country. They burned 2,000 bales of Miller cotton. When the Yankee wagons crossed Bayou Creek the bridge gave way and quite a number of soldiers and horses were seriously injured.

For many years after the War folks would find bullets in the ground. Some of the bullets were 'twins' fastened together with a chain.

Master Miller settled my father upon a piece of land after the War and we stayed on it several years, doing well.

I moved to Muskogee in 1902, coming on to Tulsa in 1907, the same year Oklahoma was made a state. My six wives are all dead,—Liza, Lizzie, Ellen, Lula, Elizabeth and Henrietta. Six children, too. George, Anna, Salomon, Nelson, Garfield, Cosmos—all good children. They remember the Tulsa riot and don't aim ever to come back to Oklahoma.

When the riot started in 1922 (I think it was), I had a place on the corner of Pine and Owasso Streets. Two hundred of my people gathered at my place, because I was so well known everybody figured we wouldn't be molested. I was wrong. Two of my horses was shot and killed. Two of my boys, Salomon and Nelson, was wounded, one in the hip, the other in the shoulder. They wasn't bad and got well alright. Some of my people wasn't so lucky. The dead wagon hauled them away!

White men came into the negro district and gathered up the homeless. The houses were most all burned. No place to go except to the camps where armed whites kept everybody quiet. They took my clothes and all my money—$298.00—and the police couldn't do nothing about my loss when I reported it to them.

That was a terrible time, but we people are better off today that any time during the days of slavery. We have some privileges and they are worth more than all the money in the world!

Oklahoma Writers' Project
Ex-Slaves

PHYLLIS PETITE
Age 83 yrs.
Fort Gibson, Okla.

I was born in Rusk County, Texas, on a plantation about eight miles east of Belleview. There wasn't no town where I was born, but they had a church.

My mammy and pappy belonged to a part Cherokee named W. P. Thompson when I was born. He had kinfolks in the Cherokee Nation, and we all moved up here to a place on Fourteen-Mile Creek close to where Hulbert now is, 'way before I was big enough to remember anything. Then, so I been told, old master Thompson sell my pappy and mammy and one of my baby brothers and me back to one of his neighbors in Texas name of John Harnage.

Mammy's name was Letitia Thompson and pappy's was Riley Thompson. My little brother was named Johnson Thompson, but I had another brother sold to a Vann and he always call hisself

Harry Vann. His Cherokee master lived on the Arkansas river close to Webber's Falls and I never did know him until we was both grown. My only sister was Patsy and she was borned after slavery and died at Wagoner, Oklahoma.

I can just remember when Master John Harnage took us to Texas. We went in a covered wagon with oxen and camped out all along the way. Mammy done the cooking in big wash kettles and pappy done the driving of the oxen. I would set in a wagon and listen to him pop his whip and holler.

Master John took us to his plantation and it was a big one, too. You could look from the field up to the Big House and any grown body in the yard look like a little body, it was so far away.

We negroes lived in quarters not far from the Big House and ours was a single log house with a stick and dirt chimney. We cooked over the hot coals in the fireplace.

I just played around until I was about six years old I reckon, and then they put me up at the Big House with my mammy to work. She done all the cording and spinning and weaving, and I done a whole lot of sweeping and minding the baby. The baby was only about six months old I reckon. I used to stand by the cradle and rock it all day, and when I quit I would go to sleep right by the cradle sometimes before mammy would come and get me.

The Big House had great big rooms in front, and they was fixed up nice, too. I remember when old Mistress Harnage tried me out sweeping up the front rooms. They had two or three great big pictures of some old people hanging on the wall. They was full blood Indians it look like, and I was sure scared of them pictures! I would go here and there and every which-a-way, and anywheres I go them big pictures always looking straight at me and watching me sweep! I kept my eyes right on them so I could run if they moved, and old Mistress take me back to the kitchen and say I can't sweep because I miss all the dirt.

We always have good eating, like turnip greens cooked in a kettle with hog skins and crackling grease, and skinned corn, and rabbit or possum stew. I liked big fish tolerable well too, but I was afraid of the bones in the little ones.

That skinned corn aint like the boiled hominy we have today. To make it you boil some wood ashes, or have some drip lye from the hopper to put in the hot water. Let the corn boil in the lye water until the skin drops off and the eyes drop out and then wash that corn in fresh water about a dozen times, or just keep carrying water from the spring until you are wore out, like I did. Then you put the corn in a crock and set it in the spring, and you got good skinned corn as long as it last, all ready to warm up a little batch at a time.

Master had a big, long log kitchen setting away from the house, and we set a big table for the family first, and when they was gone we negroes at the house eat at that table too, but we don't use the china dishes.

The negro cook was Tilda Chisholm. She and my mammy didn't do no out-work. Aunt Tilda sure could make them corn-dodgers. Us children would catch her eating her dinner first out of the kettles and when we say something she say: "Go on child, I jest tasting that dinner."

162

In the summer we had cotton homespun clothes, and in winter it had wool mixed in. They was dyed with copperas and wild indigo.

My brother, Johnson Thompson, would get up behind old Master Harnage on his horse and go with him to hunt squirrels so they would go 'round on Master's side so's he could shoot them. Master's old mare was named "Old Willow", and she knowed when to stop and stand real still so he could shoot.

His children was just all over the place! He had two houses full of them! I only remember Bell, Ida, Maley, Mary and Will, but they was plenty more I don't remember.

That old horn blowed 'way before daylight, and all the field negroes had to be out in the row by the time of sun up. House negroes got up too, because old Master always up to see everybody get out to work.

Old Master Harnage bought and sold slaves most all the time, and some of the new negroes always acted up and needed a licking. The worst ones got beat up good, too! They didn't have no jail to put slaves in because when the Masters got done licking them they didn't need no jail.

My husband was George Petite. He tell me his mammy was sold away from him when he was a little boy. He looked down a long lane after her just as long as he could see her, and cried after her. He went down to the big road and set down by his mammy's barefooted tracks in the sand and set there until it got dark, and then he come on back to the quarters.

I just saw one slave try to get away right in hand. They caught him with bloodhounds and brung him back in. The hounds had nearly tore him up, and he was sick a long time. I don't remember his name, but he wasn't one of the old regular negroes.

In Texas we had a church where we could go. I think it was a white church and they just let the negroes have it when they got a preacher sometimes. My mammy took me sometimes, and she loved to sing them salvation songs.

We used to carry news from one plantation to the other I reckon, 'cause mammy would tell about things going on some other plantation and I know she never been there.

Christmas morning we always got some brown sugar candy or some molasses to pull, and we children was up bright and early to get that 'lasses pull, I tell you! And in the winter we played skeeting on the ice when the water froze over. No, I don't mean skating. That's when you got iron skates, and we didn't have them things. We just get a running start and jump on the ice and skeet as far as we could go, and then run some more.

I nearly busted my head open, and brother Johnson said: "Try it again," but after that I was scared to skeet any more.

Mammy say we was down in Texas to get away from the War, but I didn't see any war and any soldiers. But one day old Master stay after he eat breakfast and when us negroes come in to eat he say: "After today I ain't your master any more. You all as free as I am." We just stand and look and don't know what to say about it.

After while pappy got a wagon and some oxen to drive for a white man who was coming to the Cherokee Nation because he had folks here. His name was Dave Mounts and he had a boy named John.

We come with them and stopped at Fort Gibson where my own grand mammy was cooking for the soldiers at the garrison. Her name was Phyllis Brewer and I was named after her. She had a good Cherokee master. My mammy was born on his place.

We stayed with her about a week and then we moved out on Four Mile Creek to live. She died on Fourteen-Mile Creek about a year later.

When we first went to Four Mile Creek I seen negro women chopping wood and asked them who they work for and I found out they didn't know they was free yet.

After a while my pappy and mammy both died, and I was took care of by my aunt Elsie Vann. She took my brother Johnson too, but I don't know who took Harry Vann.

I was married to George Petite, and I had on a white underdress and black high-top shoes, and a large cream colored hat, and on top of all I had a blue wool dress with tassels all around the bottom of it. That dress was for me to eat the terrible supper in. That what we called the wedding supper because we eat too much of it. Just danced all night, too! I was at Mandy Foster's house in Fort Gibson, and the preacher was Reverend Barrows, I had that dress a long time, but its gone now. I still got the little sun bonnet I wore to church in Texas.

We had six children, but all are dead but George, Tish, and Annie now.

Yes, they tell me Abraham Lincoln set me free, and I love to look at his picture on the wall in the school house at Four Mile branch where they have church. My grand mammy kind of help start that church, and I think everybody ought to belong to some church.

I want to say again my Master Harnage was Indian, but he was a good man and mighty good to us slaves, and you can see I am more than six feet high, and they say I weighs over a hundred and sixty, even if my hair is snow white.

Oklahoma Writers' Project
Ex-Slaves

MATILDA POE
Age 80 yrs.
McAlester, Okla.

I was born in Indian Territory on de plantation of Isaac Love. He was old Master, and Henry Love was young Master. Isaac Love was a full blood Chickasaw Indian but his wife was a white woman.

Old Master was sure good to his slaves. The young niggers never done no heavy work till dey was fully grown. Dey would carry water to de men in de field and do other light jobs 'round de place.

De Big House set way back from de road 'bout a quarter of a mile. It was a two-story log house, and the rooms was awful big and they was purty furniture in it. The furniture in de parlor was red plush and I loved to slip in and rub my hand over it, it was so soft like. The house was made of square logs and de cracks was filled out even with the edges of de logs. It was white washed and my but it was purty. They was a long gallery clean across de front of de house and big posts to support de roof. Back a ways from de house was de kitchen and nearby was de smokehouse. Old Master kept it well filled with meat, lard and molasses all de time. He seen to it that we always had plenty to eat. The old women done all de cooking in big iron pots that hung over the fire. De slaves was all served together.

The slave quarters was about two hundred yards back of de Big House. Our furniture was made of oak 'cepting de chairs, and dey was made out of hackberry. I still have a chair dat belonged to my mammy.

The boys didn't wear no britches in de summer time. Dey just wore long shirts. De girls wore homespun dresses, either blue or gray.

Old Master never hired no overseer for his slaves, but he looked after 'em hisself. He punished dem hisself too. He had to go away one time and he hired a white man to oversee while he was gone. The only orders he left was to keep dem busy. Granny Lucy was awful old but he made her go to the field. She couldn't hold out to work so he ups and whips her. He beat her scandalous. He cut her back so bad she couldn't wear her dress. Old Master come home and my, he was mad when he see Granny Lucy. He told de man to leave and iffen he ever set foot on his ground again he's shoot him, sure!

Old Master had a big plantation and a hundred or more slaves. Dey always got up at daylight and de men went out and fed de horses. When de bell rang dey was ready to eat. After breakfast dey took de teams and went out to plow. Dey come in 'bout half past 'leven and at twelve de bell rung agin. Dey eat their dinner and back to plowing dey went. 'Bout five o'clock dey come in again, and den they'd talk, sing and jig dance till bedtime.

Old Master never punished his niggers 'cepting dey was sassy or lazy. He never sold his slaves neither. A owner once sold several babies to traders. Dey stopped at our plantation to stay awhile. My mammy and de other women had to take care of dem babies for two days, and teach dem to nuss a bottle or drink from a glass. Dat was awful, dem little children crying for they mothers. Sometimes dey sold de mothers away from they husbands and children.

Master wasn't a believer in church but he let us have church. My we'd have happy times singing an shouting. They'd have church when dey had a preacher and prayer meeting when dey didn't.

Slaves didn't leave de plantation much on 'count of de Patrollers. De patroller was low white trash what jest wanted a excuse to shoot niggers. I don't think I ever saw one but I heard lots of 'em.

I don't believe in luck charms and things of the such. Iffen you is in trouble, there ain't nothing gonna save you but de Good Lawd. I heard of folks keeping all kind of things for good luck charms. When I was a child different people gave me buttons to string and we called them our charm string and wore 'em round our necks. If we was mean dey would tell us "Old Raw Head and Bloody Bones" would git us. Grand mammy told us ghost stories after supper, but I don't remember any of dem.

I never did know I was a slave, 'cause I couldn't tell I wasn't free. I always had a good time, didn't have to work much, and allus had something to eat and wear and that was better than it is with me now.

When de War was over old Master told us we was free. Mammy she say, "Well, I'm heading for Texas." I went out and old Master ask me to bring him a coal of fire to light his pipe. I went after it and mammy left pretty soon. My pappy wouldn't leave old Master right then but old Master told us we was free to go where we pleased, so me an' pappy left and went to Texas where my mammy was. We never saw old Master any more. We stayed a while in Texas and then come back to de Indian Territory.

Abe Lincoln was a good man, everybody liked him. See, I've got his picture. Jeff Davis was a good man too, he just made a mistake. I like Mr. Roosevelt, too.

Oklahoma Writers' Project
Ex-Slaves

HENRY F. PYLES
Age 81 yrs.
Tulsa, Okla.

Little pinch o' pepper——

Little bunch o' wool——

Mumbledy—Mumbledy——

Two, three Pammy Christy beans——

Little piece o' rusty iron——

Mumbledy—Mumbledy——

Wrop it in a rag and tie it wid hair,

Two fum a hoss an' one fum a mare——

Mumbledy, Mumbledy, Mumbledy——

Wet it in whiskey

Boughten wid silver;

Dat make you wash so hard your sweat pop out,

And he come to pass, sho'!

That's how the niggers say old Bab Russ used to make the hoodoo "hands" he made for the young bucks and wenches, but I don't know, 'cause I was too trusting to look inside de one he make for me, and anyways I lose it, and it no good nohow!

Old Bab Russ live about two mile from me, and I went to him one night at midnight and ask him to make me de hand. I was a young strapper about sixteen years old, and thinking about wenches pretty hard and wanting something to help me out wid the one I liked best.

Old Bab Russ charge me four bits for dat hand, and I had to give four bits more for a pint of whiskey to wet it wid, and it wasn't no good nohow!

Course dat was five-six years after de War. I wasn't yet quite eleven when de War close. Most all the niggers was farming on de shares and whole lots of them was still working for their old Master yet. Old Bab come in there from deep South Carolina two-three years befo', and live all by hisself. De gal I was worrying about had come wid her old pappy and mammy to pick cotton on de place, and dey was staying in one of de cabins in the "settlement", but dey didn't live there all de time.

I don't know whether I believed in conjure much or not in dem days, but anyways I tried it that once and it stirred up sech a rumpus everybody called me "Hand" after that until after I was married and had a pack of children.

Old Bab Russ was coal black, and he could talk African or some other unknown tongue, and all the young bucks and wenches was mortal 'fraid of him!

Well sir, I took dat hand he made for me and set out to try it on dat gal. She never had give me a friendly look even, and when I would speak to her polite she just hang her head and say nothing!

We was all picking cotton, and I come along up behind her and decided to use my "Hand." I had bought me a pint of whiskey to wet the hand wid, but I was scared to take out of my pocket and let the other niggers see it, so I jest set down in de cotton row and taken a big mouthful. I figgered to hold it in my mouth until I catched up wid that gal and then blow it on the hand jest before I tech her on the arm and speak to her.

Well, I take me a big mouthful, but it was so hot and scaldy it jest slip right on down my throat! Then I had to take another, and when I was gitting up I kind of stumbled and it slip down, too!

Then I see all the others get way on ahead, and I took another big mouthful—the last in the bottle—and drap the bottle under a big stalk and start picking fast and holding the whiskey in my mouth this time. I missed about half the cotton I guess, but at last I catch up with de rest and git close up behind dat purty gal. Then I started to speak to her, but forgot I had de whiskey in mouth and I lost most of it down my neck and all over my chin, and then I strangled a little on the rest, so as when I went to squirt it on de "hand" I didn't have nothing left to squirt but a little spit.

That make me a little nervous right then, but anyways I step up behind dat gal and lay my hand on her arm and speak polite and start to say something, but I finish up what I start to say laying on my neck with my nose shoved up under a cotton stalk about four rows away!

De way that gal lam me across the head was a caution! We was in new ground, and she jest pick up a piece of old root and whopped me right in de neck with it!

That raise sech a laugh on me that I never say nothing to her for three-four days, but after while I gets myself wound up to go see her at her home. I didn't know how she going to act, but I jest took my foot in my hand and went on over.

Her old pappy and mammy was asleep in the back of the room on a pallet, and we set in front of the fireplace on our hunches and jest looked at the fire and punched it up a little. It wasn't cold, but de malary fog was thick all through de bottoms.

After while I could smell the whiskey soaked up in dat "hand" I had in my pocket, and I was scared she could smell it too. So I jest reached in my pocket and teched it for luck, then I reached over and teched her arm. She jerked it back so quick she knocked over the churn and spilled buttermilk all over de floor! Dat make de old folks mad, and dey grumble and holler and told de gal, "Send dat black rapscallion on out of here!" But I didn't go.

I kept on moving over closer and she kept on backing away, but after while I reach over and put my hand on her knee. All I was going to do was say something but I shore forgot what it was the next minnit, 'cause she jest whinnied lak a scared hoss and give me a big push. I was settin straddledy-legged on the floor, and that push sent me on my head in the hot ashes in the fur corner of the chimney.

Then the old man jump up and make for me and I make for the door! It was dark, all 'cepting the light from the chimney, and I fumble all up and down the door jamb before I find de latch pin. The old man shorely git me if he hadn't stumble over the eating table and whop his hand right down in de dish of fresh made butter. That make him so mad he jest stand and holler and cuss.

I git de pin loose and jerk de door open so quick and hard I knock de powder gourd down what was hanging over it, and my feet git caught in the string. The stopper gits knocked out, and when I untangle it from my feet and throw it back in de house it fall in the fireplace.

I was running all de time, but I hear dat gourd go "Blammity Blam!" and then all de yelling, but I didn't go back to see how dey git the hot coals all put out what was scattered all over de cabin!

I done drap dat "hand" and I never did see it again. Never did see the gal but two-three times after that, and we never mention about dat night. Her old pappy was too old to work, so I never did see him neither, but she must of told about it because all the young bucks called me "Hand" after that for a long time.

Old Bab kept on trying to work his conjure with the old niggers, but the young ones didn't pay him much mind cause they was hearing about the Gospel and de Lord Jesus Christ. We was all free then, and we could go and come without a pass, and they was always some kind of church meeting going on close enough to go to. Our niggers never did hear about de Lord Jesus until after we was free, but lots of niggers on de other plantations had masters that told them all about him, and some of dem niggers was pretty good at preaching. Then de good church people in de North was sending white preachers amongst us all the time too. Most of de young niggers was Christians by that time.

One day old Bab was hoeing in a field and got in a squabble about something with a young gal name Polly, same name as his wife. After while he git so mad he reach up with his fingers and wet them on his tongue and point straight up and say, "Now you got a trick on you! Dere's a heavy trick on you now! Iffen you don't change your mind you going pass on before de sun go down!"

All de young niggers looked like they want to giggle but afraid to, and the old ones start begging old Bab to take the trick off, but that Polly git her dander up and take in after him with a hoe!

She knocked him down, and he jest laid there kicking his feet in the air and trying to keep her from hitting him in the head!

Well, that kind of broke up Bab's charm, so he set out to be a preacher. The Northern whites was paying some of the Negro preachers, so he tried to be one too. He didn't know nothing about de Bible but to shout loud, so the preacher board at Red Mound never would give him a paper to preach. Then he had to go back to tricking and trancing again.

One day he come in at dinner and told his wife to git him something to eat. She told him they aint nothing but some buttermilk, and he says give me some of that. He hollered around till she fix him a big ash cake and he ate that and she made him another and he ate that. Then he drunk the rest of de gallon of buttermilk and went out and laid down on a tobacco scaffold in de yard and nearly died.

After while he jest stiffened out and looked like he was dead, and nobody couldn't wake him up. 'Bout forty niggers gathered round and tried but it done no good. Old mammy Polly got scared and sent after the white judge, old Squire Wilson, and he tried, and then the white preacher Reverend Dennison tried and old man Gorman tried. He was a infidel, but that didn't do no good.

By that time it was getting dark, and every nigger in a square mile was there, looking on and acting scared. Me and my partner who was a little bit cripple but mighty smart come up to see what all the rumpus was about, and we was jest the age to do anything.

He whispered to me to let him start it off and then me finish it while he got a head running start. I ast him what he talking about.

Then he fooled round the house and got a little ball of cotton and soaked it in kerosene from a lamp. It was a brass lamp with a hole and a stopper in the side of the bowl. Wonder he didn't burn his fool head off! Then he sidle up close and stuck dat cotton 'tween old Bab's toes. Old Bab had the biggest feet I ever see, too.

'Bout that time I lit a corn shuck in de lamp and run out in de yard and stuck it to de cotton and jest kept right on running!

My partner had a big start but I catch up wid him and we lay down in de bresh and listened to everybody hollering and old Bab hollering louder than anybody. Old Bab moved away after that.

All that foolishness happen after the War, but before de War while I was a little boy they wasn't much foolishness went on I warrant you.

I was born on de 15th of August in 1856, and belonged to Mister Addison Pyles. He lived in town, in Jackson, Tennessee, and was a old man when de War broke. He had a nephew named Irvin T. Pyles he raised from a baby, and Mister Irvin kept a store at de corner of de roads at our plantation. The plantation covered about 300 or 400 acres I reckon, and they had about 25 slaves counting de children.

The plantation was about 9 miles north of Red Mound, close to Lexington, Tennessee, and about a mile and a half from Parker's Crossroads where they had a big battle in de War.

They wasn't no white overseer on the place, except Mister Irvin, and he stayed in de store or in town and didn't bother about the farm work. We had a Negro overlooker who was my stepdaddy. His name was Jordan, and he run away wid de Yankees about de middle of de War and was in a Negro Yankee regiment. After he left we jest worked on as usual because we was afraid not to. Several of de men got away like that but he was de only one that got in de army.

They was a big house in de middle of de place and a settlement of Negro cabins behind and around it. We called it de settlement, but on other plantations where white folks lived there too they called it de quarters. We always kept this big house clean and ready, and sometimes de white folks come out from town and stay a few days and hunt and fish and look over de crops.

We all worked at farm work. Cotton and corn and tobacco mostly. We all laid off Sunday after noontime, but we didn't have no church nor preaching and we didn't hear anything 'bout Jesus much until after de emancipation.

I reckon old Master wasn't very religious, 'cause he never tell us 'bout the Holy Word. He jest said to behave ourselves and tell him when we wanted to marry, and not have but one wife.

We had little garden patches and cotton patches we could work on Sunday and what de stuff brung we could sell and keep the money. Old Master let us have what we made that way on Sunday. We could buy ribbons and hand soap and coal oil and such at de store. Master Irvin was always honest 'bout continuing de money, too.

We didn't have no carders and spinners nor no weavers on de plantation. They cost too much money to buy just for 25 niggers, and they cost a lot more than field niggers. So we got our clothes sent out to us from in town, and sometimes we was give cloth from de store to make our clothes out of.

We got de shorts and seconds from de mill when we had wheat ground, and so we had good wheat bread as well as corn pone, and de big smokehouse was on de place and we had all de meat we wanted to eat. Old Master sent out after de meat he wanted every day or so and we kept him in garden sass that way too.

We was right between de forks of Big Beaver and Little Beaver and we could go fishing without getting far off de place. We couldn't go far away without a pass, though, and they wasn't nobody on the place to write us a pass, so we couldn't go to meeting and dances and sech.

But de niggers on de other plantations could get passes to come to our place, and so we had parties sometimes there at our place. We always had them on Sundays, 'cause in the evening we would be too tired to work if we set up, and the other masters wouldn't give passes to their niggers to come over in de evening.

We had a white doctor lived at de next plantation, and old Master had a contract with old Dr. Brown to look after us. He had a beard as long as your arm. He come for all kinds of misery except bornings. Then we had a mid-wife who was a white woman lived down below us. They was poor people renting or living on war land. Nearly all de white folks in that country been there a long time and their old people got de land from de government for fighting in the

Revolutionary War. Most all was from North Carolina—way back. I think old Master's pappy was from dere in de first place.

Old Master had two sons named Newton and Willis. Newton was in de War and was killed, and Willis went to war later and was sick a long time and come home early. Old Master was too old to go.

There was two daughters, Mary, de oldest, married a Holmes, and Miss Laura never did marry I don't think.

My mammy's name was Jane, and she was born on de 10th day of May in 1836. I know de dates 'cause old Master kept his book on all his niggers de same as on his own family. Mammy was the nurse of all de children but I think old Master sent her to de plantation about the time I was born. I don't think I had any pappy. I think I was jest one of them things that happened sometimes in slavery days, but I know old Master didn't have nothing to do with it—I'm too black.

Mammy married a man named Jordan when I was a little baby. He was the overlooker and went off to de Yankees, when dey come for foraging through dat country de first time.

He served in de Negro regiment in de battle at Fort Piller and a lot of Sesesh was killed in dat battle, so when de War was over and Jordan come back home he was a changed nigger and all de whites and a lot of de niggers hated him. All 'cepting old Master, and he never said a word out of de way to him. Jest told him to come on and work on de place as long as he wanted to.

But Jordan had a hard time, and he brung it on his self I reckon.

'Bout de first thing, he went down to Wildersville Schoolhouse, about a mile from Wildersville, to a nigger and carpet bagger convention and took me and mammy along. That was de first picnic and de first brass band I ever see. De band men was all white men and they still had on their blue soldier clothes.

Lots of de niggers there had been in de Union army too, and they had on parts of their army clothes. They took them out from under their coats and their wagon seats an put them on for de picnic.

There was a saloon over in Wildersville, and a lot of them went over there but they was scared to go in, most of them. But a colored delegate named Taylor and my pappy went in and ordered a drink. The bartender didn't pay them no mind.

Then a white man named Billy Britt walked up and throwed a glass of whiskey in Jordan's face and cussed him for being in de Yankee army. Then a white man from the North named Pearson took up the fight and him and Jordan jumped on Billy Britt, but de crowd stopped them and told pappy to git on back to whar he come from.

He got elected a delegate at de convention and went on down to Nashville and helped nominate Brownlow for governor. Then he couldn't come back home for a while, but finally he did.

Old Master was uneasy about de way things was going on, and he come out to de farm and stayed in de big house a while.

One day in broad daylight he was on de gallery and down de road come 'bout 20 bushwhackers in Sesesh clothes on horses and rid up to de gate. Old Master knowed all of them, and Captain Clay Taylor, who had been de master of de nigger delegate, was at the head of them.

They had Jordan Pyles tied with a rope and walked along on de ground betwixt two horses.

"Whar you taking my nigger?", Old Master say. He run down off de gallery and out in de road.

"He ain't your nigger no more—you know that", old Captain Taylor holler back.

"He jest as much my nigger as that Taylor nigger was your nigger, and you ain't laid hands on him! Now you jest have pity on my nigger!"

"Your nigger Jordan been in de Yankee army, and he was in de battle at Fort Piller and help kill our white folks, and you know it!" Old Captain Taylor say, and argue on like that, but old Master jest take hold his bridle and shake his head.

"No, Clay", he say, "that boy maybe didn't kill Confederates, but you and him both know my two boys killed plenty Yankees, and you forgot I lost one of my boys in de War. Ain't that enough to pay for letting my nigger alone?"

And old Captain Taylor give the word to turn Jordan loose, and they rid on down de road.

That's one reason my stepdaddy never did leave old Master's place, and I stayed on dere till I was grown and had children.

The Yankees come through past our place three-four times, and one time they had a big battle jest a mile and a half away at Parker's Crossroads.

I was in de field hoeing, and I remember I hadn't watered the cows we had hid way down in de woods, so I started down to water them when I first heard de shooting.

We had de stock hid down in de woods and all de corn and stuff hid too, 'cause the Yankees and the Sesesh had been riding through quite a lot, and either one take anything they needed iffen they found it.

First I hear something way off say "Br-r-rump!" Then again, and again. Then something sound like popcorn beginning to pop real slow. Then it git faster and I start for de settlement and de big house.

All Master's folks was staying at de big house then, and couldn't git back to town 'count of de soldiers, so they all put on they good clothes, with de hoop skirts and little sunshades and the lace pantaloons and got in the buggy to go see de battle!

They rid off and it wasn't long till all the niggers was following behind. We all got to a hill 'bout a half a mile from the crossroads and stopped when we couldn't see nothing but thick smoke all over de whole place.

We could see men on horses come in and out of de smoke, going this way and that way, and then some Yankees on horses broke through de woods right close to us and scattered off down through de field. One of de white officers rid up close and yelled at us and took off his hat, but I couldn't hear nothing he said.

Then he rid on and catch up with his men. They had stopped and was turning off to one side. He looked back and waved his hat again for us to git away from that, and jest then he clapped his hand to his belly and fell off his hoss.

Our white folks turned their buggy round and made it for home and no mistake! The niggers wasn't fur behind neither!

They fit on back toward our plantation, and some of the fighting was inside it at one corner. For three-four days after that they was burying soldiers 'round there, and some of de graves was on our old place.

Long time afterwards people come and moved all them to other graveyards at Shiloh and Corinth and other places. They was about a hundred killed all around there.

After de War I married Molly Timberlake and we lived on there 'til 1902, when we come to Indian Territory at Haskell. They wasn't no Haskell there then, and I helped to build dat town, doing carpenter work and the like.

We had two boys, Bill and Jim Dick, and eight daughters, Effie, Ida, Etta, Eva, Jessie, Tommie, Bennie and Timmie. Her real name is Timberlake after her mammy. They all went to school and graduated in the high schools.

My wife has been dead about ten years.

Oklahoma Writers' Project
Ex-Slaves
10-13-37
[Date stamp: NOV 5 1937]

CHANEY RICHARDSON
Age 90 years
Fort Gibson, Okla.

I was born in the old Caney settlement southeast of Tahlequah on the banks of Caney Creek. Off to the north we could see the big old ridge of Sugar Mountain when the sun shine on him first thing in the morning when we all getting up.

I didn't know nothing else but some kind of war until I was a grown woman, because when I first can remember my old Master, Charley Rogers, was always on the lookout for somebody or other he was lined up against in the big feud.

My master and all the rest of the folks was Cherokees, and they'd been killing each other off in the feud ever since long before I was borned, and jest because old Master have a big farm and three-four families of Negroes them other Cherokees keep on pestering his stuff all the time. Us children was always afeared to go any place less'n some of the grown folks was along.

We didn't know what we was a-feared of, but we heard the Master and Mistress keep talking 'bout "another Party killing" and we stuck close to the place.

Old Mistress' name was Nancy Rogers, but I was a orphan after I was a big girl and I called her "Aunt" and "Mamma" like I did when I was little. You see my own mammy was the house woman and I was raised in the house, and I heard the little children call old mistress "mamma" and so I did too. She never did make me stop.

My pappy and mammy and us children lived in a one-room log cabin close to the creek bank and jest a little piece from old Master's house.

My pappy's name was Joe Tucker and my mammy's name was Ruth Tucker. They belonged to a man named Tucker before I was born and he sold them to Master Charley Rogers and he just let them go on by the same name if they wanted to, because last name didn't mean nothing to a slave anyways. The folks jest called my pappy "Charley Rogers' boy Joe."

I already had two sisters, Mary and Mandy, when I was born, and purty soon I had a baby brother, Louis. Mammy worked at the Big House and took me along every day. When I was a little bigger I would help hold the hank when she done the spinning and old Mistress done a lot of the weaving and some knitting. She jest set by the window and knit most all of the time.

When we weave the cloth we had a big loom out on the gallery, and Miss Nancy tell us how to do it.

Mammy eat at our own cabin, and we had lots of game meat and fish the boys get in the Caney Creek. Mammy bring down deer meat and wild turkey sometimes, that the Indian boys git on Sugar Mountain.

Then we had corn bread, dried bean bread and green stuff out'n Master's patch. Mammy make the bean bread when we git short of corn meal and nobody going to the mill right away. She take and bile the beans and mash them up in some meal and that make it go a long ways.

The slaves didn't have no garden 'cause they work the old Master's garden and make enough for everybody to have some anyway.

When I was about 10 years old that feud got so bad the Indians was always talking about getting their horses and cattle killed and their slaves harmed. I was too little to know how bad it was until one morning my own mammy went off somewhere down the road to git some stuff to dye cloth and she didn't come back.

Lots of the young Indian bucks on both sides of the feud would ride around the woods at night, and old Master got powerful oneasy about my mammy and had all the neighbors and slaves out looking for her, but nobody find her.

It was about a week later that two Indian men rid up and ast old master wasn't his gal Ruth gone. He says yes, and they take one of the slaves along with a wagon to show where they seen her.

They find her in some bushes where she'd been getting bark to set the dyes, and she been dead all the time. Somebody done hit her in the head with a club and shot her through and through with a bullet too. She was so swole up they couldn't lift her up and jest had to make a deep hole right along side of her and roll her in it she was so bad mortified.

Old Master nearly go crazy he was so mad, and the young Cherokee men ride the woods every night for about a month, but they never catch on to who done it.

I think old Master sell the children or give them out to somebody then, because I never see my sisters and brother for a long time after the Civil War, and for me, I have to go live with a new mistress that was a Cherokee neighbor. Her name was Hannah Ross, and she raised me until I was grown.

I was her home girl, and she and me done a lot of spinning and weaving too. I helped the cook and carried water and milked. I carried the water in a home-made pegging set on my head. Them peggings was kind of buckets made out of staves set around a bottom and didn't have no handle.

I can remember weaving with Miss Hannah Ross. She would weave a strip of white and one of yellow and one of brown to make it pretty. She had a reel that would pop every time it got to a half skein so she would know to stop and fill it up again. We used copperas and some kind of bark she bought at the store to dye with. It was cotton clothes winter and summer for the slaves, too, I'll tell you.

When the Civil War come along we seen lots of white soldiers in them brown butternut suits all over the place, and about all the Indian men was in it too. Old master Charley Rogers' boy Charley went along too. Then pretty soon—it seem like about a year—a lot of the Cherokee men come back home and say they not going back to the War with that General Cooper and some of them go off the Federal side because the captain go to the Federal side too.

Somebody come along and tell me my own pappy have to go in the war and I think they say he on the Copper side, and then after while Miss Hannah tell me he git kilt over in Arkansas.

I was so grieved all the time I don't remember much what went on, but I know pretty soon my Cherokee folks had all the stuff they had et up by the soldiers and they was jest a few wagons and mules left.

176

All the slaves was piled in together and some of the grown ones walking, and they took us way down across the big river and kept us in the bottoms a long time until the War was over.

We lived in a kind of a camp, but I was too little to know where they got the grub to feed us with. Most all the Negro men was off somewhere in the War.

Then one day they had to bust up the camp and some Federal soldiers go with us and we all start back home. We git to a place where all the houses is burned down and I ask what is that place. Miss Hannah say: "Skullyville, child. That's where they had part of the War."

All the slaves was set out when we git to Fort Gibson, and the soldiers say we all free now. They give us grub and clothes to the Negroes at that place. It wasn't no town but a fort place and a patch of big trees.

Miss Hannah take me to her place and I work there until I was grown. I didn't git any money that I seen, but I got a good place to stay.

Pretty soon I married Ran Lovely and we lived in a double log house here at Fort Gibson. Then my second husband was Henry Richardson, but he's been dead for years, too. We had six children, but they all dead but one.

I didn't want slavery to be over with, mostly because we had the War I reckon. All that trouble made me the loss of my mammy and pappy, and I was always treated good when I was a slave. When it was over I had rather be at home like I was. None of the Cherokees ever whipped us, and my mistress give me some mighty fine rules to live by to git along in this world, too.

The Cherokee didn't have no jail for Negroes and no jail for themselves either. If a man done a crime he come back to take his punishment without being locked up.

None of the Negroes ran away when I was a child that I know of. We all had plenty to eat. The Negroes didn't have no school and so I can't read and write, but they did have a school after the War, I hear. But we had a church made out of a brush arbor and we would sing good songs in Cherokee sometimes.

I always got Sunday off to play, and at night I could go git a piece of sugar or something to eat before I went to bed and Mistress didn't care.

We played bread-and-butter and the boys played hide the switch. The one found the switch got to whip the one he wanted to.

When I got sick they give me some kind of tea from weeds, and if I et too many roasting ears and swole up they biled gourds and give me the liquor off'n them to make me throw up.

I've been a good church-goer all my life until I git too feeble, and I still understand and talk Cherokee language and love to hear songs and parts of the Bible in it because it make me think about the time I was a little girl before my mammy and pappy leave me.

Oklahoma Writers' Project
Ex-Slaves
[Date stamp: AUG 16 1937]

RED RICHARDSON
Age 75 yrs.
Oklahoma City, Oklahoma

I was born July 21, 1862, at Grimes County, Texas. Smith Richardson was my father's name, and Eliza Richardson my mother's. My father came from Virginia. My mother she was born in Texas.

We lived in so many places round there I can't tell jest what, but we lived in a log house most of the time. We slept on the flo' on pallets on one quilt. We ate cornbread, beans, vegetables, and got to drink plenty milk. We ate rabbits, fish, possums and such as that but we didn't get no chicken. I don't have no fav'rite food, I don't guess.

We wore shirts, long shirts slit up the side. I didn't know what pants was until I was 14. In Grimes County it ain't even cold these days, and I never wore no shoes. I married in a suit made of broad cloth. It had a tail on the coat.

Master Ben Hadley, and Mistress Minnie Hadley, they had three sons: Josh, Henry and Charley. Didn't have no overseer. We had to call all white folks, poor or rich, Mr. Master and Mistress. Master Hadley owned 'bout 2,000 acres. He had a big number of slaves. They used to wake 'em up early in the mornings by ringing a large bell. They said they used to whip 'em, drive 'em, and sell 'em away from their chillun,—I'd hear my old folks talk about it. Say they wasn't no such a thing as going to jail. The master stood good for anything his nigger done. If the master's nigger killed 'im another nigger, the old master stood good.

They never had no schools for the Negro chillun. I can't remember the date of the first school—its in a book someplace—but anyway I went to one of the first schools that was established for the education of Negro chillun.

You know Mr. Negro always was a church man, but he don't mean nothing. I don't have no fav'rite spiritual. All of them's good ones. Whenever they'd baptise they'd sing:

"Harp From the Tune the Domeful Sound."

Which starts like this:

"Come live in man and view this ground

where we must sho'ly lie."

I'm a member of Tabernacle Baptist Church myself, and I think all people should be religious 'cause Jesus died for us all.

The patrollers used to run after me but I'd jump 'em. They used to have a permit to go from one plantation to another. You had to go to old master and say, "I want to go to such and such a place." And if you had a permit they didn't bother you. The pateroller would stop you and say, "Where you going? You got a permit to go to such and such a place?" You'd say, yes suh, and show that pass. Den he wouldn't bother you and iffen he did old master would git on 'em.

When 10 o'clock come which was bed time the slaves would go to their cabins and some of 'em would go stealing chickens, hogs, steal sweet potatoes, and cook and eat 'em. Jest git in to all kind of devilment.

Old master would give 'em Sadday afternoon off, and they'd have them Sadday night breakdowns. We played a few games such as marbles, mumble peg, and cards—jest anything to pass off the time. Heahs one of the games we'd play an' I sho did like it too:

She is my sweetheart as I stand,

Come and stand beside of me,

Kiss her sweet and;

Hug her near.

On Christmas they'd make egg nog, drink whiskey and kiss their girls.

Some wore charms to ward off the devil, but I don't believe in such. I do believe in voodoo like this: People can put propositions up to you and fool you. Don't believe in ghost. Tried to see 'em but I never could.

Old master didn't turn my father loose and tell 'em we was free. They didn't turn us loose 'til they got the second threat from President Lincoln. Good old Lincoln; they wasn't nothing like 'im. Booker T. Washington was one of the finest Negro Educators in the world, but old Jefferson Davis was against the cullud man.

I think since slavery is all over, it has been a benefit to the cullud man. He's got more freedom now.

Oklahoma Writer's Project
Ex-Slaves

BETTY ROBERTSON
Age 93 yrs.
Fort Gibson, Oklahoma

I was born close to Webber's Falls, in the Canadian District of the Cherokee Nation, in the same year that my pappy was blowed up and killed in the big boat accident that killed my old Master.

I never did see my daddy excepting when I was a baby and I only know what my mammy told me about him. He come from across the water when he was a little boy, and was grown when old Master Joseph Vann bought him, so he never did learn to talk much Cherokee. My mammy was a Cherokee slave, and talked it good. My husband was a Cherokee born negro, too, and when he got mad he forgit all the English he knowed.

Old Master Joe had a mighty big farm and several families of negroes, and he was a powerful rich man. Pappy's name was Kalet Vann, and mammy's name was Sally. My brothers was name Sone and Frank. I had one brother and one sister sold when I was little and I don't remember the names. My other sisters was Polly, Ruth and Liddie. I had to work in the kitchen when I was a gal, and they was ten or twelve children smaller than me for me to look after, too. Sometime Young Master Joe and the other boys give me a piece of money and say I worked for it, and I reckon I did for I have to cook five or six times a day. Some of the Master's family was always going down to the river and back, and every time they come in I have to fix something to eat. Old Mistress had a good cookin' stove, but most Cherokees had only a big fireplace and pot hooks. We had meat, bread, rice, potatoes and plenty of fish and chicken. The spring time give us plenty of green corn and beans too. I couldn't buy anything in slavery time, so I jest give the piece of money to the Vann children. I got all the clothes I need from old Mistress, and in winter I had high top shoes with brass caps on the toe. In the summer I wear them on Sunday, too. I wore loom cloth clothes, dyed in copperas what the old negro women and the old Cherokee women made.

The slaves had a pretty easy time I think. Young Master Vann never very hard on us and he never whupped us, and old Mistress was a widow woman and a good Christian and always kind. I sure did love her. Maybe old Master Joe Vann was harder, I don't know, but that was before my time. Young Master never whip his slaves, but if they don't mind good he sell them off sometimes. He sold one of my brothers and one sister because they kept running off. They wasn't very big either, but one day two Cherokees rode up and talked a long time, then young Master came to the cabin and said they were sold because mammy couldn't make them mind him. They got on the horses behind the men and went off.

Old Master Joe had a big steam boat he called the Lucy Walker, and he run it up and down the Arkansas and the Mississippi and the Ohio river, old Mistress say. He went clean to Louisville, Kentucky, and back. My pappy was a kind of a boss of the negroes that run the boat, and they all belong to old Master Joe. Some had been in a big run-away and had been brung back, and wasn't so good, so he keep them on the boat all the time mostly. Mistress say old Master and my pappy on the boat somewhere close to Louisville and the boiler bust and tear the boat up. Some niggers say my pappy kept hollering, "Run it to the bank! Run it to the bank!" but it sunk and him and old Master died.

Old Master Joe was a big man in the Cherokees, I hear, and was good to his negroes before I was born. My pappy run away one time, four or five years before I was born, mammy tell me, and at that time a whole lot of Cherokee slaves run off at once. They got over in the Creek country and stood off the Cherokee officers that went to git them, but pretty soon they give up and come home. Mammy say they was lots of excitement on old Master's place and all the negroes mighty scared, but he didn't sell my pappy off. He jest kept him and he was a good negro after that. He had to work on the boat, though, and never got to come home but once in a long while.

Young Master Joe let us have singing and be baptized if we want to, but I wasn't baptized till after the War. But we couldn't learn to read or have a book, and the Cherokee folks was afraid to tell us about the letters and figgers because they have a law you go to jail and a big fine if you show a slave about the letters.

When the War come they have a big battle away west of us, but I never see any battles. Lots of soldiers around all the time though.

One day young Master come to the cabins and say we all free and can't stay there less'n we want to go on working for him just like we'd been, for our feed and clothes. Mammy got a wagon and we traveled around a few days and go to Fort Gibson. When we git to Fort Gibson they was a lot of negroes there, and they had a camp meeting and I was baptized. It was in the Grand River close to the ford, and winter time. Snow on the ground and the water was muddy and all full of pieces of ice. The place was all woods, and the Cherokees and the soldiers all come down to see the baptizing.

We settled down a little ways above Fort Gibson. Mammy had the wagon and two oxen, and we worked a good size patch there until she died, and then I git married to Cal Robertson to have somebody to take care of me. Cal Robertson was eighty-nine years old when I married him forty years ago, right on this porch. I had on my old clothes for the wedding, and I aint had any good clothes since I was a little slave girl. Then I had clean warm clothes and I had to keep them clean, too!

I got my allotment as a Cherokee Freedman, and so did Cal, but we lived here at this place because we was too old to work the land ourselves. In slavery time the Cherokee negroes do like anybody else when they is a death—jest listen to a chapter in the Bible and all cry. We had a good song I remember. It was "Don't Call the Roll, Jesus, Because I'm Coming Home." The only song I remember from the soldiers was: "Hang Jeff Davis to a Sour Apple Tree", and I remember that because they said he used to be at Fort Gibson one time. I don't know what he done after that.

I don't know about Robert Lee, but I know about Lee's Creek.

I been a good Christian ever since I was baptized, but I keep a little charm here on my neck anyways, to keep me from having the nose bleed. Its got a buckeye and a lead bullet in it. I had a silver dime on it, too, for a long time, but I took it off and got me a box of snuff. I'm glad the War's over and I am free to meet God like anybody else, and my grandchildren can learn to read and write.

Oklahoma Writers' Project
Ex-slaves
[Date stamp: AUG 18 1937]

HARRIET ROBINSON
Age 95 yrs.
500 Block N. Fonshill
Oklahoma City, Oklahoma.

I was born September 1, 1842, in Bastrop, Texas, on Colorado River. My pappy was named Harvey Wheeler and my mammy was named Carolina Sims. My brothers and sisters was named Alex, Taylor, Mary, Cicero, Tennessee, Sarah, Jeff, Ella and Nora. We lived in cedar log houses with dirt floors and double chimneys, and doors hung on wooden hinges. One side of our beds was bored in the walls and had one leg on the other. Them white folks give each nigger family a blanket in winter.

I nussed 3 white chillun, Lulu, Helen Augusta, and Lola Sims. I done this before that War that set us free. We kids use to make extra money by toting gravel in our aprons. They'd give us dimes and silver nickles.

Our clothes was wool and cotton mixed. We had red rustic shoes, soles one-half inch thick. They'd go a-whick a-whack. The mens had pants wid one seam and a right-hand pocket. Boys wore shirts.

We ate hominy, mush, grits and pone bread for the most part. Many of them ate out of one tray with wooden spoons. All vittles for field hands was fixed together.

Women broke in mules throwed 'em down and roped 'em. They'd do it better'n men. While mammy made some hominy one day both my foots was scalded and when they clipped them blisters, they jest put some cotton round them and catched all dat yellow water and made me a yellow dress out of it. This was 'way back yonder in slavery, before the War.

Whenever white folks had a baby born den all de old niggers had to come thoo the room and the master would be over 'hind the bed and he'd say, "Here's a new little mistress or master you got to work for." You had to say, "Yessuh Master" and bow real low or the overseer would crack you. Them was slavery days, dog days.

I remember in slavery time we had stages. Them devilish things had jest as many wrecks as cars do today. Only thing, we jest didn't have as many.

My mammy belonged to Master Colonel Sam Sims and his old mean wife Julia. My pappy belonged to Master Meke Smith and his good wife Harriett. She was sho' a good woman. I was named after her. Master Sam and Master Meke was partners. Ever year them rich men would send so many wagons to New Mexico for different things. It took 6 months to go and come.

Slaves was punished by whip and starving. Decker was sho' a mean slave-holder. He lived close to us. Master Sam didn't never whip me, but Miss Julia whipped me every day in the mawning. During the war she beat us so terrible. She say, "Your master's out fighting and losing blood trying to save you from them Yankees, so you kin git your'n here." Miss Julia would take me by my ears and butt my head against the wall. She wanted to whip my mother, but old Master told her, naw sir. When his father done give my mammy to Master Sam, he told him not to beat her, and iffen he got to whar he jest had to, jest bring her back and place her in his yard from whar he got her.

White folks didn't 'low you to read or write. Them what did know come from Virginny. Mistress Julia used to drill her chillun in spelling any words. At every word them chillun missed, she gived me a lick 'cross the head for it. Meanest woman I ever seen in my whole life.

This skin I got now, it ain't my first skin. That was burnt off when I was a little child. Mistress used to have a fire made on the fireplace and she made me scour the brass round it and my skin jest blistered. I jest had to keep pulling it off'n me.

We didn't had no church, though my pappy was a preacher. He preached in the quarters. Our baptizing song was "On Jordan's Stormy Bank I stand" and "Hark From The Tomb." Now all dat was before the War. We had all our funerals at the graveyard. Everybody, chillun and all picked up a clod of dirt and throwed in on top the coffin to help fill up the grave.

Taling 'bout niggers running away, didn't my step-pappy run away? Didn't my uncle Gabe run away? The frost would jest bite they toes most nigh off too, whiles they was gone. They put Uncle Isom (my step-pappy) in jail and while's he was in there he killed a white guardman. Then they put in the paper, "A nigger to kill", and our Master seen it and bought him. He was a double-strengthed man, he was so strong. He'd run off so help you God. They had the blood hounds after him once and he caught the hound what was leading and beat the rest of the dogs. The white folks run up on him before he knowed it and made them dogs eat his ear plumb out. But don't you know he got away anyhow. One morning I was sweeping out the hall in the big house and somebody come a-knocking on the front door and I goes to the door. There was Uncle Isom wid rags all on his head. He said, "Tell ole master heah I am." I goes to Master's door and says, "Master Colonel Sam, Uncle Isom said heah he am." He say, "Go 'round to the kitchen and tell black mammy to give you breakfast." When he was thoo' eating they give him 300 lashes and, bless my soul, he run off again.

When we went to a party the nigger fiddlers would play a chune dat went lak this:

I fooled Ole Mastah 7 years

Fooled the overseer three;

Hand me down my banjo

And I'll tickle your bel-lee.

We had the same doctors the white folks had and we wore asafetida and garlic and onions to keep from taking all them ailments.

I 'member the battle being fit. The white folks buried all the jewelry and silver and all the gold in the Blue Ridge Mountains, in Orange, Texas. Master made all us niggers come together and git ready to leave 'cause the Yankees was coming. We took a steamer. Now this was in slavery time, sho' 'nuff slavery. Then we got on a steamship and pulled out to Galveston. Then he told the captain to feed we niggers. We was on the bay, not the ocean. We left Galveston and went on trains for Houston.

One, my sister Liza, was mulatto and Master Colonel Sims' son had 3 chillun by her. We never seen her no more after her last child was born. I found out though that she was in Canada.

After the War, Master Colonel Sims went to git the mail and so he call Daniel Ivory, the overseer, and say to him, "Go round to all the quarters and tell all the niggers to come up, I got a paper to read to 'em. They're free now, so you kin git you another job, 'cause I ain't got no more niggers which is my own." Niggers come up from the cabins nappy-headed, jest lak they gwine to the field. Master Colonel Sims say, "Caroline (that's my mammy), you is free as me. Pa said bring you back and I'se gwina do jest that. So you go on and work and I'll pay you and your three oldest chillun $10.00 a month a head and $4.00 fer Harriet," that's me, and then he turned to the rest and say "Now all you'uns will receive $10.00 a head till the crops is laid by." Don't you know before he got half way thoo', over half them niggers was gone.

Them Klu Klux Klans come and ask for water with the false stomachs and make lak they was drinking three bucketsful. They done some terrible things, but God seen it all and marked it down.

We didn't had no law, we had "bureau." Why, in them days iffen somebody stole anything from you, they had to pay you and not the Law. Now they done turned that round and you don't git nothing.

One day whiles master was gone hunting, Mistress Julia told her brother to give Miss Harriett (me) a free whipping. She was a nigger killer. Master Colonel Sam come home and he said, "You infernal sons o' bitches don't you know there is 300 Yankees camped out here and iffen they knowed you'd whipped this nigger the way you done done, they'd kill all us. Iffen they find it out, I'll kill all you all." Old rich devils, I'm here, but they is gone.

God choosed Abraham Lincoln to free us. It took one of them to free us so's they couldn't say nothing.

Doing one 'lection they sung:

Clark et the watermelon

J. D. Giddings et the vine!

Clark gone to Congress

An' J. D. Giddings left behind.

They hung Jeff Davis up a sour apple tree. They say he was a president, but he wasn't, he was a big senator man.

Booker T. Washington was all right in his way, I guess, but Bruce and Fred Douglass, or big mens jest sold us back to the white folks.

I married Haywood Telford and had 13 head of chillun by him. My oldest daughter is the mammy of 14. All my chillun but four done gone to heaven before me.

I jined the church in Chapel Hill, Texas. I am born of the Spirit of God sho' nuff. I played with him seven years and would go right on dancing at Christmas time. Now I got religion. Everybody oughta live right, though you won't have no friends iffen you do.

Our overseer was a poor man. Had us up before day and lak-a-that. He was paid to be the head of punishment. I jest didn't like to think of them old slavery days, dogs' days.

Oklahoma Writers' Project
Ex-Slaves
[HW: (photo)]
[Date stamp: AUG 16 1937]

KATIE ROWE
Age 88 yrs.
Tulsa, Oklahoma

I can set on de gallery, whar de sunlight shine bright, and sew a powerful fine seam when my grandchillun wants a special purty dress for de school doings, but I ain't worth much for nothing else I reckon.

These same old eyes seen powerful lot of tribulations in my time, and when I shets 'em now I can see lots of l'il chillun jest lak my grandchillun, toting hoes bigger dan dey is, and dey pore little black hands and legs bleeding whar dey scratched by de brambledy weeds, and whar dey got whuppings 'cause dey didn't git out all de work de overseer set out for 'em.

I was one of dem little slave gals my own self, and I never seen nothing but work and tribulations till I was a grown up woman, jest about.

De niggers had hard traveling on de plantation whar I was born and raised, 'cause old Master live in town and jest had de overseer on de place, but iffen he had lived out dar hisself I speck it been as bad, 'cause he was a hard driver his own self.

He git biling mad when de Yankees have dat big battle at Pea Ridge and scatter de 'Federates all down through our country all bleeding and tied up and hungry, and he jest mount on his hoss and ride out to de plantation whar we all hoeing corn.

He ride up and tell old man Saunders—dat de overseer—to bunch us all up round de lead row man—dat my own uncle Sandy—and den he tell us de law!

"You niggers been seeing de 'Federate soldiers coming by here looking purty raggedy and hurt and wore out," he say, "but dat no sign dey licked!

"Dem Yankees ain't gwine git dis fur, but iffen dey do you all ain't gwine git free by 'em, 'cause I gwine free you befo' dat. When dey git here dey going find you already free, 'cause I gwine line you up on de bank of Bois d' Arc Creek and free you wid my shotgun! Anybody miss jest one lick wid de hoe, or one step in de line, or one clap of dat bell, or one toot of de horn, and he gwine be free and talking to de debil long befo' he ever see a pair of blue britches!"

Dat de way he talk to us, and dat de way he act wid us all de time.

We live in de log quarters on de plantation, not far from Washington, Arkansas, close to Bois d' Arc Creek, in de edge of de Little River bottom.

Old Master's name was Dr. Isaac Jones, and he live in de town, whar he keep four, five house niggers, but he have about 200 on de plantation, big and little, and old man Saunders oversee 'em at de time of de War. Old Mistress name was Betty, and she had a daughter name Betty about grown, and then they was three boys, Tom, Bryan, and Bob, but they was too young to go to de War. I never did see 'em but once or twice 'til after de War.

Old Master didn't go to de War, 'cause he was a doctor and de onliest one left in Washington, and purty soon he was dead anyhow.

Next fall after he ride out and tell us dat he gwine shoot us befo' he let us free he come out to see how his steam gin doing. De gin box was a little old thing 'bout as big as a bedstead, wid a long belt running through de side of de gin house out to de engine and boiler in de yard. De boiler burn cord wood, and it have a little crack in it whar de nigger ginner been trying to fix it.

Old Master come out, hopping mad 'cause de gin shet down, and ast de ginner, old Brown, what de matter. Old Brown say de boiler weak and it liable to bust, but old Master jump down off'n his hoss and go 'round to de boiler and say, "Cuss fire to your black heart! Dat boiler all right! Throw on some cordwood, cuss fire to your heart!"

Old Brown start to de wood pile grumbling to hisself and old Master stoop down to look at de boiler again, and it blow right up and him standing right dar!

Old Master was blowed all to pieces, and dey jest find little bitsy chunks of his clothes and parts of him to bury.

De wood pile blow down, and old Brown land way off in de woods, but he wasn't killed.

Two wagons of cotton blowed over, and de mules run away, and all de niggers was scared nearly to death 'cause we knowed de overseer gwine be a lot worse, now dat old Master gone.

Before de War when Master was a young man de slaves didn't have it so hard, my mammy tell me. Her name was Fanny and her old mammy name was Nanny. Grandma Nanny was alive during de War yet.

How she come in de Jones family was dis way: old Mistress was jest a little girl, and her older brother bought Nanny and give her to her. I think his name was Little John, anyways we called him Master Little John. He drawed up a paper what say dat Nanny allus belong to Miss Betty and all de chillun Nanny ever have belong to her, too, and nobody can't take 'em for a debt and things like dat. When Miss Betty marry, old Master he can't sell Nanny or any of her chillun neither.

Dat paper hold good too, and grandmammy tell me about one time it hold good and keep my own mammy on de place.

Grandmammy say mammy was jest a little gal and was playing out in de road wid three, four other little chillun when a white man and old Master rid up. The white man had a paper about some kind of a debt, and old Master say take his pick of de nigger chillun and give him back de paper.

Jest as Grandmammy go to de cabin door and hear him say dat de man git off his hoss and pick up my mammy and put her up in front of him and start to ride off down de road.

Pretty soon Mr. Little John come riding up and say something to old Master, and see grandmammy standing in de yard screaming and crying. He jest job de spur in his hoss and go kiting off down de road after dat white man.

Mammy say he ketch up wid him jest as he git to Bois d' Arc Creek and start to wade de hoss across. Mr. Little John holler to him to come back wid dat little nigger 'cause de paper don't kiver dat child, 'cause she old Mistress' own child, and when de man jest ride on, Mr. Little John throw his big old long hoss-pistol down on him and make him come back.

De man hopping mad, but he have to give over my mammy and take one de other chillun on de debt paper.

Old Master allus kind of techy 'bout old Mistress having niggers he can't trade or sell, and one day he have his whole family and some more white folks out at de plantation. He showing 'em all de quarters when we all come in from de field in de evening, and he call all de niggers up to let de folks see 'em.

He make grandmammy and mammy and me stand to one side and den he say to the other niggers, "Dese niggers belong to my wife but you belong to me, and I'm de only one you is to call Master.

"Dis is Tom, and Bryan, and Bob, and Miss Betty, and you is to call 'em dat, and don't you ever call one of 'em Young Master or Young Mistress, cuss fire to your black hearts!" All de other white folks look kind of funny, and old Mistress look 'shamed of old Master.

My own pappy was in dat bunch, too. His name was Frank, and after de War he took de name of Frank Henderson, 'cause he was born under dat name, but I allus went by Jones, de name I was born under.

Long about de middle of de War, after old Master was killed, de soldiers begin coming 'round de place and camping. Dey was Southern soldiers and dey say dey have to take de mules and most de corn to git along on. Jest go in de barns and cribs and take anything dey want, and us niggers didn't have no sweet 'taters nor Irish 'taters to eat on when dey gone neither.

One bunch come and stay in de woods across de road from de overseer's house, and dey was all on hosses. Dey lead de hosses down to Bois d' Arc Creek every morning at daylight and late every evening to git water. When we going to de field and when we coming in we allus see dem leading big bunches of hosses.

Dey bugle go jest 'bout de time our old horn blow in de morning and when we come in dey eating supper, and we smell it and sho' git hungry!

Before old Master died he sold off a whole lot of hosses and cattle, and some niggers too. He had de sales on de plantation, and white men from around dar come to bid, and some traders come. He had a big stump whar he made de niggers stand while dey was being sold, and de men and boys had to strip off to de waist to show dey muscle and iffen dey had any scars or hurt places, but de women and gals didn't have to strip to de waist.

De white men come up and look in de slave's mouth jest lak he was a mule or a hoss.

After old Master go, de overseer hold one sale, but mostly he jest trade wid de traders what come by. He make de niggers git on de stump, through. De traders all had big bunches of slaves and dey have 'em all strung out in a line going down de road. Some had wagons and de chillun could ride, but not many. Dey didn't chain or tie 'em 'cause dey didn't have no place dey could run to anyway.

I seen chillun sold off and de mammy not sold, and, sometimes de mammy sold and a little baby kept on de place and give to another woman to raise. Dem white folks didn't care nothing 'bout how de slaves grieved when dey tore up a family.

Old man Saunders was de hardest overseer of anybody. He would git mad and give a whipping some time and de slave wouldn't even know what it was about.

My uncle Sandy was de lead row nigger, and he was a good nigger and never would tech a drap of likker. One night some de niggers git hold of some likker somehow, and dey leave de jug half full on de step of Sandy's cabin. Next morning old man Saunders come out in de field so mad he was pale.

He jest go to de lead row and tell Sandy to go wid him, and start toward de woods along Bois d' Arc Creek wid Sandy follering behind. De overseer always carry a big heavy stick, but we didn't know he was so mad, and dey jest went off in de woods.

Purty soon we hear Sandy hollering and we know old overseer pouring in on, den de overseer come back by his self and go on up to de house.

Come late evening he come and see what we done in de day's work, and go back to de quarters wid us all. Then he git to mammy's cabin, whar grandmammy live too, he say to grandmammy, "I sent Sandy down in de woods to hunt a hoss, he gwine come in hungry purty soon. You better make him a extra hoe cake," and he kind of laugh and go on to his house.

Jest soon as he gone we all tell grandmammy we think he got a whipping, and sho' nuff he didn't come in.

De next day some white boys find uncle Sandy whar dat overseer done killed him and throwed him in a little pond, and dey never done nothing to old man Saunders at all!

When he go to whip a nigger he make him strip to de waist, and he take a cat-o-nine tails and bring de blisters, and den bust de blisters wid a wide strap of leather fastened to a stick handle. I seen de blood running out'n many a back, all de way from de neck to de waist!

189

Many de time a nigger git blistered and cut up so dat we have to git a sheet and grease it wid lard and wrap 'em up in it, and dey have to wear a greasy cloth wrapped around dey body under de shirt for three-four days after dey git a big whipping!

Later on in de War de Yankees come in all around us and camp, and de overseer git sweet as honey in de comb! Nobody git a whipping all de time de Yankees dar!

Dey come and took all de meat and corn and 'taters dey want too, and dey tell us, "Why don't you poor darkeys take all de meat and molasses you want? You made it and it's your's much as anybody's!" But we know dey soon be gone, and den we git a whipping iffen we do. Some niggers run off and went wid de Yankees, but dey had to work jest as hard for dem, and dey didn't eat so good and often wid de soldiers.

I never forget de day we was set free!

Dat morning we all go to de cotton field early, and den a house nigger come out from old Mistress on a hoss and say she want de overseer to come into town, and he leave and go in. After while de old horn blow up at de overseer's house, and we all stop and listen, 'cause it de wrong time of day for de horn.

We start chopping again, and dar go de horn again.

De lead row nigger holler "Hold up!" And we all stop again. "We better go on in. Dat our horn," he holler at de head nigger, and de head nigger think so too, but he say he afraid we catch de devil from de overseer iffen we quit widout him dar, and de lead row man say maybe he back from town and blowing de horn hisself, so we line up and go in.

When we git to de quarters we see all de old ones and de chillun up in de overseer's yard, so we go on up dar. De overseer setting on de end of de gallery wid a paper in his hand, and when we all come up he say come and stand close to de gallery. Den he call off everybody's name and see we all dar.

Setting on de gallery in a hide-bottom chair was a man we never see before. He had on a big broad black hat lak de Yankees wore but it din't have no yaller string on it lak most de Yankees had, and he was in store clothes dat wasn't homespun or jeans, and dey was black. His hair was plumb gray and so was his beard, and it come way down here on his chest, but he didn't look lak he was very old, 'cause his face was kind of fleshy and healthy looking. I think we all been sold off in a bunch, and I notice some kind of smiling, and I think they sho' glad of it.

De man say, "You darkies know what day dis is?" He talk kind, and smile.

We all don't know of course, and we jest stand dar and grin. Pretty soon he ask again and de head man say, No, we don't know.

"Well dis de fourth day of June, and dis is 1865, and I want you all to 'member de date, 'cause you allus going 'member de day. Today you is free, Jest lak I is, and Mr. Saunders and your Mistress and all us white people," de man say.

190

"I come to tell you", he say, "and I wants to be sho' you all understand, 'cause you don't have to git up and go by de horn no more. You is your own bosses now, and you don't have to have no passes to go and come."

We never did have no passes, nohow, but we knowed lots of other niggers on other plantations got 'em.

"I wants to bless you and hope you always is happy, and tell you got all de right and lief [TR: sic] dat any white people got", de man say, and den he git on his hoss and ride off.

We all jest watch him go on down de road, and den we go up to Mr. Saunders and ask him what he want us to do. He jest grunt and say do lak we dam please, he reckon, but git off dat place to do it, less'n any of us wants to stay and make de crop for half of what we make.

None of us know whar to go, so we all stay, and he split up de fields and show us which part we got to work in, and we go on lak we was, and make de crop and git it in, but dey ain't no more horn after dat day. Some de niggers lazy and don't git in de field early, and dey git it took away from 'em, but dey plead around and git it back and work better de rest of dat year.

But we all gits fooled on dat first go-out! When de crop all in we don't git half! Old Mistress sick in town, and de overseer was still on de place and he charge us half de crop for de quarters and de mules and tools and grub!

Den he leave, and we gits another white man, and he sets up a book, and give us half de next year, and take out for what we use up, but we all got something left over after dat first go-out.

Old Mistress never git well after she lose all her niggers, and one day de white boss tell us she jest drap over dead setting in her chair, and we know her heart jest broke.

Next year de chillun sell off most de place and we scatter off, and I and mammy go into Little Rock and do work in de town. Grandmammy done dead.

I git married to John White in Little Rock, but he died and we didn't have no chillun. Den in four, five years I marry Billy Rowe. He was a Cherokee citizen and he had belonged to a Cherokee name Dave Rowe, and lived east of Tahlequah before de War. We married in Little Rock, but he had land in de Cherokee Nation, and we come to east of Tahlequah and lived 'til he died, and den I come to Tulsa to live wid my youngest daughter.

Billy Rowe and me had three chillun, Ellie, John, and Lula. Lula married a Thomas, and it's her I lives with.

Lots of old people lak me say dat dey was happy in slavery, and dat dey had de worst tribulations after freedom, but I knows dey didn't have no white master and overseer lak we all had on our place. Dey both dead now I reckon, and dey no use talking 'bout de dead, but I know I been gone long ago iffen dat white man Saunder didn't lose his hold on me.

It was de fourth day of June in 1865 I begins to live, and I gwine take de picture of dat old man in de big black hat and long whiskers, setting on de gallery and talking kind to us, clean into my grave wid me.

No, bless God, I ain't never seen no more black boys bleeding all up and down de back under a cat o' nine tails, and I never go by no cabin and hear no poor nigger groaning, all wrapped up in a lardy sheet no more!

I hear my chillun read about General Lee, and I know he was a good man, I didn't know nothing about him den, but I know now he wasn't fighting for dat kind of white folks.

Maybe dey dat kind still yet, but dey don't show it up no more, and I got lots of white friends too. All my chillun and grandchillun been to school, and dey git along good, and I know we living in a better world, what dey ain't nobody "cussing fire to my black heart!"

I sho' thank de good Lawd I got to see it.

Oklahoma Writers' Project
Ex-Slaves

MORRIS SHEPPARD
Age 85 yrs.
Fort Gibson, Okla.

Old Master tell me I was borned in November 1852, at de old home place about five miles east of Webber's Falls, mebbe kind of northeast, not far from de east bank of de Illinois River.

Master's name was Joe Sheppard, and he was a Cherokee Indian. Tall and slim and handsome. He had black eyes and mustache but his hair was iron gray, and everybody liked him because he was so good-natured and kind.

I don't remember old Mistress' name. My mammy was a Crossland negro before she come to belong to Master Joe and marry my pappy, and I think she come wid old Mistress and belong to her. Old Mistress was small and mighty pretty too, and she was only half Cherokee. She inherit about half a dozen slaves, and say dey was her own and old Master can't sell one unless she give him leave to do it.

Dey only had two families of slaves wid about twenty in all, and dey only worked about fifty acres, so we sure did work every foot of it good. We git three or four crops of different things out of dat farm every year, and something growing on dat place winter and summer.

Pappy's name was Caesar Sheppard and Mammy's name was Easter. Dey was both raised 'round Webber's Falls somewhere. I had two brothers, Silas and George, dat belong to Mr. George Holt in Webber's Falls town. I got a pass and went to see dem sometimes, and dey was both treated mighty fine.

The Big House was a double log wid a big hall and a stone chimney but no porches, wid two rooms at each end, one top side of de other. I thought it was mighty big and fine.

Us slaves lived in log cabins dat only had one room and no windows so we kept de doors open most of de time. We had home-made wooden beds wid rope springs, and de little ones slept on trundle beds dat was home made too.

At night dem trundles was jest all over de floor, and in de morning we shove dem back under de big beds to git dem out'n de way. No nails in none of dem nor in de chairs and tables. Nails cost big money and old Master's blacksmith wouldn't make none 'cepting a few for old Master now and den, so we used wooden dowels to put things together.

They was so many of us for dat little field we never did have to work hard. Up at five o'clock and back in sometimes about de middle of de evening, long before sundown, unless they was a crop to git in before it rain or something like dat.

When crop was laid by de slaves jest work 'round at dis and dat and keep tol'able busy. I never did have much of a job, jest tending de calves mostly. We had about twenty calves and I would take dem out and graze 'em while some grown-up negro was grazing de cows so as to keep de cows milk. I had me a good blaze-faced horse for dat.

One time old Master and another man come and took some calves off and Pappy say old Master taking dem off to sell. I didn't know what "sell" meant and I ast Pappy, "Is he going to bring 'em back when he git through selling them?" I never did see no money neither, until time of de War or a little before.

Master Joe was sure a good provider, and we always had plenty of corn pone, sow belly and greens, sweet potatoes, cow peas and cane molasses. We even had brown sugar and cane molasses most of de time before de War. Sometimes coffee, too.

De clothes wasn't no worry neither. Everything we had was made by my folks. My aunt done de carding and spinning and my mammy done de weaving and cutting and sewing, and my pappy could make cowhide shoes wid wooden pegs. Dey was for bad winter only.

Old Master bought de cotton in Ft. Smith because he didn't raise no cotton, but he had a few sheep and we had wool-mix for winter.

Everything was stripedy 'cause Mammy like to make it fancy. She dye wid copperas and walnut and wild indigo and things like dat and make pretty cloth. I wore a stripedy shirt till I was about eleven years old, and den one day while we was down in de Choctaw Country old Mistress see me and nearly fall off'n her horse! She holler, "Easter, you go right now and make dat big buck of a boy some britches!"

193

We never put on de shoes until about late November when de frost begin to hit regular and split our feet up, and den when it git good and cold and de crop all gathered in anyways, they is nothing to do 'cepting hog killing and a lot of wood chopping, and you don't git cold doing dem two things.

De hog killing mean we gits lots of spare-ribs and chitlings, and somebody always git sick eating too much of dat fresh pork. I always pick a whole passel of muskatines for old Master and he make up sour wine, and dat helps out when we git the bowel complaint from eating dat fresh pork.

If somebody bad sick he git de doctor right quick, and he don't let no negroes mess around wid no poultices and teas and sech things like cupping-horns neither!

Us Cherokee slaves seen lots of green corn shootings and de like of dat, but we never had no games of our own. We was too tired when we come in to play any games. We had to have a pass to go any place to have singing or praying, and den they was always a bunch of patrollers around to watch everything we done. Dey would come up in a bunch of about nine men on horses, and look at all our passes, and if a negro didn't have no pass dey wore him out good and made him go home. Dey didn't let us have much enjoyment.

Right after de War de Cherokees that had been wid the South kind of pestered the freedmen some, but I was so small dey never bothered me; jest de grown ones. Old Master and Mistress kept on asking me did de night riders persecute me any but dey never did. Dey told me some of dem was bad on negroes but I never did see none of dem night riding like some said dey did.

Old Master had some kind of business in Fort Smith, I think, 'cause he used to ride in to dat town 'bout every day on his horse. He would start at de crack of daylight and not git home till way after dark. When he get home he call my uncle in and ask about what we done all day and tell him what we better do de next day. My uncle Joe was de slave boss and he tell us what de Master say do.

When dat Civil War come along I was a pretty big boy and I 'remember it good as anybody. Uncle Joe tell us all to lay low and work hard and nobody bother us, and he would look after us. He sure stood good with de Cherokee neighbors we had, and dey all liked him. There was Mr. Jim Collins, and Mr. Bell, and Mr. Dave Franklin, and Mr. Jim Sutton and Mr. Blackburn that lived around close to us and dey all had slaves. Dey was all wid the South, but dey was a lot of dem Pin Indians all up on de Illinois River and dey was wid de North and dey taken it out on de slave owners a lot before de War and during it too.

Dey would come in de night and hamstring de horses and maybe set fire to de barn, and two of 'em named Joab Scarrel and Tom Starr killed my pappy one night just before de War broke out.

I don't know what dey done it for, only to be mean, and I guess they was drunk.

Them Pins was after Master all de time for a while at de first of de War, and he was afraid to ride into Fort Smith much. Dey come to de house one time when he was gone to Fort Smith and us children told dem he was at Honey Springs, but they knowed better and when he got home he said somebody shot at him and bushwhacked him all the way from Wilson's Rock to dem Wildhorse Mountains, but he run his horse like de devil was setting on his tail and dey never did hit him. He never seen them neither. We told him 'bout de Pins coming for him and he just laughed.

When de War come old Master seen he was going into trouble and he sold off most of de slaves. In de second year of de War he sold my mammy and my aunt dat was Uncle Joe's wife and my two brothers and my little sister. Mammy went to a mean old man named Peper Goodman and he took her off down de river, and pretty soon Mistress tell me she died 'cause she can't stand de rough treatment.

When Mammy went old Mistress took me to de Big House to help her, and she was kind to me like I was part of her own family. I never forget when they sold off some more negroes at de same time, too, and put dem all in a pen for de trader to come and look at.

He never come until the next day, so dey had to sleep in dat pen in a pile like hogs.

It wasn't my Master done dat. He done already sold 'em to a man and it was dat man was waiting for de trader. It made my Master mad, but dey didn't belong to him no more and he couldn't say nothing.

The man put dem on a block and sold 'em to a man dat had come in on a steamboat, and he took dem off on it when de freshet come down and de boat could go back to Fort Smith. It was tied up at de dock at Webber's Falls about a week and we went down and talked to my aunt and brothers and sister. De brothers was Sam and Eli. Old Mistress cried jest like any of de rest of us when de boat pull out with dem on it.

Pretty soon all de young Cherokee menfolks all gone off to de War, and de Pins was riding 'round all de time, and it aint safe to be in dat part around Webber's Falls, so old Master take us all to Fort Smith where they was a lot of Confederate soldiers.

We camp at dat place a while and old Mistress stay in de town wid some kinfolks. Den old Master get three wagons and ox teams and take us all way down on Red River in de Choctaw Nation.

We went by Webber's Falls and filled de wagons. We left de furniture and only took grub and tools and bedding and clothes, 'cause they wasn't very big wagons and was only single-yoke.

We went on a place in de Red River bottoms close to Shawneetown and not far from de place where all de wagons crossed over to go into Texas. We was at dat place two years and made two little crops.

One night a runaway negro come across from Texas and he had de blood hounds after him. His britches was all muddy and tore where de hounds had cut him up in de legs when he clumb a tree in de bottoms. He come to our house and Mistress said for us negroes to give him something to eat and we did.

Then up come de man from Texas with de hounds and wid him was young Mr. Joe Vann and my uncle that belong to young Joe. Dey called young Mr. Joe "Little Joe Vann" even after he was grown on account of when he was a little boy before his pappy was killed. His pappy was old Captain "Rich Joe" Vann, and he been dead ever since long before de War. My uncle belong to old Captain Joe nearly all his life.

Mistress try to get de man to tell her who de negro belong to so she can buy him, but de man say he can't sell him and he take him on back to Texas wid a chain around his two ankles. Dat was one poor negro dat never got away to de North, and I was sorry for him 'cause I know he must have had a mean master, but none of us Sheppard negroes, I mean the grown ones, tried to git away.

I never seen any fighting in de War, but I seen soldiers in de South army doing a lot of blacksmithing 'long side de road one day. Dey was fixing wagons and shoeing horses.

After de War was over, old Master tell me I am free but he will look out after me 'cause I am just a little negro and I aint got no sense. I know he is right, too.

Well, I go ahead and make me a crop of corn all by myself and then I don't know what to do wid it. I was afraid I would get cheated out of it 'cause I can't figure and read, so I tell old Master about it and he bought it off'n me.

We never had no school in slavery and it was agin the law for anybody to even show a negro de letters and figures, so no Cherokee slave could read.

We all come back to de old place and find de negro cabins and barns burned down and de fences all gone and de field in crab grass and cockleburrs. But de Big House aint hurt 'cepting it need a new roof. De furniture is all gone, and some said de soldiers burned it up for firewood. Some officers stayed in de house for a while and tore everything up or took it off.

Master give me over to de National Freedmen's Bureau and I was bound out to a Cherokee woman name Lizzie McGee. Then one day one of my uncles named Wash Sheppard come and tried to git me to go live wid him. He say he wanted to git de family all together agin.

He had run off after he was sold and joined de North army and discharged at Fort Scott in Kansas, and he said lots of freedmen was living close to each other up by Coffeyville in de Coo-ee-scoo-ee District.

I wouldn't go, so he sent Isaac and Joe Vann dat had been two of old Captain Joe's negroes to talk to me. Isaac had been Young Joe's driver, and he told me all about how rich Master Joe was and how he would look after us negroes. Dey kept after me 'bout a year, but I didn't go anyways.

But later on I got a freedman's allotment up in dat part close to Coffeyville, and I lived in Coffeyville a while but I didn't like it in Kansas.

I lost my land trying to live honest and pay my debts. I raised eleven children just on de sweat of my hands and none of dem ever tasted anything dat was stole.

When I left Mrs. McGee's I worked about three years for Mr. Sterling Scott and Mr. Roddy Reese. Mr. Reese had a big flock of peafowls dat had belonged to Mr. Scott and I had to take care of dem.

Whitefolks, I would have to tromp seven miles to Mr. Scott's house two or three times a week to bring back some old peafowl dat had got out and gone back to de old place!

Poor old Master and Mistress only lived a few years after de War. Master went plumb blind after he move back to Webber's Falls and so he move up on de Illinois River 'bout three miles from de Arkansas, and there old Mistress take de white swelling and die and den he die pretty soon. I went to see dem lots of times and they was always glad to see me.

I would stay around about a week and help 'em, and dey would try to git me to take something but I never would. Dey didn't have much and couldn't make anymore and dem so old. Old Mistress had inherited some property from her pappy and dey had de slave money and when dey turned everything into good money after de War dat stuff only come to about six thousand dollars in good money, she told me. Dat just about lasted 'em through until dey died, I reckon.

By and by I married Nancy Hildebrand what lived on Greenleaf Creek, 'bout four miles northwest of Gore. She had belonged to Joe Hildebrand and he was kin to old Steve Hildebrand dat owned de mill on Flint Creek up in de Going Snake District. She was raised up at dat mill, but she was borned in Tennessee before dey come out to de Nation. Her master was white but he had married into de Nation and so she got a freedmen's allotment too. She had some land close to Catoosa and some down on Greenleaf Creek.

We was married at my home in Coffeyville, and she bore me eleven children and then went on to her reward. A long time ago I came to live wid my daughter Emma here at dis place, but my wife just died last year. She was eighty three.

I reckon I wasn't cut out on de church pattern, but I raised my children right. We never had no church in slavery, and no schooling, and you had better not be caught wid a book in your hand even, so I never did go to church hardly any.

Wife belong to de church and all de children too, and I think all should look after saving their souls so as to drive de nail in, and den go about de earth spreading kindness and hoeing de row clean so as to clinch dat nail and make dem safe for Glory.

Of course I hear about Abraham Lincoln and he was a great man, but I was told mostly by my children when dey come home from school about him. I always think of my old Master as de one dat freed me, and anyways Abraham Lincoln and none of his North people didn't look after me and buy my crop right after I was free like old Master did. Dat was de time dat was de hardest and everything was dark and confusion.

Oklahoma Writers' Project
Ex-Slaves
[Date stamp: AUG 16 1937]

ANDREW SIMMS
Age 80
Sapulpa, Okla.

My parents come over on a slave ship from Africa about twenty year before I was born on the William Driver plantation down in Florida. My folks didn't know each other in Africa but my old Mammy told me she was captured by Negro slave hunters over there and brought to some coast town where the white buyers took her and carried her to America.

She was kinder a young gal then and was sold to some white folks when the boat landed here. Dunno who they was. The same thing happen to my pappy. Must have been about the same time from the way they tells it. Maybe they was on the [HW: same] boat, I dunno.

They was traded around and then mammy was sold to William Driver. The plantation was down in Florida. Another white folks had a plantation close by. Mister Simms was the owner. Bill Simms—that's the name pappy kept after the War.

Somehow or other mammy and pappy meets 'round the place and the first thing happens they is in love. That's what mammy say. And the next thing happen is me. They didn't get married. The Master's say it is alright for them to have a baby. They never gets married, even after the War. Just jumped the broomstick and goes to living with somebody else I reckon.

Then when I was four year old along come the War and Master Driver takes up his slaves and leaves the Florida country and goes way out to Texas. Mammy goes along, I goes along, all the children goes along. I don't remember nothing about the trip but I hears mammy talk about it when I gets older.

Texas, that was the place, down near Fairfield. That's where I learn to do the chores. But the work was easy for the Master was kind as old Mammy herself and he never give me no hard jobs that would wear me down. All the slaves on our place was treated good. All the time. They didn't whip. The Master feeds all the slaves on good clean foods and lean meats so's they be strong and healthy.

Master Driver had four children, Mary, Julia, Frank and George. Every one of them children kind and good just the old Master. They was never mean and could I find some of 'em now hard times would leave me on the run! They'd help this old man get catched up on his eating!

Makes me think of the old song we use to sing:

Don't mind working from Sun to Sun,

Iffen you give me my dinner—

When the dinner time comes!

Nowadays I gets me something to eat when I can catch it. The trouble is sometimes I don't catch! But that ain't telling about the slave days.

In them times it was mostly the overseers and the drivers who was the mean ones. They caused all the misery. There was other whitefolks caused troubles too. Sneak around where there was lots of the black children on the plantation and steal them. Take them poor children away off and sell them.

There wasn't any Sunday Schooling. There was no place to learn to read and write—no big brick schools like they is now. The old Master say we can teach ourselves but we can't do it. Old Elam Bowman owned the place next door to Mister Driver. If he catch his slaves toying with the pencil, why, he cut off one of their fingers. Then I reckon they lost interest in education and get their mind back on the hoe and plow like he say for them to do.

I didn't see no fighting during of the War. If they was any Yankees soldiering around the country I don't remember nothing of it.

Long time after the War is over, about 1885, I meets a gal named Angeline. We courts pretty fast and gets married. The wedding was a sure enough affair with the preacher saying the words just like the whitefolks marriage. We is sure married.

The best thing we do after that is raise us a family. One of them old fashioned families. Big 'uns! Seventeen children does we have and twelve of them still living. Wants to know they names? I ain't never forgets a one! There was Lucy, Bill, Ebbie, Cora, Minnie, George, Frank, Kizzie, Necie, Andrew, Joe, Sammie, David, Fannie, Jacob, Bob and Myrtle.

All good children. Just like their old pappy who's tried to care for 'em just like the old Master takes care of their old daddy when he was a boy on that plantation down Texas way.

When the age comes on a man I reckon religion gets kind of meanful. Thinks about it more'n when he's young and busy in the fields. I believes in the Bible and what it says to do. Some of the Colored folks takes to the voodoo. I don't believe in it. Neither does I believe in the fortune telling or charms. I aims to live by the Bible and leave the rabbit foots alone!

Oklahoma Writers' Project
Ex-Slaves
10-19-38
718 words

LIZA SMITH
Age 91
Muskogee, Oklahoma

Both my mammy and pappy was brought from Africa on a slave boat and sold on de Richmond (Va.) slave market. What year dey come over I don't know. My mammy was Jane Mason, belonging to Frank Mason; pappy was Frank Smith, belonging to a master wid de same name. I mean, my pappy took his Master's name, and den after my folks married mammy took de name of Smith, but she stayed on wid de Masons and never did belong to my pappy's master. Den, after Frank Mason took all his slaves out of de Virginia county, mammy met up wid another man, Ben Humphries, and married him.

In Richmond, dat's where I was born, 'bout 1847, de Master said; and dat make me more dan 90-year old dis good year. I had two brothers named Webb and Norman, a half-brother Charley, and two half-sisters, Mealey and Ann. Me, I was born a slave and so was my son. His father, Toney, was one of de Mason slave boys; de Master said I was 'bout 13-year old when de boy was born.

Frank Mason was a young man when de War started, living wid his mother. Dey had lots of slaves, maybe a hundred, and dey always try to take good care of 'em; even after de War was over he worried 'bout trying to get us settled so's we wouldn't starve. De Master had overseer, but dere was no whuppings.

All de way from Richmond to a place dey call Waco, Texas, we traveled by ox-wagon and boats, and den de Master figures we all be better off over in Arkansas and goes to Pine Bluff.

What wid all de running 'round de slaves was kept clean and always wid plenty to eat and good clothes to wear. De Master was a plenty rich man and done what his mother, Mrs. Betsy Mason, told him when we all left de Big Mansion, way back dere in Richmond. De Mistress said, "Frank, you watch over dem Negroes cause dey's good men and women; keep dem clean!" Dat's what he done, up until we was freed, and den times was so hard nobody wanted us many Negroes around, and de work was scarce, too. Hard times! Folks don't know what hard times is.

When a Negro get sick de master would send out for herbs and roots. Den one of de slaves who knew how to cook and mix 'em up for medicine use would give de doses. All de men and women wore charms, something like beads, and if dey was any good or not I don't know, but we didn't have no bad diseases like after dey set us free.

I was at Pine Bluff when de Yankees was shooting all over de place. De fighting got so hot we all had to leave; dat's the way it was all de time for us during de War—running away to some place or de next place, and we was all glad when it stopped and we could settle down in a place.

We was back at Waco when de peace come, but Master Frank was away from home when dat happen. It was on a Sunday when he got back and called all de slaves up in de yard and counted all of dem, young and old.

The first thing he said was, "You men and women is all free! I'm going back to my own mammy in old Virginia, but I ain't going back until all de old people is settled in cabins and de young folks fix up wid tents!"

Den he kinder stopped talking. Seem now like he was too excited to talk, or maybe he was feeling bad and worried 'bout what he going to do wid all of us. Pretty soon he said, "You men and women, can't none of you tell anybody I ain't always been a good master. Old folks, have I ever treated you mean?" He asked. Everybody shout, "No, sir!" And Master Frank smiled; den he told us he was going 'round and find places for us to live.

He went to see Jim Tinsley, who owned some slaves, about keeping us. Tinsley said he had cabins and could fix up tents for extra ones, if his own Negroes was willing to share up with us. Dat was the way it worked out. We stayed on dere for a while, but times was so hard we finally get dirty and ragged like all de Tinsley Negroes. But Master Frank figure he done the best he could for us.

After he go back to Virginia we never hear no more of him, but every day I still pray if he has any folks in Richmond dey will find me someway before I die. Is dere someway I could find dem, you s'pose?

Oklahoma Writers' Project
Ex-Slaves
[Date Stamp: Aug 12 1937]

LOU SMITH
Age 83 yrs.
Platter, Okla.

Sho', I remembers de slavery days! I was a little gal but I can tell you lots of things about dem days. My job was nussing de younguns. I took keer of them from daylight to dark. I'd have to sing them to sleep too. I'd sing:

"By-lo Baby Bunting

Daddy's gone a-hunting

To get a rabbit skin

To wrap Baby Bunting in."

Sometimes I'd sing:

"Rock-a-bye baby, in a tree top

When de wind blows your cradle'll rock.

When de bough breaks de crad'll fall

Down comes baby cradle'n all."

My father was Jackson Longacre and he was born in Mississippi. My mother, Caroline, was born in South Carolina. Both of them was born slaves. My father belonged to Huriah Longacre. He had a big plantation and lots of niggers. He put up a lot of his slaves as security on a debt and he took sick and died so they put them all on de block and sold them. My father and his mother (my grandma) was sold together. My old Mistress bought my grandmother and old Mistress' sister bought my grandma's sister. These white women agreed that they would never go off so far that the two slave women couldn't see each other. They allus kept this promise. A Mr. Covington offered old Master $700 for me when I was about ten years old, but he wouldn't sell me. He didn't need to for he was rich as cream and my, how good he was to us.

Young Master married Miss Jo Arnold and old Master sent me and my mother over to live with them. I was small when I was took out of old man McWilliams' yard. It was his wife that bought my grandmother and my father. My mother's folks had always belonged to his family. They all moved to Texas and we all lived there until after the surrender.

Miss Jo wasn't a good Mistress and mother and me wasn't happy. When young Master was there he made her treat us good but when he was gone she made our lives a misery to us. She was what we called a "low-brow." She never had been used to slaves and she treated us like dogs. She said us kids didn't need to wear any clothes and one day she told us we could jest take'em off as it cost too much to clothe us. I was jest a little child but I knowed I oughten to go without my clothes. We wore little enough as it was. In summer we just wore one garment, a sort of slip without any sleeves. Well, anyway she made me take off my clothes and I just crept off and cried. Purty soon young Master come home.

He wanted to know what on earth I was doing without my dress on. I told him, and my goodness, but he raised the roof. He told her if she didn't treat us better he was going to take us back to old Master. I never did have any more good times 'cepting when I'd get to go to visit at old Master's. None of our family could be sold and that was why old Master just loaned us to young Master. When old Master died, dey put all our names in a hat and all the chilluns draw out a name. This was done to 'vide us niggers satisfactory. Young Master drawed my mother's name and they all agreed that I should go with her, so back we went to Miss Jo. She wouldn't feed us niggers. She'd make me set in a corner like a little dog. I got so hungry and howled so loud they had to feed me. When the surrender come, I was eleven years old, and they told us we was free. I ran off and hid in the plum orchard and I said over'n over, "I'se free, I'se free; I ain't never going back to Miss Jo." My mother come out and got me and in a few days my father came and lived with us. He worked for young Master and the crops was divided with him. Miss Jo died and we lived on there. My mother took over the charge of the house and the chillun for young Master and we was all purty happy after that.

They was a white man come into our settlement and bought a plantation and some slaves. My, but he treated them bad. He owned a boy about fifteen years old. One day he sent him on a errand. On the way home he got off his mule and set down in the shade of a tree to rest. He fell asleep and the mule went home. When he woke up he was scared to go home and he stayed out in de woods for several days. Finally they caught him and took him home and his master beat him nearly to death. He then dug a hole and put him in it and piled corn shucks all around him. This nearly killed him 'cause his body was cut up so with the whip. One of the niggers slipped off and went to the jining plantation and told about the way the boy was being treated and a bunch of white men came over and made him take the child out and doctor his wounds. This man lived there about ten years and he was so mean to his slaves 'til all the white men round who owned niggers finally went to him and told him they would just give him so long to sell out and leave. They made him sell his slaves to people there in the community, and he went back north.

My mother told me that he owned a woman who was the mother of several chillun and when her babies would get about a year or two of age he'd sell them and it would break her heart. She never got to keep them. When her fourth baby was born and was about two months old she just studied all the time about how she would have to give it up and one day she said, "I just decided I'm not going to let old Master sell this baby; he just ain't going to do it." She got up and give it something out of a bottle and purty soon it was dead. 'Course didn't nobody tell on her or he'd of beat her nearly to death. There wasn't many folks that was mean to their slaves.

Old Master's boys played with the nigger boys all the time. They'd go swimming, fishing and hunting together. One of his boys name was Robert but everybody called him Bud. They all would catch rabbits and mark them and turn them loose. One day a boy come along with a rabbit he had caught in a trap. Old Master's boy noticed that it had Bud's mark on it and they made him turn it loose.

Old Master was his own overseer, but my daddy was the overlooker. He was purty hard on them too, as they had to work just like they never got tired. The women had to do housework, spinning, sewing and work in the fields too. My mother was housewoman and she could keep herself looking nice. My, she went around with her hair and clothes all Jenny-Lynned-up all the time until we went to live with Miss Jo. She took all the spirit out of poor mother and me too.

I remember she allus kept our cabin as clean and neat as a pin. When other niggers come to visit her they would say, "My you are Buckry Niggers (meaning we tried to live like white folks)."

I love to think of when we lived with old Master. We had a good time. Our cabin was nice and had a chimbley in it. Mother would cook and serve our breakfast at home every morning and dinner and supper on Sundays. We'd have biscuit every Sunday morning for our breakfast. That was something to look forward to.

We all went to church every Sunday. We would go to the white folks church in the morning and to our church in the evening. Bill McWilliams, old Master's oldest boy, didn't take much stock in church. He owned a nigger named Bird, who preached for us. Bill said, "Bird, you can't preach, you can't read, how on earth can you get a text out of the Bible when you can't even read? How'n hell can a man preach that don't know nothing?" Bird told him the Lord had called him to preach and he'd put the things in his mouth that he ought to say. One night Bill went to church and Bird preached the hair-raisingest sermon you ever heard. Bill told him all right to go and preach, and he gave Bird a horse and set him free to go anywhere he wanted to and preach.

Old Master and old Mistress lived in grand style. Bob was the driver of their carriage. My, but he was always slick and shiny. He'd set up in front with his white shirt and black clothes. He looked like a black martin (bird) with a white breast. The nurse set in the back with the chillun. Old Master and Mistress set together in the front seat.

Old Master and Mistress would come down to the quarters to eat Christmas dinners sometimes and also birthday dinners. It was sho' a big day when they done that. They'd eat first, and the niggers would sing and dance to entertain them. Old Master would walk 'round through the quarters talking to the ones that was sick or too old to work. He was awful kind. I never knowed him to whip much. Once he whipped a woman for stealing. She and mother had to spin and weave. She couldn't or didn't work as fast as Ma and wouldn't have as much to show for her days work. She'd steal hanks of Ma's thread so she couldn't do more work than she did. She'd also steal old Master's tobacco. He caught up with her and whipped her.

I never saw any niggers on the block but I remember once they had a sale in town and I seen them pass our house in gangs, the little ones in wagons and others walking. I've seen slaves who run away from their masters and they'd have to work in the field with a big ball and chain on their leg. They'd hoe out to the end of the chain and then drag it up a piece and hoe on to the end of the row.

Times was awful hard during the War. We actually suffered for some salt. We'd go to the smoke house where meat had been salted down for years, dig a hole in the ground and fill it with water. After it would stand for a while we'd dip the water up carefully and strain it and cook our food in it. We parched corn and meal for coffee. We used syrup for sugar. Some folks parched okra for coffee. When the War was over you'd see men, women and chillun walk out of their cabins with a bundle under their arms. All going by in droves, just going nowhere in particular. My mother and father didn't join them; we stayed on at the plantation. I run off and got married when I was twenty. Ma never did want me to get married. My husband died five years ago. I never had no chillun.

I reckon I'm a mite superstitious. If a man comes to your house first on New Years you will have good luck; if a woman is your first visitor you'll have bad luck. When I was a young woman I knowed I'd be left alone in my old age. I seen it in my sleep. I dreamed I spit every tooth in my head right out in my hand and something tell me I would be a widow. That's a bad thing to dream about, losing your teeth.

Once my sister was at my house. She had a little baby and we was setting on the porch. They was a big pine tree in front of the house, and we seen something that looked like a big bird light in the tree. She begun to cry and say that's a sign my baby is going to die. Sho' nuff it just lived two weeks. Another time a big owl lit in a tree near a house and we heard it holler. The baby died that night. It was already sick, we's setting up with it.

I don't know where they's hants or not but I'se sho heard things I couldn't see.

We allus has made our own medicines. We used herbs and roots. If you'll take poke root and cut it in small pieces and string it and put it 'round a baby's neck it will cut teeth easy. A tea made out of dog fennel or corn shucks will cure chills and malaria. It'll make 'em throw up. We used to take button snake root, black snake root, chips of anvil iron and whiskey and make a tonic to cure consumption. It would cure it too.

Oklahoma Writers' Project
Ex-Slaves
10-13-37
[Date stamp: NOV 5 1937]

JAMES SOUTHALL
Age 82 years,
Oklahoma City, Okla.

I was born in Clarksville, Tenn. My father was Wesley and my mother was Hagar Southall. Our owner was Dr. John Southall, an old man. Father always belonged to him but he bought my mother when she was a young girl and raised her. She never knew anything 'bout her people but my father's mother lived with us in de quarter's at Master Southall's. Master John never sold any of his slaves.

We was known as "Free Niggers." Master said he didn't believe it was right to own human beings just because dey was black, and he freed all his slaves long before de War. He give 'em all freedom papers and told dem dat dey was as free as he was and could go anywhere dey wanted. Dey didn't have no where to go so we all stayed on wid him. It was nice though to know we could go where we pleased 'thout having to get a pass and could come back when we pleased even if we didn't take advantage of it.

He told his slaves dat dey could stay on at his farm but dey would have to work and make a living for deyselves and families. Old Master managed de farm and bought all de food and clothes for us all. Everybody had to work, but dey had a good time.

We had good clothes, plenty of food and good cabins. We had what was known as Georgia bedsteads. Dey was wooden bedsteads wid holes bored in de side pieces and in de foot and head-boards. Ropes was laced back and forth across and this took de place of both slats and springs. De ropes would git loose and we had what was called a "following-pin" to tighten 'em wid. We'd take a block of wood wid a notch in it and catch de rope and hold it till de following-pin could be driven in and den we'd twist de ropes tight again. We had grass or cotton beds and we slept good, too.

We had tin plates but no knives or forks so we et with our fingers. Old Master was a doctor and we had good attention when we was sick. We had no wish to take advantage of our freedom for we was a lot better off even than we is now and we knowed it. We never had to worry about anything.

De quarters was about a half mile from de "Big House" as we called Master John's house. It really wasn't such a big house as it had only four or five rooms in it. It was a common boxed house, painted white and wid a long gallery across de front. Maybe it was de gallery dat made it look so big to us. We liked to set on de steps at night and listen to Master John talk and to hear old Mistress and de girls sing. Sometimes we'd join in wid dem and fairly make de woods ring. Everybody thought dey was crazy to let us have so much freedom but dey wasn't nothing any of us black folks wouldn't a-done for that family.

He never employed any overseers as he done his own overseeing. He'd tell de older hands what he wanted done and dey would see it was done. We was never punished. Just iffen dey didn't work dey didn't have nothing to eat and wear and de hands what did work wouldn't divide wid 'em iffen dey didn't work. Old Master sho' was wise fer he knowed iffen we was ever set free dat we would have to work and he sure didn't bide no laziness in his hands. Dey got up 'bout four o'clock in de morning and was at work as soon as dey could see. Dey would work and sing as happy as you please.

We used to hear stories 'bout how slaves was punished but we never saw any of it. Dey would punish 'em by whupping 'em or by making 'em stand on one foot for a long time, tie 'em up by de thumbs as high as dey could reach and by making 'em do hard tasks and by going without food for two-three days.

Niggers was very religious and dey had church often. Dey would annoy de white folks wid shouting and singing and praying and dey would take cooking pots and put over dey mouths so de white folks couldn't hear 'em. Dey would dig holes in de ground too, and lie down when dey prayed.

Old Master let us have church in de homes. We had prayer-meeting every Wednesday night. All our cullud preachers could read de Bible. He let dem teach us how to read iffen we wanted to learn.

In de evening when we was through wid our work dey would gather at one of de cabins and visit and sing or dance. We'd pop corn, eat walnuts, peanuts, hickory nuts, and tell ghost stories. We didn't have any music instruments so de music we danced by wasn't so very good. Everybody sang and one or two would beat on tin pans or beat bones together.

Us boys played marbles. I got to be a professional. I could hit de middler ever time. We made a square and put a marble in each corner and one in de middle and got off several feet from de ring and shot at de marbles. Iffen you hit de middler you got de game. I could beat 'em all.

Old Master kept us through de War. We saw Yankee soldiers come through in droves lak Coxsey's Army. We wasn't afraid for ourselves but we was afraid dey would catch old Master or one of de boys when dey would come home on a furlough. We'd hep 'em git away and just swear dat dey hadn't been home a-tall.

After de war we stayed until old Master died. It broke us all up for we knowed we had lost de best friend dat we ever had or ever would have. He was a sort of father to all of us. Old Mistress went to live with her daughter and we started wandering 'round. Some folks from de North come down and made de cullud folks move on. I guess dey was afraid dat we'd hep our masters rebuild dey homes again. We lived in a sort of bondage for a long time.

De white folks in de South as well as de cullud folks lost de best friend dey had when Abe Lincoln was killed. He was God's man and it was a great loss when he died.

God created us all free and equal. Somewhere along de road we lost out.

Cullud folks would have been better off iffen dey had been left alone in Africa. We'd a-had better opportunities. We should have some compensation fer what we have suffered. Yes, we could be sent back and we'd like it if dey would help us to get started out again. Dat's where our forefathers come from.

I learned a long time ago dat dey was nothing to charms. How could a rabbit's foot bring me good luck? De Bible teaches me better'n dat. I believes in dreams though. I've seen de end of time in my dreams. Saw de great trouble we going through right now, years ago in a dream. It's clear in my mind how de world is coming to a end.

I believe all Christians should all join up together as dat makes 'em stronger. I believe in praying fer what we want and need. I'm a licensed preacher in de Baptist church. I've been a member for forty years but have just been a licensed preacher about ten years.

Oklahoma Writers' Project
Ex-Slaves

BEAUREGARD TENNEYSON
Age 87 yrs.
West Tulsa, Okla.

My mother and father just about stocked Jess Tenneyson's plantation with slaves. That's a fact. The old folks had one big family—twenty-three Children was the number. With the old folks that make twenty-five (there were only five more slaves), so I reckon they done mighty well by Master Jess.

The Master done well by them, too. Master Jess and Mistress Lula was Christian peoples. They raised their two sons, Henry and George, the same way.

There was so many of us children I don't remember all the names. Three of the boys was named after good southern gentlemen who soldiered in the War. Price, Lee and Beaugard. Beaugard is me. Proud of that name just like I'm proud of the Master's name.

My folks named Patrick and Harriett. Mother worked round the house And father was the field boss. They was close by the Master all the time.

The plantation was down in Craig County, Texas. Nine hundred acre it was. They raise everything, but mostly corn and cotton. Big times when come the harvest. Master fix up a cotton gin right on the place. It was an old-fashioned press. Six horses run it with two boys tromping down the cotton with their feets.

In the fall time was the best of all. Come cotton picking time, all the master from miles around send in their best pickers—and how they'd work, sometimes pick the whole crop in one day! The one who picked the most win a prize. Then come noon and the big feast, and at night come the dancing.

Something like that when the corn was ready. All the folks have the biggest time. Log rollings. Clearing the new ground for planting. Cutting the trees, burning the bresh, making ready for the plow. The best worker wins hisself a prize at these log rollings, too.

Them kind of good times makes me think of Christmas. Didn't have no Christmas tree, but they set up a long pine table in the house and that plank table was covered with presents and none of the Negroes was ever forgot on that day.

Master Jess didn't work his slaves like other white folks done. Wasn't no four o'clock wake-up horns and the field work started at seven o'clock. Quitting time was five o'clock—just about union hours nowadays. The Master believed in plenty of rest for the slaves and they work better that way, too.

One of my brother took care of the Master's horse while on the plantation. When the Master join in with rebels that horse went along. So did brother. Master need them both and my brother mighty pleased when he get to go.

When Master come back from the War and tell us that brother is dead, he said brother was the best boy in all the army.

The Tenneyson slaves wasn't bothered with patrollers, neither the Klan. The Master said we was all good Negroes—nobody going to bother a good Negro.

We was taught to work and have good manners. And to be honest. Just doing them three things will keep anybody out of trouble.

Oklahoma Writers' Project
Ex-Slaves

WILLIAM WALTERS
Age 85 yrs.
Tulsa, Oklahoma.

Mammy Ann (that was my mother) was owned by Mistress Betsy, and lived on the Bradford plantation in Relsford County, Tennessee, when I was born in 1852.

My daddy, Jim Walters, then lived in Nashville, where my mammy carried me when she ran away from the Mistress after the Rebs and Yanks started to fight. My daddy died in Nashville in 1875.

We were runaway slaves. The slipper-offers were often captured, but Mammy Ann and her little boy William (that's me) escaped the sharp eyes of the patrollers and found refuge with a family of northern symphatizers living in Nashville.

Nashville was a fort town, filled with trenches and barricades. Right across the road from where we stayed was a vacant block used by the Rebs as an emergency place for treating the wounded.

I remember the boom of cannons one whole day, and I heard the rumble of army wagons as they crossed through the town. But there was nothing to see as the fog of powder smoke became thicker with every blast of Sesesh cannon.

When the smoke fog cleared away I watched the wounded being carried to the clearing across the road—fighting men with arms shot off, legs gone, faces blood smeared—some of them just laying there cussing God and Man with their dying breath!

Those were awful times. Yet I have heard many of the older Negroes say the old days were better.

Such talk always seemed to me but an expression of sentiment for some good old master, or else the older Negroes were just too handicapped with ignorance to recognize the benefits of liberty or the opportunities of freedom.

But I've always been proud of my freedom, and proud of my old mother who faced death for her freedom and mine when she escaped from the Bradford plantation a long time before freedom came to the Negro race as a whole.

Oklahoma Writers' Project
Ex-Slaves
570 words
10-19-1938

MARY FRANCES WEBB
Grand daughter of Sarah Vest, aged 92, (deceased)
McAlester, Okla.

I've heard my grandmother tell a lot of her experiences during slavery. She remembered things well as she was a grown woman at the time of the War of the Rebellion.

Her home was at Sedalia, Mo., and her owner was Baxter West, a prominent farmer and politician. He was very kind and good to his slaves. He provided them with plenty of food and good clothes. He would go to town and buy six or eight bolts of cloth at a time and the women could pick out two dresses apiece off it. These would be their dresses for dressing up. They wove the cloth for their everyday clothes.

The men wore jeans suits in winter. He bought shoes for all his slaves, young and old. He had about twenty slaves counting the children.

My grandmother was a field hand. She plowed and hoed the crops in the summer and spring, and in the winter she sawed and cut cord wood just like a man. She said it didn't hurt her as she was as strong as an ox.

She could spin and weave and sew. She helped make all the cloth for their clothes and in the spring one of the jobs for the women was to weave hats for the men. They used oat-straw, grass, and cane which had been split and dried and soaked in hot water until it was pliant, and they wove it into hats. The women wore a cloth tied around their head.

They didn't have many matches so they always kept a log heap burning to keep a fire. It was a common thing for a neighbor to come in to borrow a coal of fire as their fire had died out.

On wash days all the neighbors would send several of their women to the creek to do the family wash. They all had a regular picnic of it as they would wash and spread the clothes on the bushes and low branches of the trees to dry. They would get to spend the day together.

They had no tubs or wash boards. They had a large flat block of wood and a wooden paddle. They'd spread the wet garment on the block, spread soap on it and paddle the garment till it was clean. They would rinse the clothes in the creek. Their soap was made from lye, dripped from ashes, and meat scraps.

The slaves had no lamps in their cabins. In winter they would pile wood on the fire in their fireplace and have the light from the fire.

The colored men went with their master to the army. They made regular soldiers and endured the same hardships that the white soldiers did. They told of one battle when so many men were killed that a little stream seemed to be running pure blood as the water was so bloody.

After the war the slaves returned home with their masters and some of the older ones stayed on with them and helped them to rebuild their farms. None of them seemed to think it strange that they had been fighting on the wrong side in the army as they were following their white folks.

Those who stayed with their old master were taught to read and write and were taught to handle their own business and to help themselves in every way possible to take their place in life.

Oklahoma Writers' Project
Ex-Slaves
10-14-37
[Date stamp: NOV 5 1937]

EASTER WELLS
Age 83
Colbert, Okla.

I was born in Arkansas, in 1854, but we moved to Texas in 1855. I've heard 'em tell about de trip to Texas. De grown folks rode in wagons and carts but de chaps all walked dat was big enuff. De men walked and toted their guns and hunted all de way. Dey had plenty of fresh game to eat.

My mother's name was Nellie Bell. I had one sister, Liza. I never saw my father; in fact, I never heard my mammy say anything about him and I don't guess I ever asked her anything about him for I never thought anything about not having a father. I guess he belonged to another family and when we moved away he was left behind and he didn't try to find us after de War.

My mammy and my sister and me belonged to young Master Jason Bell. We was his onliest slaves and as he wasn't married and lived at home wid his parents we was worked and bossed by his father, Cap'n William Bell and his wife, Miss Mary.

After we moved to Texas, old Master built a big double log house, weather-boarded on de inside and out. It was painted white. Dey was a long gallery clean across de front of de house and a big open hall between de two front rooms. Dey was three rooms on each side of de hall and a wide gallery across de back. De kitchen set back from de house and dey was a board walk leading to it. Vines was planted 'round de gallery and on each side of de walk in de summer time. De house was on a hill and set back from de big road about a quarter of a mile and dey was big oak and pine trees all 'round de yard. We had purty flowers, too.

We had good quarters. Dey was log cabins, but de logs was peeled and square-adzed and put together with white plaster and had shuttered windows and pine floors. Our furniture was home made but it was good and made our cabins comfortable.

Old Master give us our allowance of staple food and it had to run us, too. We could raise our own gardens and in dat way we had purty plenty to eat. Dey took good care of us sick or well and old Mistress was awful good to us.

My mammy was de cook. I remember old Master had some purty strict rules and one of 'em was iffen you burnt de bread you had to eat it. One day mammy burnt de bread. She was awful busy and forgot it and it burnt purty bad. She knowed dat old Master would be mad and she'd be punished so she got some grub and her bonnet and she lit out. She hid in de woods and cane brakes for two weeks and dey couldn't find her either. One of de women slipped food out to her. Finally she come home and old Master give her a whipping but he didn't hurt her none. He was glad to git her back. She told us dat she could'a slipped off to de North but she didn't want to leave us children. She was afraid young Master would be mad and sell us and we'd a-had a hard time so she come back. I don't know whether she ever burnt de bread any more or not.

Once one of de men got his 'lowance and he decided he'd have de meat all cooked at once so he come to our cabin and got mammy to cook it for him. She cooked it and he took it home. One day he was at work and a dog got in and et de meat all up. He didn't have much food for de rest of de week. He had to make out wid parched corn.

We all kept parched corn all de time and went 'round eating it. It was good to fill you up iffen you was hungry and was nourishing, too.

When de niggers cooked in dere own cabins dey put de food in a sort of tray or trough and everybody et together. Dey didn't have no dishes. We allus ate at de Big House as mammy had to do de cooking for de family.

I never had to work hard as old Master wanted us to grow up strong. He'd have mammy boil Jerusalem Oak and make a tea for us to drink to cure us of worms and we'd run races and get exercise so we would be healthy.

Old Mistress and old Master had three children. Dey was two children dead between Master Jason and Miss Jane. Dey was a little girl 'bout my age, named Arline. We played together all de time. We used to set on de steps at night and old Mistress would tell us about de stars. She'd tell us and show us de Big Dipper, Little Dipper, Milky Way, Ellen's Yard, Job's Coffin, and de Seven Sisters. I can show 'em to you and tell you all about 'em yet.

I scared Arline and made her fall and break her leg twice. One time we was on de porch after dark one night and I told her dat I heard something and I made like I could see it and she couldn't so she got scared and run and hung her toe in a crack and fell off de high porch and broke her leg. Another time while de War was going on we was dressed up in long dresses playing grown-ups. We had playhouses under some big castor-bean bushes. We climbed up on de fence and jest for fun I told her dat I seen some Yankees coming. She started to run and got tangled up in her long dress and fell and broke her leg again. It nigh broke my heart for I loved her and she loved me and she didn't tell on me either time. I used to visit her after she was married and we'd sure have a good visit talking 'bout de things we used to do. We was separated when we was about fifteen and didn't see [HW: each] other any more till we was both married and had children. I went to visit her at Bryant, Brazos County, Texas and I ain't seen her since. I don't know whether she is still living or not.

I 'members hearing a man say dat once he was a nigger trader. He'd buy and trade or sell 'em like they was stock. He become a Christian and never sold any more.

Our young Master went to de War and got wounded and come home and died. Old Master den took full charge of us and when de War ended he kept us because he said we didn't have no folks and he said as our owner was dead we wasn't free. Mother died about a year after de War, and some white folks took my sister but I was afraid to go. Old Master told me iffen I left him he would cut my ears off end I'd starve and I don't know what all he did tell me he'd do. I must a-been a fool but I was afraid to try it.

I had so much work to do and I never did git to go anywhere. I reckon he was afraid to let me go off de place for fear some one would tell me what a fool I was, so I never did git to go anywhere but had to work all de time. I was de only one to work and old Mistress and de girls never had done no work and didn't know much about it. I had a harder time den when we was slaves.

I got to wanting to see my sister so I made up my mind to run off. One of old Master's motherless nephews lived with him and I got him to go with me one night to the potato bank and I got me a lap full of potatoes to eat so I wouldn't starve like old Master said I would. Dis white boy went nearly to a house where some white folks lived. I went to de house and told 'em I wanted to go to where my sister was and dey let me stay fer a few days and sent me on to my sister.

I saw old Master lots of times after I run away but he wasn't mad at me. I heard him tell de white folks dat I lived wid dat he raised me and I sure wouldn't steal nor tell a lie. I used to steal brown sugar lumps when mammy would be cooking but he didn't know 'bout dat.

On holidays we used to allus have big dinners, 'specially on Christmas, and we allus had egg-nog.

We allus had hog-jowl and peas on New Years Day 'cause iffen you'd have dat on New Years Day you'd have good luck all de year.

Iffen you have money on New Years' Day you will have money all de year.

My husband, Lewis Wells, lived to be one-hundred and seven years old. He died five years ago. He could see witches, spirits and ghosts but I never could. Dere are a few things dat I've noticed and dey never fail.

Dogs howling and scritch owls hollering is allus a warning. My mother was sick and we didn't think she was much sick. A dog howled and howled right outside de house. Old Master say, "Nellie gonna die." Sure nuff she died dat night.

Another time a gentle old mule we had got after de children and run 'em to de house and den he lay down and wallow and wallow. One of our children was dead 'fore a week.

One of our neighbors say his dog been gone 'bout a week. He was walking and met de dog and it lay down and stretch out on de ground and measure a grave wid his body. He made him git up and he went home jest as fast as he could. When he got dere one of his children was dead.

Iffen my left eye quiver I know I'm gwineter cry and iffen both my eyes quiver I know I gwinter laugh till I cry. I don't like for my eyes to quiver.

We has allus made our own medicine. Iffen we hadn't we never could astood de chills and fevers. We made a tea out'n bitter weeds and bathed in it to cure malaria. We also made bread pills and soaked 'em in dis tea and swallowed 'em. After bathing in dis tea we'd go to bed and kiver up and sweat de malaria out.

Horse mint and palm of crystal (Castor-bean) and bullnettle root boiled together will make a cure fer swelling. Jest bathe de swollen part in dis hot tea.

Anvil dust and apple vinegar will cure dropsy. One tea cup of anvil dust to a quart of vinegar. Shake up well and bathe in it. It sure will cure de worse kind of a case.

God worked through Abraham Lincoln and he answered de prayers of dem dat was wearing de burden of slavery. We cullud folks all love and honor Abraham Lincoln's memory and don't you think we ought to?

I love to hear good singing. My favorite songs are: "Am I A Soldier Of The Cross", an "How Can I Live In Sin and Doubt My Savior's Love." I belongs to de Baptist church.

Oklahoma Writers' Project
Ex-Slaves
Revision of story sent in 8-13-37.

JOHN WHITE
Age 121 years
Sand Springs, Okla.

Of all my Mammy's children I am the first born and the longest living. The others all gone to join Mammy. She was named Mary White, the same name as her Mistress, the wife of my first master, James White.

About my pappy. I never hear his name and I never see him, not even when I was the least child around the old Master's place 'way back there in Georgia more'n one-hundred twenty years ago!

Mammy try to make it clear to me about my daddy. She married like the most of the slaves in them days.

He was a slave on another plantation. One day he come for to borrow something from Master White. He sees a likely looking gal, and the way it work out that gal was to be my Mammy. After that he got a paper saying it was all right for him to be off his own plantation. He come a'courting over to Master White's. After a while he talks with the Master. Says he wants to marry the gal, Mary. The Master says it's all right if it's all right with Mary and the other white folks. He finds out it is and they makes ready for the wedding.

Mary says a preacher wedding is the best but Master say he can marry them just as good. There wasn't no Bible, just an old Almanac. Master White read something out of that. That's all and they was married. The wedding was over!

Every night he gets a leave paper from his Master and come over to be with his wife, Mary. The next morning he leaves her to work in the fields. Then one night Mammy says he don't come home. The next night is the same, and the next. From then on Mammy don't see him no more— never find out what happen to my pappy.

When I was born Mammy named me John, John White. She tells me I was the blackest 'white' boy she ever see. I stays with her till I was eleven year old. The Master wrote down in the book when I was born, April 10, 1816, and I know it's right. Mammy told me so, and Master told me when I was eleven and he sold me to Sarah Davenport.

Mistress Sarah lived in Texas. Master White always selling and trading to folks all over the country. I hates to leave on account of Mammy and the good way Master White fared the slaves—they was good people. Mammy cry but I has to go just the same. The tears are on my face a long time after the leaving. I was hoping all the time to see Mammy again, but that's the last time.

We travels and travels on the stage coach. Once we cross the Big River (Mississippi) on the boat and pick up with the horses on the other side. A new outfit and we rides some more. Seems like we going to wear out all the horses before we gets to the place.

The Davenport plantation was way north of Linden, Texas, up in the Red River country. That's where I stayed for thirty-eight year. There I was drug through the hackles by the meanest master that ever lived. The Mistress was the best white woman I ever knew but Master Presley used his whip all the time, reason or no reason, and I got scars to remember by!

I remembers the house. A heavy log house with a gallery clear across the front. The kitchen was back of the house. I work in there and I live in there. It wasn't built so good as the Master's house. The cold winds in the winter go through the cracks between the logs like the walls was somewheres else, and I shivers with the misery all the time.

The cooking got to be my job. The washing too. Washday come around and I fills the tub with clothes. Puts the tub on my head and walks half a mile to the spring where I washes the clothes. Sometimes I run out of soap. Then I make ash soap right by the spring. I learns to be careful about streaks in the clothes. I learns by the bull whip. One day the Master finds a soapy streak in his shirt. Then he finds me.

The Military Road goes by the place and the Master drives me down the road and ties me to a tree. First he tears off the old shirt and then he throws the bull whip to me. When he is tired of beating me more torture is a-coming. The salt water cure. It don't cure nothing but that's what the white folks called it. "Here's at you," the Master say, and slap the salt water into the bleeding cuts. "Here's at you!" The blisters burst every time he slap me with the brine.

Then I was loosened to stagger back into the kitchen. The Mistress couldn't do nothing about it 'cept to lay on the grease thick, with a kind word to help stop the misery.

Ration time was Saturday night. Every slave get enough fat pork, corn meal and such to last out the week. I reckon the Master figure it to the last bite because they was no leavings over. Most likely the shortage catch them!

Sometimes they'd borrow, sometimes I'd slip somethings from out the kitchen. The single women folks was bad that way. I favors them with something extra from the kitchen. Then they favors me—at night when the overseer thinks everybody asleep in they own places!

I was always back to my kitchen bed long before the overseer give the get-up-knock. I hear the knock, he hear me answer. Then he blow the horn and shout the loud call, ARE YOU UP, and everybody know it was four o'clock and pour out of the cabins ready for the chores.

Sometimes the white folks go around the slave quarters for the night. Not on the Davenport plantation, but some others close around. The slaves talked about it amongst themselves.

After a while they'd be a new baby. Yellow. When the child got old enough for chore work the master would sell him (or her). No difference was it his own flesh and blood—if the price was right!

I traffic with lots of the women, but never marries. Not even when I was free after the War. I sees too many married troubles to mess up with such doings!

Sometimes the master sent me alone to the grinding mill. Load in the yellow corn, hitch in the oxen, I was ready to go. I gets me fixed up with a pass and takes to the road.

That was the trip I like best. On the way was a still. Off in the bresh. If the still was lonely I stop, not on the way to but on the way back. Mighty good whiskey, too! Maybe I drinks too much, then I was sorry.

Not that I swipe the whiskey, just sorry because I gets sick! Then I figures a woods camp meeting will steady me up and I goes.

The preacher meet me and want to know how is my feelings. I says I is low with the misery and he say to join up with the Lord.

I never join because he don't talk about the Lord. Just about the Master and Mistress. How the slaves must obey around the plantation—how the white folks know what is good for the slaves. Nothing about obeying the Lord and working for him.

I reckon the old preacher was worrying more about the bull whip than he was the Bible, else he say something about the Lord! But I always obeys the Lord—that's why I is still living!

The slaves would pray for to get out of bondage. Some of them say the Lord told them to run away. Get to the North. Cross the Red River. Over there would be folks to guide them to the Free State (Kansas).

The Lord never tell me to run away. I never tried it, maybe, because mostly they was caught by patrollers and fetched back for a flogging—and I had whippings enough already!

Before the Civil War was the fighting with Mexico. Some of the troops on they way south passed on the Military Road. Wasn't any fighting around Linden or Jefferson during the time.

They was lots of traveling on the Military Road. Most of the time you could see covered wagons pulled by mules and horses, and sometimes a crawling string of wagons with oxen on the pulling end.

From up in Arkansas come the stage coach along the road. To San Antonio. The drivers bring news the Mexicans just about all killed off and the white folks say Texas was going to join the Union. The country's going to be run different they say, but I never see no difference. Maybe, because I ain't white folks.

Wasn't many Mexicans around the old plantation. Come and go. Lots of Indians. Cherokees and Choctaws. Living in mud huts and cabin shacks. I never see them bother the whites, it was the other way around.

During the Civil War, when the Red River was bank high with muddy water, the Yankee's made a target of Jefferson. That was a small town down south of Linden.

Down the river come a flat barge with cannon fastened to the deck. The Yankee soldiers stopped across the river from Jefferson and the shooting started.

When the cannon went to popping the folks went arunning—hard to tell who run the fastest, the whites or the blacks! Almost the town was wiped out. Buildings was smashed and big trees cut through with the cannon balls.

And all the time the Yankee drums was a-beating and the soldiers singing:

We'll hang Jeff Davis on a sour apple tree,

As we go marching on!

Before the Civil War everybody had money. The white folks, not the negroes. Sometimes the master take me to the town stores. They was full of money. Cigar boxes on the counter, boxes on the shelf, all filled with money. Not the crinkley paper kind, but hard, jingley gold and silver! Not like these scarce times!

After the War I stay on the plantation 'til a soldier man tells me of the freedom. The master never tell us—negroes working just like before the War.

That's when I leave the first time. Slip off, saying nothing, to Jefferson. There I found some good white folks going to New Orleans. First place we go is Shreveport, by wagon. They took me because I fix up with them to do the cooking.

On to the Big River (Mississippi) and boards a river steamboat for New Orleans. Lots of negroes going down there—to work on the canal.

The whole town was built on logs covered with dirt. Trying to raise itself right out of the swamp. Sometimes the water get high and folks run for the hills. When I got there almost was I ready to leave.

I like Texas the best. Back to Jefferson is where I go. Fifteen-twenty mile below Linden. Almost the first person I see was Master Davenport.

He says, "Black rascal, you is coming with me." And I do. He tried to keep his slaves and just laugh when I tell him about the freedom. I worked for food and quarters 'til his meanness come cropping out again.

That wasn't long and he threatened me with the whip and the buck and gag. The buck and gag was maybe worse. I got to feeling that iron stick in my mouth, fastened around my head with chains, pressing hard on my tongue. No drinking, no eating, no talking!

So I slip off again. That night I goes through Linden. Crawling on my hands and knees! Keeping in the dark spots, hiding from the whites, 'til I pass the last house, then my feets hurries me to Jefferson, where I gets a ride to Arkansas.

In Russelville is where I stop. There I worked around in the yards, cutting the grass, fancying the flower beds, and earned a little money for clothes and eats, with some of it spent for good whiskey.

That was the reason I left Arkansas. Whiskey. The law got after me to tell where was a man's whiskey still. I just leave so's I won't have to tell.

But while I was making a little money in Russelville, I lose out on some big money, account some white folks beat me to it.

I was out in the hills west of town, walking along the banks of a little creek, when I heard a voice. Queer like. I called out who is that talking and I hears it again.

"Go to the white oak tree and you will find Ninety Thousand Dollars!" That's what I hear. I look around, nobody in sight, but I see the tree. A big white oak tree standing taller than all the rest 'round about.

Under the tree was a grave. An old grave. I scratch around but finds no money and thinks of getting some help.

I done some work for a white man in town and told him about the voice. He promised to go with me, but the next day he took two white mens and dug around the tree. Then he says they was nothing to find.

To this day I know better. I know wherever they's a ghost, money is around someplace! That's what the ghost comes back for.

Somebody dies and leaves buried money. The ghost watches over it 'til it sees somebody it likes. Then ghost shows himself—lets know he's around. Sometimes the ghost tells where is the money buried, like that time at Russelville.

That ain't the only ghost I've seen or heard. I see one around the yard where I is living now. A woman. Some of these times she'll tell me where the buried money is.

Maybe the ghost woman thinks I is too old to dig. But I been a-digging all these long years. For a bite to eat and a sleep-under cover.

I reckon pretty soon she's going to tell where to dig. When she does, then old Uncle John won't have to dig for the eats no more!

Oklahoma Writers' Project
Ex-Slaves
[HW: (photo)]
[Date stamp: AUG 16 1937]

CHARLEY WILLIAMS
Age 94 yrs.
Tulsa, Okla.

Iffen I could see better out'n my old eyes, and I had me something to work with and de feebleness in my back and head would let me 'lone, I would have me plenty to eat in de kitchen all de time, and plenty tobaccy in my pipe, too, bless God!

And dey wouldn't be no rain trickling through de holes in de roof, and no planks all fell out'n de flo' on de gallery neither, 'cause dis one old nigger knows everything about making all he need to git along! Old Master done showed him how to git along in dis world, jest as long as he live on a plantation, but living in de town is a different way of living, and all you got to have is a silver dime to lay down for everything you want, and I don't git de dime very often.

But I aint give up! Nothing like dat! On de days when I don't feel so feeble and trembly I jest keep patching 'round de place. I got to keep patching so as to keep it whar it will hold de winter out, in case I git to see another winter.

Iffen I don't, it don't grieve me none, 'cause I wants to see old Master again anyways. I reckon maybe I'll jest go up an ask him what he want me to do, and he'll tell me, and iffen I don't know how he'll show me how, and I'll try to do it to please him. And when I git it done I wants to hear him grumble like he used to and say, "Charley, you ain't got no sense but you is a good boy. Dis here ain't very good but it'll do, I reckon. Git yourself a little piece o' dat brown sugar, but don't let no niggers see you eating it—if you do I'll whup your black behind!"

Dat ain't de way it going be in Heaven, I reckon, but I can't set here on dis old rottendy gallery and think of no way I better like to have it!

I was a great big hulking buck of a boy when de War come along and bust up everything, and I can 'member back when everybody was living peaceful and happy, and nobody never had no notion about no war.

I was borned on the 'leventh of January, in 1843, and was old enough to vote when I got my freedom, but I didn't take no stock in all dat politics and goings on at dat time, and I didn't vote till a long time after old Master passed away, but I was big enough before de War to remember everything pretty plain.

Old Master name was John Williams, and old Mistress name was Miss Betty, and she was a Campbell before she married. Young Missy was named Betty after her mommy, and Young Master was named Frank, but I don't know who after. Our overseer was Mr. Simmons, and he was mighty smart and had a lot of patience, but he wouldn't take no talk nor foolishness. He didn't whup nobody very often, but he only had to whup 'em jest one time! He never did whup a nigger at de time the nigger done something, but he would wait till evening and have old Master come and watch him do it. He never whupped very hard 'cept when he had told a nigger about something and promised a whupping next time and the nigger done it again. Then that nigger got what he had been hearing 'bout!

De plantation was about as big as any. I think it had about three hundred acres, and it was about two miles northwest of Monroe, Louisiana. Then he had another one not so big, two—three miles south of the big one, kind of down in the woodsy part along the White river bottoms. He had another overseer on that place and a big passel of niggers, but I never did go down to that one. That was where he raised most of his corn and shoats, and lots of sorghum cane.

Our plantation was up on higher ground, and it was more open country, but still they was lots of woods all around and lots of the plantations had been whacked right out of de new ground and was full of stumps. Master's place was more open, though, and all in the fields was good plowing.

The big road runned right along past our plantation, and it come from Shreveport and run into Monroe. There wasn't any town at Monroe in them days, jest a little cross roads place with a general store and a big hide house. I think there was about two big hide houses, and you could smell that place a mile before you got into it. Old Master had a part in de store, I think.

De hide houses was jest long sheds, all open along de sides and kivered over wid cypress clapboards.

Down below de hide houses and de store was jest a little settlement of one or two houses, but they was a school for white boys. Somebody said there was a place where they had been an old fort, but I never did see it.

Everything boughten we got come from Shreveport, and was brung in by the stage and the freighters, and that was only a little coffee or gunpowder, or some needles for the sewing, or some strap iron for the blacksmith, or something like dat. We made and raised everything else we needed right on the place.

I never did even see any quinine till after I was free. My mammy knowed jest what root to go out and pull up to knock de chills right out'n me. And de bellyache and de running off de same way, too.

Our plantation was a lot different from some I seen other places, like way east of there, around Vicksburg. Some of them was fixed up fancier but dey didn't have no more comforts than we had.

Old Master come out into that country when he was a young man, and they didn't have even so much then as they had when I was a boy. I think he come from Alabama or Tennessee, and way back his people had come from Virginia, or maybe North Carolina, 'cause he knowed all about tobacco on the place. Cotton and tobacco was de long crops on his big place, and of course lots of horses and cattle and mules.

De big house was made out'n square hewed logs, and chinked wid little rocks and daubed wid white clay, and kivered wid cypress clapboards. I remember one time we put on a new roof, and de niggers hauled up de cypress logs and sawed dem and frowed out de clapboards by hand.

De house had two setting rooms on one side and a big kitchen room on de other, wid a wide passage in between, and den about was de sleeping rooms. They wasn't no stairways 'cepting on de outside. Steps run up to de sleeping rooms on one side from de passageway and on de other side from clean outside de house. Jest one big chimbley was all he had, and it was on de kitchen end, and we done all de cooking in a fireplace dat was purty nigh as wide as de whole room.

In de sleeping rooms day wasn't no fires 'cepting in brazers made out of clay, and we toted up charcoal to burn in 'em when it was cold mornings in de winter. Dey kept warm wide de bed clothes and de knitten clothes dey had.

Master never did make a big gallery on de house, but our white folks would set out in de yard under de big trees in de shade. They was long benches made out'n hewed logs and all padded wid gray moss and corn shuck padding, and dey set pretty soft. All de furniture in de house was home-made, too. De beds had square posts as big around as my shank and de frame was mortised into 'em, and holes bored in de frame and home-made rope laced in to make it springy. Den a great big mattress full of goose feathers and two—three comforts as thick as my foot wid carded wool inside! Dey didn't need no fireplaces!

De quarters was a little piece from de big house, and dey run along both sides of de road dat go to de fields. All one-room log cabins, but dey was good and warm, and every one had a little open shed at de side whar we sleep in de summer to keep cool.

They was two or three wells at de quarters for water, and some good springs in de branch at de back of de fields. You could ketch a fish now and den in dat branch, but Young Master used to do his fishing in White River, and take a nigger or two along to do de work at his camp.

It wasn't very fancy at de Big House, but it was mighty pretty jest de same, wid de gray moss hanging from de big trees, and de cool green grass all over de yard, and I can shet my old eyes and see it jest like it was before de War come along and bust it up.

I can see old Master setting out under a big tree smoking one of his long cheroots his tobacco nigger made by hand, and fanning hisself wid his big wide hat another nigger platted out'n young inside corn shucks for him, and I can hear him holler at a big bunch of white geeses what's gitting in his flower beds and see 'em string off behind de old gander towards de big road.

When de day begin to crack de whole plantation break out wid all kinds of noises, and you could tell what going on by de kind of noise you hear.

Come de daybreak you hear de guinea fowls start potracking down at de edge of de woods lot, and den de roosters all start up 'round de barn and de ducks finally wake up and jine in. You can smell de sow belly frying down at the cabins in de "row", to go wid de hoecake and de buttermilk.

Den purty soon de wind rise a little, and you can hear a old bell donging way on some plantation a mile or two off, and den more bells at other places and maybe a horn, and purty soon younder go old Master's old ram horn wid a long toot and den some short toots, and here come de overseer down de row of cabins, hollering right and left, and picking de ham out'n his teeth wid a long shiny goose quill pick.

Bells and horns! Bells for dis and horns for dat! All we knowed was go and come by de bells and horns!

Old ram horn blow to send us all to de field. We all line up, about seventy-five field niggers, and go by de tool shed and git our hoes, or maybe go hitch up de mules to de plows and lay de plows out on de side so de overseer can see iffen de points is shart. Any plow gits broke or de point gits bungled up on de rocks it goes to de blacksmith nigger, den we all git on down in de field.

Den de anvil start dangling in de blacksmith shop: "Tank! Deling-ding! Tank! Deling-ding!", and dat ole bull tongue gitting straightened out!

Course you can't hear de shoemaker awling and pegging, and de card spinners, and de old mammy sewing by hand, but maybe you can hear de old loom going "frump, frump", and you know it all right iffen your clothes do be wearing out, 'cause you gwine git new britches purty soon!

We had about a hundred niggers on dat place, young and old, and about twenty on de little place down below. We could make about every kind of thing but coffee and gunpowder dat our whitefolks and us needed.

When we needs a hat we gits inside cornshucks and weave one out, and makes horse collars de same way. Jest tie two little soft shucks together and begin plaiting.

All de cloth 'cepting de Mistress' Sunday dresses come from de sheep to de carders and de spinners and de weaver, den we dye it wid "butternut" and hickory bark and indigo and other things and set it wid copperas. Leather tanned on de place made de shoes, and I never see a store boughten wagon wheel 'cepting among de stages and de freighters along de big road.

We made purty, long back-combs out'n cow horn, and knitting needles out'n second hickory. Split a young hickory and put in a big wedge to prize it open, then cut it down and let it season, and you got good bent grain for wagon hames and chair rockers and such.

It was jest like dat until I was grown, and den one day come a neighbor man and say we in de War.

Little while young Master Frank ride over to Vicksburg and jine de Sesesh army, but old Master jest go on lak nothing happen, and we all don't hear nothing more until long come some Sesesh soldiers and take most old Master's hosses and all his wagons.

I bin working on de tobacco, and when I come back to de barns everything was gone. I would go into de woods and git good hickory and burn it till it was all coals and put it out wid water to make hickory charcoal for curing de tobacco. I had me some charcoal in de fire trenches under de curing houses, all full of new tobacco, and overseer come and say bundle all de tobacco up and he going take it to Shreveport and sell it befo' de soldiers take it too.

After de hosses all gone and most de cattle and de cotton and de tobacco gone too, here come de Yankees and spread out all over de whole country. Dey had a big camp down below our plantation.

One evening a big bunch of Yankee officers come up to de Big House and old Master set out de brandy in de yard and dey act purty nice. Next day de whole bunch leave on out of dat part.

When de hosses and stuff all go old Master sold all de slaves but about four, but he kept my pappy and mammy and my brother Jimmie and my sister Betty. She was named after old Mistress. Pappy's name was Charley and mammy's was Sally. De niggers he kept didn't have much work without any hosses and wagons, but de blacksmith started in fixing up more wagons and he kept them hid in de woods till they was all fixed.

Den along come some more Yankees, and dey tore everything we had up, and old Master was afeared to shoot at them on account his womenfolks, so he tried to sneak the fambly out but they kotched him and brung him back to de plantation.

We niggers didn't know dat he was gone until we seen de Yankees bringing dem back. De Yankees had done took charge of everything and was camping in de big yard, and us was all down at de quarters scared to death, but dey was jest letting us alone.

It was night when de white folks tried to go away, and still night when de Yankees brung dem back, and a house nigger come down to de quarters wid three—four mens in blue clothes and told us to come up to de Big House.

De Yankees didn't seem to be mad wid old Master, but jest laughed and talked wid him, but he didn't take de jokes any too good.

Den dey asked him could he dance and he said no, and dey told him to dance or make us dance. Dar he stood inside a big ring of dem mens in blue clothes, wid dey brass buttons shining in de light from de fire dey had in front of de tents, and he jest stood and said nothing, and it look lak he wasn't wanting to tell us to dance.

So some of us young bucks jest step up and say we was good dancers, and we start shuffling while de rest of de niggers pat.

Some nigger women go back to de quarters and git de gourd fiddles and de clapping bones made out'n beef ribs, and bring dem back so we could have some music. We git all warmed up and dance lak we never did dance befo'! I speck we invent some new steps dat night!

We act lak we dancing for de Yankees, but we trying to please Master and old Mistress more than anything, and purty soon he begin to smile a little and we all feel a lot better.

Next day de Yankees move on away from our place, and old Master start gitting ready to move out. We git de wagons we hid, and de whole passel of us leaves out for Shreveport. Jest left de old place standing like it was.

In Shreveport old Master git his cotton and tobacco money what he been afraid to have sent back to de plantation when he sell his stuff, and we strike out north through Arkansas.

Dat was de awfullest trip any man ever make! We had to hide from everybody until we find out if dey Yankees or Sesesh, and we go along little old back roads and up one mountain and down another, through de woods all de way.

After a long time we git to the Missouri line, and kind of cut off through de corner of dat state into Kansas. I don't know how we ever git across some of dem rivers but we did. Dey nearly always would be some soldiers around de fords, and dey would help us find de best crossing. Sometimes we had to unload de wagons and dry out de stuff what all got wet, and camp a day or two to fix up again.

Purty soon we git to Fort Scott, and that was whar de roads forked ever whichaways. One went on north and one east and one went down into de Indian country. It was full of soldiers coming and going back and forth to Arkansas and Fort Gibson.

We took de road on west through Kansas, and made for Colorado Springs.

Fort Scott was all run down, and the old places whar dey used to have de soldiers was all fell in in most places. Jest old rackety walls and leaky roofs, and a big pole fence made out'n poles sot in de ground all tied together, but it was falling down too.

They was lots of wagons all around what belong to de army, hauling stuff for de soldiers, and some folks told old Master he couldn't make us niggers go wid him, but we said we wanted to anyways, so we jest went on west across Kansas.

When we got away on west we come to a fork, and de best road went kinda south into Mexico, and we come to a little place called Clayton, Mexico whar we camped a while and then went north.

Dat place is in New Mexico now, but old Master jest called it Mexico. Somebody showed me whar it is on de map, and it look lak it a long ways off'n our road to Colorado Springs, but I guess de road jest wind off down dat ways at de time we went over it. It was jest two or three houses made out'n mud at dat time, and a store whar de soldiers and de Indians come and done trading.

About dat time old Master sell off some of de stuff he been taking along, 'cause de wagons loaded too heavy for de mountains and he figger he better have de money than some of de stuff, I reckon.

On de way north it was a funny country. We jest climb all day long gitting up one side of one bunch of mountains, and all de nigger men have to push on de wheels while de mules pull and den scotch de wheels while de mules rest. Everybody but de whitefolks has to walk most de time.

Down in de valleys it was warm like in Louisiana, but it seem lak de sun aint so hot on de head, but it look lak every time night come it ketch us up on top of one of dem mountains, and it almost as cold as in de winter time!

All de niggers had shoes and plenty warm clothes and we wrop up at night in everything we can git.

We git to Fort Scott again, and den de Yankee officers come and ask all us niggers iffen we want to leave old Master and stay dar and work, 'cause we all free now. Old Master say we can do what we please about it.

A few of de niggers stay dar in Fort Scott, but most of us say we gwine stay wid old Master, and we don't care iffen we is free or not.

When we git back to Monroe to de old place us niggers git a big surprise. We didn't hear about it, but some old Master's kinfolks back in Virginia done come out dar an fix de place up and kept it for him while we in Colorado, and it look 'bout as good as when we left it.

He cut it up in chunks and put us niggers out on it on de halves, but he had to sell part of it to git de money to git us mules and tools and found to run on. Den after while he had to sell some more, and he seem lak he git old mighty fast.

Young Master bin in de big battles in Virginia, and he git hit, and den he git sick, and when he come home he jest lak a old man he was so feeble.

About dat time they was a lot of people coming into dat country from de North, and dey kept telling de niggers dat de thing for dem to do was to be free, and come and go whar dey please.

Dey try to git de darkeys to go and vote but none us folks took much stock by what dey say. Old Master tell us plenty time to mix in de politics when de younguns git educated and know what to do.

Jest de same he never mind iffen we go to de dances and de singing and sech. He allus lent us a wagon iffen we want to borry one to go in, too.

Some de niggers what work for de white folks from de North act purty uppity and big, and come pestering 'round de dance places and try to talk up ructions amongst us, but it don't last long.

De Ku Kluckers start riding 'round at night, and dey pass de word dat de darkeys got to have a pass to go and come and to stay at de dances. Dey have to git de pass from de white folks dey work for, and passes writ from de Northern people wouldn't do no good. Dat de way de Kluckers keep the darkies in line.

227

De Kluckers jest ride up to de dance ground and look at everybody's passes, and iffen some darkey dar widout a pass or got a pass from de wrong man dey run him home, and iffen he talk big and won't go home dey whop him and make him go.

Any nigger out on de road after dark liable to run across de Kluckers, and he better have a good pass! All de dances got to bust up at about 'leven o'clock, too.

One time I seen three-four Kluckers on hosses, all wrapped up in white, and dey was making a black boy git home. Dey was riding hosses and he was trotting down de road ahead of 'em. Ever time he stop and start talking dey pop de whip at his heels and he start trotting on. He was so made he was crying, but he was gitting on down de road jest de same.

I seen 'em coming and I gits out my pass young Master writ so I could show it, but when dey ride by one in front jest turns in his saddle and look back at tother men and nod his head, and they jest ride on by widout stopping to see my pass. Dat man knowed me, I reckon. I looks to see iffen I knowed de hoss, but de Kluckers sometime swapped dey hosses 'round amongst 'em, so de hoss maybe wasn't hisn.

Dey wasn't very bad 'cause de niggers 'round dar wasn't bad, but I hear plenty of darkeys git whopped in other places 'cause dey act up and say dey don't have to take off dey hats in de white stores and such.

Any nigger dat behave hisself and don't go running 'round late at night and drinking never had no trouble wid de Kluckers.

Young Mistress go off and git married, but I don't remember de name 'cause she live off somewhar else, and de next year, I think it was, my pappy and mammy go on a place about five miles away owned by a man named Mr. Bumpus, and I go 'long wid my sister Betty and brother Jimmie to help 'em.

I live around dat place and never marry till old mammy and pappy both gone, and Jimmie and Betty both married and I was gitting about forty year old myself, and den I go up in Kansas and work around till I git married at last.

I was in Fort Scott, and I married Mathilda Black in 1900, and she is 73 years old now and was born in Tennessee. We went to Pittsburg, Kansas, and lived from 1907 to 1913 when we come to Tulsa.

Young Master's children writ to me once in a while and told me how dey gitting 'long up to about twenty year ago, and den I never heard no more about 'em. I never had no children, and it look lak my wife going outlive me, so my mainest hope when I goes on is seeing Mammy and Pappy and old Master. Old overseer, I speck, was too devilish mean to be thar!

'Course I loves my Lord Jesus same as anybody, but you see I never hear much about Him until I was grown, and it seem lak you got to hear about religion when you little to soak it up and put much by it. Nobody could read de Bible when I was a boy, and dey wasn't no white preachers talked to de niggers. We had meeting sometimes, but de nigger preacher jest talk about bein a good nigger and "doing to please de Master," and I allus thought he meant to please old Master, and I allus wanted to do dat anyways.

So dat de reason I allus remember de time old Master pass on.

It was about two years after de War, and old Master been mighty porely all de time. One day we was working in de Bumpus field and a nigger come on a mule and say old Mistress like to have us go over to de old place 'cause old Master mighty low and calling mine and Pappy's and Mammy's name. Old man Bumpus say go right ahead.

When we git to de Big House old Master setting propped up in de bed and you can see he mighty low and out'n his head.

He been talking about gitting de oats stacked, 'cause it seem to him lak it gitting gloomy-dark, and it gwine to rain, and hail gwine to ketch de oats in de shocks. Some nigger come running up to de back door wid an old horn old Mistress sent him out to hunt up, and he blowed it so old Master could hear it.

Den purty soon de doctor come to de door and say old Master wants de bell rung 'cause de slaves should ought to be in from de fields, 'cause it gitting too dark to work. Somebody git a wagon tire and beat on it like a bell ringing, right outside old Master's window, and den we all go up on de porch and peep in. Every body was snuffling kind of quiet, 'cause we can't help it.

We hear old Master say, "Dat's all right, Simmons. I don't want my niggers working in de rain. Go down to de quarters and see dey all dried off good. Dey ain't got no sense but dey all good niggers." Everybody around de bed was crying, and we all was crying too.

Den old Mistress come to de door and say we can go in and look at him if we want to. He was still setting propped up, but he was gone.

I stayed in Louisiana a long time after dat, but I didn't care nothing about it, and it look lak I'm staying a long time past my time in dis world, 'cause I don't care much about staying no longer only I hates to leave Mathilda.

But any time de Lord want me I'm ready, and I likes to think when He ready He going tell old Master to ring de bell for me to come on in.

Oklahoma Writers' Project
Ex-Slaves

SARAH WILSON
Age 87 yrs.
Fort Gibson, Okla.

I was a Cherokee slave and now I am a Cherokee freedwoman, and besides that I am a quarter Cherokee my own self. And this is the way it is.

I was born in 1850 along the Arkansas river about half way between Fort Smith and old Fort Coffee and the Skullyville boat landing on the river. The farm place was on the north side of the river on the old wagon road what run from Fort Smith out to Fort Gibson, and that old road was like you couldn't hardly call a road when I first remember seeing it. The ox teams bog down to they bellies in some places, and the wagon wheel mighty nigh bust on the big rocks in some places.

I remember seeing soldiers coming along that old road lots of times, and freighting wagons, and wagons what we all know carry mostly wiskey, and that was breaking the law, too! Them soldiers catch the man with that whiskey they sure put him up for a long time, less'n he put some silver in they hands. That's what my Uncle Nick say. That Uncle Nick a mean Negro, and he ought to know about that.

Like I tell you, I am quarter Cherokee. My mammy was named Adeline and she belong to old Master Ben Johnson. Old Master Ben bring my grandmammy out to that Sequoyah district way back when they call it Arkansas, mammy tell me, and God only know who my mammy's pa is, but mine was old Master Ben's boy, Ned Johnson.

Old Master Ben come from Tennessee when he was still a young man, and he bring a whole passel of slaves and my mammy say they all was kin to one another, all the slaves I mean. He was a white man that married a Cherokee woman, and he was a devil on this earth. I don't want to talk about him none.

White folks was mean to us like the devil, and so I jest let them pass. When I say my brothers and sisters I mean my half brothers and sisters, you know, but maybe some of them was my whole kin anyways, I don't know. They was Lottie that was sold off to a Starr because she wouldn't have a baby, and Ed, Dave, Ben, Jim and Ned.

My name is Sarah now but it was Annie until I was eight years old. My old Mistress' name was Annie and she name me that, and Mammy was afraid to change it until old Mistress died, then she change it. She hate old Mistress and that name too.

Lottie's name was Annie, too, but Mammy changed it in her own mind but she was afraid to say it out loud, a-feared she would get a whipping. When sister was sold off Mammy tell her to call herself Annie when she was leaving but call herself Lottie when she git over to the Starrs. And she done it too. I seen her after that and she was called Lottie all right.

The Negroes lived all huddled up in a bunch in little one-room log cabins with stick and mud chimneys. We lived in one, and it had beds for us children like shelves in the wall. Mammy need to help us up into them.

Grandmammy was mighty old and Mistress was old too. Grandmammy set on the Master's porch and minded the baby mostly. I think it was Young Master's. He was married to a Cherokee girl. They was several of the boys but only one girl, Nicie. The old Master's boys were Aaron, John, Ned, Cy and Nathan. They lived in a double log house made out of square hewed logs, and with a double fireplace out of rock where they warmed theirselves on one side and cooked on the other. They had a long front porch where they set most of the time in the summer, and slept on it too.

There was over a hundred acres in the Master's farm, and it was all bottom land too, and maybe you think he let them slaves off easy! Work from daylight to dark! They all hated him and the overseer too, and before slavery ended my grandmammy was dead and old Mistress was dead and old Master was mighty feeble and Uncle Nick had run away to the North soldiers and they never got him back. He run away once before, about ten years before I was born, Mammy say, but the Cherokees went over in the Creek Nation and got him back that time.

The way he made the Negroes work so hard, old Master must have been trying to get rich. When they wouldn't stand for a whipping he would sell them.

I saw him sell a old woman and her son. Must have been my aunt. She was always pestering around trying to get something for herself, and one day she was cleaning the yard he seen her pick up something and put it inside her apron. He flew at her and cussed her, and started like he was going to hit her but she just stood right up to him and never budged, and when he come close she just screamed out loud and ran at him with her fingers stuck out straight and jabbed him in the belly. He had a big soft belly, too, and it hurt him. He seen she wasn't going to be afraid, and he set out to sell her. He went off on his horse to get some men to come and bid on her and her boy, and all us children was mighty scared about it.

They would have hangings at Fort Smith courthouse, and old Master would take a slave there sometimes to see the hanging, and that slave would come back and tell us all scary stories about the hanging.

One time he whipped a whole bunch of the men on account of a fight in the quarters, and then he took them all to Fort Smith to see a hanging. He tied them all in the wagon, and when they had seen the hanging he asked them if they was scared of them dead men hanging up there. They all said yes, of course, but my old uncle Nick was a bad Negro and he said, "No, I aint a-feared of them nor nothing else in this world", and old Master jumped on him while he was tied and beat him with a rope, and then when they got home he tied old Nick to a tree and took his shirt off and poured the cat-o-nine-tails to him until he fainted away and fell over like he was dead.

I never forget seeing all that blood all over my uncle, and if I could hate that old Indian any more I guess I would, but I hated him all I could already I reckon.

Old Master wasn't the only hellion neither. Old Mistress just as bad, and she took most of her wrath out hitting us children all the time. She was afraid of the grown Negroes. Afraid of what they might do while old Master was away, but she beat us children all the time.

She would call me, "Come here Annie!" and I wouldn't know what to do. If I went when she called "Annie" my mammy would beat me for answering to that name, and if I didn't go old Mistress would beat me for that. That made me hate both of them, and I got the devil in me and I wouldn't come to either one. My grandmammy minded the Master's yard, and she set on the front porch all the time, and when I was called I would run to her and she wouldn't let anybody touch me.

When I was eight years old old Mistress died, and Grandmammy told me why old Mistress picked on me so. She told me about me being half Mister Ned's blood. Then I knowed why Mister Ned would say, "Let her along, she got big big blood in her", and then laugh.

Young Mister Ned was a devil, too. When his mammy died he went out and "blanket married." I mean he brung in a half white and half Indian woman and just lived with her.

The slaves would get rations every Monday morning to do them all week. The Overseer would weigh and measure according to how many in the family, and if you run out you just starve till you get some more. We all know the overseer steal some of it for his own self but we can't do anything, so we get it from the old Master some other way.

One day I was carrying water from the spring and I run up on Grandmammy and Uncle Nick skinning a cow. "What you-all doing?", I say, and they say keep my mouth shut or they kill me. They was stealing from the Master to piece out down at the quarters with. Old Master had so many cows he never did count the difference.

I guess I wasn't any worse than any the rest of the Negroes, but I was bad to tell little lies. I carry scars on my legs to this day where Old Master whip me for lying, with a rawhide quirt he carry all the time for his horse. When I lie to him he just jump down off'n his horse and whip me good right there.

In slavery days we all ate sweet potatoes all the time. When they didn't measure out enough of the tame kind we would go out in the woods and get the wild kind. They growed along the river sand betaween where we lived and Wilson's Rock, out west of our place.

Then we had boiled sheep and goat, mostly goat, and milk and wild greens and corn pone. I think the goat meat was the best, but I aint had no teeth for forty years now, and a chunk of meat hurts my stomach. So I just eats grits mostly. Besides hoeing in the field, chopping sprouts, shearing sheep, carrying water, cutting firewood, picking cotton and sewing I was the one they picked to work Mistress' little garden where she raised things from seed they got in Fort Smith. Green peas and beans and radishes and things like that. If we raised a good garden she give me a little of it, and if we had a poor one I got a little anyhow even when she didn't give it.

For clothes we had homespun cotton all the year round, but in winter we had a sheep skin jacket with the wool left on the inside. Sometimes sheep skin shoes with the wool on the inside and sometimes real cow leather shoes with wood peggings for winter, but always barefooted in summer, all the men and women too.

Lord, I never earned a dime of money in slave days for myself but plenty for the old Master. He would send us out to work the neighbors field and he got paid for it, but we never did see any money.

I remember the first money I ever did see. It was a little while after we was free, and I found a greenback in the road at Fort Gibson and I didn't know what it was. Mammy said it was money and grabbed for it, but I was still a hell cat and I run with it. I went to the little sutler store and laid it down and pointed to a pitcher I been wanting. The man took the money and give me the pitcher, but I don't know to this day how much money it was and how much was the pitcher, but I still got that pitcher put away. It's all blue and white stripedy.

Most of the work I done off the plantation was sewing. I learned from my Granny and I loved to sew. That was about the only thing I was industrious in. When I was just a little bitsy girl I found a steel needle in the yard that belong to old Mistress. My mammy took it and I cried. She put it in her dress and started for the field. I cried so old Mistress found out why and made Mammy give me the needle for my own.

We had some neighbor Indians named Starr, and Mrs. Starr used me sometimes to sew. She had nine boys and one girl, and she would sew up all they clothes at once to do for a year. She would cut out the cloth for about a week, and then send the word around to all the neighbors, and old Mistress would send me because she couldn't see good to sew. They would have stacks of drawers, shirts, pants and some dresses all cut out to sew up.

I was the only Negro that would set there and sew in that bunch of women, and they always talked to me nice and when they eat I get part of it too, out in the kitchen.

One Negro girl, Eula Davis, had a mistress sent her too, one time, but she wouldn't sew. She didn't like me because she said I was too white and she played off to spite the white people. She got sent home, too.

When old Mistress die I done all the sewing for the family almost. I could sew good enough to go out before I was eight years old, and when I got to be about ten I was better than any other girl on the place for sewing.

I can still quilt without my glasses, and I have sewed all night long many a time while I was watching Young Master's baby after old Mistress died.

They was over a hundred acres in the plantation, and I don't know how many slaves, but before the War ended lots of the men had run away. Uncle Nick went to the North and never come home, and Grandmammy died about that time.

We was way down across the Red river in Texas at that time, close to Shawneetown of the Choctaw Nation but just across the river on the other side in Texas bottoms. Old Master took us there in covered wagons when the Yankee soldiers got too close by in the first part of the War. He hired the slaves out to Texas people because he didn't make any crops down there, and we all lived in kind of camps. That's how some of the men and my uncle Nick got to slip off to the north that way.

Old Master just rant and rave all the time we was in Texas. That's the first time I ever saw a doctor. Before that when a slave sick the old women give them herbs, but down there one day old Master whip a Negro girl and she fall in the fire, and he had a doctor come out to fix her up where she was burnt. I remember Granny giving me clabber milk when I was sick, and when I was grown I found out it had had medicine in it.

Before freedom we didn't have no church, but slipped around to the other cabins and had a little singing sometimes. Couldn't have anybody show us the letters either, and you better not let them catch you pick up a book even to look at the pictures, for it was against a Cherokee law to have a Negro read and write or to teach a Negro.

Some Negroes believed in buckeyes and charms but I never did. Old Master had some good boys, named Aaron, John, Ned, Cy and Nat and they told me the charms was no good. Their sister Nicie told me too, and said when I was sick just come and tell her.

They didn't tell us anything about Christmas and New Year though, and all we done was work.

When the War was ended we was still in Texas, and when old Master got a letter from Fort Smith telling him the slaves was free he couldn't read, and Young Miss read it to him. He went wild and jumped on her and beat the devil out of her. Said she was lying to him. It near about killed him to let us loose, but he cooled down after awhile and said he would help us all get back home if we wanted to come.

Mammy told him she could bear her own expenses. I remember I didn't know what "expenses" was, and I thought it was something I was going to have to help carry all the way back.

It was a long time after he knew we was free before he told us. He tried to keep us, I reckon, but had to let us go. He died pretty soon after he told us, and some said his heart just broke and some said some Negroes poisoned him. I didn't know which.

Anyways we had to straggle back the best way we could, and me and mammy just got along one way and another till we got to a ferry over the Red River and into Arkansas. Then we got some rides and walked some until we got to Fort Smith. They was a lot of Negro camps there and we stayed awhile and then started out to Fort Gibson because we heard they was giving rations out there. Mammy knew we was Cherokee anyway, I guess.

That trip was hell on earth. Nobody let us ride and it took us nearly two weeks to walk all that ways, and we nearly starved all the time. We was skin and bones and feet all bloody when we got to the Fort.

We come here to Four Mile Branch to where the Negroes was all setting down, and pretty soon Mammy died.

I married Oliver Wilson on January second, 1878. He used to belong to Mr. DeWitt Wilson of Tahlequah, and I think the old people used to live down at Wilson Rock because my husband used to know all about that place and the place where I was borned. Old Mister DeWitt Wilson give me a pear tree the next year after I was married, and it is still out in my yard and bears every year.

I was married in a white and black checkedy calico apron that I washed for Mr. Tim Walker's mother Lizzie all day for, over close to Ft. Gibson, and I was sure a happy woman when I married that day. Him and me both got our land on our Cherokee freedman blood and I have lived to bury my husband and see two great grandchildren so far.

I bless God about Abraham Lincoln. I remember when my mammy sold pictures of him in Fort Smith for a Jew. If he give me my freedom I know he is in Heaven now.

I heard a lot about Jefferson Davis in my life. During the War we hear the Negroes singing the soldier song about hand Jeff Davis to a apple tree, and old Master tell about the time we know Jeff Davis. Old Master say Jeff Davis was just a dragoon soldier out of Fort Gibson when he bring his family out here from Tennessee, and while they was on the road from Fort Smith to where they settled young Jeff Davis and some more dragoon soldiers rid up and talked to him a long time. He say my grandmammy had a bundle on her head, and Jeff Davis say, "Where you going Aunty?" and she was tired and mad and she said, "I don't know, to Hell I reckon", and all the white soldiers laughed at her and made her that much madder.

I joined the Four Mile Branch church in 1879 and Sam Solomon was a Creek negro and the first preacher I ever heard preach. Everybody ought to be in the church and ready for that better home on the other side.

All the old slaves I know are dead excepting two, and I will be going pretty soon I reckon, but I'm glad I lived to see the day the Negroes get the right treatment if they work good and behave themselves right. They don't have to have no pass to walk abroad no more, and they can all read and write now, but it's a tarnation shame some of them go and read the wrong kind of things anyways.

Oklahoma Writers' Project
Ex-Slaves
10-19-38
1,534 words

TOM W. WOODS
Age 83.
Alderson, Okla.

Lady, if de nigger hadn't been set free dis country wouldn't ever been what it is now! Poor white folks wouldn't never had a chance. De slave holders had most of de money and de land and dey wouldn't let de poor white folks have a chance to own any land or anything else to speak of. Dese white folks wasn't much better off den we was. Dey had to work hard and dey had to worry 'bout food, clothes and shelter and we didn't. Lots of slave owners wouldn't allow dem on deir farms among deir slaves without orders from de overseer. I don't know why, unless he was afraid dey would stir up discontent among de niggers. Dere was lots of "underground railroading" and I rekon dat was what Old Master and others was afraid of.

Us darkies was taught dat poor white folks didn't amount to much. Course we knowed dey was white and we was black and dey was to be respected for dat, but dat was about all.

White folks as well as niggers profited by emancipation. Lincoln was a friend to all poor white folks as well as black ones and if he could a' lived things would a'been different for ever'body.

Dis has been a good old world to live in. I always been able to make a purty good living and de only trouble I ever had has been sickness and death. I've had a sight of dat kind of trouble. I've outlived two wives and eight children. I had 13 brothers and sisters and I was de oldest, and I'm de only one left.

I sits here at night by myself and gits to wondering what de good Lord is sparing me for. I reckon it's for some good reason, and I'd like to live to be a hundred if He wants me to. I'm not tired of living yet!

I was born in Florence, Alabama. My father's name was Thomas Woods and my mammy was Frances Foster. Mammy belonged to Wash Foster and father was owned by Moses Woods, who lived on an adjoining plantation. He worked for his Master ever' day but spent each night wid us. He walked 'bout a mile to his work ever' day.

Master Wash was a poor man when he married Miss Sarah Watkins of Richmond, Virginia. Her father was as rich as cream, he owned 7 plantations and 200 slaves to each plantation. When Master Wash and Miss Sarah got married her father give her 50 slaves. Ever'body said Miss Mary jest married Master Wash because he was a purty boy, and he sure was a fine looking man.

He was good and kind to all his slaves when he was sober, but he was awful crabbed and cross when he was drunk, and he was drunk most of de time. He was hard to please and sometimes he would whip de slaves. I remember seeing Master Wash whup two men once. He give 'em 200 lashes.

Miss Sarah was de best woman in de world. It takes a good woman to live wid a drunkard.

Two of the men ran away one time and was gone till dey got tired of staying away. Master Wash wouldn't let anyone hunt 'em. When dey finally come home he had dem strapped in stocks and den deir bodies bared to de waist and he sure did ply de lash. I guess he whupped 'em harder dan he would if he hadn't been so full of whisky.

He never did sell any of his slaves. He kept the 50 dat Miss Sarah's father give 'em and deir increase. He bought some ever' time dey had a sale. He owned two plantations and dey was about a hundred slaves on each one. Him and his family lived in town.

Me and a boy named John was sized and put to work when we was about nine or ten years old. We was so bad dey had to put us to work as dey couldn't do any thing else with us. We'd chase de pigs and ride de calves and to punish us dey made us tote water to de hands. Dey was so many hands to water dat it kept us busy running back and forth with de water. De next year dey put me to plowing and him to hoeing. We made regular hands from den on.

If we had behaved ourselves we wouldn't a'had to go to work till we was fourteen or fifteen anyway. Slave owners was awful good to deir nigger chaps for dey wanted 'em to grow up to be strong men and women.

Dey was about thirty children on our plantation. Two women looked after us and took care of us till our parents come in from de field. Dey cooked for us and always gave us our supper and sent us home to our parents for de night.

Our food was placed on a long table in a trough. Each child had a spoon and four of us eat out of one trough. Our food at night was mostly milk and bread. At noon we had vegetables, bread, meat and milk. He gave us more and better food than he did his field hands. He said he didn't want none of us to be stunted in our growing.

He bought our shoes for us but cloth for our clothes was spun and wove right there on de farm. In summer us boys wore long tailed shirts and no pants. I've plowed dat way a many a day. We was glad to see it git warm in de spring so we could go barefooted and go wid out our pants.

Our overseers lived near de quarters and every morning about four o' clock dey'd blow a horn [HW: to] wake us up. We knowed it meant to git up and start de day. We was in de field by de time we could see. We always fed our teams at night. We'd give 'em enough to keep 'em eating all night so we wouldn't have to feed 'em in de morning.

Master Wash Foster and his family lived in de finest house in Florence, Ala. It was a fine, large two-story house, painted white as nearly all de houses was in dem days. Dere was big gallery in front and back and a fine lawn wid big cedar and chestnut trees all 'round de house.

He had a fine carriage and a pair of spanking bays dat cost him $500 apiece. Old Monroe was his coachman and dey made a grand sight. Monroe kept de nickel plated harness and carriage trimmings shining and de team was brushed slick and clean and dey sure stepped out.

We lived on de plantation about eight miles from town and we liked for de family to come out to de farm. Dey was four children, Wash, Jack, Sarah and Sally and dey always played with us. When dey come we always had a regular feast as dey children would eat wid us children. Dey had dishes though to eat out of. After dinner we would run and play Peep Squirrel. I think dey call it hide-and-seek now.

My mother was a regular field hand till Miss Sarah decided to take her into town to take care of her children. Dey all called her Frank instead of Frances. I used to get to go to town to visit my mother and we'd have glorious times I tell you.

We'd go out and gather hickory nuts, hazel nuts, pig nuts, and walnuts. We'd all set around de fire and eat nuts and tell ghost tales ever' night. Master Wash raised lots of apples too, and we had all that we wanted of dem to eat.

I saw lots of Yankee soldiers. Sherman and Grant's armies marched by our house and camped at DeCatur, Ala. It took dem three days to pass. We wasn't afraid of dem.

In the second year of de war some Yankee soldiers come through and gathered up all de slaves and took us to Athens, Ala., and put us on a Government farm. We stayed dere till de end of de War. My father died jest before dey took us away.

My mother and us children were on de farm together and dey treated us all mighty good. We had plenty of good food and clothes.

Master Wash came to see us while we was on de Government farm. He was left in a bad shape and we was all sorry for him. A lot of his hands went back to him after de Surrender but we never did. Mother married another man named Goodloe and we all went to Arkansas, near Little Rock. Dis was his former home. I was about nineteen or twenty years old at this time.

I never sent to school. My wife taught me how to read de Bible but I never learned to write. I have good eyesight. I guess dat is cause I never put dem out reading and going to moving picture shows.

When any of my family was sick I always sent for de doctor. We had a few of our own home remedies dat we used also. We boiled poke root and bathed in it for a cure for rheumatism.

A tea made from May apples was used for a physic.

Oklahoma Writers' Project
Ex-Slaves

ANNIE YOUNG
Age 86
Oklahoma City, Okla.

I was born in 1851, makes me 86 years old. I was born in Middle Tennessee, Summers County. My mother was put on a block and sold from me when I was a child. I don't remember my father real good. Sister Martha, Sister Sallie, nor Sister Jane wasn't sold. But my brother John was. My mother's name is Rachel Donnahue. We lived in a log hut. The white folks lived in a frame white building sitting in a big grove yard. Old master owned a big farm.

We ate molasses, bread and butter and milk in wooden bowls and crumbled our bread up in it. Old master had big smokehouses of meat. Dey ate chickens, possums and coons, and my old auntie would barbecue rabbits for de white folks. We ate ash cakes too.

I washed dishes, swept de yard, and kept de yard clean wid weed brush brooms. I never earned no money. All de slaves had gardens, and chickens too. My auntie, dey let her have chickens of her own and she raised chickens, and had a chicken house and garden down in de woods.

I remember in time of de War dey'd send me down in de woods to pick up chips and git wood. All de men had gone to de army. One morning and t'was cold dey sent me down in de woods and my hands got frostbitten. All de skin come off and dey had to tie my hands up in roasted turnips. Sallie she had gloves, and didn't get frostbitten. After my old master died, Master Donnahue was his name, his old son-in-law come to take over de plantation. He was mean, but my sister whipped him.

We had no nigger driver or overseer. We raised wheat, corn and vegetables, not much cotton, jest enough to spun de clothes out of.

At night when we'd go to our cabins we'd pick cotton from de seeds to make our clothes. Boys and girls alike wore dem long shirts slit up de side nearly to your necks. They'd have cornshuckings sometimes all night long. You see I didn't have no mother, no father, nobody to lead me, teach me or tell me, and so jest lived with anybody was good enough to let me stay and done what they did. They'd have log rollings, with all de whiskey dey could drink.

I remember going to church, de Methodist Church dey call it. We used to sing dis song and I sho did like it too:

"I went down in de valley to pray,

Studying dat good old way."

I been a Christian long before most of dese young niggers was born. My other favorites are:

"Must Jesus bear This Cross Alone."

and

"The Consecrated Cross I'll Bear 'til

Death Shall Set Me Free,

Yea, There's a Crown for Everyone,

And There's a Crown for Me."

Yes Lawd, there sho is.

One day a nigger killed one of his master's shoats and he catch him and when he'd ask him, "What's that you got there?" The nigger said, "a possum." De master said, "Let me see." He looked and seen it was a shoat. De nigger said, "Master it may be a shoat now, but it sho was a possum while ago when I put 'im in dis sack."

Dey didn't whip our folks much, but one day I saw a overseer on another place. He staked a man down with two forked sticks 'cross his wrist nailed in de ground and beat him half to death with a hand saw 'til it drawed blisters. Den he mopped his back wid vinegar, salt and pepper. Sometimes dey'd drop dat hot rosin from pine knots on dose blisters.

When de Yanks come, business took place. I remember white folks was running and hiding, gitting everything dey could from de Yanks. Dey hid dey jewelry and fine dishes and such. Dose Yanks had on big boots. Dey'd drive up, feed dey hosses from old Master's corn, catch dey chickens, and tell old Master's cook to cook 'em, and they'd shoot down old Master's hogs and skin 'em.

De Yanks used to make my nephew drunk, and have him sing (dis is kind of bad):

"I'll be God O'Mighty

God Dammed if I don't

Kill a nigger,

Oh Whooey boys! Oh Whooey!

Oh Whooey boys! Oh Whooey!"

I don't remember never seeing no funerals. Jest took 'em off and buried 'em. I remember dat old Master's son-in-law dat my sister whipped, he called hisself a doctor and he killed Aunt Clo. Give her some medicine but he didn't know what he was doing and killed her.

I married William Young and we had a pretty good wedding. Married in Crittington County Arkansas. When I left Tennessee and went to Arkansas I followed some hands. You know after de War dey immigrated niggers from one place to another. I owned a good farm in Arkansas. I came out here some 42 years ago.

I have three daughters. Mattie Brockins runs a rooming house in Kansas City. Jessie Cotton, lives right up de street here. Osie Olla Anderson is working out in North town.

Well I think Abraham Lincoln is more than a type a man than Moses. I believe he is a square man, believe in union that every man has a right to be a free man regardless to color. He was a republican man. Don't know much 'bout Jeff Davis but I think Booker T. Washington was a pretty good man. He's a right good man I guess, but he is dead ain't he?

I can remember once my auntie's old Master tried to have her and she run off out in de woods, and when he put those blood hounds or nigger hounds on her trail he catched her and hit her in de head wid something like de stick de police carry, and he knocked a hole in her head and she bled like a hog, and he made her have him. She told her mistress, and mistress told her to go ahead and be wid him 'cause he's gonna kill you. And he had dem two women and she had some chillun nearly white, and master and dey all worked in de fields side by side.

HISTORIC PUBLISHING
SLAVE NARRATIVE SERIES™

1) *The WPA Slave Narratives of Oklahoma: A Folk History of Slavery in the United States From Interviews With Former Slaves.* ISBN: 978-1-64227-020-4

2) *Anti-Slavery Leaders Of North Carolina & 75 WPA South Carolina Slave Narratives: A Folk History of Slavery in the United States From Interviews with Former Slaves & The Story of North Carolina's Leading Abolitionists.* ISBN: 978-1642270181

3) *Kansas Slave Narratives & Slave Songs. 136 Authentic Slave Songs With Sheet Music: A Folk History of Slavery in the United States From Interviews with Former Slaves Residing In The State of Kansas. An Original Compilation.* ISBN: 978-1642270174

4) *The WPA Arkansas Slave Narratives Collection. Part VII: A Folk History of Slavery in the United States from Interviews with Former Slaves.* ISBN: 978-1642270167

5) *Kentucky Slave Narratives & The Narrative of the Life of J. D. Green: A Runaway Slave From Kentucky, Containing an Account of His Three Escapes, in 1839, 1846, and 1848. An Original Compilation,* ISBN: 978-1642270150

6) *Alabama WPA Slave Narratives: From Interviews With Former Slaves* ISBN: 978-1642270259

7) Texas Slave Narratives & Photographs: A Traditional History of Slavery in the United States From Interviews with Former Slaves Illustrated with Photographs. Part 3. ISBN-13: 978-1642270129

8) *Texas Slave Narratives & Photographs: A Folk History of Slavery in the United States From Interviews with Former Slaves, Illustrated with Photographs. Part 4.* ISBN: 978-1642270228

9) *Former Slave Narratives & Interviews: From the States of Kentucky and Georgia* ISBN: 978-1642270112

10) *Recorded Audio Slave Narratives & Interviews Transcript Collection: Transcribed from Actual Recordings of Former Slaves.* ISBN-13: 978-1642270235

11) *Florida Slave Narratives: A Folk History of Slavery in the United States From Interviews with Former Slaves,* ISBN-13: 978-1642270013

12) *South Carolina Slave Narratives: A Folk History of Slavery in the United States From Interviews with Former Slaves.* ISBN-13: 978-1946640598

PREPARED FOR PUBLICATION BY
HISTORIC PUBLISHING
All Rights Reserved
San Antonio, Texas
©2017

Texas Slave Narratives & Photographs:

A Folk History of Slavery in the United States From Interviews with Former Slaves, Illustrated with Photographs.

Part 4

TYPEWRITTEN RECORDS PREPARED BY
THE FEDERAL WRITERS' PROJECT
1936-1938
ASSEMBLED BY
THE LIBRARY OF CONGRESS PROJECT
WORK PROJECTS ADMINISTRATION
FOR THE DISTRICT OF COLUMBIA
SPONSORED BY THE LIBRARY OF CONGRESS

Illustrated with Photographs

WASHINGTON 1941

VOLUME XVI

TEXAS NARRATIVES—PART 4

Prepared by the Federal Writers' Project of

the Works Progress Administration for the State of Texas

PREPARED FOR PUBLICATION

BY

HISTORIC PUBLISHING SERIES™

Slave Narratives: A Folk History of Slavery in the United States From Interviews with Former Slaves
©2017 All Rights Reserved

HISTORIC PUBLISHING
©2017 All Rights Reserved

Slavery Books & African American History Courses & Resources

https://africanamericanhistorybooks.blogspot.com

HISTORIC PUBLISHING
WWW.HISTORICPUBLISHING.COM

INFORMANTS (S-Y)

1. Mazique Sanco
2. Clarissa Scales
3. Hannah Scott
4. Abram Sells
5. George Selman
6. Callie Shepherd
7. Betty Simmons
8. George Simmons
9. Ben Simpson
10. Giles Smith
11. James W. Smith
12. Jordon Smith
13. Millie Ann Smith
14. Susan Smith
15. John Sneed
16. Mariah Snyder
17. Patsy Southwell
18. Leithean Spinks
19. Guy Stewart
20. William Stone
21. Yach Stringfellow
22. Bert Strong
23. Emma Taylor
24. Mollie Taylor
25. Jake Terriell
26. J.W. Terrill
27. Allen Thomas
28. Bill and Ellen Thomas
29. Lucy Thomas
30. Philles Thomas

31. William M. Thomas
32. Mary Thompson
33. Penny Thompson
34. Albert Todd
35. Aleck Trimble
36. Reeves Tucker
37. Lou Turner
38. Irella Battle Walker
39. John Walton
40. Sol Walton
41. Ella Washington
42. Rosa Washington
43. Sam Jones Washington
44. William Watkins
45. Dianah Watson
46. Emma Watson
47. James West
48. Adeline White
49. Sylvester Sostan Wickliffe
50. Daphne Williams
51. Horatio W. Williams
52. Lou Williams
53. Millie Williams
54. Rose Williams
55. Steve Williams
56. Wayman Williams
57. Willie Williams
58. Lulu Wilson
59. Wash Wilson
60. Willis Winn
61. Rube Witt

62. Ruben Woods
63. Willis Woodson
64. James G. Woorling
65. Caroline Wright
66. Sallie Wroe
67. Fannie Yarbrough
68. Litt Young
69. Louis Young
70. Teshan Young

Transcriber's Note:

[HW:] Handwritten note

[TR:] Transcriber's note

TEXAS SLAVE NARRATIVES
Volume XVI: Texas Narratives — Part 4

ILLUSTRATIONS

1.   Mazique Sanco

2.   Clarissa Scales

3.   Abram Sells

4.   George Selman

5.   Callie Shepherd

6.   Betty Simmons

7.   George Simmons

8.   Giles Smith

9.   James W. Smith

10. Jordon Smith

11. Millie Ann Smith

12. John Sneed

13. Mariah Snyder

14. Leithean Spinks

15. William Stone

16. Yach Stringfellow

17. Bert Strong

18. Emma Taylor

19. Allen Thomas

20. Bill and Ellen Thomas

21. Lucy Thomas

22. Philles Thomas

23. William M. Thomas

24. Mary Thompson

25. Penny Thompson

26. Albert Todd

27. Reeves Tucker

28. Lou Turner

29. Sol Walton

30. Rosa Washington

31. Sam Jones Washington

32. William Watkins

33. Emma Watson

34. James West

35. Adeline White

36. Daphne Williams

37. Lou Williams

38. Lou Williams' House

39. Millie Williams

40. Steve Williams

41. Wayman Williams and Henry Freeman

42. Willie Williams

43. Lulu Wilson

44. Wash Wilson

45. Willis Winn

46. Rube Witt

47. Ruben Woods

48. Willis Woodson

49. Sallie Wroe

50. Litt Young

51. Louis Young

52. Teshan Young

Mazique Sanco

Mazique Sanco was born a slave of Mrs. Louisa Green, in Columbia, South Carolina, on February 10, 1849. Shortly after Mazique was freed, he enlisted in the army and was sent with the Tenth Cavalry to San Angelo, then Fort Concho, Texas. After Mazique left the army he became well-known as a chef, and worked for several large hotels. Mazique uses little dialect. When asked where Mazique is, his young wife says, "In his office," and upon inquiry as to the location of this office, she replies mirthfully, "On de river," for since he is too old to work, Mazique spends most of his time fishing.

"My mistress owned a beautiful home and three hundred twenty acres of land in the edge of Columbia, in South Carolina, just back of the state house. Her name was Mrs. Louisa Green and she was a widow lady. That's where I was born, but when her nephew, Dr. Edward Flemming, married Miss Dean, I was given to him for a wedding present, and so was my mother and her other children. I was a very small boy then, and when I was ten Dr. Flemming gave me to his crippled mother-in-law for a foot boy. She got crippled in a runaway accident, when her husband was killed. He had two fine horses, fiery and spirited as could be had. He called them Ash and Dash, and one day he and his wife were out driving and the horses ran the carriage into a big pine tree, and Mr. Dean was killed instantly, and Mrs. Dean couldn't ever help herself again. I waited on her. I had a good bed and food and was let to earn ten cent shin plasters.

"When the war was over she called up her five families of slaves and told us we could go or stay. Some went and some stayed. I was always an adventurer, wanting to see and learn things, so I left and went back to my mother with Mrs. Flemming.

Mazique Sanco

"I only stayed there a few months and hired out to Major Legg, and worked for him several years. I felt I wasn't learning enough, so I joined the United States Army and with a hundred and eighty-five boys went to St. Louis, Missouri. From there we were transferred with the Tenth Cavalry to Fort Concho. I helped haul the lumber from San Antonio to finish the buildings at the fort. I was there five years.

"After I went to work at private employment I did some carpenter work, but most of the houses were adobe or pecan pole buildings, so I got a job from Mr. Jimmy Keating as mechanic for awhile, and then drifted to Mexico. Odd jobs were all I could get for awhile, so I landed in El Paso and got a job in a hotel.

"That was the start of my success, for I learned to be a skilled chef and superintended the kitchens in some of the largest hotels in Texas. I made as high as $80.00, in Houston. My last work was done at the St. Angelus Hotel here in San Angelo and if you don't believe I'm a good cook, just look at my wife over there. When I married her she was fourteen years old and weighed a hundred and fifteen pounds. Now it's been a long time since I could get her on the scales, not since she passed the two hundred pound mark."

Clarissa Scales

Clarissa Scales, 79, was born a slave of William Vaughan, on his plantation at Plum Creek, Texas. Clarissa married when she was fifteen. She owns a small farm near Austin, but lives with her son, Arthur, at 1812 Cedar Ave., Austin.

"Mammy's name was Mary Vaughan and she was brung from Baton Rouge, what am over in Louisiana, by our master. He went and located on Plum Creek, down in Hays County.

"Mammy was a tall, heavy-set woman, more'n six foot tall. She was a maid-doctor after freedom. Dat mean she nussed women at childbirth. She allus told me de last thing she saw when she left Baton Rouge was her mammy standin' on a big, wood block to be sold for a slave. Dat de last time she ever saw her mammy. Mammy died 'bout fifty years ago. She was livin' on a farm on Big Walnut Creek, in Travis County. Daddy done die a year befo' and she jes' grieves herself to death. Daddy was sho' funny lookin', 'cause he wore long whiskers and what you calls a goatee. He was field worker on de Vaughan plantation.

"Master Vaughan was good and treated us all right. He was a great white man and didn't have no over seer. Missy's name was Margaret, and she was good, too.

"My job was tendin' fires and herdin' hawgs. I kep' fire goin' when de washin' bein' done. Dey had plenty wood, but used corn cobs for de fire. Dere a big hill corn cobs near de wash kettle. In de evenin' I had to bring in de hawgs. I had a li'l whoop I druv dem with, a eight-plaited rawhide whoop on de long stick. It a purty sight to see dem hawgs go under de slip-gap, what was a rail took down from de bottom de fence, so de hawgs could run under.

"Injuns used to pass our cabin in big bunches. One time dey give mammy some earrings, but when they's through eatin' they wants dem earrings back. Dat de way de Injuns done. After feedin' dem, mammy allus say, 'Be good and kind to everybody.'

"One day Master Vaughan come and say we's all free and could go and do what we wants. Daddy and mammy rents a place and I stays until I's fifteen. I wanted to be a teacher, but daddy kep' me hoein' cotton most de time. Dat's all he knowed. He allus told me it was 'nough larnin' could I jes' read and write. He never even had dat much. But he was de good farmer and good to me and mammy.

"Dere was a school after freedom. Old Man Tilden was de teacher. One time a bunch of men dey calls de Klu Klux come in de room and say, 'You git out of here and git 'way from dem niggers. Don' let us cotch you here when we comes back.' Old Man Tilden sho' was scart, but he say, 'You all come back tomorrow.' He finishes dat year and we never hears of him 'gain. Dat a log schoolhouse on Williamson Creek, five mile south of Austin.

Clarissa Scales

"Den a cullud teacher named Hamlet Campbell come down from de north. He rents a room in a big house and makes a school. De trustees hires and pays him and us chillen didn't have to pay. I got to go some, and I allus tells my granddaughter how I's head of de class when I does go. She am good in her studies, too.

"When I's fifteen I marries Benjamin Calhoun Scales and he was a farmer. We had five chillen and three boys is livin'. One am a preacher and Arthur am a cement laborer and Chester works in a printin' shop.

"Benjie dies on February 15th, dis year (1937). I lives with Arthur and de gov'ment gives me $10.00 de month. I has de li'l farm of nineteen acres out near Oak Hill and Floyd, de preacher, lives on dat. All my boys is good to me. Dey done good, and better'n we could, 'cause we couldn't git much larnin' dem days. I's had de good life. But we 'preciated our chance more'n de young folks does nowadays. Dey has so much dey don't have to try so hard. If we'd had what dey got, we'd thunk we was done died and gone to Glory Land. Maybe dey'll be all right when deys growed."

Hannah Scott

Hannah Scott was born in slavery, in Alabama. She does not know her age but says she was grown when her last master, Bat Peterson, set her free. Hannah lives with her grandson in a two-room house near the railroad tracks, in Houston, Texas. Unable to walk because of a paralytic stroke, Hannah asked her grandson to lift her from the bed to a chair, from which she told her story.

"Son, move de chair a mite closer to de stove. Dere, dat's better, 'cause de heat kind of soople me up. Ain't nothin' left of me but some skin and bones, nohow.

"Lemme see now. I's born in Alabama and I think dey calls it Fayette County. Mama's name was Ardissa and she 'long to Marse Clark Eccles, but us chillen allus call him White Pa. Miss Hetty, his wife, we calls her White Ma.

"I never knowed my own pa, 'cause he 'long to 'nother man and was sold away 'fore I's old 'nough to know him. Mama has five us chillen, but dey all dead 'ceptin' me. Dey didn't have no marriage back den like now. Dey just puts black folks together in de sight of man and not in de sight of Gawd, and dey puts dem asunder, too.

"Marse Eccles didn't have no big place and only nine slaves. I guess he what you calls 'poor folks,' but he mighty good to he black folks. I 'member when he sold us to Bat Peterson. He and White Ma break down and cry when old Bat puts us in de wagon and takes us off to Arkansas. I heared mama say something 'bout White Pa sellin' us for debt and he gits a hunerd dollars for me.

"Whoosh, it sho' was a heap dif'ent from Alabama. Marse Bat had niggers. I reckon he must of had a hunerd of dem and two nigger drivers, Uncle Green and Uncle Jake, and a overseer. Marse Bat was mean, too, and work he slaves from daylight till nine o'clock at night. I carries water for de hands. I carries de bucket on my head and 'fore long I ain't got no more hair on my head den you has on de palm of you hand. No, suh!

"When I gits bigger, de overseer puts me in de field with de rest. Marse Bat grow mostly cotton and it don't make no dif'ence is you big or li'l, you better keep up or de drivers burn you up with de whip, sho' 'nough. Old Marse Bat never put a lick on me all de years I 'longs to him, but de drivers sho' burnt me plenty times. Sometime I gits so tired come night, I draps right in de row and gone to sleep. Den de driver come 'long and, wham, dey cuts you 'cross de back with de whip and you wakes up when it lights on you, yes, suh! 'Bout nine o'clock dey hollers 'cotton up' and dat de quittin' signal. We goes to de quarters and jes' drap on de bunk and go to sleep without nothin' to eat.

"On old Bat's place dat all us know, is work and more work. De onlies' time we has off am Sunday and den we has to wash and mend clothes. De first Sunday of de month a white preacher come, but all he say is 'bedience to de white folks, and we hears 'nough of dat without him tellin' us.

"I 'member when White Pa come to try git mama and us chillen back. We been in Arkansas five, six year, and, whoosh, I sho' wants to go back to my White Pa, but old Bat wouldn't let us go. He come to our quarters dat night and tell mama if she or us chillen try to run off he'll kill us. Dey sho' watch us for awhile.

"Sometimes one of de niggers runs off but he ain't gone long. He gits hungry and comes back. Den he gits a burnin' with de bullwhip. Does he run 'way again, Marse Bat say he got too much rabbit in him and chains him up till he goes to Little Rock and sells him.

"I heared some white folks treat dey slaves good and give dem time off, but Marse Bat don't. We has plenty to eat and clothes, but dat all. Dat de way it was till we's freed, only it wasn't in Arkansas. It was down to Richmond, here in Texas, 'cause Marse Bat rents a farm at Richmond. He thunk if he brung us to Texas he wouldn't have to set us free. But he got fooled, 'cause a gov'ment man come tell us we's free. We had de crop planted and old Bat say if we'll stay through pickin' he'll pay us. Mama and us stayed awhile.

"I gits married legal with Richard Scott and we comes to Harrisburg and he gits a job on de section of de railroad. I's lived here ever since. My husban' and me raises five chillen, but only de one gal am alive now. My grandson takes care of me. He tells me iffen my husband lived so long, he be 107 years old. I know he was older dan me, but not 'xactly how much.

"Sometime I feel I's been here too long, 'cause I's paralyzed and can't move round none. But maybe de Lawd ain't ready for me yet, and de Debbil won't have me."

Abram Sells

Abram Sells was born a slave on the Rimes Plantation, which was located about 18 miles southeast of Newton, Texas. He does not know his age, but must be well along in the 80's, as his recollections of slavery days are keen. He lives at Jamestown, Texas.

"I was birthed on the Rimes Plantation, now called Harrisburg. My great-grand-daddy's name was Bowser Rimes and he was brung to Texas from Louisiana and die at 138 year old. He's buried on the old Ben Powell place close to Jasper. My grand-daddy, that's John, he lives to be 103 year old and he buried on the Eddy plantation at Jasper. My daddy, Mose Rimes, he die young at 86 and he buried in Jasper County, too. My mammy's name was Phoebe and she was birthed a Rimes nigger and brung to Texas from back in Louisiana. The year slaves was freed I was inherit by a man named Sells, what marry into the Rimes family and that's why my name's Sells, 'cause it change 'long with the marriage. Us was jes' ready to be ship back to Louisiana to the new massa's plantation when the end of the war break up the trip.

"You see, we all had purty good time on Massa Rimes's plantation. None of them carin' 'bout being sot free. They has to work hard all time, but that don' mean so much, 'cause they have to work iffen they was on they own, too. The old folks was 'lowed Saturday evenin' off or when they's sick, and us little ones, us not do much but bring in the wood and kindle the fires and tote water and he'p wash clothes and feed the little pigs and chickens.

"Us chillen hang round close to the big house and us have a old man that went round with us and look after us, white chillen and black chillen, and that old man was my great grand-daddy. Us sho' have to mind him, 'cause iffen we didn't, us sho' have bad luck. He allus have the pocket full of things to conjure with. That rabbit foot, he took it out and he work that on you till you take the creeps and git shakin' all over. Then there's a pocket full of fish scales and he kind of squeak and rattle them in the hand and right then you wish you was dead and promise to do anything. Another thing he allus have in the pocket was a li'l old dry-up turtle, jes' a mud turtle 'bout the size of a man's thumb, the whole thing jes' dry up and dead. With that thing he say he could do mos' anything, but he never use it iffen he ain't have to. A few times I seed him git all tangle up and boddered and he go off by hisself and sot down in a quiet place, take out this very turtle and put it in the palm of the hand and turn it round and round and say somethin' all the time. After while he git everything ontwisted and he come back with a smile on he face and maybe whistlin'.

"They fed all us nigger chillen in a big trough made out'n wood, maybe more a wood tray, dug out'n soft timber like magnolia or cypress. They put it under a tree in the shade in summer time and give each chile a wood spoon, then mix all the food up in the trough and us goes to eatin'. Mos' the food was potlicker, jes' common old potlicker; turnip green and the juice, Irish 'taters and the juice, cabbages and peas and beans, jes' anything what make potlicker. All us git round like so many li'l pigs and then us dish in with our wood spoon till it all gone.

"We has lots of meat at times. Old grand-daddy allus ketchin' rabbit in some kind of trap, mostly make out'n a holler log. He sot 'em round in the garden and sho' kotch the rabbits. And possums, us have a good possum dog, sometimes two or three, and every night you heered them dogs barkin' in the field down by the branch. Sho' 'nuf, they git possum treed and us go git him and parbile him and put him in the oven and bake him plumb tender. Then we stacks sweet 'taters round him and po' the juice over the whole thing. Now, there is somethin' good 'nuf for a king.

"There was lots of deer and turkey and squirrel in the wil' wood and somebody out huntin' nearly every day. Course Massa Rime's folks couldn't eat up all this meat befo' it spile and the niggers allus git a great big part of it. Then we kilt lots of hawgs and then talk 'bout eatin'! O, them chitlin's, sousemeat and the haslets, thats the liver and the lights all biled up together. Us li'l niggers fill up on sich as that and go to bed and mos' dream us is li'l pigs.

"Us allus have plenty to eat but didn't pay much 'tention to clothes. Boys and gals all dress jes' alike, one long shirt or dress. They call it a shirt iffen a boy wear it and call it a dress iffen the gal wear it. There wasn't no difference, 'cause they's all made out'n somethin' like duck and all white. That is, they's white when you fus' put them on, but after you wears them a while they git kind of pig-cullud, kind of grey, but still they's all the same color. Us all go barefoot in summer, li'l ones and big ones, but in winter us have homemake shoes. They tan the leather at home and make the shoe at home, allus some old nigger that kin make shoe. They was more like moc'sin, with lace made of deerskin. The soles was peg on with wood pegs out'n maple and sharpen down with a shoe knife.

"Us have hats make out'n pine straw, long leaf pine straw, tied together in li'l bunches and platted round and round till it make a kinder hat. That pine straw great stuff in them days and us use it in lots of ways. Us kivered sweet 'taters with it to keep them from git freeze and hogs made beds out'n it and folks too. Yes, sir, us slep' on it. The beds had jes' one leg. They bored two hole in the wall up in the corner and stuck two pole in them holes and lay plank on that like slats and pile lots of pine straw on that. Then they spread a homemake blanket or quilt on that and sometime four or five li'l niggers slep' in there to keep us warm.

"The li'l folks slep' mos' as long as they want to in daylight, but the big niggers have to come out'n that bed 'bout fo' o'clock when the big horn blow. The overseer have one nigger, he wake up early for to blow the horn and when he blow this horn he make sich a holler then all the res' of the niggers better git out'n that bed and 'pear at the barn 'bout daylight. He might not whip him for being late the fus' time, but that nigger better not forgit the secon' time and be late!

"Massa Rimes didn't whip them much, but iffen they was bad niggers he jes' sold them offen the place and let somebody else do the whippin'. Never have no church house or school, but Massa Rimes, he call them in and read the Bible to them. Then he turn the service over to some good, old, 'ligious niggers and let them finish with the singin' and prayin' and 'zorting. After peach [HW: "?"] cleared, a school was 'stablish and a white man come from the north to teach the cullud chillen, but befo' that they didn' take no pains to teach the niggers nothin' 'ceptin' to work, and the white chillen didn't have much school neither.

"That was one plantation what was run 'sclusively by itself. Massa Rimes have a commissary or sto' house, whar he kep' whatnot things—them what make on the plantation and things the slaves couldn' make for themselfs. That wasn't much, 'cause we make us own clothes and shoes and plow and all farm tools and us even make our own plow line out'n cotton and iffen us run short of cotton sometime make them out'n bear grass and we make buttons for us clothes out'n li'l round pieces of gourds and kiver them with cloth.

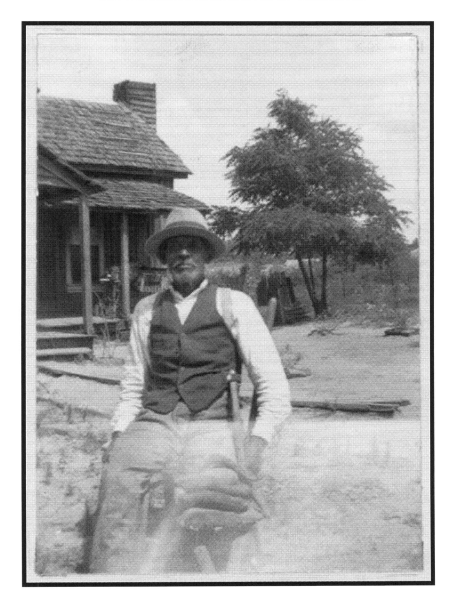

Abram Sells

"That wasn't sich a big plantation, 'bout a t'ousand acre and only 'bout forty niggers. There was'n no jail and they didn't need none. Us have no real doctor, but of course there was a doctor man at Jasper and one at Newton, but a nigger have to be purty sick 'fore they call a doctor. There's allus some old time nigger what knowed lots of remedies and knowed all dif'rent kinds of yarbs and roots. My grand-daddy, he could stop blood, and he could conjure off the fever and rub his fingers over warts and they'd git away. He make ile out'n rattlesnake for the rheumatis'. For the cramp he git a kind of bark offen a tree and it done the job, too. Some niggers wo' brass rings to keep off the rheumatis' and punch hole in a penny or dime and wear that on the ankle to keep off sickness.

267

"'Member the war? Course I does. I 'member how some of them march off in their uniforms, lookin' so grand, and how some of them hide out in the wood to keep from lookin' so grand. They was lots of talkin' 'bout fighting, and rubbing and scrubbing the old shotgun. The oldes' niggers was settin' round the fire late in the night, stirrin' the ashes with the poker and rakin' out the roas' 'taters. They's smokin' the old corn cob pipe and homemake tobacco and whisperin' right low and quiet like what they's gwineter do and whar they's gwineter to when Mister Lincoln, he turn them free.

"The more they talk, the more I git scared that the niggers is going to git sot free and wondering what I's gwine to do if they is. No, I guess I don't want to live back in them times no mo', but I sho' seed lots of niggers not doin' so well as they did when they was slaves and not havin' nigh as much to eat."

George Selman

George Selman was born in 1852, five miles east of Alto, Texas. His father was born in Virginia and his mother in South Carolina, and were brought to Texas by Mr. Dan Lewis. Green has been a Baptist minister since his youth. He lives in Jacksonville, Texas.

"We was a big fam'ly, nine children. I was born a slave of the Selmans, Marster Tom and Missus Polly, and they lived in Mississippi. Mother's name was Martha and my father's name was John Green Selman.

"Marster's folks come from Mississippi a long ways back and they had a big house made from hewed logs with a big hallway down the middle. The kitchen was out in the yard, 'bout forty steps from the house. The yard had five acres in it and a big garden was in it. Marster had five slave families and our cabins was built in a half circle in the back yard. I seemed to be the pet and always went with Marster Tom to town or wherever he was goin'. Then I learned to plow by my mother letting me hold the handles and walk along with her. Finally she let me go 'round by myself.

"Marster Tom was always good to us and he taught me religion. He was the best man I ever knew. Then Saturday noon come, they blew the horn and we quit workin'. We went to church one Sunday a month and we sat on one side and the white folks on the other.

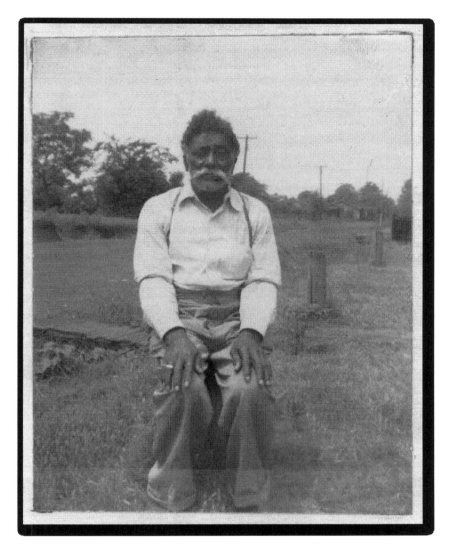

George Selman

"I never learnt to read and write, but I learned to work in the house and the fields. Late in the day Aunt Dicey, who was the cook, called all us children out under the big trees and give us supper. This was in summer, but nobody ever fed us but Aunt Dicey. We all ate from one bowl, or maybe I'd call it a tray 'cause it was made of wood, like a bread tray but bigger, big enough to hold three, four gallons. She put the food in the tray and give each chil' a spoon. Mostly we had pot likker and corn-bread. In winter we ate from the same tray, but in the kitchen.

"I never seen runaway slaves, but Marster Tom had a neighbor mean to slaves and sometimes when they was whipped we could hear 'em holler. The neighbor had one slave called Sallie, and she was a weaver and was so mean she had to wear a chain. After she died, I heered her ghost one night. I was stayin' with a white man who had the malaria-typhoid-pneumonia fever, and one night I heered Sallie scream and seen her chain drag back and forth. I tol' the man I knowed it was Sallie, 'cause I'd heered that scream for years. But the man said she was dead, so it mus' have been her ghost. I heered her night after night, screamin' and draggin' her chain up and down.

"When Marster Tom says we's free, I goes to his sister, Miss Ca'line and works for her. After sev'ral years I larned to preach and I's the author of most the Baptist churches in this county."

Callie Shepherd

Callie Shepherd, age 84, lives at 4701 Spring Ave., Dallas, Texas. She was born near Gilmer, Texas, in 1852, a slave of the Stevens family. At present she is cared for by her 68 year old son and his wife.

"Course I kin tell you. I got 'memberance like dey don't have nowadays. Dat 'cause things is goin' round and round too fast without no settin' and talkin' things over.

"I's native born right down here at Gilmer on de old place and Miss Fannie could tell you de same if she could be in your presence, but she went on to Glory many a year ago. She de one what raised me, right in de house with her own chillen. I slep' right in de house, in de chillens' room, in a little trundle bed what jus' pushed back under de big bed when de mornin' come. If her chillen et one side de table I et t'other side, right by Miss Fannie's elbow.

"Miss Fannie, she Dr. Steven's wife and dey from Georgia and lived near Gilmer till de doctor goes off to de war and takes a sickness what he ain't never get peart from and died. Died right there on de old place. He was a right livin' man and dey allus good to me and my mammy, what dey done brought from Georgia and she de main cook.

"My mammy don't think they ain't nobody like Miss Fannie. My mammy, she a little red-Indian nigger woman not so big as me, and Miss Fanny tell her, 'Don't you cry 'cause dey tryin' make freedom, 'cause de doctor done say we is gwine help you raise your babies.'

"Some de niggers don't like de treatment what dey white folks gives 'em and dey run away to de woods. I'd hear de nigger dogs a-runnin' and when dey cotch de niggers dey bites 'em all over and tears dey clothes and gits de skin, too. And de niggers, dey'd holler. I seed 'em whip de niggers, 'cause dey tolt de chillen to look. Dey buckled 'em down on de groun' and laid it on dey backs. Sometimes dey laid on with a mighty heavy hand. But I ain't never git no whippin' 'cause I never went with de cullud gen'ration. I set right in de buggy with de white chillen and went to hear Gospel preachin'.

Callie Shepherd

"I danced at de balls in de sixteen figure round sets and everybody in dem parts say I de principal dancer, but I gits 'ligion and left de old way to live in de 'termination to live beyon' dis vale of tears.

"I have my trib'lations after my old daddy die, 'cause he good to us little chillen. But my next daddy a man mighty rough on us. Dat after Miss Fannie done gone back to Georgia and my back done hurt me all de time from pullin' fodder and choppin' cotton. It make a big indif'rence after Miss Fannie gone, and de war de cause of it all. I heered de big cannons goin' on over there jus' like de bigges' clap of thunder.

"Me and de little chillen playin' in de road makin' frog houses out of sand when we hear de hosses comin'. We looks and see de budallions shinin' in de sun and de sojers have tin cups tied on side dere saddles and throwed dem cups to us chillen as dey passed. Dey say war is over and we is free. Miss Fannie say she a Seay from Georgia and she go back dere, but I jus' stay on where I's native born."

Betty Simmons

Betty Simmons, 100 or more, was born a slave to Leftwidge Carter, in Macedonia, Alabama. She was stolen when a child, sold to slave traders and later to a man in Texas. She now lives in Beaumont, Texas.

"I think I's 'bout a hunnerd and one or two year old. My papa was a free man, 'cause his old massa sot him free 'fore I's born, and give him a hoss and saddle and a little house to live in.

"My old massa when I's a chile, he name Mr. Leftwidge Carter and when he daughter marry Mr. Wash Langford, massa give me to her. She was call Clementine. Massa Langford has a little store and a man call Mobley go in business with him. Dis man brung down he two brothers and dey fair clean Massa Langford out. He was ruint.

"But while all dis goin' on I didn't know it and I was happy. Dey was good to me and I don't work too hard, jus' gits in de mischief. One time I sho' got drunk and dis de way of it. Massa have de puncheon of whiskey and he sell de whiskey, too. Now, in dem days, dey have frills 'round de beds, dey wasn't naked beds like nowdays. Dey puts dis puncheon under de beds and de frills hides it, but I's nussin' a little boy in dat room and I crawls under dat bed and drinks out of de puncheon. Den I poke de head out and say 'Boo' at de little boy, and he laugh and laugh. Den I ducks back and drinks a little more and I say 'Boo' at him 'gain, and he laugh and laugh. Dey was lots of whiskey in dat puncheon and I keeps drinkin' and sayin' 'Boo'. My head, it gits funny and I come out with de puncheon and starts to de kitchen, where my aunt Adeline was de cook. I jes' a-stompin' and sayin' de big words. Dey never lets me 'round where dat puncheon is no more.

"When Massa Langford was ruint and dey goin' take de store 'way from him, dey was trouble, plenty of dat. One day massa send me down to he brudder's place. I was dere two days and den de missy tell me to go to de fence. Dere was two white men in a buggy and one of 'em say, 'I thought she bigger dan dat.' Den he asks me, 'Betty, kin you cook?' I tells him I been cook helper two, three month, and he say, 'You git dressed and came on down three mile to de other side de post office.' So I gits my little bundle and whan I gits dere he say, 'Gal, you want to go 'bout 26 mile and help cook at de boardin' house?' He tries to make me believe I won't be gone a long time, but when I gits in de buggy dey tells me Massa Langford done los' everything and he have to hide out he niggers for to keep he credickers from gittin' dem. Some of de niggers he hides in de woods, but he stole me from my sweet missy and sell me so dem credickers can't git me.

"When we gits to de crossroads dere de massa and a nigger man. Dat another slave he gwine to sell, and he hate to sell us so bad he can't look us in de eye. Dey puts us niggers inside de buggy, so iffen de credickers comes along dey can't see us.

"Finally dese slave spec'laters puts de nigger man and me on de train and takes us to Memphis, and when we gits dere day takes us to de nigger traders' yard. We gits dere at breakfast time and waits for de boat dey calls de 'Ohio' to git dere. De boat jus' ahead of dis Ohio, Old Capt. Fabra's boat, was 'stroyed and dat delay our boat two hours. When it come, dey was 258 niggers out of dem nigger yards in Memphis what gits on dat boat. Dey puts de niggers upstairs and goes down de river far as Vicksburg, dat was de place, and den us gits offen de boat and gits on de train 'gain and dat time we goes to New Orleans.

"I's satisfy den I los' my people and ain't never goin' to see dem no more in dis world, and I never did. Dey has three big trader yard in New Orleans and I hear de traders say dat town 25 mile square. I ain't like it so well, 'cause I ain't like it 'bout dat big river. We hears some of 'em say dere's gwineter throw a long war and us all think what dey buy us for if we's gwine to be sot free. Some was still buyin' niggers every fall and us think it too funny dey kep' on fillin' up when dey gwineter be emptyin' out soon.

"Dey have big sandbars and planks fix 'round de nigger yards and dey have watchmans to keep dem from runnin 'way in de swamp. Some of de niggers dey have jus' picked up on de road, dey steals dem. Dey calls dem 'wagon boy' and 'wagon gal.' Dey has one bit mulatto boy dey stole 'long de road dat way and he massa find out 'bout him and come and git him and take him 'way. And a woman what was a seamster, a man what knowed her seed her in de pen and he done told her massa and he come right down and git her. She sho' was proud to git out. She was stole from 'long de road, too. You sees, if dey could steal de niggers and sell 'em for de good money, dem traders could make plenty money dat way.

"At las' Col. Fortescue, he buy me and kep' me. He a fighter in de Mexican war and he come to New Orleans to buy he slaves. He takes me up de Red River to Shreveport and den by de buggy to Liberty, in Texas.

"De Colonel, he a good massa to us. He 'lows us to work de patch of ground for ourselves, and maybe have a pig or a couple chickens for ourselves, and he allus make out to give us plenty to eat.

"De massa, when a place fill up, he allus pick and move to a place where dere ain't so much people. Dat how come de Colonel fus' left Alabama and come to Texas, and to de place dey calls Beef Head den, but calls Gran' Cane now.

"When us come to Gran' Cane a nigger boy git stuck on one us house girls and he run away from he massa and foller us. It were a woodly country and de boy outrun he chasers. I heered de dogs after him and he torn and bleedin' with de bresh and he run upstair in de gin house. De dogs sot down by de door and de dog-man, what hired to chase him, he drug him down and throw him in de Horse Hole and tells de two dogs to swim in and git him. De boy so scairt he yell and holler but de dogs nip and pinch him good with de claws and teeth.

When dey lets de boy out de water hole he all bit up and when he massa larn how mean de dog-man been to de boy he 'fuses to pay de fee.

"I gits married in slavery time, to George Fortescue. De massa he marry us sort of like de justice of de peace. But my husban', he git kilt in Liberty, when he cuttin' down a tree and it fall on him. I ain't never marry no more.

"I sho' was glad when freedom come, 'cause dey jus' ready to put my little three year old boy in de field. Dey took 'em young. I has another baby call Mittie, and she too young to work. I don't know how many chillen I's have, and sometimes I sits and tries to count 'em. Dey's seven livin' but I had 'bout fourteen.

Betty Simmons

"Dey was pretty hard on de niggers. Iffen us have de baby us only 'lowed to stay in de house for one month and card and spin, and den us has to get out in de field. Dey allus blow de horn for us mammies to come up and nuss de babies.

"I seed plenty soldiers 'fore freedom. Dey's de Democrats, 'cause I never seed no Yankees. Us niggers used to wash and iron for dem. At night us seed dose soldiers peepin' 'round de house and us run 'way in de bresh.

"When freedom come us was layin' by de crop and de massa he give us a gen'rous part of dat crop and us move to Clarks place. We gits on all right after freedom, but it hard at first 'cause us didn't know how to do for ourselves. But we has to larn."

George Simmons

George Simmons, born in Alabama in 1854, was owned by Mr. Steve Jaynes, who lived near Beaumont, Texas. George has a good many memories of slavery years, although he was still a child when he was freed. He now lives in Beaumont, Tex.

"I's bo'n durin' slavery, somewhar in Alabama, but I don' 'member whar my mammy said. Dey brung me here endurin' de War and I belonged to Massa Steve Jaynes, and he had 'bout 75 other niggers. It was a big place and lots of wo'k, but I's too little to do much 'cept errands 'round de house.

"Massa Jaynes, he raised cotton and co'n and he have 'bout 400 acres. He 'spected de niggers to wo'k hard from mornin' till sundown, but he was fair in treatin' 'em. He give us plenty to eat and lots of cornbread and black-eye' peas and plenty hawg meat and sich. We had possum sometimes, too. Jus' took a nice, fat possum we done cotched in de woods and skinned 'im and put 'im in a oven and roas' 'im with sweet 'tatoes all 'round and make plenty gravy. Dat was good.

"Massa Jaynes, he 'lowed de slaves who wanted to have a little place to make garden, veg'tables and dose kin' of things. He give 'em seed and de nigger could have all he raised in his little garden. We was all well kep' and I don' see whar freedom was much mo' better, in a way. Course, some massas was bad to dere slaves and whipped 'em so ha'd dey's nearly dead. I know dat, 'cause I heered it from de neighbors places. Some of dere slaves would run away and hide in de woods and mos' of 'em was kotched with dogs. Fin'ly dey took to puttin' bells on de slaves so iffen dey run away, dey could hear 'em in de woods. Dey put 'em on with a chain, so dey couldn' get 'em off.

"We could have church on Sunday and our own cullud church. Sam Watson, he was de nigger preacher and he's a slave, too.

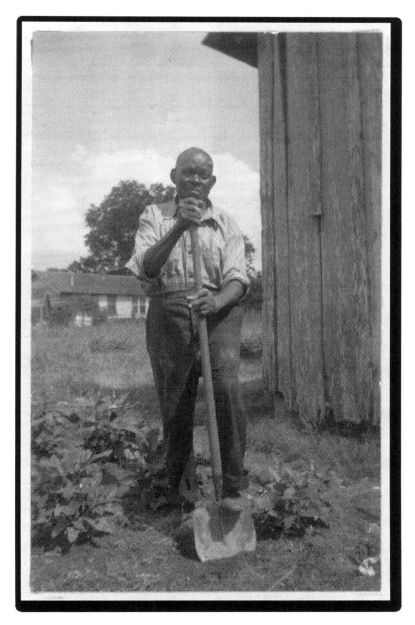

George Simmons

"I didn' know much 'bout de war, 'cause we couldn' read and de white folks didn' talk war much 'fore us. But we heered things and I 'member de sojers on dere way back after it's all over. Dey wasn' dressed in a uniform and dey clothes was mos'ly rags, dey was dat tore up. We seed 'em walkin' on de road and sometimes dey had ole wagons, but mos' times dey walk. I 'member some Yankee sojers, too. Dey have canteens over de shoulder, and mos' of 'em has blue uniforms on.

"Massa, he tell us when freedom come, and some of us stays 'round awhile, 'cause whar is we'uns goin'? We didn' know what to do and we didn' know how to keep ourselves, and what was we to do to get food and a place to live? Dose was ha'd times, 'cause de country tore up and de business bad.

"And de Kluxes dey range 'round some. Dey soon plays out but dey took mos' de time to scare de niggers. One time dey comes to my daddy's house and de leader, him in de long robe, he say, 'Nigger, quick you and git me a drink of water.' My daddy, he brung de white folks drinkin' gourd and dat Klux, he say, 'Nigger, I say git me a big drink—bring me dat bucket. I's thirsty.' He drinks three buckets of water, we thinks he does, but what you think we learns? He has a rubber bag under his robe and is puttin' dat water in dere!"

Ben Simpson

Ben Simpson, 90, was born in Norcross, Georgia, a slave of the Stielszen family. He had a cruel master, and was afraid to tell the truth about his life as a slave, until assured that no harm would come to him. Ben now lives in Madisonville, Texas, and receives a small old age pension.

"Boss, I's born in Georgia, in Norcross, and I's ninety years old. My father's name was Roger Stielszen and my mother's name was Betty. Massa Earl Stielszen captures them in Africa and brung them to Georgia. He got kilt and my sister and me went to his son. His son was a killer. He got in trouble there in Georgia and got him two good-stepping hosses and the covered wagon. Then he chains all he slaves round the necks and fastens the chains to the hosses and makes then walk all the way to Texas. My mother and my sister had to walk. Emma was my sister. Somewhere on the road it went to snowin' and massa wouldn't let us wrap anything round our feet. We had to sleep on the ground, too, in all that snow.

"Massa have a great, long whip platted out of rawhide and when one the niggers fall behind or give out, he hit him with that whip. It take the hide every time he hit a nigger. Mother, she give out on the way, 'bout the line of Texas. Her feet got raw and bleedin' and her legs swoll plumb out of shape. Then massa, he jus' take out he gun and shot her, and whilst she lay dyin' he kicks her two, three times and say, 'Damn a nigger what can't stand nothin'.' Boss, you know that man, he wouldn't bury mother, jus' leave her layin' where he shot her at. You know, then there wasn't no law 'gainst killin' nigger slaves.

"He come plumb to Austin through that snow. He taken up farmin' and changes he name to Alex Simpson, and changes our names, too. He cut logs and builded he home on the side of them mountains. We never had no quarters. When night-time come he locks the chain round our necks and then locks it round a tree. Boss, our bed were the ground. All he feed us was raw meat and green corn. Boss, I et many a green weed. I was hongry. He never let us eat at noon, he worked us all day without stoppin'. We went naked, that the way he worked us. We never had any clothes.

"He brands us. He brand my mother befo' us left Georgia. Boss, that nearly kilt her. He brand her in the breast, then between the shoulders. He brand all us.

"My sister, Emma, was the only woman he have till he marries. Emma was wife of all seven Negro slaves. He sold her when she's 'bout fifteen, jus' befo' her baby was born. I never seen her since.

"Boss, massa was a outlaw. He come to Texas and deal in stolen hosses. Jus' befo' he's hung for stealin' hosses, he marries a young Spanish gal. He sho' mean to her. Whips her 'cause she want him to leave he slaves alone and live right. Bless her heart, she's the best gal in the world. She was the best thing God ever put life in the world. She cry and cry every time massa go off. She let us a-loose and she feed us good one time while he's gone. Missy Selena, she turn us a-loose and we wash in the creek clost by. She jus' fasten the chain on us and give us great big pot cooked meat and corn, and up he rides. Never says a word but come to see what us eatin'. He pick up he whip and whip her till she falls. If I could have got a-loose I'd kilt him. I swore if I ever got a-loose I'd kill him. But befo' long after that he fails to come home, and some people finds him hangin' to a tree. Boss, that long after war time he got hung. He didn't let us free. We wore chains all the time. When we work, we drug them chains with us. At night he lock us to a tree to keep us from runnin' off. He didn't have to do that. We were 'fraid to run. We knew he'd kill us. Besides, he brands us and they no way to get it off. It's put there with a hot iron. You can't git it off.

"If a slave die, massa made the rest of us tie a rope round he feet and drug him off. Never buried one, it was too much trouble.

"Massa allus say he be rich after the war. He stealin' all the time. He have a whole mountain side where he keep he stock. Missy Selena tell us one day we sposed to be free, but he didn't turn us a-loose. It was 'bout three years after the war they hung him. Missy turned us a-loose.

"I had a hard time then. All I had to eat was what I could find and steal. I was 'fraid of everybody. I jus' went wild and to the woods, but, thank God, a bunch of men taken they dogs and run me down. They carry me to they place. Gen. Houston had some niggers and he made them feed me. He made them keep me till I git well and able to work. Then he give me a job. I marry one the gals befo' I leaves them. I'm plumb out of place there at my own weddin'. Yes, suh, boss, it wasn't one year befo' that I'm the wild nigger. We had thirteen chillen.

"I farms all my life after that. I didn't know nothin' else to do. I made plenty cotton, but now I'm too old. Me and my wife is alone now. This old nigger gits the li'l pension from the gov'ment. I not got much longer to stay here. I's ready to see God but I hope my old massa ain't there to torment me again."

Giles Smith

Giles Smith, 79, now residing at 3107 Blanchard St., Fort Worth, Texas, was born a slave of Major Hardway, on a plantation near Union Springs, Alabama. The Major gave Giles to his daughter when he was an infant and he never saw his parents again. In 1874 Frank Talbot brought Giles to Texas, and he worked on the farm two years. He then went to Brownwood and worked in a gin seventeen years. In 1908 he moved to Fort Worth and worked for a packing company. Old age led to his discharge in 1931 and he has since worked at any odd jobs he could find.

"My name am Giles Smith, 'cause my pappy was born on the Smith plantation and I took his name. I's born at Union Springs, in Alabama and Major Hardway owned me and 'bout a hundred other slaves. But he gave me to Mary, his daughter, when I's only a few months old and had to be fed on a bottle, 'cause she am jus' married to Massa Miles. She told me how she carried me home in her arms. She say I was so li'l she have a hard time to make me eat out the bottle, and I put up a good fight so she nearly took me back.

"I don't 'member the start of the war, but de endin' I does. Massa Miles called all us together and told us we's free and it give us all de jitters. He treated all us fine and nobody wanted to go. He and Missy am de best folks de Lawd could make. I stayed till I was sixteen years old.

"It am years after freedom Missy Mary say to me what massa allus say, 'If the nigger won't follow orders by kind treatin', sich nigger am wrong in the head and not worth keepin'. He didn't have to rush us. We'd just dig in and do the work. One time Massa clearin' some land and it am gittin' late for breakin' the ground. Us allus have Saturday afternoon and Sunday off. Old Jerry says to us, 'Tell yous what us do,—go to the clearin' this afternoon and Sunday and finish for the Massa. That sho' make him glad.'

"Saturday noon came and nobody tells the massa but go to that clearin' and sing while us work, cuttin' bresh and grubbin' stomps and burnin' bresh. Us sing

"'Hi, ho, ug, hi, ho, ug.
De sharp bit, de strong arm,
Hi, ho, ug, hi, ho, ug,
Dis tree am done 'fore us warm.'

"De massa come out and his mouth am slippin' all over he face and he say, 'What this all mean? Why you workin' Saturday afternoon?'

"Old Jerry am a funny cuss and he say, 'Massa, O, massa, please don't whop us for cuttin' down yous trees.'

"I's gwine whop you with the chicken stew,' Massa say. And for Sunday dinner dere am chicken stew with noodles and peach cobbler.

"So I stays with massa and after I's fifteen he pays me $2.00 the month, and course I gits my eats and my clothes, too. When I gits the first two I don't know what to do, 'cause it the first money I ever had. Missy make the propulation to keep the money and buy for me and teach me 'bout it. There ain't much to buy, 'cause we make nearly everything right there. Even the tobaccy am made. They put honey 'twixt the leaves and put a pile of it 'twixt two boards with weights. It am left for a month and that am a man's tobaccy. A weaklin' better stay off that kind tobaccy.

"First I works in the field and then am massa's coachman. But when I's 'bout sixteen I gits a idea to go off somewheres for myself. I hears 'bout Mr. Frank Talbot, whom am takin' some niggers to Texas and I goes with him to the Brazos River bottom, and works there two years. I's lonesome for massa and missy and if I'd been clost enough, I'd sho' gone back to the old plantation. So after two years I quits and goes to work for Mr. Winfield Scott down in Brownwood, in the gin, for seventeen years.

"Well, shortly after I gits to Brownwood I meets a yaller gal and after dat I don't care to go back to Alabama so hard. I's married to Dee Smith on December the eighteenth, in 1880, and us live together many years. She died six years ago. Us have six chillen but I don't know where one of them are now. They all forgit their father in his old age! They not so young, either.

Giles Smith

"My woman could write a little so she write missy for me, and she write back and wish us luck and if we ever wants to come back to the old home we is welcome. Us write back' forth with her. Finally, us git the letter what say she sick, and then awful low. That 'bout twenty-five years after I marries. That am too much for me, and I catches the next train back to Alabama but I gits there too late. She am dead, and I never has forgive myself, 'cause I don't go back befo' she die, like she ask us to, lots of times.

"I comes here fifteen years ago and here I be. The last six year I can't work in the packin' plants no more. I's too old. Anything I can find to do I does, but it ain't much no more.

"The worst grief I's had, am to think I didn't go see missy 'fore she die. I's never forgave myself for that."

James W. Smith

James W. Smith, 77, was born a slave of the Hallman family, in Palestine, Texas. James became a Baptist minister in 1895, and preached until 1931, when poor health forced him to retire. He and his wife live at 1306 E. Fourth St., Fort Worth, Texas.

"Yes, suh, I'm birthed a slave, but never worked as sich, 'cause I's too young. But I 'members hearin' my mother tell all about her slave days and our master. He was John Hallman and owned a place in Palestine, with my mother and father and fifty other slaves. My folks was house servants and lived a little better'n the field hands. De cabins was built cheap, though, no money, only time for buildin' am de cost. Dey didn't use nails and helt de logs in place by dovetailin'. Dey closed de space between de logs with wedges covered with mud and straw. De framework for de door was helt by wooden pegs and so am de benches and tables. Master Hallman always had some niggers trained for carpenter work, and one to be blacksmith and one to make shoes and harness.

"We was lucky to have de kind master, what give us plenty to eat. If all de people now could have jus' so good food what we had, there wouldn't be no beggin' by hungry folks or need for milk funds for starved babies.

"We didn't have purty clothes sich as now, with all de dif'rent colors mixed up, but dey was warm and lastin', dyed brown and black. De black oak and cherry made de dyes. Our shoes wasn't purty, either. I has to laugh when I think of de shoes. There wasn't no careful work put on dem, but dey covered de feets and lasted near forever.

"Master always wanted to help his cullud folks live right and my folks always said de best time of they lives was on de old plantation. He always 'ranged for parties and sich. Yes, suh, he wanted dem to have a good time, but no foolishment, jus' good, clean fun. There am dancin' and singin' mostest every Saturday night. He had a little platform built for de jiggin' contests. Cullud folks comes from all round, to see who could jig de best. Sometimes two niggers each put a cup of water on de head and see who could jig de hardest without spillin' any. It was lots of fun.

"I must tell you 'bout de best contest we ever had. One nigger on our place was de jigginest fellow ever was. Everyone round tries to git somebody to best him. He could put de glass of water on his head and make his feet go like triphammers and sound like de snaredrum. He could whirl round and sich, all de movement from his hips down. Now it gits noised round a fellow been found to beat Tom and a contest am 'ranged for Saturday evenin'. There was a big crowd and money am bet, but master bets on Tom, of course.

"So dey starts jiggin'. Tom starts easy and a little faster and faster. The other fellow doin' de same. Dey gits faster and faster and dat crowd am a-yellin'. Gosh! There am 'citement. Dey jus' keep a-gwine. It look like Tom done found his match, but there am one thing yet he ain't done—he ain't made de whirl. Now he does it. Everyone holds he breath, and de other fellow starts to make de whirl and he makes it, but jus' a spoonful of water sloughs out his cup, so Tom am de winner.

"When freedom come, the master tells his slaves and says, 'What you gwine do?' Wall, suh, not one of dem knows dat. De fact am, dey's scared dey gwine be put off de place. But master says dey can stay and work for money or share crop. He says they might be trouble 'twixt de whites and niggers and likely it be best to stay and not git mixed in dis and dat org'ization. Mostest stays, only one or two goes away. My folks stays for five years after de war. Den my father moves to Bertha Creek, where he done 'range for a farm of his own. They hated to leave master's plantation, he's so good and kind.

"Some the cullud folks thinks they's to take charge and run the gov'ment. They asks my father to jine their org'ization. He goes once and some eggs am served. Dey am served by de crowd and dem eggs ain't fresh yard eggs. Father 'cides he wants his eggs served dif'rent, and he likes dem fresh, so he takes master's advice and don't jine nothing.

"When de Klux come, de cullud org'ization made their scatterment. Plenty gits whipped round our place and some what wasn't 'titled to it. Den soldiers comes and puts order in de section. Dey has trouble about votin'. De cullud folks in dem days was non-knowledge, so how could dey vote 'telligent? Dat am foolishment to 'sist on de right to vote. It de non-knowledge what hurts. Myself, I never voted and am too far down de road now to start.

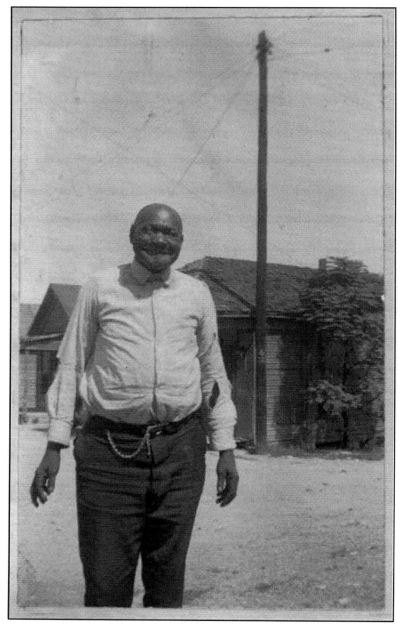

James W. Smith

"I worked at farmin' till 1895 when I starts preachin' in de Baptist church. I kept that up till 1931, but my health got too bad and I had to quit. I has de pressure bad. When I preaches, I preaches hard, and de doctor says dat am danger for me.

"The way I learns to preach am dis: after surrender, I 'tends de school two terms and den I studies de Bible and I's a nat'ral talker and gifted for de Lawd's work, so I starts preachin'.

"Jennie Goodman and me marries in 1885 and de Lawd never blessed us with any chillen. We gits de pension, me $16.00 and her $14.00, and gits by on dat. It am for de rations and de eats, but de clothes am a question!"

Jordon Smith

Jordon Smith, 86, was born in Georgia, a slave of the Widow Hicks. When she died, Jordon, his mother and thirty other slaves were willed to Ab Smith, his owner's nephew, and were later refugeed from Georgia to Anderson Co., Texas. When freed, Jordon worked on a steamboat crew on the Red River until the advent of railroads. For thirty years Jordon worked for the railroad. He is now too feeble to work and lives with his third wife and six children in Marshall, Texas, supported by the latter and his pension of $10.00 a month.

"I's borned in Georgia, next to the line of North Car'lina, on Widow Hick's place. My papa died 'fore I's borned but my mammy was called Aggie. My ole missus died and us fell to her nephew, Ab Smith. My granma and granpa was full-blooded Africans and I couldn't unnerstand their talk.

"My missus was borned on the Chattahoochee River and she had 2,000 acres of land in cul'vation, a thousand on each side the river, and owned 500 slaves and 250 head of work mules. She was the richest woman in the whole county.

"Us slaves lived in a double row log cabins facin' her house and our beds was made of rough plank and mattresses of hay and lynn bark and shucks, make on a machine. I's spinned many a piece of cloth and wove many a brooch of thread.

"Missus didn't 'low her niggers to work till they's 21, and the chillen played marbles and run round and kick their heels. The first work I done was hoeing and us worked long as we could see a stalk of cotton or hill of corn. Missus used to call us at Christmas and give the old folks a dollar and the rest a dinner. When she died me and my mother went to Ab Smith at the dividement of the property. Master Ab put us to work on a big farm he bought and it was Hell 'mong the yearlin's if you crost him or missus either. It was double trouble and a cowhidin' whatever you do. She had a place in the kitchen where she tied their hands up to the wall and cowhided them and sometimes cut they back 'most to pieces. She made all go to church and let the women wear some her old, fine dresses to hide the stripes where she'd beat them. Mammy say that to keep the folks at church from knowin' how mean she was to her niggers.

"Master Ab had a driver and if you didn't do what that driver say, master say to him, 'Boy, come here and take this nigger down, a hunerd licks this time.' Sometimes us run off and go to a dance without a pass and 'bout time they's kickin' they heels and getting sot for the big time, in come a patterroller and say, 'Havin' a big time, ain't you? Got a pass?' If you didn't, they'd git four or five men to take you out and when they got through you'd sho' go home.

"Master Ab had hunerds acres wheat and made the women stack hay in the field. Sometimes they got sick and wanted to go to the house, but he made them lay down on a straw-pile in the field. Lots of chillen was borned on a straw-pile in the field. After the chile was borned he sent them to the house. I seed that with my own eyes.

"They was a trader yard in Virginia and one in New Orleans and sometimes a thousand slaves was waitin' to be sold. When the traders knowed men was comin' to buy, they made the slaves all clean up and greased they mouths with meat skins to look like they's feedin' them plenty meat. They lined the women up on one side and the men on the other. A buyer would walk up and down 'tween the two rows and grab a woman and try to throw her down and feel of her to see how she's put up. If she's purty strong, he'd say, 'Is she a good breeder?' If a gal was 18 or 19 and put up good she was worth 'bout $1,500. Then the buyer'd pick out a strong, young nigger boy 'bout the same age and buy him. When he got them home he'd say to them, 'I want you two to stay together. I want young niggers.'

"If a nigger ever run off the place and come back, master'd say, 'If you'll be a good nigger, I'll not whip you this time.' But you couldn't 'lieve that. A nigger run off and stayed in the woods six month. When he come back he's hairy as a cow, 'cause he lived in a cave and come out at night and pilfer round. They put the dogs on him but couldn't cotch him. Fin'ly he come home and master say he won't whip him and Tom was crazy 'nough to 'lieve it. Master say to the cook, 'Fix Tom a big dinner,' and while Tom's eatin', master stand in the door with a whip and say, 'Tom, I's change my mind; you have no business runnin' off and I's gwine take you out jus' like you come into the world.

"Master gits a bottle whiskey and a box cigars and have Tom tied up out in the yard. He takes a chair and say to the driver, 'Boy, take him down, 250 licks this time.' Then he'd count the licks. When they's 150 licks it didn't look like they is any place left to hit, but master say, 'Finish him up.' Then he and the driver sot down, smoke cigars and drink whiskey, and master tell Tom how he must mind he master. Then he lock Tom up in a log house and master tell all the niggers if they give him anything to eat he'll skin 'em alive. The old folks slips Tom bread and meat. When he gits out, he's gone to the woods 'gain. They's plenty niggers what stayed in the woods till surrender.

"I heared some slaves say they white folks was good to 'em, but it was a tight fight where us was. I's thought over the case a thousand times and figured it was 'cause all men ain't made alike. Some are bad and some are good. It's like that now. Some folks you works for got no heart and some treat you white. I guess it allus will be that way.

"They was more ghosts and hants them days than now. It look like when I's comin' up they was common as pig tracks. They come in different forms and shapes, sometimes like a dog or cat or goat or like a man. I didn't 'lieve in 'em till I seed one. A fellow I knowed could see 'em every time he went out. One time us walkin' 'long a country lane and he say,

'Jordon, look over my right shoulder.' I looked and see a man walkin' without a head. I broke and run plumb off from the man I's with. He wasn't scart of 'em.

"I's refugeed from Georgia to Anderson County 'fore the war. I see Abe Lincoln onct when he come through, but didn't none of know who he was. I heared the president wanted 'em to work the young niggers till they was twenty-one but to free the growed slaves. They say he give 'em thirty days to 'siderate it. The white folks said they'd wade blood saddle deep 'fore they'd let us loose. I don't blame 'em in a way, 'cause they paid for us. In 'nother way it was right to free us. We was brought here and no person is sposed to be made a brute.

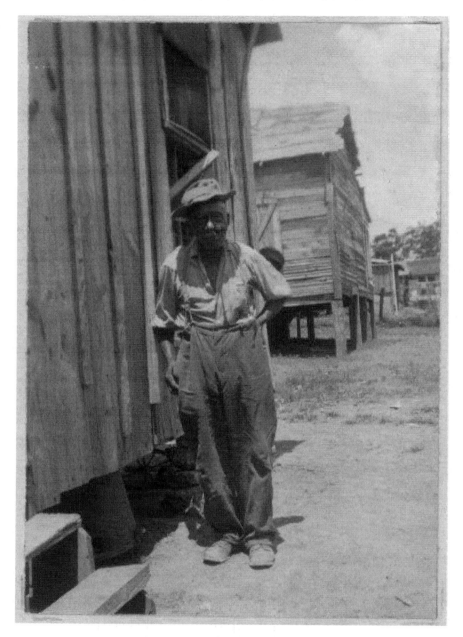

Jordon Smith

"After surrender, Massa Ab call us and say we could go. Mammy stayed but I left with my uncles and aunts and went to Shreveport where the Yanks was. I didn't hear from my mammy for the nex' twenty years.

"In Ku Klux times they come to our house and I stood tremblin', but they didn't bother us. I heared 'em say lots of niggers was took down in Sabine bottom and Kluxed, just 'cause they wanted to git rid of 'em. I think it was desperados what done that, 'stead of the Ku Klux. That was did in Panola County, in the Bad Lands. Bill Bateman and Hulon Gresham and Sidney Farney was desperados and would kill a nigger jus' to git rid of him. Course, lots of folks was riled up at the Kluxers and blamed 'em for everything.

"I's voted here in Marshall. Every nation has a flag but the cullud race. The flag is what protects 'em. We wasn't invited here, but was brought here, and don't have no place else to go. We was brought under this government and it's right we be led and told what to do. The cullud folks has been here more'n a hunerd years and has help make the United States what it is. The only thing that'll help the cause is separation of the races. I'll not be here when it comes, but it's bound to, 'cause the Bible say that some day all the races of people will be separated. Since 1865 till now the cullud race have done nothing but go to destruction. There was a time a man could control his wife and family, but you can't do that now.

"After surrender I went to Shreveport and steamboated from there to New Orleans, then to Vicksburg. Old hands was paid $15.00 a trip. I come here in 1872 and railroaded 30 years, on the section gang and in the shops. Since then I farmed and I's had three wives and nineteen chillen and they are scattered all over the state. Since I's too old to farm I work at odd jobs and git a $10.00 a month pension."

Millie Ann Smith

Millie Ann Smith was born in 1850, in Rusk Co., Texas, a slave of George Washington Trammell, a pioneer planter of the county. Trammell bought Millie's mother and three older children in Mississippi before Millie's birth, and brought them to Texas, leaving Millie's father behind. Later he ran away to Texas and persuaded Trammell to buy him, so he could be with his family.

"I's born 'fore war started and 'members when it ceased. I guess mammy's folks allus belonged to the Trammells, 'cause I 'member my grandpa, Josh Chiles, and my grandma, call Jeanette. I's a strappin' big girl when they dies. Grandpa used to say he come to Texas with Massa George Trammell's father when Rusk County was jus' a big woods, and the first two years he was hunter for the massa. He stay in the woods all the time, killing deer and wild hawgs and turkeys and coons and the like for the white folks to eat, and the land's full of Indians. He kinda taken up with them and had holes in the nose and ears. They was put there by the Indians for rings what they wore. Grandpa could talk mos' any Indian talk and he say he used to run off from his massa and stay with the Indians for weeks. The massa'd go to the Indian camp looking for grandpa and the Indians hided him out and say, 'No see him.'

"How mammy and we'uns come to Texas, Massa George brung his wife and three chillen from Mississippi and he brung we'uns. Pappy belonged to Massa Moore over in Mississippi and Massa George didn't buy him, but after mammy got here, that 'fore I's born, pappy runs off and makes his way to Texas and gits Massa George to buy him.

"Massa George and Missy America lived in a fine, big house and they owned more slaves and land than anybody in the county and they's the richest folks 'round there. Us slaves lived down the hill from the big house in a double row of log cabins and us had good beds, like our white folks. My grandpa made all the beds for the white folks and us niggers, too. Massa didn't want anything shoddy 'round him, he say, not even his nigger quarters.

"I's sot all day handin' thread to my mammy to put in the loom, 'cause they give us homespun clothes, and you'd better keep 'em if you didn't want to go naked.

"Massa had a overseer and nigger driver call Jacob Green. If a nigger was hard to make do the right thing, they ties him to a tree, but Massa George never whip 'em too hard, jus' 'nough to make 'em 'have.

"The slaves what worked in the fields was woke up 'fore light with a horn and worked till dark, and then there was the stock to tend to and cloth to weave. The overseer come 'round at nine o'clock to see if all is in the bed and then go back to his own house. When us knowed he's sound asleep we'd slip out and run 'round, sometimes. They locked the young men up in a house at night and on Sunday to keep 'em from runnin' 'round. It was a log house and had cracks in it and once a little nigger boy pokes his hand in tryin' to tease them men and one of 'em chops his fingers off with the ax.

"Massa didn' 'low no nigger to read and write, if he knowed it. George Wood was the only one could read and write and how he larn, a little boy on the 'jining place took up with him and they goes off in the woods and he shows George how to read and write. Massa never did find out 'bout that till after freedom.

"We slips off and have prayer but daren't 'low the white folks know it and sometime we hums 'ligious songs low like when we's workin'. It was our way of prayin' to be free, but the white folks didn't know it. I 'member mammy used to sing like this:

> "'Am I born to die, to lay this body down.
> Must my tremblin' spirit fly into worlds unknown,
> The land of deepes' shade,
> Only pierce' by human thought.'

"Massa George 'lowed them what wanted to work a little ground for theyselves and grandpa made money sellin' wild turkey and hawgs to the poor white folks. He used to go huntin' at night or jus' when he could.

Millie Ann Smith

"Them days we made our own med'cine out of horsemint and butterfly weed and Jerusalem oak and bottled them teas up for the winter. Butterfly Weed tea was for the pleurisy and the others for the chills and fever. As reg'lar as I got up I allus drank my asafoetida and tar water.

"I 'member Massa George furnishes three of his niggers, Ed Chile and Jacob Green and Job Jester, for mule skinners. I seed the government come and take off a big bunch of mules off our place. Mos' onto four year after the war, three men comes to Massa George and makes him call us up and turn us loose. I heered 'em say its close onto four year we's been free, but that's the first we knowed 'bout it.

"Pappy goes to work at odd jobs and mammy and I goes to keep house for a widow woman and I stays there till I marries, and that to Tom Smith. We had five chillen and now Tom's dead and I lives on that pension from the government, what is $16.00 a month, and I's glad to git it, 'cause I's too old to work."

Susan Smith

Susan Smith is not sure of her age, but appears to be in the late eighties. She was a slave of Charles Weeks, in Iberia, Louisiana. Susan was dressed in a black and white print, a light blue apron and a black velvet hat when interviewed, and seemed to be enjoying the generous quid of tobacco she took as she started to tell her story.

"I 'lieve I was nine or ten when freedom come, 'cause I was nursing for the white folks. Old massa was Charlie Weeks and he lived in Iberia. His sons, Willie and Ned, dey run business in de court house. One of dem tax collector and de other lookin' after de land, and am de surveyor. Old missus named Mag Weeks.

"My pa named Dennis Joe and ma named Sabry Joe, and dey borned and raised on Weeks Island, in Louisiana. After dey old massa die, dey was 'vided up and falls to Massa Charlie Weeks, and dat where I borned, in Iberia on Bayou Teche.

"Massa Charlie, he live in de big brick house with white columns and everybody what pass dere know dat place. Dey have de great big tomb in corner de yard, where dey buries all dey folks, but buries de cullud folks back of de quarters. Dey's well fix in Louisiana, but not so good after dey come to Texas.

"Dey used to have big Christmas in Louisiana and lots of things for us, and a big table and kill hawgs and have lots to eat. But old Missus Mag, she allus treat me like her own chillen and make me set at de table with dem and eat.

"I was with Missus Mag on a visit to Mansfield when de war starts at six o'clock Sunday and go till six o'clock Monday. I went over dat battlefield and look at dem sojers dey kill. David McGill, a young massa, he git kill. He uncle, William Weeks, what done hired him to jine the army in he place, he goes to the battlefield to look for Massa David. De only way he knowed it was him, he have two gold eyeteeth with diamonds in dem. Some dem hurt sojers was prayin' and some cussin'. You could hear some dem hollerin', 'Oh, Gawd, help me.' Dey was layin' so thick you have to step over dem.

"I seed de sojers in Iberia. Dey take anythin' dey wants. Dey cotch de cow and kill it and eat it. Dey have de camp dere and dey jus' carry on. I used to go to de camp, 'cause dey give me crackers and sardines. But after dat Mansfield battle dey have up white flags and dey ain't no more war dere. But while it gwine on, I go to de camp and sometimes dem sojers give me meat and barbecue. Dey one place dere a lump salt big as dis house, and dey set fire to de house and left dat big lump salt. Anywhere dey camp dey burns up de house.

"I didn't know I'm free till a man say to me, 'Sissy, ain't you know you ain't got no more massa or missus?' I say, 'No, suh.' But I stays with dem till I git marry, and slep' right in dey house and nuss for dem. Dey give me de big weddin', too. De noter public in Iberia, he marry us. My husband name Henry Smith and dat when I'm fifteen year old. I so big-limb and fat den I bigger den what I is now.

"I ain't had no husband for a time. I can't cast de years, he been dead so long. Us have fifteen chillen, and seven livin' now.

"Sperrits? I used to see dem. I scart of dem. Sometime dey looks nat'ral and sometime like de shadow. Iffen dey look like de shadow, jus' keep on lookin' at dem till dey looks nat'ral. Iffen you walks 'long, dey come right up side you. Iffen you looks over you left shoulder, you see dem. Dey makes de air feel warm and you hair rise up, and sometime dey gives you de cold chills. You can feel it when dey with you. I set here and seed dem standin' in dat gate. Dey goes round like dey done when dey a-livin'. Some say dey can't cross water.

"I heared talk of de bad mouth. A old woman put bad mouth on you and shake her hand at you, and befo' de day done you gwine be in de acciden'.

"I seed de Klu Klux. Po' Cajuns and redbones, I calls dem. Dey ought to be sleepin'. One time I seed a man hangin' in de wood when I'n pickin' blackberries. His tongue hangin' out and de buzzards fly down on he shoulder. De breeze sot him to swingin' and de buzzards fly off. I tells de people and dey takes him down to bury. He a fine, young cullud man. I don't know why dey done it. Dat after peace and de Yankees done gone back home.

"I been here in Texas a good while, and it such a rough road it got my 'membrance all stir up. I never been to school, 'cause I bound out to work. I lives with my daughter and dis child here my grandchild. I can't 'member no more, 'cause my head ain't good as it used to be."

John Sneed

John Sneed, born near Austin, Texas, does not know his age, but was almost grown when he was freed. He belonged to Dr. Sneed and stayed with him several years after Emancipation.

"I's borned on de old Sneed place, eight miles south of Austin, and my mammy was Sarah Sneed and pappy was Ike. Dey come from Tennessee and dere five boys and two gals. De boys am Dixie and Joe and Jim and Bob and me, and de gals name Katy and Lou. Us live in quarters what was log huts. Dere's one long, log house where dey spinned and weaved de cloth. Dere sixteen spinnin' wheels and eight looms in dat house and my job was turnin' one dem wheels when they'd thresh me out and git me to do it. Mos' all de clothes what de slaves and de white folks have was made in dat house.

"Mos' and usual de chillen sleept on de floor, unless with de old folks. De bedsteads make of pieces of split logs fasten with wooden pegs and rope criss-cross. De mattress make of shucks tear into strips with maybe a li'l cotton or prairie hay. You could go out on de prairie mos' any time and get 'nough grass to make de bed, and dry it 'fore it put in de tick. De white folks have bought beds haul by ox teams from Austin and feather beds.

"Dr. Sneed raise cotton and corn and wheat. Sometime five or six oxen hitch to de wagon and 25 or 30 wagons make what am call de wagon train. Dey haul cotton and corn and wheat to Port Lavaca what am de nearest shipping point. On de return trip, dey brung sugar and coffee and cloth and other things what am needed on de plantation. First time massa 'low me go with dat ox-train, I thunk I's growed.

"Dere a big gang of white and cullud chillen on de plantation but Dr. Sneed didn't have no chillen of he own. De neighbor white chillen come over dere and played. Us rip and play and fight and kick up us heels, and go on. Massa never 'low no whippin' of de chillen. He make dem pick rocks up and make fences out dem, but he didn't 'low no chillen work in de field till dey 'bout fourteen. De real old folks didn't work in de fields neither. Dey sot 'round and knit socks and mend de shoes and harness and stuff.

"Massa John mighty good to us chillen. He allus give us a li'l piece money every Sunday. When he'd git in he buggy to go to Austin to sell butter, de chillen pile in dat buggy and all over him so you couldn't see him and he'd hardly see to drive.

"Us had possum and rabbit and fish and trap birds for eatin'. Dere all kind wild green dem days. Us jus' go in de woods and git wild lettuce and mustard and leather-britches and polk salad and watercress, all us want to eat. Us kilt hawgs and put up de lard by de barrel. Us thresh wheat and take it to de li'l watermill at Barton Creek to grind. Dey'd only grind two bushel to de family, no matter how big dat family, 'cause dere so many folks and it such a small mill.

"Each family have de li'l garden and raise turnips and cabbage and sweet 'taters and put dem in de kiln make from corn stalks and cure dem for winter eatin'. Us have homemake clothes and brogan shoes, come from Austin or some place. Us chillen wear shirt-tail till us 'bout thirteen.

"Massa live in de big two-story rock house and have he office and drug-store in one end de house. Missy Ann have no chillen so she 'dopt one from Tennessee, name Sally.

"Dere 'bout four or five hunerd acres and 'bout sixty slaves. Dey git up 'bout daylight and come from de field in time to feed and do de chores 'fore dark. After work de old folks sot 'round, fiddle and play de 'cordian and tell stories. Dat mostly after de crops laid by or on rainy days. On workin' time, dey usually tired and go to bed early. Dey not work on Saturday afternoon or Sunday, 'cept dey gatherin' de crop 'gin a rain. Old man Jim Piper am fiddler and play for black and white dances. On Sunday massa make us go to church. Us sing and pray in a li'l log house on de plantation and sometimes de preacher stop and hold meetin'.

"Massa John Sneed doctored from Austin to Lockhart and Gonzales and my own mammy he train to be midwife. She good pneumonia doctor and massa 'low her care for dem.

"On Christmas all us go to de big house and crowd 'round massa. He a li'l man and some black boys'd carry him 'round on dere shoulders. All knowed dey gwine git de present. Dere a big tree with present for everyone, white and black. Lots of eggnog and turkey and baked hawgs and all kind good things. Dere allus lots of white folks company at massa's house and big banquets and holidays and birthdays. Us like dem times, 'cause work slack and food heavy. Every las' chile have he birthday celebrate with de big cake and present and maybe de quarter in silver from old massa, bless he soul. Us play kissin' games and ring plays and one song am like dis:

> "'I'm in de well,
> How many feet?
> Five. Who'd git you out?'

"Iffen it a man, he choose de gal and she have to kiss him to git him out de well. Iffen a gal in de well, she choose a man.

"I well 'member de day freedom 'clared. Us have de tearin'-down dinner dat day. De niggers beller and cry and didn't want leave massa. He talk to us and say long as he live us be cared for, and us was. Dere lots of springs on he place and de married niggers pick out a spring and Massa Doctor give dem stuff to put up de cabin by dat spring, and dey take what dey have in de quarters. Dey want to move from dem slave quarters, but not too far from massa. Dey come to de big house for flour and meal and meat and sich till massa die. He willed every last one he slaves somethin'. Mos' of 'em git a cow and a horse and a pig and some chickens. My mammy git two cows and a pair horses and a wagon and 70 acres land.

She marries 'gain when my daddy die and dat shif'less nigger she marry git her to sign some kind paper and she lose de land.

"My wife was Nanny Madeira and us have six chillen and five is livin'. I followed cattle till I's 'bout 26. I's went up de Chisholm Trail eight or nine times and druv for Massa Blocker and Jedge Brackenridge and others. On one stampede I rode 24 hours straight and after we rounds up all de cattle, I goes to sleep under a tree. Dat day I has on a buckskin coat I in gen'ral wore and I feels somethin' grab dat coat and bite my side. I rouses up and sees de big panther draggin' me off to de thicket. I has de six-gun but I couldn't git to it. Every once in a while dat panther lay me down and sniff at my nose. I jes' hold de breath, 'cause if dat panther cotch me breathin' dat been de end of me. He drug me to some bushes and den goes off a li'l way and give de yell. Dat yell make me turn cold, 'cause it sound jes' like a man screamin'. Den dat cat dug a shallow hole. I eases out my old gun, takes careful aim and den says, 'Thank you, old man,' and he turns to look at me and I shoots him right 'tween he eyes. After 'while, dat cat's mate and cub come runnin', 'cause he yell for dem, and I kilt dem, too.

John Sneed

"'Nother time, I seed de panther a-draggin' a white man off and I slips up jes' as de cat seizes him and shoots dat cat. Us have to run dat man down and cotch him, 'cause he scared stiff when dat dead cat fall on him.

"Some time after dat I works for a man what freights supplies 'round Austin and I's one de drivers. Us start in September with sev'ral six-wheel wagons, 'nough to las' a town de year, and not git back to Austin till January. Sometimes de mud so bad it take six oxen to pull de wagon out.

"One time us movin' and stampedin' de bunch cattle and me and my brother gits los' from de rest and was los' three days and nights. All us eat am parched corn. De grass nearly waist high to a man and us scoop out de hole in de ground and cut off tops de grass and weeds and make de fire. Den us drap de corn on de fire and parch it. De woods full wild animals and panthers and wolves. De wolves de worst. Dey slip up on us to git de chicken us has with us. At last us come to a house and finds us folks."

Mariah Snyder

Mariah Snyder, 89, was born in Mississippi, a slave of Sam Miller, who brought her to Texas when she was five. Since Mariah's second husband died, twenty-two years ago, she has earned her living by washing and cooking. Now too old to do much, she is cared for by her only living daughter, with the aid of a $10.00 monthly pension.

"I's borned in Mississippi. Yes, sar. I 'longed to Massa Miller and he name am Sam, and my name am Mariah. My pappy was Weldon and my mammy, Ann. Massa Sam fotches all us to Texas when I's jes' five year old and we come in wagons and hossback. He done buy my mammy and pappy in the slave market, so I don't know nothin' 'bout none my other 'lations.

"Massa Sam live in a great big, ceiled house, and had plenty land and niggers. The quarters was logs and any kind beds we could git. We wore lowell clothes and I never seed no other kind of dress till after surrender. We et meat and collards and cornbread and rough grub, and they biled all the victuals in a big, black pot what hung on a rack in the kitchen fireplace. We had red russet, flat shoes and no stockin's, but in winter we made wool panties to wear on our legs.

"Missy was name Patsy and she was purty good, and Massa Sam was purty good, too. He'd whip us if we needed it. He'd pull off our clothes and whip in the field. But he wouldn't 'low the driver to whip us if we didn't need it. No, sar. And he wouldn't have no patterrollers on the place.

"The driver come round and woke everybody up and had 'em in the field by daybreak. I's seed a whole field of niggers abreast, hoein'. The rows of cotton was so long you couldn't make but one 'fore dinnertime. I driv the gin, what was run by two mules. The cotton was wropped in baggin' and tied with ropes. It was a long time after 'fore I seed cotton tied with steel like they bales it now.

"I seed plenty niggers whipped while I driv that gin. They tied the feets and hands and rawhided 'em good. They tied a bell on one woman what run away all the time. They locks it round her head.

"I seed lots of niggers put on the block and bid off and carry away in chains. One woman name Venus raises her hands and hollers, 'Weigh dem cattle,' whilst she's bein' bid off.

"The big folks dances all night Sat'day. That's all the fun we had. We used to sing

"I'm in a lady's garden, I'm in a lady's garden,
So let me out. I'm sufferin' for water and wine.

"The slaves most allus sings whilst theys workin' in the field, and one song was

       "When I's here you calls me honey,
       When I's gone you honies everybody.

or

       "The raccoon am de funny thing,
       Ramblin' round in de dark.

"Massa Sam have a cullud man what give us our ABC's. I still got mine, but didn't never git no further.

Mariah Snyder

"Massa Sam git kilt 'fore the war. A mule throwed him. He had plenty good hosses but allus rid a mule. He come in from a neighbor's one day and the mule throwed him on a stob 'fore

301

he got to the house. We heared a hollerin' down the road, but didn't pay no 'tention, 'cause they's allus all kind racket gwine on. Fin'ly somebody say, 'That sound like a man,' and we goes down there and it was massa. 'Fore he die he calls all the cullud chillen to him and shakes hands and tells 'em to be good.

"We 'longs to he son, Ruben, then, and stays with him three years after surrender. Lordy me! How I hates to think of 'em talkin' 'bout that war! Young missy cry a whole week, 'cause she fear her men folks gwine git kilt. They did, too. Her two boys, George and Frank, gits kilt, and heap of the neighbors boys gits kilt, too.

"Fin'ly us leaves Massa Ruben and goes to Shreveport and I marries Snyder. The 'Progo' Marshal marries us. We raises two gals and I lives with Mary. Snyder died twenty-two years ago and all them years I made a livin' washin' and ironin' and cookin', up to six years ago. I gits a pension from the gov'ment now and it am $10.00 a month. It's mighty good of the white folks to take care of this old nigger, but I'd rather work, only I ain't able no more."

Patsy Southwell

Patsy Southwell, 83, was born in Jasper Co., Texas. She has lived on or near the old plantation all her life. Her master was Bill Trailor.

"My name Patsy Southwell and I lives at Rock Hill. I been livin' on dat plantation all my life, but not allus in the very same place. I think the house was move and 'nother builded.

"My pappy was John Redd and he 'longed to Bill Trailor and he brung here from Virginny. Mammy's name Rose Redd and she a yaller nigger, come from South Carolina and maybe she white and Indian, too. My brothers call Dennis, George, William, and Charles and dey all dead.

"We all live in the quarters and massa a tol'able good one 'sidering others what cut and slashes bad. Pappy and mammy work in the field and dey send pappy and he sons off six months at the time, over to Alexandria, to make salt.

"My brothers hunt all the time and brung in deer and wild turkey, so we has lots to eat. We has butter and milk and honey and pappy allus have he li'l garden patch.

"We wears slip homespun dress make outten cloth from us loom. I never have shoes and us has no Sunday clothes. Massa was tol'ably good to the old folks and not so mean to the chillen. He wasn't no barbarian like some what whip the slaves every Monday mornin' befo' dey starts to work.

"Massa plantation have fifteen hunnerd acre in it and he didn't have 'nough slaves so they works awful hard. I seed 'em hit my mammy five hunnerd licks and my pappy six hunnerd. Pappy have run 'way and been gone long time and they cotch him in de water in the Neches River. He have meat and stuff and they say mammy feedin' him, but I think it the other way. I think he gittin' and sendin' her stuff.

"The white folks has the big church with the bar 'cross it and the cullud folks sit behin' the bar. If any wants to jine us tell massa and he tell the preacher, and he old man Southwell. They baptise at the mill pond.

"I marries Jerry Southwell and us git marry at home. Jerry wears the black suit and I wears the dotted white Swiss dress with the overskirt.

"When freedom breaks and massa say we free, we goes to the Haynes' place and my pappy farms for hisself. We gits on better den in slavery days and after 'while pappy buys him some land and den we all right. Me and my husban', we stays on with pappy awhile, but we gits our own farm and farm all us life."

Leithean Spinks

Leithean Spinks, 82, was born a slave to Fay Thompson, in Rankin County, Mississippi. Soon after Leithean's birth, Mr. Thompson moved to E. Feliciana Parish, Louisiana. Leithean was happy in slave days, and stayed with her master two years after she was freed. She lives at 2600 Merrick St., Fort Worth, Texas.

"Does I look old 'nough to be birthed in slavery? I's eighty-two years old and mammy had it right there in de Bible, marked when I's birthed, in 1855. I's birthed in Mississippi but a little while after, massa goes to Louisiana, over in East Feliciana Parish, and when I's old 'nough to 'member, we'uns am there, 'twixt New Roads and Jackson, right near the Mississippi River.

"Massa Thompson had a awful big plantation and more'n 300 cullud folks, and three rows of cabins 'bout two blocks long, and 'bout one family to a cabin. No floors in dem cabins, you stands on dirt, and de furniture am something you knows ain't there. Why, man, there am jus' benches to sit on and a homemake table and bunks. Dere am de fireplace but all de main cookin' am done in de big cookin' shed, and old Mammy Dice done it, with four to holp her.

"De bell am rung when meal time comes and all de slaves lines up, with their pans and cups and passes de service table, and de food am put on dere pans and milk in de cup. Dat de one time massa could allus 'pend on de niggers. When de bell say, 'Come and git it,' all us am there. Us takes de food to de cabins and eats it.

"Dis old nigger come near gwine to Glory once when mammy am gone to de cook shed. How 'twas am dis-a-way. She latches de door on de outside to keep us three chillen in de cabin, my sis and brudder and me. Well, in dem days, us uses tallow candles for light and pine knots when candles am short. Mammy lights de pine knot befo' she leaves and after she am gone, it falls off de hook and hits de ground and rolls a couple feet under de bunk. There am straw in de tick and right off de whole shebang am on fire. There am three of us with de door latch and all de grown-ups in de cook shed. Us hollers and yells but it am no use, and de hollerin' don't last long, 'cause de smoke gittin' thick. De fire am spreadin' fast and de bunks starts burnin'. Us am huddle togedder, skeert plumb out our wits and chokin' and coughin'.

"Den my brudder gits de idea and he grabs de big spoon and de iron poker and starts diggin' de dirt from under de log next de door. De smoke ain't so bad next de ground, and did yous ever see de dog diggin' in de rabbit hole? Dat how us digs, and seems it never gwine come a hole. Finally, a hole busted through and lets in fresh air, and den us dig some more, and it am big 'nough for my little sis to crawl through. Den us dig some more and I crawls out and my brudder starts but he gits he head outside and his shoulders wedges and there he am, stucked. Us pull and pull, but nary a inch could us budge him. He try to back up but he shirt caught on a knot and he can't do dat. So us runs for de cook shed and yells, 'Mammy, de cabin on fire.' Everybody starts to holler, 'Fire,' and mammy busts in de door and yanks brudder out dat hole, and he am sweatin' like a latherin' mare. After dey puts de fire out with de water buckets, mammy say, 'When sis gits out, why didn't she unlatch de door?' 'Cause de 'citement, us never think of dat!

"Us have plenty hawg meat and veg'tables and butter and 'lasses and honey. De food ain't short no time 'round massa, 'cause he say niggers works better when dey feeds good. De mammies leaves de babies in de nursery durin' de day and dem chillen am take good care of and has lots of milk and am all fat like hawgs.

"In de mornin' when de bell ring, everybody goes to work, but I is little and does de chores and am gap tender. De cattle am 'lowed to run where dey wants, here, there and all over. Fences am 'round de fields and yards and there am gates to go through, but us calls dem gaps. It am my job to open and close dem, 'cause somebody allus wantin' to drive or walk through dem gaps.

"MY sis am de fly chaser. She has de big fan make from de tail feathers of de peacock. 'Twas awful purty thing. She stands 'round de white folks and shoo off de flies.

"Massa Fay ain't hard on he cullud folks. He works dem steady but don't drive dem. Lots de slaves goes fishin' in de river on Saturday afternoon and Sunday, and dey cotches plenty fish.

"Us has parties and singin' and dancin' and fiddle music. Oh, Lawdy! How lonesome I gits when I thinks 'bout dem days, and de music and singin'. Sometimes 'bout a hunerd sings to once and dat sound purty and jus' go all through me.

Leithean Spinks

"For runnin' off am de only hard whuppin's massa give. De run-off am tie to de log and massa lay de whuppin' on he back. De plantation am near de river and dere am lots of caves and cliffs to hide in. Massa cotch de run-offs with de nigger hounds and if he don't, dey git hongry and sneaks back. Only one gits clear away.

"One Sunday mornin' 'bout ten o'clock, massa have de bell ring and calls all us to de front gallery and makes de talk. He say, 'I's happy to tell yous is free and, 'cording to de law, yous am all citizens. Dem what wants to stay with me I'll pay de wages or dey can work on shares.' He gives us all de paper, with de name and age and where us am birthed. Me and mammy stays two years after freedom. I marries Sol Pleasant in 1872 and us has two chillen. Us sep'rate in 1876. De trouble am, he wants to be de boss of de job and let me do de work. I 'cides I don't need no boss, so I transports him, and says, 'Nigger, git out of here and don't never come back. If you comes back, I'll smack you down.'

"In 1876 I marries Frank Spinks and us has eight chlllen and he dies in 1930. All dem eight chillen lives here and I's livin' with one of dem, Mrs. Covy Kelly. 'Tain't many years befo' old Gabriel blow he horn, and I's waitin' for him."

Guy Stewart

Guy Stewart, 87, 209 Austin Ave., Ft. Worth, was born Nov. 26, 1850, a slave of Jack Taylor, who also owned Guy's parents, 3 brothers and 3 sisters. They lived in Mansfield Parish, La. Stewart started work in the fields at seven years, and remained with his owner three years after he was freed. He then moved onto his own farm where he lived until 1898, when he moved to Fort Worth.

"Yas, suh, I'se an ol' slave and I'se 'bout 11 years ol' when de War starts. My marster am Jack Taylor and my family belongs to him.

"I 'members de war well, 'cause we'uns hears shootin' and see soldiers. Dey comes to marster's place and takes hosses and vittals. One time dey wants some of de niggers for to help fix for de battle. Dere am heap of 'citement and de marster's 'fraid de battle come too close. He say, 'It's too close for saftment.' And he say, 'Put dis and dat away so de soldier cain't find it.'

"I starts work long 'fore dat, when I'se seven, in de cotton and co'n field. I just peddles 'round first. Marster sho' am good to us and so good dat de other white folks calls us de 'free niggers.'

"We'uns have cabins for to live in and sleep in bunks with straw ticks on 'em. We'uns has lots to eat, all we wants. And we'uns have all de clothes we needs.

"Sho, we went to church with de marster. Dey tol' us 'bout Heaven and de devil and sich. But dey never 'lows us to have books in de hands. Dey says it wasn' good for us to larn readin' or writin.' "We'uns has lots of music on dat place 'cause de marster, he am de good fiddler and he learns some of us niggers to play de fiddle and de banjo. We gits together and has de music, sing and dance. If I thinks 'bout dem days now, I can see we'uns dancin' and hear de singin' of dem ol' songs, sich like Ol' Black Joe and Swanee River. Iffen I thinks too much 'bout dem days, tears comes in dis ol' nigger's eyes. Dem were de happy days of my life. In dem days, we'uns not know what am money, never have any. What for we'uns need it? I'se more happy den, dan I been since, with money.

"De marster am scart for to lose all de hosses and everything, 'cause dey takes it for de army man, so he gits to thinkin' 'bout movin' to Texas. De war warn't over when he goes to Texas and takes all us niggers with him. De roads dem days am not so good. No bridges over de rivers, 'cept de bigges' ones. Lots of times we'uns has to push for help de hosses pull de wagons outta de mudhole, and we'uns is over a month gettin' to Williams County. De marster rents de land dere and we stays for one crop, and den we all goes to Travis County, whar marster settle for to raise de wheat.

"When freedom comes, de marster says we'uns has to work for wages and buy all de food and de clothes and everything dat we'uns gits. Dat's not so easy. At first he pays me $5.00 a month and den pays me $10.00 de month. After three years I quits and rents a farm and works for myself, I gits married in 1877 and my wife dies in 1915. We'uns has one chile. In 1898 I comes to Fort Worth and gits me a job in de woodyard and sich.

"White man, I sho' likes for to see dat ol' plantation down in Louisiana and it would do dis ol' darky good. I sits here and thinks of de marster and de good times. And de fishin down dere! Is dere good fishin'? De folks here don' know what am fishin'.

"You has dis nigger thinkin' heaps 'bout de ol' plantation and de good times. If I don' stop talkin' 'bout dat, I gits to cryin'."

William Stone

William Stone was born in a covered wagon, on the way from Alabama to Texas, about 1863. Though he was too small to remember slave days, he does recall many things told him by his parents and other ex-slaves. William lives in Mart, Texas.

"My parents done told me where I's borned. It am in a covered wagon on de way from Alabama to Texas, two years 'fore freedom. Old Marse, Lem Stone, he left Alabama for Texas, where de war not so bad, and brung some he slaves with him. He done lost so much in Alabama, Yankees burnin' he house and cotton and killin' he stock, he want to git 'way from dere.

"First he come to Rusk County, den goes back to Shreveport and stays till freedom. Pappy and mammy was Louis and Car'line Stone. I lived in Louisiana till I's growed.

"Mammy and pappy done told me all 'bout de old plantation. It am hundreds of acres of land, part worked and part jus' timber and pasture. It was near Montgomery, and dey raised more cotton den anything else, but had some corn and peas and cane. Dey made sorghum and ribbon cane 'lasses and had boilin' vats for sugar, too.

"De soldiers come through. Dey named, Yankees. Dey make mammy cook somethin' to eat and den kilt all de hawgs and took de meat with dem, and burn de barn and house. Old Marse had pens to put cotton in, hid way out in de bresh. Dey picked it in gunny sacks and hides it, and slips it out to de gin by night and tries to sell it 'fore dem Yankees finds it and burns it.

"Mammy say dey all went to church and had to drive four horses when de roads muddy in winter and sand deep in summer. Dey allus carry dinner and stay all day. Den in de evenin', after de niggers had dey preachin', dey all go home. Sometimes a preacher come out to de plantation and hold church for de white folks in de mornin' and in de evenin' for de niggers, out under a big oak tree.

"De Lawd say iffen us trusts him and help to be good he gwine make our path straight. Dis was true in de days of den, 'cause our white folks tooken care of us, befo' dey was freedom and sech. Now, us gittin' old, and gits de old age pension when us too old to work.

"I works all up and down de old river when I's growed. De plantations has long staple cotton. Dey raise sugar cane and dere be twenty wagons haulin' cane to de boilin' mills. We was happy to do dat work, 'cause we knowed it mean us have plenty 'lasses in winter. Lawdy, I wish I knowed I could have all de 'lasses and bread I wanted dis winter! Dem was good times, Lawd! Us sing dis song:

"'We'll stick to de hoe till de sun go down,

We'll rise when de rooster crow,

And go to de field where de sunshine hot,

To de field where de sugar cane grow.

Yes, chilluns, we'll all go.'

"I can jes' see dem long rows of cotton and niggers drivin' de oxen and mules. I know 'nother song:

"Nigger mighty happy when he layin' by de corn,

Nigger mighty happy when he hear dat dinner horn;

But he more happy when de night come on,

Dat' sun's a'slantin', as sho's you born!

Dat old cow's a shakin' dat great big bell,

And de frogs tunin' up, 'cause de dew's done fell.'

"Dat jes' after freedom. Dey have plantations and overseers like slavery, but most de overseers niggers, and dey didn't whip you den. On Saturday night de overseer pay us, mostly in rations. He give us five, maybe ten pounds rations of meat, and a peck or two or meal, and some coffee and 'lasses.

"'Dat ration day come once a week,

Old massa rich as Gundy.

But he give 'lasses all de week,

And buttermilk for Sunday.

"'Old massa give a pound of meat,

I et it all on Monday;

Den I et 'lasses all de week,

And buttermilk for Sunday.'

"All dis was down on de Mississippi bottom. Old Man River was sho' purty in de fall, when dem wild geeses come in droves and de blossoms red and yaller. De fogs come hang over and chills and fever gits started. De woman sot by de fire piecin' quilts and spinnin' thread, and de old men weave cotton baskets and chair bottoms, and de young men work on da levees, so dey hold Old Man River back when he start prowlin' round 'gain.

William Stone

"Floods come down, no matter what time of year. One day Old Man River be runnin' 'long, jes' as peaceful and quiet, and everybody happy. Everybody meet de boats at de landin'. Den way in de night you wake up and hear a roarin' like thunder and dat river be on a tear. Folks know he am in de ugly mood, and starts movin' to higher ground. Everybody what have a wagon and mule gits out. Some jes' gits to de levee. It look like my folks told me when dey run from de Yankees, only dis time it's de river. Old Man River sho' treach'ous. After he go on one he rarin' and tearin' spells, den he gwine be so peaceful and quiet like. Look like he try to make up for he meanness.

"I gits married and moves clost to de Trinity River, and stays till my family done raised. Dey has free schools in Texas den. I works in de sawmill and dere so much wild game us can eat easy. Dem days on de Mississippi bottom is like a dream, but when I hears talk 'bout Old Man River, I can dem big waters roarin' down."

Yach Stringfellow

Yach Stringfellow, 90, was born a slave of Frank Hubert, in Brenham, Texas. His memory is poor and, though he recalled a good many incidents of slavery days, he had little to say about his life from 1865 to the present. He now lives in Watt, Texas.

"I'll be ninety-one years old next May, and I was borned in Brenham. My massa and missus was Frank Hubert and Sarah Ann Hubert. My daddy come from de old Africa and was tall and straight as a arrow. He was sold to a man what tooked him to California in de gold rush in 1849 and me and mammy stays with Massa Hubert. Dat how come my name ain't de same as massa have.

"I got so much misery in de head I can't 'member like I should. But I know us live in little log houses all kind of group together, and us eat in a long lean-to builded on to the big house. Us chillen had a long, scooped-out dish on a split log table. What we had to eat was dumped in dat trough and us ate it like slop. But it sho' taste good when you been huntin' for eggs or calves or gittin' in chips or breakin' bresh.

"When I's big 'nough I carries water, sometimes from de spring and sometimes from de deep well. Dere danger a little child fall in and drown and massa, he say niggers too valu'ble to risk dem dat way. It was hard work to tote water for niggers workin', 'cause allus somebody hollerin' for de water. I had to trot down de slippery bank through de thorns to de spring or pull de heavy sweep to git it out de well, and carry two buckets most de time.

"Us cut two saplin's de right size to fasten together at de end and stick dem in holes in de wall, to make de bed. Us use lace cowhide strings or any kind rope across de poles to hold de bed up. Den put hay or corn shucks and a little cotton in de ticks.

"Us eat bacon and cornbread and greens, but de white folks had more'n better. Dey didn't have to eat string victuals like us; us have to eat something to stick to de ribs. Right 'bout de time dis state come to be de United States, and de Mexicans raisin' de old billy, us cook most usual on de fireplace and have ovens by de side to make bread, and cranes for de pots.

"Us slaves used pine torches and sometimes a little bit of candle. De women make all de candles demselves for de white folks. Us didn't need much light at night, 'cause us tired after de long day, workin' from can see to can't see, and us git in de bed early.

"I wore shirt tail till I's fourteen, den de homespun britches and shirt. My weddin' suit was de dark jeans and I was fix up fine as any nigger on de plantation. She wore white and massa fix supper and git de fiddler and all sich.

"Massa have John to oversee, and he sho' de stepper. He be every place you didn't think he gwine come. He have de big, boom voice and allus slingin', and wail, 'Look along, black man, look along, dere trouble comin' sho'.' Iffen de black boy or woman lyin' in de corn row, dey git up quick and be mighty bust right soon, 'cause dat black snake whip reach for dem. Dey scramble deyself together and be de busiest in de bunch by time John git dere.

Yach Stringfellow

"In de long winter days de men sat round de fire and whittle wood and make butter paddles and troughs for de pigs and sich, and ax handles and hoe handles and box traps and figure-four traps. Dey make combs to git de wool clean for de spinnin'. Us take de long strip

315

of leather and put wire in it and bend dem so dey stay, den cut dem comb-like teef and dere you are.

"Come Christmas us slaves have de big dinner and eat all day and dance till nex' mornin'. Some de niggers from near plantations git dey passes and come jine us. Course dey a drap egg nog round and candy for de chillen. De white folks have dey big carriage full of visitors and big goin's on dey come to from miles round. Us didn't have no money, but didn't have no place to go to spend it, neither.

"At night, us sat round de fire sometimes and de women sew and knit and de men whittle and told things. Dey talk 'bout charms and sich. You gwine have lots of luck iffen you cotch de rabbit in de graveyard on de dark of de moon and cut off he hind leg and wear it. Iffen you chews de piece of shoe-string root, jus' you ask anybody a favor and you sho' gwine git it."

Bert Strong

Bert Strong was born in 1864, a slave of Dave Cavin. He and his mother remained in the service of the Cavin family for ten years after they were freed. Bert has farmed in Harrison County all his life and now lives alone on Long's Camp Road, twelve miles northeast of Marshall. He is supported by a $15.00 per month pension.

"I been livin' here all my life. I was birthed a year and more 'fore the war stopped and 'longed to old Dave Cavin. All my folks 'longed to him over in Montgomery, in Alabama. Massa Dave buyed my mammy's papa off a 'baccy farm in Richmond, in Virginny. I heared Massa Dave say he done come to Texas 'cause he heared in Alabama this was a rich country—hawgs walkin' round with a knife in they back and you could shake money off the trees. His folks and 'bout thirty slaves cone to Texas in wagons. They was on the road three months.

"I heared my grand-people tell 'bout holpin' run the Indians out of Texas. Big Lake, on Caddo Lake, was jus' a small kind of stream them days. My grandpa was name Gloster and he died at a hunerd five years.

"Massa Cavin had 'bout four hunerd acres and builded us all good quarters with chimnies and fireplaces, and good beds and plenty food. I's too little to know all this 'fore the war, but my folks stayed with massa ten years after freedom and things was jus' the same as in slave times, only they got a little money, so I can 'member.

"My grandma was cook and there was plenty wild game, turkey and deer and pigeon and rabbits and squirrels. I 'member once they's grumblin' 'bout what they have to eat and old massa comes to the quarters and say, 'What you fussin' 'bout? They's a gallon good potlicker in the pot." I's raise on greens and pork and potlicker and 'taters and ash-cake. Dat am good food, too. I ain't never hope to see no better food dan dat.

"Massa give he slaves two sets clothes a year and one pair 'bachelor' brogan shoes with brass toes. The white folks larnt us Negroes to read and write, at night and on Sunday, and we could go to church. We had our own preacher, and massa let us have fun'rals when a slave died. They wasn't no undertakers then. They jus' made the coffin and planed the boards and lined it with black cloth. The white folks and the cullud folks, too, was put 'way nice on our place.

"They was a overseer a while, but massa fires him for cuttin' and slashin' he niggers. He made my uncle Freeman overlooker. We is heared slaves on farms close by hollerin' when they git beat. Some the neighbors works they hands till ten at night and weighed the last weighin' by candles. If the day's pickin' wasn't good 'nough, they beat them till it a pity.

"Christmas was the big time. Massa kilt the hawg or beef and sometimes a mutton, and give the slaves the big dinner. Us all hang the stockin' up on massa's gallery and it was a run to see what we'd git. He give the chillen toys and apples and the big folks somethin' to wear. He'd 'low the chillen to have candy pullin' Saturday nights and the growed folks parties. My cousin, Tom, was songster and call the plays at all the dances, and they turned 'cordin' to what he'd sing.

"When young massa went to war they calls all the slaves to tell him good-bye. They blowed the horn. He come home two times on a furlough and says, 'I's smellin' and seein' the Devil.' Then the nex' time he come home he say, 'Las' time I tells you 'bout smellin' the Devil. I's smellin' and seein' Hell now.' When the war am over, he come home and say to old massa, 'Ain't you read the 'lamation to you niggers yet?' Massa say he hasn't, and young massa blowed the horn and calls us all up and tells us we's free as he is and could work for who we please, but he like us to stay till the crop am out. He say he'd hire us and make a contrac'. Me and my mammy stays ten years, 'cause they so good it ain't no use to leave. One of the young massas am livin' here now, Mr. Tom, and I goes to see him.

317

Bert Strong

"I stays with mammy till I marries and then farms for myself. That all I ever done and I'd be doin' it now if I was able. I raises two boys but they am both dead now.

"I votes once in the county 'lection and once in the president 'lection. I think any man should vote, but it ain't 'tended for women to vote.

"Mos' the young niggers am gwine to Hell. They don't 'preciate things. They has lots more'n we ever did. They can go to school and all, but they don't 'preciate it."

Emma Taylor

Emma Taylor, 89, was born a slave of the Greer family, in Mississippi. She and her mother were sold to a Texas man, whose name Emma has forgotten. Emma lives with one of her children, in Tyler, Texas.

"My maw and paw lived in Mississippi, and belonged to Marse Greer. Dat dere name, too. All the slaves tooken dere master's name, 'cause dey hadn't no use for a name, nohow.

"De first thing I 'members is followin' my maw in the cotton patch. She allus went ahead, pickin' cotton, and made a clean place with her sack draggin' on the ground. But de first work I ever done was feed de chickens and geese and shell corn to feed dem.

"Us nigger chillen couldn't play with de white chillen. De worstest whippin' I ever got was fer playin' with a doll what belonged to one marse's chillen. I 'members it yet and I ain't never seed a doll purty as dat doll was to me. It was make out a corncob with arms and legs what moved and a real head, with eyes and hair and mouth painted on. It had a dress out of silk cloth, jist like one my missus weared when she went to meetin'. Dat li'l gal done leave de doll under de tree, but missus found me playin' with it and whipped me hard.

"We lived in a cabin in de back field 'hind de big house, one room and a shed room, where maw done all de cookin' for de whole family. I had three brothers and three sisters, all dead, I supposes. Dey all older'n what I was. We cooked on a fireplace, and a big pot hanged on poles over de fire and de bread cook on dat fire in a skillet what was made of two pieces of iron, turn up all round. We puts de dough in one and turns de other one over it, den buries it in de coals a few minutes till it brown on de top and bottom. It was good, jist as good as nowadays, baked in a oven. Our beds was made out of straw and old rags, but we kept warm sleepin' a whole lot in one bed in winter, but we slept outside in summer.

"I was sold one time. Marse, he gittin' old and 'cide he didn't need so many slaves, so he have de sale and a man come and put us all up on a big platform. We pulls off nearly all our clothes, so as to show how big we was, and he 'gins hollerin' 'bout who gwineter buy, who gwineter buy. I was scart and thunk I has to leave maw, so I 'gins hollerin' jist as loud as he does. He turn 'round and say, 'Shut up, you li'l coon, you. I can't hear nothin'.' I hides my face in maw's apron and didn't know no more till we's all loaded in a wagon and starts to de new home. We gits dere and is give new clothes and shoes, de first ones I ever had on and it taken me a long time to larn to wear dem things on my feet.

"Us niggers has to git up at four in de mornin', and work, work till us can't see no more. Den dey work at night. De men chops wood and hauls poles to build fences and make wood, and de women folks has to spin four cuts of thread every night and make all de clothes. Some has to card cotton to make quilts and some weave and knits stockin's. Marse give each one a chore to do at night and iffen it warn't did when we went to bed, we's whipped.

319

One time I falls plumb asleep befo' I finishes shellin' some corn, but I didn't git a bad whippin' dat time.

"Sometimes de niggers danced and played de fiddle and us chillen played in de yard. We could stay up all night dem times, but had to work next day, and hardly ever stayed up all night. Dat durin' harvest or at Christmas time.

"All de victuals was issued out by de overseer and he give 'nough for one week, den iffen us eat it all up too soon, it am jist go without. Lots of times, I went down to de 'tato patch a long time after everybody am in bed, and stole 'tatoes, so we wouldn't be hungry next day. I allus covered de hole up good and never did git cotched. De dogs got after me one time, but I put pepper in dey eyes and dey stopped. I allus carried pepper with me.

Emma Taylor

"I marries when I's fifteen, not so long befo' I'm free. Nigger men didn't git no license to marry dey gals den. Dey jist picked her out and asked marse, and iffen he 'grees, dey's married. But iffen he don't want it, dat man has to find heself 'nother gal. De men what lived on 'nother plantation couldn't see dere wives but onct every two weeks. Marse buyed my husban', Rube Taylor, and he come to live with me.

"One day marse say we's all free and we has a big celebration, eatin' and dancin'. But we near all stayed on his place for a long time after day. He paid us thirty-five cents de day and let us live in de same old houses.

"After we done left him, we jist drifts 'round, workin' for white folks, till we manages to git a farm. Rube done died a long time back, and I lives with my baby child."

Mollie Taylor

Mollie Taylor, 84, was born a slave to John Wilson, at Campbell, Texas. After she was freed, Mollie moved with her family to an adjoining farm which they worked on shares. Mollie now lives at 522 Seaton St., Fort Worth, Texas.

"Now den, I's no record of when I's born and just what de white folks tells me is all I knows. I'll be 84 this coming October, but just what day I don't know. I's born on Massa John Wilson's farm at Campbell, Texas and him owned my father and mother and 'bout 20 more slaves. Dere was 'bout four or five chillen in we'uns family. My father died and I don't 'member much 'bout him, but his name was Anson Wilson and my mother name was Hattie Wilson. We'uns gits de name from de massa.

"Us slaves lived in log houses back of massa's house, and they was two and three-room houses with dirt floors and de rock fireplace and just holes for windows. De flies come in de door and go out de window, but most of 'em stayed in de house. Dere was no furniture like am today. No, suh, it was homemake stuff. De bunks was built 'gainst de wall and full of straw or hay and de tables was made of split logs. Dere was de cook room and de eatin' room where all de slaves meals cooked and they ate, 'tween de slaves quarters and de massa's house.

"Massa Wilson, him feed us purty good, with de cornmeal and 'lasses and plenty coffee and milk. We has white flour once a week and massa git de sugar by de barrel. De slaves could have dere own gardens and dey raised most dere vegetables. All de chillen ate out of de wooden trough with wooden spoons. It was a sight to watch them, day just like de bunch of pigs.

"De overseer, him ring de bell 'bout half past four in de mornin' and everybody what work go to de fields. De massa purty reason'ble with de work and didn't whip much. On Sundays de old slaves goes to de church and de chillen plays.

"When war come dere lots of soldiers allus ridin' by de place, all deck out in de uniform with big, shiny buttons on de coat. When us chillen seed dem we took to de woods.

"After freedom we'uns moves to de next farm and works and I stays dere with my family till I's 'bout 25 year old, and den I marries Tom Gould and move to McLennan County. But he so mean I didn't stay with him very long, and 'bout six months of his foolishness and I ups and leaves him. After two years I marries George Taylor and I lives with dat man for 12 years and took 'nough of his foolishness, so I leaves him. I's had four chillen but Tom Gould nor George Taylor wasn't de father of any of 'em. No, suh, I just found dem chillen."

Jake Terriell

Jake Terriell, born a slave of Felix Terriell in Raleigh, South Carolina, does not know his age. He was grown and married at the close of the Civil War, so is probably in the 90's. He lives in Madisonville, Texas.

"Pappy and mammy was called Tom and Jane and they's cotched in Africy and brung to America and sold. My brother was called James and my sisters Lucindy and Sally. Massa Felix Terriell owned me and pappy and mammy but when I's still a chile he done give me to he son, Massa Dalton Terriell.

"My papy was de wild man and he so wild Massa Felix have to keep him locked up at night and in de chains by day to keep him from runnin' off. He had to wear de chains in de field and den he couldn't run fast.

"Massa Dalton growed de tobaccy. He was a good massa and give me de nickel and de dime sometime and I'd buy candy. He have lots of slaves and de cook fix our grub in big old skillets. We allus have de cornbread and de syrup and some meat. I likes possum cooked with sweet 'taters.

"Missy Mary try larn me read and write but I never did care for de book larnin'. Massa wake us 'bout four o'clock with de great iron and hammer and us work long as us could see.

"Massa didn't have to whip us but I seed pappy whip, with de rawhide with nine tails. He got thirty-nine licks and every lick, it brung de blood.

"I seed slaves sold and you has heared cattle bawl when de calves took from de mammy and dat de way de slaves bawls. When massa sell de slave he make 'em wash up and grease de face good and stand up straight and he fatten 'em jus' like you do hawgs to sell. I had de good massa. He was good to black debbils, what he call us niggers. Us could rest when us git to de quarters or go by de big tank and take de bath, and every Saturday night us git de holiday and have banjo and tin pan beatin' and dance. On Christmas massa kilt de big hawg and us fix it jus' like us wants and have big dinner.

"Massa have doctor when us sick. He say us too val'ble. If us sold us brung 'bout $1,000. Old mammy could fix de charm and git us well. She gather bark and make de tea. Most us sickness chill and fever. Sometime a slave git leg broke and massa say he no more 'count and finish him up with de club.

"Massa nearly kilt in de fightin' and he had he doctor write missy to set us free. I had two wives and missy said I couldn't keep but one, so I takes Mary and us starts out for Texas, a-foot. Us most starved to death 'fore us got here and then us have hard time. But dere plenty wild meat and dat what us lived on three, four year. Us had two chillen and den she dies and I marry a half-Indian gal and she died. Us jus' 'greed to live together in dem days, no weddin'. Then I marries Lucie Grant and us have 11 chillen and de preacher calls us man and wife. I's pappy to 17 chillen and I don't know how many grandchillen. Lucie say more'n a hun'erd."

J.W. Terrill

J.W. Terrill was born in DeSoto Parish, Louisiana, and is about 100 years old. His master was his father. He now lives in Madisonville, Texas.

"My father took me away from my mother when at age of six weeks old and gave me to my grandmother, who was real old at the time. Jus' befo' she died she gave me back to my father, who was my mammy's master. He was a old batchelor and run saloon and he was white, but my mammy was a Negro. He was mean to me.

"Finally my father let his sister take me and raise me with her chillen. She was good to me, but befo' he let her have me he willed I must wear a bell till I was 21 year old, strapped 'round my shoulders with the bell 'bout three feet from my head in steel frame. That was for punishment for bein' born into the world a son of a white man and my mammy, a Negro slave. I wears this frame with the bell where I couldn't reach the clapper, day and night. I never knowed what it was to lay down in bed and get a good night's sleep till I was 'bout 17 year old, when my father died and my missy took the bell offen me.

"Befo' my father gave me to his sister, I was tied and strapped to a tree and whipped like a beast by my father, till I was unconscious, and then left strapped to a tree all night in cold and rainy weather. My father was very mean. He and he sister brung me to Texas, to North Zulch, when I 'bout 12 year old. He brung my mammy, too, and made her come and be his mistress one night every week. He would have kilt every one of his slaves rather than see us go free, 'specially me and my mammy.

"My missy was purty good to me, when my father wasn't right 'round. But he wouldn't let her give me anything to eat but cornbread and water and little sweat 'taters, and jus' 'nough of that to keep me alive. I was allus hongry. My mammy had a boy called Frank Adds and a girl called Marie Adds, what she give birth to by her cullud husban', but I never got to play with them. Missy worked me on the farm and there was 'bout 100 acres and fifteen slaves to work 'em. The overseer waked us 'bout three in the mornin' and then he worked us jus' long as we could see. If we didn't git 'round fast 'nough, he chain us to a tree at night with nothin' to eat, and nex' day. if we didn't go on the run he hit us 39 licks with a belt what was 'bout three foot long and four inches wide.

"I wore the bell night and day, and my father would chain me to a tree till I nearly died from the cold and bein' so hongry. My father didn't 'lieve in church and my missy 'lieved there a Lord, but I wouldn't have 'lieved her if she try larn me 'bout 'ligion, 'cause my father tell me I wasn't any more than a damn mule. I slep' on a chair and tried to res' till my father died, and then I sang all day, 'cause I knowed I wouldn't be treated so mean. When missy took that bell offen me I thinks I in Heaven 'cause I could lie down and go to sleep. When I did I couldn't wake up for a long time and when I did wake up I'd be scairt to death I'd see my father with his whip and that old bell. I'd jump out of bed and run till I give out, for fear he'd come back and git me.

"I was 'bout 17 year old then and I so happy not to have that bell on me. Missy make us work hard but she have plenty to eat and I could sleep. On Christmas she cook us a real dinner of beef meat.

"Plenty time I listens to the cannon popping till I mos' deaf, and I was messenger boy and spy on the blue bellies. When I'd git back to the Southern sojers I he'ped 'em bury they dead and some what was jus' wounded I he'ped carry home.

"When we heered was was over and we's free, we all jus' jumped up and hollers and dances. Missy, she cries and cries, and tells us we is free and she hopes we starve to death and she'd be glad, 'cause it ruin her to lose us. They was a big bunch of us niggers in town and we stirrin' 'round like bees workin' in and out a hive. We was jus' that way. I went wild and the first year I went north, but I come back 'gain to Texas.

"After 'while I marries a Indian maid. It was nothin' much but Indians 'round and there wasn't much law. I lived with her 'bout two year and then the Indians come and captured her jus' befo' she was to give birth. They kilt her or carried her 'way and lef' me for dead, and I never seed or heered of her since. While I was sick a outlaw, what was Tomas Jafferies, he'ped me git well and then I turns outlaw and follows all signs of Indians, all over the earth. But I never could git word of my wife.

"It mus' be 'bout 15 year after that, I marries Feline Ford, by a preacher. My first weddin' was common weddin' with the Indian maid. I jus' give her deerskin in front of Tomas Jefferies and she my wife."

Allen Thomas

Allen Thomas, 97, was owned by several ranchers of Jefferson and Orange Counties, Texas, but recalls Moise Broussard of Hamshire the best. Ill health has affected his memory and his story is not coherent. He is a familiar figure on the streets of Beaumont, Texas, a small man clad in none too clean and somewhat ragged clothes, with a tow sack across his shoulders, into which he puts such things as he finds in his wanderings about the city. Rumor has it that Allen is fairly well to do and that his begging attitude is assumed, for reasons of his own.

"I figgers I's gwine be 97 year old on de fourth of August, I's borned over in Duncan Woods, over in Orange County. My daddy's name was Lockin Thomas. I never see my daddy. He git drown in de river here at Beaumont. My mammy's Hetty Anderson.

"I 'longed to three masters. One John Adam and he was mean. One Stowers, and he was mean but not so mean to me. Den dere Moise Broussard, he was purty mean, but he never beat me. De las' man what finish raise me was Amos Harrison and he purty good man. He wife name Mag and dey lives on Turtle Bayou over in Chambers County. He buy me from Lewis Pinder. He was good. My brudder was Kelly Idonia and I had a sister Lessie Williams. Dey beat her with clubs. I's walk over many a dead person. Dey beat 'em to death.

"Us had tins dishes dem times, master and slaves, too. Dey have wooden paddles what us take de food out de dishes with. De white folks sot at one table and de cullud folks have table to deyself, but 'bout what de white folks has.

"Us have watermilion and sugar cane and milk and butter. Den us have de possum. Us clean him and put him top de house and 'low de frost fall on him. Den us fill him full salt and pepper and put him in de oven. Sometime put sweet 'taters all 'round him. Us have de long, square oven with de lid on it.

"Us wore knitted shirt make on dem looms and dey gives us boots with brass toes on 'em. Me and mammy work on de spinnin' wheel many a night up to one or two o'clock. I used to card de bats.

Allen Thomas

"Dere plenty hawgs and hosses and dem cattle what am longhorn. Us have plenty meat and raise veg'tables, too.

"I never seed no sojers but I heared de cannons. I disremember when peace am corral'. I come up here to Beaumont when I thank I's a man and I's been here every Gawd's since.

"I see some sperrits, but I see 'em only special times. You see 'em twict a year, 'tween spring and summer and den 'gain 'twixt fall and winter. Sometime dey comes right 'long and den sometime dey jis' standin' still. When you looks at 'em dey looks kinder vagueish. I can allus tell when sperrits 'round. Dey got a queer scent. When you walk 'bout 20 feet, steam gwineter hit you in de face. I can tell dey dere iffen I can't see 'em. Dey look like men. Dey ain't white but dey got a pale look."

Bill and Ellen Thomas

Bill and Ellen Thomas live in the Old Slave Settlement, 3 miles north of Hondo. Bill is 88 and Ellen is 81. They seem to be happy; their fields are tilled, a horse and a cow graze near the house; a kitchen garden is under way and several broods of baby chicks are in the yard. They were dressed in simple, clean clothes, and Ellen wears a string of nutmegs around her neck, to 'make yer eyes strong.'

Uncle Bill's Story

"Does you want me to start right at the beginnin'? Well, I'll tell you jes' how I went to this country. I left Falls County where I belonged to the man there that kept the post office. He was named Chamlin. He had lots of land, I reckin about 50 acres. They kep' us in a little house right in their yard. Reckin how old I was when he bought me? Jus' five years old! He give $500 for me, but he bought my mother and my sisters, too. He had to buy me, 'cause my mother, she wouldn't go without me. No, suh, she tol' 'em she wouldn't go if they didn' buy me, too. An' the man he bought us f'om, he wanted to keep me, so he wouldn't take less than $500 for me. Massa Chamblin bought the whole family, 'cept my father. They sold him and we never laid eyes on him again.

"My mother cooked. Massa Chamlin, he always fed us plenty, an' whatever they had, we had. If he cooked sausage, you had it too; if he cooked ham, you got it too; if he cooked lye hominy, you got it; an' if he had puddin', you got some.

"When I was 6 or 7 years old I chopped cotton and I plowed too, and I could lay as straight rows with oxen as any you ever saw.

"The massa whipped me with a dogwood switch, but he never did bring no blood. But it taken 7 men to whip my father.

"I'll tell you how I got away f'om there. Massa bought cotton and carried it to Mexico. He taken his 2 boys with him and we had 3 wagons and I drove one. I had 4 oxen and I had 3 bales of cotton on my wagon; he had 6 oxen and 6 bales of cotton, and the last wagon, it had 10 bales on it and 6 oxen. He had to ship it acrost the Rio Grande. If a Mexican bought it, he come across and took it over hisself. Reckin how much he got for that cotton? He got 60¢ a pound. Yes'm, he sho' did. Cotton was bringin' that then.

327

"I was freed over there in Mexico. I was about 14 years old. Massa Chamlin, he stayed over there till the country was free. He didn't believe in that fightin'.

"I cooked in a hotel over there in Mexico. I cooked two years at $1.00 a day.

"When Massa owned me, he always give us good clothes. Our pants was made out of duckin' like wagon sheets, but my mother took some kind of bark and dyed 'em. I think it was blackjack bark. He give us shoes, too. They was half-tan leather brogans."

"I used to play the fiddle for dances when I was young, but not after I joined the church. I played for the white people. Oh, yes'm, the cullud folks had dances, they sho' did dance.

"Yes'm, I saw a ghost onct. One night after I was livin' down here, I was goin' to Sabinal, me and another man, and a great long thing passed right in front of us. It was the blackest thing you ever saw. It was about six feet long. Yes'm, it sho' was a ghost or sumpin; it disappeared, and me lookin' at it. The other fellow that was with me, he seen it, too.

"Yes, they was lots of panthers and bears here. If this ghost was a bear, he sho' was a big 'un. We had a ghost down here on the creek we called the 'Ball Water Hole Ghost.' He was seen lots of times. He used to stay down there, but he ain't been seen lately. My wife, she seen him."

Aunt Ellen's Story

"Yes'm, I seen him walkin' 'long the trail ahead of us. He had on a black hat, like a tall stovepipe hat, and a long black coat, and when we got up close he jes' disappeared. He was a big man, and tall, too. We didn' know which way he went; he jes' seemed to disappear. My oldest daughter saw him too. Lots of folks did. He was always seen down at that water hole somewhere.

"Another time, I was stayin' with Mrs. Reedes. Mr. Reedes was killed and all night long he'd come back and grind coffee and sprinkle it all over us. I was so bad scared I nearly died. Next mornin' there'd be coffee all over the floor. We supposed it was Mr. Reede's ghost. They say if a person was wicked they come back like that. Onct he pulled Mrs. Reedes outta bed and pitched her on the floor, and he would take the dishes out of the shelves and throw 'em down. I couldn't stand it but a night or two and I said I was goin' home. Yes, ma'am, it sho' was a ghost. He sho' did tear up that house every night. Why, they'd be a light shine in that room just as plain as daylight, nearly. They say ghosties will run you, but I never had any to run me."

"I was born in Mississippi. We come to Texas and my mother died, so grandma raised me. I was jes' a baby when we come to Texas. Mr. Harper owned us. I remember the war, but it's so long ago I don't remember much. I remember when John Harper read the free paper to us. He had a big lot of slaves, but

when he read, the free papers they jes' flew out like birds. But I didn't. I was stickin' to my grandmother. She was on crutches and she stayed on at the Harper place.

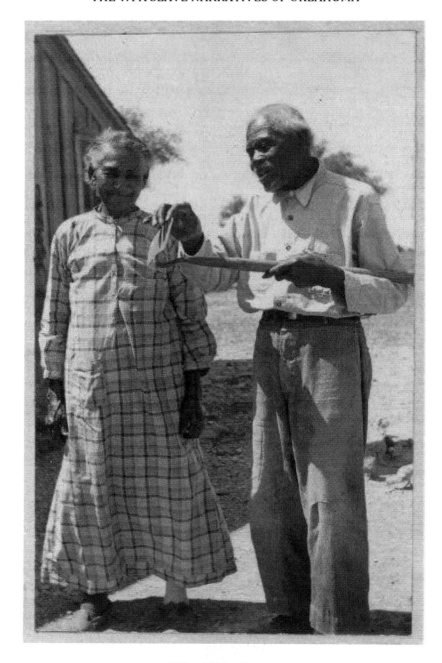

Bill and Ellen Thomas

"After we was free I worked for them a long time. I cooked, washed, ironed, milked the cows. He was pretty good to us, Judge Harper was. I went along with him when he went to war, his wife and chillun did too, and I nursed them, I'd give a young baby shuck tea to break him out with the hives. For chills and fever I give quinine weed. It don't grow here.

"When Judge Harper went up to Hondo my grandma grabbed me and kept me. So I stayed and worked. I was still a young girl, but I plowed, hauled and grubbed. I used to wear 'cotton stripes.' I remember 'em well. It was a homespun cloth. I know how to spin and weave and I could knit a pair of socks in two nights.

"I never did hear much about hard times. I was treated good but I got switched many a time. Oh, yes'm. I've been whipped, but not like some of 'em was. They used to tie some of 'em down. I've heered tell, they shore whopped 'em. They used to be a runaway that got away and went to Mexico now and then, and if they caught him they shore whopped him awful.

"That old piano in there, my daughter bought a long time ago. The varnish is off, but a man tol' us it could be sandpapered and refinished and it would be a beautiful thing. It's about 75 years old."

Lucy Thomas

Lucy Thomas,86, was born in Harrison Co., Texas, a slave of Dr. William Baldwin. She stayed with her master until 1868. In 1869 she married Anthony Thomas. She now lives with her son at Baldwin Switch, sixteen miles northeast of Marshall, Texas, on part of the land originally owned by the Baldwins.

"My name am Lucy Baldwin Thomas and I's birthed right here in Harrison County, on the old Baldwin place at Fern Lake. The log cabin where I's birthed sot in a grove of trees right by the lake. The Baldwin place jined the Haggerty and Major Andrews places.

"The best statement I can make of my age am I's 'bout fourteen the last year of Abe Lincoln's war. It was true, 'cause I starts hoein' in the field when I's nine years old and I'd been hoein' a long time.

"They called my papa, Ike. The Baldwins bought him out of Alabama, and mama's name was Nancy and she's birthed in Virginny, and the Baldwins bought her out the New Orleans slave market for $1,100.00. I's heared my gran'ma, Barbara, tell how some Alabama owners drug they niggers with a mule and laid dem face down in a hole and beat dem till they's raw as beefsteak. But her folks wasn't like that and the Baldwins wasn't neither. They was good white folks, and Missy was named May Amelia and then there was Old Marse Doctor William. He was a doctor but he worked a hundred acres land and owned 'bout eighty-five niggers, what lived in log quarters. They had son-of-a-gun beds peg to the walls, and wore bachelor brogan shoes and blue and stripe lowel clothes made on the place, and had lots to eat. My mama say she had a lots better time in slavery than after.

"All hands was up and in the field by daylight and Marse Baldwin allus kep' a fifty gallon barrel whiskey on the place and a demijohn on the front porch all the time for the niggers to git they drink on way to the field. But nobody ever got drunk.

"Marse's brother-in-law, Marse Lewis Brantly, was overseer, but never kicked and beat the niggers. He give us a light breshin' when we needed it. We would go mos' anywhere but had to git a pass first, and had play parties on Saturday night.

Lucy Thomas

"I went to school three months. A Yankee named Old Man Mills run a school and I quit workin' in the field to go. Them days, the Klu Kluxers was runnin' round and I seed big bunches of niggers with they heads tied up, goin' to report the Kluxers to the Progee Marshal.

"Three years after it was all over, my folks moved to the Haggerty place. I know lots 'bout old Col. Haggerty's widow. She was an Indian and her first husband was a big chief of the Caddo Indians on Caddo Lake. He betrayed the Indians to the white folks and he and her hid on a cave on the lake, and she slipped out to git food, and the Indians took him away. They say they scalped him like they done white folks. Then she married Col. Haggerty and he got kilt on a gamblin' spree and left her a lot of land and 'bout three hundred slaves. She kept a nigger woman chained to a loom for a year and when she knew the slaves was gittin' free, she poisoned a lot of dem and buried dem at night. We'd hear the other slaves moanin' and cryin' at night for the dead ones. That widow Haggerty was somthin'!

"I seed the 'Mattie Stephens' boat the day after it burned and kilt sixty people. Me and Anthony Thomas went to Marshall and married the day 'fore it burnt. That was on February 12th, in 1869. I lived with him fifty-five years and raised seven chillen, and after he died I kep' on farmin' until 'bout three years ago. Then I come to live with one my son's here and this land we're on right now was part the land old Marse Baldwin owned. I gits $10.00 a month from the gov'ment. They sho' is good to me, and my son is good, too, so I's happy in my old age."

Philles Thomas

Philles Thomas, 77, was born a slave of Dave Miles, who owned a plantation in Brazoria Co., Texas. Philles does not remember her father, but was told by her mother that he was sent to the Confederate Army and was fatally injured at Galveston, Texas. Philles stayed with her family until she was seventeen, then married William Thomas. They now live at 514 Hayes St., Fort Worth, Tex.

"I don't 'member much 'bout de war, 'cause I's jus' a young'un when it start and too small to have much mem'randum when it stop. I's still on de place where I's born when surrender come, de Lowoods Place, own by Massa Dave Miles, 'twixt Brazoria and Columbia. Massa Dave sho' have de big plantation but I don' know how many slaves.

"When I's a young'un, us kids didn't run round late. We'uns am put to bed. When sundown come, my mammy see dat my feets am wash and de gown put on, and in de bunk I goes.

"I can't 'member my daddy, but mammy told me him am sent to de 'Federate Army and am kilt in Galveston. She say dey puttin' up breastworks and de Yanks am shootin' from de ships. Well, daddy am watchin' de balls comin' from dem guns, fallin' round dere, and a car come down de track loaded with rocks and hit him. Dat car kilt him.

"Mammy marries Bill Bailey after freedom and moves to de Barnum Place, what Massa John Miles own. I stays with mammy till I's seventeen and holp dem share crop. Den I leaves. Dat de way with chillen, dey gives you lots of trouble raisin' dem and den off dey goes. When my chillen am young'uns dey's on my lap, and when dey's growed up, dey's on my heart.

"Us have de hard time share croppin'. Times was hard den and de niggers didn't know much 'bout takin' care demselves. Course, dey better off free, but dey have to larn. Us work hard and make 'nough to live on de first year us free. Us raise cotton and veg'tables and when I's not helpin' mammy I goes out and gits a li'l work here and yonder.

"I marries in Galveston, to dat old cuss, settin' right dere, William Thomas am he name and I's stood for him ever since. Him am dock wallopin' when I's marry to him. Sho', him am a dock walloper. If you wants to talk big, you calls it stev'dore on de wharf.

"Dat cullud gen'man of mine allus brung in de bacon. We'uns am never rich, but allus eats till de last few years. Us goes on de farm and it hand and mouth livin', but us eats someway. After while, us come to Fort Worth and he works as mortar man and cement mixer. We'uns live good till de few years back, when him break down in de back and can't work no more.

"It am ten chillun us raise but only five livin' now. One live at Stop Six, right here in Fort Worth, and de others am all over de world. Us don't know where dey am. Since Bill can't work no more, us git de pension from de State and dat $26.00 de month for de two of us.

"Does I ever vote? Christ for 'mighty! No. Why yous talk dat foolishment. Why for dis igno'mous old woman want to vote? No, sar, and no tother womens ought to vote. Dat am for de mens to do. My Bill votes couple times, when us in Galveston, and I tells you 'bout dat.

"Dey gives de eddication with a couple cups whiskey and de cheroot. When de whiskey and de cheroot works on Bill's brain, dere am den de smart nigger, and he votes 'telligent. I asks him what he votes for and him say, 'I's vote for what am on de ticket.' 'What am on de ticket,' I says. 'How does I know, I can't read.' Den I says, 'Better yous not vote, 'cause maybe yous vote to put youself in de jailhouse.' So I guess him think 'bout dat and him see what foolishment and troublement him maybe git into, and him quit votin'. We'uns am lucky with de trouble. Guess it 'cause we'uns knows how to 'have. When I's young my mammy larn me how to 'have and where I 'long, so de patterrollers and de Ku Klux never bother we'uns. Now, we'uns so old us can't git round, so us double safe now.

Philles Thomas

"Gosh for 'mighty! What yous want next? Now it for me to sing. Well, yous can't put de bluff on dis old nigger, so here it am:

"'Put on my long white robe,
Put on de golden crown,
Put on de golden slipper,
And forever be Jesus' lamb.'

"But I likes 'nother song better, like dis:

"'Herodias go down to de river one day,
Want to know what John Baptist have to say,

335

John spoke de words at risk of he life,
Not lawful to marry yous brudder's wife.'
"Not dat am 'nough. If I's here much longer, yous have dis old woman dancin'."

William M. Thomas

William M. Thomas, 87, now residing at 514 Hayes St., Fort Worth, Texas, was born a slave of Dr. Frank Thomas, in Lauderdale County, Miss. William's father was sold when William was a baby and his mother mated with another slave. It was seven years after they were freed that the family left their master and moved onto a tract of land. William stayed with them until he was twenty-four, then worked twelve years in Galveston, as a stevedore. He farmed until 1910, then worked as a mortar man at the Purina Mills in Fort Worth until 1931. He and his wife receive a $13.00 monthly pension.

"I knows 'zactly how old I is. Massa done give my mammy de statement. He do dat for all he niggers when dey freed. I's borned May 17th, in 1850, and dat make me eighty-eight next May. Dat's on Massa Doctor Frank Thomas's plantation, over near Meridian, in Mississippi. Dere forty-four slave families on he place and he own 'bout seven hunerd acres land, so him have plenty pasture, wood and field land. De money crop was cotton, of course.

"My mammy and sis was in de place and my step-pa. My pappy am sold and took to Texas when I's so li'l I don't 'member him. After dat, mammy done took another man.

"All de slaves live in quarters 'cept de house servants, and dey live in servants' quarters, and dere's where I's de lucky nigger. My mammy am cook for massa and I's round de kitchen what 'twas plenty of good eats. And I plays with massa's two boys, 'twas Frank and Lawrence.

"I's so li'l 'fore surrender I never really works, 'cept to be de errand boy. I fetches eggs and sich. Massa have lots of chickens and us fetch in high as a thousand eggs in one day sometimes. Us have eggs to eat, too. Massa Thamas am awful good and dere am never de holler 'bout feedin'. I bet none dem niggers done live so good after dey free.

"Us have all de meat us want, mostest pork and beef and mutton. Dey kills five hunerd hawgs when killin' time came, and make hams and bacon and sausages. If yous ever ate sich ham and bacon what am made by massa's butcher right dere on de place, you say dere never am sich. Dat sausage, it make de mouf water to think 'bout it. 'Sides de meat, us have cornbread and 'lasses and de rations ain't measure out, 'cept de white flour on Sunday mornin'. All week de meals am cook in dat kitchen and serve in de big shed, but each family cook for deyself on Sunday.

"Us go to church if us want, 'bout four miles off. Massa give anybody de pass to go dere. Dere am no parties and sich, but old Jack saw on de fiddle and us sing.

"Massa didn't whip, only once. Dat 'cause a nigger steal he fav'rite pumpkin. He am savin' dat for to git de seed and it am big as de ten gallon jug. De corn field am full of pumpkins, but dat nigger done took massa's choice one. Dat pumpkin am so big, he have to tussle with it 'fore he git it to he cabin. It like stealin' a elephant, you can't hide it in de watch pocket. Course, lots of niggers seed dat cullud gen'man with dat pumpkin, and 'fore long massa knew it.

"Well, sar, it am de funny sight to see him punish dat nigger. First, massa set him down on de ground front de quarters, where us all see him. Den he make dat nigger set down and give him de big bowl pumpkin sauce and make him eat it. Him eat and eat and git so full him can't hardly swallow and massa say, 'Eat some more, it am awful good.' Dat nigger try, but him can't eat no more. Massa give him de light breshin' and it am funny to see, dat cullud gen'man with pumpkin smear on he face and tears runnin' down he face. After dat, us chillen call him Massa Pumpkin and massa never have no more trouble with stealin' he seed pumpkins.

"When war starts I's 'bout fifteen year old. 'Bout half mile from de plantation am de crossroads and one go to New Orleans and one go to Vicksburg. Dere am a 'Federate camp dere at de start, but after 'while dey goes and de Yanks comes. Dere a battle near, and us hear de shootin' but us have to stay on de place.

"I done slip off and see de camp, though. De Yanks puts up two big tents and use dem for de hospital and de wounded am fetch dere. What I sees and hears dere, I never forgits, and it done turn dis nigger 'gainst war. Why can't dey settle dey 'sputes without killin'? Dey's moanin' and cryin' and screamin' in dem tents.

"One day de Yanks come clean de crib of all de corn and de meat house of all de meat. Massa am smart and fix it so dey don't find all de rations. Him dig a big ditch in de woods and hide lots of rations.

"Us didn't know when freedom came. It a long time after dat de Yanks come tell us, and it de same way on all de plantations round dere. De Yanks come and make massa pay us all fifty cents de day. After dat massa puts dem what wants to go on pieces of land and dey ain't charge for it till seven year after. Den dey has to pay rent and part de crop, and for de mules and tools all de time.

"I stays with my folks till I's twenty-four year old and den I's on my way to Galveston and gits work as de stevedore. Dat am on de wharf and I works dere twelve year. I votes dere two times. Some white folks done come to us, and de boss, too, and gives us de ticket. It am all mark up. Boss say us don't have to work de next day, and us to report at a place. When us comes dere, 'twas a table with meat and bread and stuff for to eat, and whiskey and cigars. Dey give us something to eat and a cup or two of dat whiskey and puts de cigar in de mouth. Us am 'portant niggers, ready to vote. With dat cup of whiskey in de stomack and dat cigar in de mouth and de hat cock on side de head, us march to de votin' place and does our duty. Fix up de way us was, us would vote to put us back in slavery. And de nigger what didn't vote, after all dat, him am in for de fixin'. I means he gits fixed. Dey pounds he head till him won't forgit to do it right next time.

"But I gits to thinkin' how massa say when us leave him, 'Don't let no white folks use you for to make trouble.' I figgers dat what am happenin' with dat votin' business, and I quits votin' and goes to farmin'. I 'lieve de cullud folks should vote, but not de igno'mous niggers like us was den.

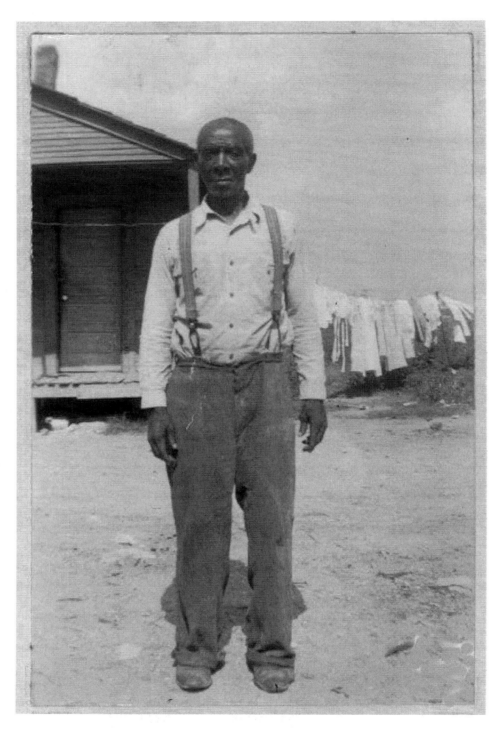

William M. Thomas

I farms till 1910 and den comes to Fort Worth, and dey am buildin' de Purina Mills Elevators on East 4th Street and I works dere at mortar work. Den I works at cement on lots de big buildin's in dis city, till 'bout ten year ago, when it git too hard for me. I has de back misery.

"I gits married to Phillis Wilson when I's twenty-nine, in Galveston, and us don't allushave lots, but us gits by and raises de family. Now us have to live on de pension from de State, what am $13.00, and sometimes us am awful short, tryin' to pay de rent and buy de rations and what clothes us needs, but us am glad to git it. Ten chillen am what us raises and five am dead and four am scattered and us don't know where, and one live here.

""Ain't it diff'rent how peoples lives? Us used to travel with de ox and now dey flies in de sky. Folks sings in New York and us sets right here and hears dem. Shucks! De way things am gwine, I's all fussed up and can't understand whether I's gwine or comin'."

Mary Thompson

Mary Thompson was born a slave 87 years ago, in Denton, Miringo County, Alabama. Her mother, Viney Askew, and father, Wesley Jones, belonged to Green Askew, a Georgian. She was 15 when she was freed. Mary now lives at 1104 East Avenue, Austin, Tex.

"I was bo'n in Alabama and my mother was Viney Askew. She belonged to Marster Green Askew. My father was Wesley Jones, 'cause he took his marster's name.

"My mother was a good cook and she cooked for de marster. She had a great big stove and she made salt-risin' bread, too. We and all de slaves lived in cabins near de big house and some of de slaves would have chillen by de marster.

"When we come home from de fields at night, de women cooked de food and den dey was so tired dey jus' went to bed. We didn' have fun in de evenin's, but on Christmas mornin' de marster give us eggnog and sich. Den we'd sing but I don' 'member de songs now.

"De crops in Alabama would be cleared by July 4 and den we'd have sev'ral days off, all de slaves. Dey'd give us pits of barbecue and pies and cakes to eat.

"When we was sick de marster would sen' for de doctor and we made teas outta herbs and sich. Alabama was full of chills and fevers in dem days and we drunk catnip tea for fevers and blue and white sage. Calamus root, looks like an onion, was good for de chillens' colic.

"My mistress' niece had a big plantation and she had a place whar she had de slaves whopped. She had a reg'lar whoppin' post. My marster jes' had a large cowhide whoop. Yes,

I got a whoppin' more'n once. Sev'ral times marster took hold my ears and bumped my head 'gainst de wall. But gen'rally dey was good to me.

"We wasn't 'lowed no whiskey, 'less we was sick. De poor white folks was good to us, better'n rich folks. Dey'd give us a quarter now'n den.

"I can 'member how de slaves was fattened like hawgs and den marched to town and 'round and auctioned off like cattle. Some of 'em had done somethin' mean and was sold off. Some of 'em brought more'n a thousand dollars down in New Orleans.

"I knows of one slave who liked to run 'round at night. She was nuss to marster's girl and she give it morphine to put it to sleep. She give de baby girl so much morphine dat her body was full of it and she died. De cullud folks got to talkin' too much and de baby was dug up and 'xamined. De slave nuss was put in jail and kep' there a long time and den she was sold.

"Heap of de slaves would run away and go up north. Dey would try to find 'em by sendin' nigger houn's after 'em. Once de houn's caught a slave and he kep' sayin', 'O, Lawd ... O, Lawd!'

Mary Thompson

"After de war, when we was free, de slaves would go here and there and a lot of 'em died. Dey'd git de black measles, go out in de woods and die. Dey didn' know how to take care of demselves.

"I stayed at marster's house eight months, den hired out at ten dollars a month. Dat was de fus' money I ever made and I didn' want to go to school, 'cause I wanted to make dat money. Dat looked like big money to me. I was proud to have it, 'cause I could git what I wanted. I cain't read or write to this day.

"I was married to General Thompson, and he'd been a slave too, in Alabama. Yes, General was his given name. I was 16 years old when I married and a white preacher married us durin' a 4th of July celebration. Yes, we had a big time and a good time.

"We come to Texas later and my husban' farmed on the Brazos. We had eight chillen, and two of 'em is livin.' My husban' died and I buried him, den I took up with a Horace Foster, and he was nothin' but a gambler. I lived with him 'bout 8 years, but he never would marry me, so I lef' him."

Penny Thompson

Penny Thompson, 86, now living at 1100 E. 12th St., Fort Worth, Texas, was born a slave to Calvin Ingram, in Coosa Co., Alabama. In 1867 Penny was brought to Tyler, Texas, and several years later she married Ike Thompson and moved to Fort Worth.

"Do I 'member slavery days? Yes, suh! How could I forgit dem? For an old person I has good 'collection. I's 10 year old when de war start and my massa am Calvin Ingram. My mammy and pappy was a weddin' present to Massa Ingram from his pappy. Mammy give birth to 15 chilluns, but I never saw any of my brothers and sisters, 'cause they all born on Massa Ingram's pappy's plantation 'fore he give my mammy to Massa Ingram.

"De plantation dat Massa Ingram have was 200 acres or mo'. Him own 'bout 20 grown-up slaves, and on dat place dey raises 'bout everything we eats and wears, includin' de vinegar and de peach brandy. Everybody am 'signed to dey duties and my mammy am chief cook for de big house. I he'ps her and feeds chickens, gits eggs and totes water.

"De treatmen' couldn't be better. Massa am de bestes' and de kindes' fellow dat ever live. He am in Heaven, for sho', but de missy mus' be in Hell, for she sho' was a debbil. Massa have de fight with her lots of times 'bout de treatment of us, but he wouldn't let her 'buse us.

"We'uns was never hongry for food, 'cause we have lots of meat, chickens and eggs and cornmeal and 'lasses and honey. De hams is smoked on de place and dey am de hams, white man, dey am de hams! Den massa have a big cellar jus' full of everything and I never forgit de big, brass key what lock dat cellar. Dere was de jams and de jellies and de preserves, and de massa give us somethin' of all of dat. Him makes de gran' peach brandy and every mornin' we could have two fingers in de glass. 'Twas de same at night. Dere was somethin' else was reg'lar every mornin' and night and dat am de prayer. He calls all us together and says de prayers. I often thinks of dat brandy and de prayers, two times every day.

"As for de whuppin,' dere wasn't any on massa's place. Him have only one nigger what am unruly and dat am Bill McClure, and a bigger thief never lived.

"On de nex' plantation dey gives de whuppin' and we hears dem niggers beller. On dat plantation dey trades and sells de niggers all de time and de speculation wagon comes by often. Sometime it am awful to see de babies sold from de mothers and de wife from de husban'. Sich bemoanin' at some of dem sales, yous jus' can't 'magine.

"But on massa's place we has no tradin' of slaves and we'uns have pass for go to church and parties and de dance. When de night for de party come on our place, de yard am cleaned off and we makes sandwiches. One time massa come to me and say, 'Jus' wait a minute, I nearly forgits de mos' 'portant part,' and he give me a new pink dress. I's so happy I cries for joy, and everybody says I looks like de Queen of Sheba.

"De other big time am de corn huskin' bee. Once a year all de neighbors comes fust to one place den to de other. At de huskin's, dey gives de prize when you finds a red ear. De prize am two fingers of dat peach brandy. When dey gits de fus' one dey works a little harder, de second still faster, and de third, Lawd-a-massy, how dem husks do fly! Dey don't git drunk, 'cause you am lucky to find as much as three red ears at one huskin'.

"We has de weddin's too, but no preacher or cer'mony. When a man sees a girl him likes and de girl am willin', dey says dey wants a weddin'. De womens cooks extra and dey gits de cedar boughs and wets dem and sprinkles flour on dem and puts dem on de table. We sits at de table and eats and sings 'ligious songs and after supper dey puts de broom on de floor an de couple takes de hands and steps over de broom, and den dey am put to bed.

Penny Thompson

"We was never bother with de patter rollers, but I 'members a song 'bout dem, like dis:
"'Up de hill and down de hollow
Patter rollers cotched nigger by de collar;
Dat nigger run, dat nigger flew,
Dat nigger tear his shirt in two.'

"In de war soldiers comes to massa's place and every time he feeds dem. You hears de clippity clop of de hosses and dey is off de saddle 'fore you gits to de door. Dey says, 'We wants de meal,' or maybe dey wants to sleep. Massa's wife say, 'I's not goin' do nothin' for dem blue bellies,' but massa make her fix de chicken. Dere was everything dere but manners, 'cause dey have de pistols drawed.

344

"After freedom, mos' of us stays with massa, 'cause we don't know where to go and we don't want to go, but 'fore long massa dies and dat was mournin' time. After de death, we all leaves.

I marries Bill Thompson but he won't work so after 15 year I gits de divorcement."

Albert Todd

Albert Todd, 86 years old, was born a slave to Capt. Hudson, in Russellville, Kentucky. His master was killed in the Civil War and he then came to Texas in a covered wagon. His "Missus" kept him a slave for three years after the War. He now lives with his wife, daughter and two sons at 703 Center St., San Antonio, Texas.

"I most suppose my memory is too jumpy, but I'll try to bring it 'long from de time I was born. I don't know de year, but it was in Russellville, Kentucky and my massa, Captain Hudson, had a fruit orchard. My reg'lar work was protectin' my young missus, Nannie Hudson. She had to walk five miles to and forth from school every day and I was her protector. I was only 8 and she was 11. I sat on the steps until she got through larnin' and then brung her home. She come to be grown and married and died, but I allus loved her.

"When war comes, my massa goes and gets kilt and my missus got 'gusted with the orchard and packs up in two covered wagons and heads crossland to Texas. We finally gets to Lavernia and gets a farm and us worked plenty hard.

Albert Todd

"Our missus was good to us, but one white man neighbor got a new set of niggers every year. He say if they didn't die, they wasn't any good work left in them after they works for him a year. He allus cut off one they ears, so if they run away he'd know 'em.

"My clothes was a long shirt, made out of a meal sack. That's all I wore them days. I was a slave three year after the others was freed, 'cause I didn't know nothin' 'bout bein' free. A Mrs. Gibbs got holt of me and makes me her slave. She was a cruel old woman and she didn't have no mercy on me. She give me one sausage and one biscuit in the mornin' and nothin' else all day. One day she gone and I stole some biscuits, and she comes back and says, 'Did you take them biscuits?' She tells me if I tells de truth she won't punish me, but she knocks me down and beats me till I not know nothin'. But after 'while her house burns and she burns up in it.

"But 'fore that I was goin' to run away and I goes to the road and sits down and then my sisters comes 'long and finds me and takes me to a place where they was livin' on the

346

ranch of a man name Widman. We works for him a long time and then I is free from that Gibbs woman."

Aleck Trimble

His skin was of an extremely dark chocolate color, his hair thin and gray. A blue shirt was about his body while blue trousers enclosed his nether limbs. His bare feet protruded as he sat on an old dilapidated chair. Under his flat nose was a gray mustache, and one eye had completely lost its vision. This small negro man was Aleck Trimble who thoughtfully told the story of his life. [HW: Veth, Tex.]

"I was bo'n in 1861. I warn't much of a chile when freedom come, but yet dey's right smart of t'ings I kin 'member in slavery times."

"My pa name was Aleck Trimble and dat's my name, too. My ma was Ellen Trimble and I was de onlies' son. I didn' hab no brudders. Ol' marster's las' name was Alexander, but I dis'member his fus' name."

"I uster hafter do a li'l wuk 'roun' de place like pullin' up weeds and drivin' de calfs. I 'member one time I was drivin' a calf up to de lot and I saw a crazy man. He didn' try to do nuffin' to me. I jis' walk up on him and he sittin' dere mumblin' and I know right den dere was sump'n' wrong wid him. He didn' try to hu't me nor run atter me, but he sho' scare me and I run away from him fas' as I kin."

"I warn't so glad when freedom come. I was a-farin' pretty well in de kitchen. I didn' t'ink 'eber see better times dan what dem was, and I ain't. I t'ought I was jis' as near hebben as I want to be. It didn' look to me like dey coulder been no betterer dan what dey was."

"I uster had jis' all I want to eat. Us hab biscuit and syrup, and plenty milk and butter. And dey give us all de collard greens and hog jowls us could hol'."

"Dey uster had lots of cows and all de milk and butter anybody want. Dey had a big bucket hangin' in de well. Dey put de butter in dat in de summer time to keep it from meltin'. How dey kep' it from sp'ilin'? Why, dey et it up, dat's how dey keep it from sp'ile."

"I neber see 'em do de slaves bad. Iffen dey did dey tek 'em off in de woods somers where nobody see 'em."

"Sometime nigger traders come 'long de road wid a big drove of niggers. I neber pay dat no min' though. It was jis' a drove of niggers to me."

"Dey gimme 'bout as good clo's as I got now. When I was doin' 'roun' de yard at Marster' house I wo' a shu't wid pleats 'cross de bosom in front."

"Dey gimme some britches befo' freedom come, and den I t'ought I's 'bout as big as anybody. Dey gimme dem when I was big 'nuff to dribe de calfs up from de lot. But I neber go in de fiel' to wuk."

"Atter freedom come I go to school to a white lady name' Mrs. Tunsten she had a son name' Waddy. She teach de school at Shiloh and all de white chillun and nigger chillun go to school in de same room. She teach her own chillun in dat school on de Huntsville road. I 'member de stages and t'ings gwine by. I t'ought she was a good teacher, but she whip me half a day one time 'cause I didn' spell "gangrene." She whip me 'till I learn how to spell it and I ain't neber forgit. I kin spell dat word yit. I's satisfy she from de Nor'f. Dere was a ol' stage stan' dere by de school house."

"I went to dat teacher and dat school t'ree or fo' year'. Atter she quit teachin' dey was other teachers what come drappin' in and teachin' t'ree or fo' months."

"My pa he uster wuk in de fiel' 'till freedom come. My ma she wuk in de kitchen. Dat how come I git so much outer de kitchen to eat. Sometime she hafter wuk in de fiel' too."

"Jis' like I say, I stay 'roun' de big house. I raise up wid de white chillun 'till I was 25 or 30 year' ol'."

"I t'ink dey stay at de ol' place a year or mo' atter freedom. Den dey 'gin to drif' 'roun' to diff'rent place w'ere dey find wuk to do. I stay wid de ol' folks and he'p s'po't (support) 'em wid what money I git for de wuk what I doin'. My ma lef' my pa at de ol' plantation, and her and me and a gal what was ol'er dan me, what was my sister, us move."

"De fus' wuk I done and de fus' money I mek was pickin' cotton for a white man. De fus' money I git I buy me a ol' Webster Blue-back speller. Lawd, I uster look at dat book sometime 'till dem A B C's all run togedder seem like."

"Dat plantation was de Johnnie Murchison plantation. Us stay dere 'bout five or six year'. Atter dat I lef' dere and went to wuk for cullud man what was name' Sam Scott. I wuk 'roun' in de fiel' and go to mill when I was on dat place."

"I 'member seein' de sojers. Dey was a big troop of 'em come marchin' down de road. Dey was all of 'em dress' up in blue coats and some of 'em had blue capes over dey shoulders. Dey had wagons and lots of sich t'ings comin' 'long behin'."

"I can't tell you much 'bout de ol' marster 'cause I didn' see him eb'ry day. Lots and lots of time I didn' hab no notion where he was."

"Dey was a large troop of cullud folks on de place. When dey want 'em dey blow a bugle or ho'n or sump'n'."

"I git marry in Houston county. I don' 'member what year it was but it was back in Cleveland's 'ministration. Den atter while she die and dat lef' me a widower. Den 'bout 28 year' ago I marry Ollie Washington. I was wukkin' for Scott befo' I marry Washington. Dat's my li'l 'dopted gran'chile dere. You see dat t'ing 'roun' her neck? Dat's hoss hair roll up in a clo'f. Dat to he'p when she teethin'. Dat good for stomach and bowel trouble, too. Long as she wear dat she ain't gwine to hab no fever in de head needer. I gwine to let her wear it 'till she finish cuttin' her teef. I jis' put dat rag 'roun' it to keep it from stickin' her. You kin see how healthy she is."

"Anudder t'ing what good for chillun when dey's teethin' is for to tek a rabbit head and 'noint (anoint) dey gums good wid rabbit brains. Some of de ol' folks wear a dime tie' 'roun' dey leg wid a hole in it for de rheumatism."

"May-apple for a good purgative too, but you got to know how to use it. Iffen you don' use it right though, it gwine to stir up your stomach and mek you sick. And you better not drink no milk when you tek dat May-apple root and you don' want to eat nuffin' needer. Dat's bitter'n quinine."

"Co'se, sometime some of de slaves die on de plantation. I know dey have home-mek coffin, but I ain't neber see 'em mekin' one. Sometime' when de corpse a-layin' dere dead dey have a wake."

"Dem what wanted 'em had a li'l patch of groun' where dey plant garden truck and veg'tables for deyself. Dey have half a day off on Sunday, and den co'se, dey have Sunday. All de slaves have big holiday on Crismus."

"Dey lib in log houses. Moss and du't (dirt) was pack' all in 'tween de logs and boards was nail' on over dat. Ol' marster he have a awful large house buil' outer plank. It had a gallery to de front and back."

"Dey had a li'l house down de way dey had preachin' in. De white preacher he do de preachin'. Seem to me dat soon play out."

"Dey had a ol' lady what ten' to de chillun when dey in de fiel' pickin' cotton. Sometime she uster sing:

'My Lord say dey's room enough,
Room enough in hebben fer us all.'
fotch (fetch) 'em a whack on de head and say:
'Come 'long wid dat row."
"Atter freedom come de darkies uster have a song what go like dis:
'Come along
Come along
Make no delayin'
Soon be so Uncle Sam give us
all a farm.
'Come from de way
Come from de nation
'Twon't be long 'till Uncle Sam

give us all a farm.'
Atter while de Klu Kluxers git atter de cullud folks. Den dey mek a song:
'Run nigger run de Klu Klux git you.'

Lots of time dey come on Sunday. One place dere was a big plum thicket 'long de road and dey dodge in dere and ketch people. Lots of cullud folks hafter pass by dere to git where dey gwine. In de day time dem Klu Kluxes was jis' in dey common clo's but when dey come in de nights dey did figger deyself wid dem high p'int hats and white t'ings wrap 'roun' 'em."

"I b'longs to de Baptis' Chu'ch. I reckon dat was de Baptis' chu'ch back in dem days, but I don' 'member no baptisms back in slavery. I 'members though that dey was a blin' cullud man what uster preach."

"I 'members dey was lots of smallpox one time. Dat was atter freedom come, 'bout 50 year' ago. De people was sho' scare' of it, wusser'n if it was a Winchester. When I fus' 'member 'bout dat smallpox dey was a man had it and dey run him 'bout a mont' and bu'n him. If dey find out you got de smallpox you jis' long gone, you better not go out nor in. Dey put de food on de gate-pos'. If you don' git better in so many days dey bu'n you and de house and eb'ryt'ing up."

"I uster farm 'till de boll weevil start in dis part of de country. Atter dat sawmillin' and public works. Jis' go from one sawmill to anudder. But I spen' my bes' days on de farm."

"When I was cut off dem sawmill and public works jobs I was done wo' out. Dey orter stop' me fifteen years befo' dey did, 'cause den I mightenter (might not have) been wo' out. Now I can't do nuffin'."

"I los' one of my eye 'bout seben year' ago. I have de fever and it settle in my eye and jis' cook. Dat was when I had meningitis."

"I can't plow no mo'. I jis' live on my li'l bit of pension and dat ain't nuttin'."

Reeves Tucker

Reeves Tucker, 98 year old Negro farmer of Harrison Co., Texas, was born in Bibb Co., Alabama, a slave of George Washington Tucker, Sr. When Reeves was six his master died and Reeves was separated from his family and brought to Texas by George Tucker, Jr. Reeves now lives with his son, who owns a farm nine miles northwest of Marshall, Texas.

"My father was Armistead Tucker and my mother Winnie Tucker and they's both born slaves of Massa George Washington Tucker. He lived over in old Alabama, between Selma and Maplesville. My brothers was Andy and John and Peter and there was two girls, Anne and Dorcus, and we was all born on Massa Tucker's plantation. My missy died 'fore I was born and my old massa died when I was jest a shirt-tail boy and his chillen had a dividement of his lands and mammy and all the chillen but me fell to the daughter and pappy was give to the son. Pappy begs too hard for me to go with him that fin'ly they lets me. I never seed my mammy after that, bein' as how Missy Emogene stays in Alabama and us come to Texas.

"Massa George settles near Gilmer and he sho' have a big place with lots of acres and a good house. He didn't 'low no beatin' on that place but I've saw slaves on other places whopped till the blood run off them onto the groun'. When they was cut loose from the tree or whippin' post they falls over like dead. But our massa was good to us and give us lots to eat and wear. We et pork meat and white flour jest like the white folks and every woman have to spin so many yards cloth 'fore she go to bed, so we allus had the clothes.

"I've saw lots of slaves bid off like stock and babies sold from their mammy's breast. Some brung 'bout $1,500, owing to how strong they is. Spec'lators used to ride all over the country near our place and buy up niggers and I've saw as many as fifty in a gang, like convicts.

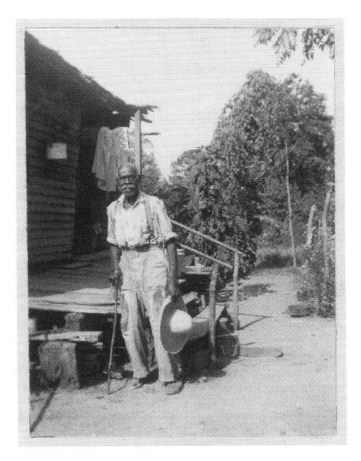

Reeves Tucker

"But Massa George wouldn't sell and buy slaves and none of 'em ever run off 'cept my pappy and one night he started to go 'cross a shirt of woods to the neighbors and young massa was a pattyroller and tells pappy to wait and go with him, but pappy hard headed as a mule and goes hisself and the pattyrollers cotches him and nigh beats him to death. Young massa was sho' mad as fire, 'cause he didn't want his niggers beat up.

"Them circuit ridin' preachers come to the white church and tries to make the white folks bring their slaves to preaching. Preacher say, 'Nigger have a soul to save same as us all.' Massa allus went to church but I don't 'lieve it done him any good, 'cause while he there at meetin' the niggers in the field stacking that fodder. He did give us Christmas Day and a big dinner and 'cept for workin' the lights outten us, gen'rally treated us decent and we had heap easier time than any other slaves 'round.

"I 'member the war and Jeff Davis and Abe Lincoln was warfaring 'bout freein' the niggers 'bout four year 'fore they fought. Massa Tucker jest grunted when we was freed, 'cause he knowed the thing was up, and he tells us if we'd stay and help the crop out he'd give us a horse and saddle, but we didn't git nothin'. So I lef' him soon as the crop laid by the year of freedom and then moved with pappy to a farm near Hallsville and stays with him till I marries. I had seven chillen to be growed and married and I farmed near Hallsville mos' my life, till I too old. My son, Reeves after me, owns this farm and we's all right. Never did have hard times after freedom, like some niggers, 'cause we just sot down on the land."

Lou Turner

Lou Turner, 89, was born at Rosedale, near Beaumont, Texas, on the Richard West plantation. She has spent her entire life within three miles of Beaumont, and now lives in her own little home, with her daughter, Sarah.

"I hears you been 'round to see me befo', but you ain't never gwine find me to home. I sho' love to go 'round visitin'. You know dey say iffen you treats the cat too good, you ain't never know where the cat is.

"I's gwine on seventeen year old when freedom come. I's born right here near Beaumont, on the big road what they calls the Concord Road, in the place what they calls Rosedale. I's a growed-up young lady befo' I ever sees Beaumont. I's gwine on 89 year old now.

"Richard West, he's my massa and Mary Guidry she my missy. Dey used to call her the 'Cattle King.' Dey have a big plantation and jes' a few slaves. Dey raises my mammy since she eleven year old. Her name Maria and she marry Sam Marble. He come from Miss'ippi.

"I stay up at the big house and missy fix my plate when she fix hers. God bless her heart, she kind to me, I know now I's sassy to her but she didn't pay me no 'tention 'cause I's li'l. I slep' on a trundle bed by missy's side and I git so smart I allus smell my bed to see iffen dey puts nice, clean sheets on mine like dey did on hers. Sometime I play sick, but old missy a good doctor and she gimme beefoot oil and it so nasty I quit playing off. She French and she so good doctor they send for her to other folks houses.

"Old missy was real rich. I's taken her money out of de wardrobe ane make tall playhouse out of gold and silver money. Iffen she have to buy somethin' she have to come and borrow it from me. Us allus has to figger how to take dat money out of de corners so de house won't fall down. I cried and cried iffen she tored it up.

"She'd take me with her when she go to see her grandchillen in de French settlement. Us come in buggy or hack and bring jelly and money and things. I thought I's gwine to Heaven, 'cause I gits to play with li'l chillen. Us play 'ring place', dat's draw a ring and hop 'round in it. Us jump rope and swing. Dey have a hair rope swing with a smooth board in it so it ain't scratch us behin'.

"Old missy so kind but what got 'way with me, I couldn't go to school. I beg and beg, but she kep' sayin', 'Some day, some day,' and I ain't never sit in a school in my life.

"Old massa didn't work 'em hard. He make 'en come in when the sun got bad, 'cause he feared dey git sunstroke. He mighty good in early days, but when he figger dey gwine loose he slaves he start bein' mean. He split 'em and sold 'em, tryin' to make he money out of 'em.

"De house what the white folks live in was make out of logs and moss and so was the quarters houses. Better'n New Orleans, dem quarters was. Us slaves have de garden patch. The white folks raises hogs and kilt 'em by the twenties. Dey smoke hams and shoulders and chittlin's and sich and hang 'em up in the smokehouse. Us allus have plenty to eat and us have good, strong clothes. Missy buy my dresses separate, though. She buy me pretty stripe cotton dress.

"Bout the only work I ever done was help watch the geese and turkeys and fill the quilts. I larn to card, too. Old missy never whip me much, she jes' like to scare me. She whip me with big, tall straw she git out the field or wet a towel and whip my legs. My old massa done a trick I never forgit while I's warm. I's big gal 'bout sixteen year old and us all 'lone on the place. He tells me to crawl under the corncrib and git the eggs. I knowed dey ain't nothin' dere but the nest egg, but I have to go. When I can't find nothin' he pull me out backwards by the feet and whip me. When old missy come home I ain't know no better'n to tell her and she say she ought to kill him, but she sho' fix him, anyway. He say she spile me and dat why he whip me.

"Old missy taken to preachin'. She was real good preacher. Dey have de big hall down the center of the house where they have services. A circuit rider come once a month and everybody stop workin' even if it wasn't Sunday.

353

Lou Turner

"When war was on us there wasn't no sojers 'round where I was, but dat battle on Atchafalia shook all the dishes off the dresser and broke 'em up. Jes' broke up all the fine Sunday and company dishes.

"After de trouble my mammy have gettin' me 'way from there when freedom come, she gits me after all. Old missy have seven li'l nigger chillen what belong to her slaves, but dey mammies and daddys come git 'em. I didn't own my own mammy. I own my old missy and call her 'mama'. Us cry and cry when us have to go with us mammy. I 'members how old missy rock me in her arms and sing to me. She sing dat 'O, Susanna' and tell me a story:

354

"'Dere a big, old brown bear what live in de woods and she have lots of li'l cub bears and dey still nussin' at de breast. Old mama bear she out huntin' one day and she come by de field where lots of darkies workin' and dere on a pallet she see fat, li'l pickaninny baby. Mama bear she up and stole dat li'l pickaninny baby and takes it home. It hongry but after she git all de cub bears fed, dere ain't no milk left for de nigger baby. Mama bear git so 'sasperated she say to her babies, 'Go long, you go way and play.' Dan she feed de li'l pickaninny baby and dat how she raise dat nigger baby.'

"Now, every time old missy come to dat place in de story, she start laughin', 'cause I allus used to ask her.

"'How come dey didn't no hair grow on dat baby.'"

Irella Battle Walker

Irella Battle Walker, 86, was born a slave at Craft's Prairie, Texas. Her parents, Mesheck and Becky Battle, belonged to Mr. Battle, but were sold while Irella was a baby to Tom Washington, of Travis County. Irella learned her A B C's from an old slave, Jack James, although it was against the rules. This was the only schooling she ever had. Irella receives a monthly old age pension of eight dollars. She lives at 2902 Cole St., Austin, Texas.

"My name was Irella Battle and I was borned on August 15th, in 1851, down at Craft's Prairie, in Bastrop County. I was 86 years old last August, and I'm blind in one eye.

"Mammy's name was Becky Battle and she was a field worker, and dat about de most work she have to do, 'cept on rainy days. She had five girls and one boy and I'm de youngest and de only livin' one now. Daddy was Mesheck Battle and when I'm a baby in mammy's arms, us sold to Massa Washington.

"Daddy had to do field work. I never knowed him do nothin' but farm. He sho' make us behave and whop us if we didn't. Massa was purty good. De massas dem times, some was good and some was bad, and about de most of dem was bad. I had to he'p round de big house and dey purty good to me. But when I still little I went to de fields. Dey give me a sack what de slaves make to pick cotton in. Dey spin de thread and make cloth on de loom and stitch it and make cotton sacks. Dey short for us chillen and de older folks had a short one to pick in and a big sack to empty in. I could pick about a hundred fifty pounds a day when I's twelve. Israel Roberts could pick five hundred a day. Us never got no money for pickin', only food and clothes and a place to stay at night. Old man Jonas watched us chillen and kept us divin' for dat cotton all de day long. Us wish him dead many a time.

"De plantation had a hoss-power gin and some days our rows of cotton tooked us right to de gin house and we'd look up and watch de slave boys settin' on de lever and drivin' dem hosses round and round.

"De cabins was log and mud and stick chimney. When one dem chimneys catch fire us git on top and throw water on it.

"In summer us go barefoot, but dere shoemakers what make shoes for winter. When a beef killed, de hide kept and cleaned and put in de tannin' trough. When de leather ready, de shoes make in de little shoe shop, and when dem shoes git dry dey hard as a rock. Daddy make us rub tallow or fried grease meat or any other kind grease into dat hard shoe leather, and it make dem soft, but when de dew and sun git on dem again dey's hard again. Times de coyotes steal dem greased shoes and make off with dem. Dat act'ly happen a lot of times.

"Old man Jack James work at day and have night school at night. He have long boards for benches and let dem down by ropes from de rafters, and have blue back spellers. He point to de letters with de long broom straw and dat's how we larn our A B C's. I can read purty good, when my eyes let me, but I can't write nothin'.

"If it rained we had to shuck and shell corn or pull weeds in de yard, and it was a big one, too. De women spin thread for de looms, two of dem and a spinnin' wheel in every cabin.

"Us have beds de men make and take wore out clothes and breeches and piece dem and stuff with cotton for quilts. When it cold us keep fire all night long. De plates am tin and a big gourd dipper to drink water with. De men make dere own cedar water pails.

"De week's rations for a growed person run like three pounds bacon and a peck cornmeal and some home-made 'lasses. No flour and no coffee, but us parch bran or wheat and make coffee. Each night dey give a pint of sweet milk. But de chillen all et in a special place in de kitchen.

"One mornin' Massa Washington call us all and he read from de big paper. He say, 'You is free to live and free to die and free to go to de devil, if you wants to.' He tell us if we gather he crops he'd pay us for it. Den he turned and walked away and started cryin'. All de families stays but one man. De highest price massa pay anybody was about $15.00, but dat seem like a lot of money to folks what wasn't used to gittin' any money at all.

"Finally my folks moved on a farm on Onion Creek, in Travis County, on rented land from Nat Watters and Dr. Shears, and farm on de third and fourth. We stays about six years and raises cotton and corn.

"But when I's twenty years old I marries Joe Walker and us move to Bastrop County, add I stays dere till he dies in 1932. Us have eleven chillen and nine of dem still livin'. I gits a pension, nine dollars de month, and it sho' am a help now I's old and nearly blind."

John Walton

John Walton, 87, was born August 15, 1849, a slave of Bill Walton, who lived in Austin, Texas, until the Civil War. He then purchased a farm in Robertson County, Texas. John and his wife, Missouri, own a little home at 1008 Juniper St., Austin. Each receives an old age pension of $10.00 a month.

"My name am John Walton, yes, suh, and I's born right here in Austin. Dat on de 15th day of August, in 1849. I done had de papers on dat but where dey is now I don't know. Pappy's named Gordon Walton and I 'member he die while de war goin' on, or jes' befo'. I disremember. My mammy was a small woman, named Mary.

"Massa Bill Walton owns all us, and he de brother of Buck Walton, and us live in Austin till it said de Yankees comin'. Some southern folks here in Austin was diggin' ground for a fort, old Fort MacGruder, jes' south of Austin. So Massa Bill takes us all 'way from Austin and up to Robertson County, 'cause he done figured de Yankees can't git up dere.

"I done field work up dere and even us kids had to pick 150 pounds cotton a day, or git de whoppin'. Us puts de cotton in de white-oak baskets and some dem hold more'n 100 pounds. It 'cordin' to de way you stamps you cotton in. De wagon with de yoke of oxen standin' in de field for to pour de cotton in and when it full, de oxen pulls dat wagon to de hoss-power gin. Us gin'rally use 'bout 1,600 pounds cotton to make de bale.

"Purty soon after Massa Walton opens he farm he die and Missus Walton den marries a Dr. Richardson and he git de overseer what purty rough on us. He want all us to stay right in line and chop 'long and keep up with de lead man. If us didn't it am de bullwhip. He ride up and down and hit us over de back if us don't do de job right. Sometimes he'd git off he hoss and have two slaves hold one down and give him de bullwhip. He'd give it to him, too.

"I helped break up de land and plant and chop cotton and a little of everything. Jes' what had to be done at de time, I goes out and does it. I run 'cross plenty snakes and one day one bit me right top de foot. Dere plenty varmints, too.

"In de fall of de year us kill plenty hawgs and put up de gamblin' racks and hang dat meat up for de night. Dere some big dogs what watched de meat and one old dog, old Jefferson, was bigger'n any dog I ever seed. He kilt many 'nother dog. One night a big panther try steal de hawg meat and old Jeff cotch him and helt him till de men comes. De panther tore Jeff up purty bad. Us heered dem panthers scream at night, and if you didn't know, you'd think it a woman. I could tell de diff'rence, 'cause de panther scream have de little growl at de end. If he half mile 'way, you'd hear dat little whang.

"One night I goes out in de bottom with my dog. I was huntin' but I don't like what I finds. A big panther follows me and old Nig, dat my big, black bulldog, scart him 'way from me. I sho' run dat night, and I never slip 'way no more at night.

"Massa's big house sot 'way from our cabins. Us have de big room where de slaves' meals all cook and de fireplace 'bout four foot 'cross and plenty ashes in de mornin' to make de ashcakes. For breakfast us have meat and ashcakes and bran-coffee or sassafras tea. You could keep dem dried sassafras roots de year 'round and dey jes' as strong. Us plowed 'em up in de field, 'cause dey growed wild.

"Us didn't have time for de playin' of games durin' de week, 'cause it dark when us goes out and it dark when us comes back. Us sho' was tired. At night dat overseer walk by our cabins and call out to us, to see if us all inside. If us don't answer he come up and find out why, and he'd find us, too.

"I larned to read and write a little jes' since freedom. Us used Webster's old blue-back spellers and I has one in de house to dis day and I wouldn't take nothing for it.

"The first year after freedom I farms with mammy and my stepdaddy. Pappy done die. Us done purty good de first year and I keeps on farmin' most my life. I marries Georgia Anne Harper in 1875 or 1876 in Limestone County. Us have four chillen and three is livin'. I marries 'gain in 1882 to Missouri Fisher and us have eight chillen and six is livin'.

"Us gits 'long on what de state give us now, and it ain't so bad. Times is diff'rent. I never done much but farm, so I don't know so much 'bout everything what goes on."

Sol Walton

Sol Walton, 88, was born in Mobile, Alabama, a slave of Sam Lampkin. Sol and his father stayed on the Lampkin Plantation, then in Mooringsport, Louisiana, until 1873, and farmed on shares. From 1876 to 1922 Sol worked in the T.& P. shops, in Marshall, Texas. Sol and his wife are supported by odd jobs Sol secures about town and they receive money from a son who is in a CCC camp.

"I was knockin' round, a good-sized chap, way back yonder in Buchanan's and Henry Clay's time. I was born in 1849, in Mobile, Alabama, and belonged to Sam Lampkin. My father was bought by the Lampkins and he allus kept the name of his first master, Walton. My mammy was a Alabama Negro and her name was Martha, and I had four brothers and four sisters, Robert, Jim, Richard, Alex, Anna, Dora, Isabella, Bettie.

"My master was Sam Lampkin and his wife was Missus Mary, and their first plantation was in Alabama, but they moved to Mississippi when I was 'bout six, and we lived on Salt Water Creek. They had a big, frame house and we lived in log quarters, slept on rough rail beds and had plenty to eat, peas, pumpkins, rice and other truck we raised on the place, and plenty of fish out of the creek.

"The first work I done in slavery was totin' water and dinner to the field hands, in gourd buckets. We didn't have tin buckets then. The hands worked from sun to sun, and if the overseer seed 'em slackin' up he cussed 'em and sometimes whacked 'em with a bullwhip. I seed 'em whipped till their shirt stuck to their back. I seed my mammy whipped for shoutin' at white folks meetin'. Old massa stripped her to the waist and whipped her with a bullwhip. Heaps of 'em was whipped jus' 'cause they could be whipped. Some owners half fed their hands and then whipped them for beggin' for grub.

"After our folks came in from the field they et supper and some went to Salt Water Creek to cotch fish and crabs. They used to spin at night, too. On Christmas Day massa allus give the slaves a little present, mostly somethin' to wear, 'cause he goin' to git that anyhow.

"Massa never had but one white overseer. He got kilt fightin'. The hands was burnin' logs and trash and the overseer knocked a old man down and made some of the niggers hold him while he bullwhipped him. The old man got up and knocked the overseer in the head with a big stick and then took a ax and cut off his hands and feet. Massa said he didn't ever want another white overseer and he made my cousin overlooker after that.

"The slaves had their own prayer meetin's and that's 'bout the biggest pleasure they had. We'd slip off sometimes to dances and parties, but the patterrollers come and run us home with hounds. The black and white children all played together and there was 'bout sixty of us.

"The old folks told us ghost stories but I never seed a ghost but once, after I was married. Me and some men was walkin' down the Shreveport road and saw a big house all lit up and fiddlin' and dancin' goin' on inside. But when we got close the music stops and the lights went out. When we got on past a piece it lit up and the fiddlin' starts 'gain. I wasn't scared, but we didn't hang round to see what made it do that way.

"Some of the cullud folks on our place could read and write. They larned it theyselves. The white folks didn't larn 'em. All they larned 'em was to work hard. But they took care of us when we was sick and old women made lots of medicine. There was boneset tea and willow tea and shuck tea and cottonseed tea for chills and fever and Jerusalum Oak for worms.

Sol Walton

"Master left Mississippi for Texas 'bout time the war got goin' good, with his fam'ly and sixty slaves. We'd been on the road three weeks when a gang of Yankees come on us one day at dinner. The niggers scatters like birds. 'Bout half of 'em never come back, but the rest of us come on and settled seven miles southwest of Mooringsport, in Louisiana. Young master went to the war after we got there and come home sev'ral times. But they didn't talk the war 'mongst us cullud folks.

"Nothin' special happened the day they said we was free, 'cept some of 'em didn't stay ten minutes. Master told 'em if they'd stay he'd give them the third and fourth. The ones who left wasn't promised nothin' and didn't git nothin'. My folks stayed for 'most twenty years after 'mancipation, workin' on the halves.

"I left my folks in '73 and come to Jimmie D. Scott's place, in Texas, 'bout eight miles east of Marshall, and worked for $10.00 the month. That's where I met Liza Montecue, who is my wife. She was born on the Scott's place the same year I was born. We moved to Marshall in '76 and I got a job in the railroad shops and worked till the big strike in 1922. I didn't belong to the strike but the strikers wouldn't let me work. After they run me off my job, I never could get back on and had to make a livin' at anythin' I could find till my boy got in the CCC camp. I been married sixty-four years and raised eight children, and three of 'em lives here and works at anythin' they can find to make a dollar."

Ella Washington

Ella Washington, 82, was born a slave of Dave Mann, in St. Mary's Parish, Louisiana. When the slaves were freed in Louisiana Ella was taken to Calvert, Texas, and put on the Barton plantation. Soon after the civil war she came to Galveston, and lives with her daughter, who supports herself and her mother by taking in washing.

"You got to 'scuse how I looks, 'cause I been out in de back yard helpin' my daughter with de washin'. She allus fuss at me 'cause I work like dat, but I tells her jes' 'cause I is a old woman ain't no reason why I got to act like one.

"I don't know for sho' jes' when I'm birthed, but my sister allus say I's one year and six months older'n her and she say she's birthed 'bout 1857. Dey didn't make no record den like now. I thinks old massa, Dave Mann, keep some kind record on us, but he been dead de long time.

"My mammy and pappy was name Meine, Car'line and Charles Meine. De slaves used to take de massa's name and sometimes when dey sold dey drap de old name and take de new massa's name. Dat how come it so hard to keep up with dem.

"Massa Mann sho' nice but him and he missy die and Massa Jim Ross step into dere shoes on de plantation. Us gits swamp den. When you git swamp dat mean you got to live with a mean man. He sho' was mean, too.

"De plantation was big and 'bout a hundred slaves on it. Dey work dem hard, too, sometimes till nine o'clock at night. A lot of dem run away but dey sic de nigger dogs on dere trail and cotch dem. When dey cotch dem dey whup dem. Dey put sticks in de ground and tie dere hands and feet to dem. Some places dey strip dem naked and whip dem.

"Sometimes Massa Jim 'low us go to de Catholic Church at Marion. Dey wouldn't 'low us to pray by ourself. But we sneaks off and have pot prayin'. Two men carry de great big hog pot dey uses to scald hogs and take it out in de woods and us stick de head in it and pray. All de noise go in de pot and you couldn't hear it outside.

"Old massa fed us good, meal and syrup and meat 'nough to last. He give us watermelons every Sunday. But Massa Jim didn't 'lieve in pamperin' niggers, he say. He didn't give us much to eat and de houses leak 'cause de walls rotten.

"One time he take de notion to sell us. He put my mother and me and sister on de block up in Marion. Us all cryin' hard, 'cause us thunk us gwine git sep'rate. Den I looks up sudden and right at my young miss, Miss Mary. She so mad she pale like de ghost. She say, 'Ella, you git 'way from dat block and come over to me, and you too, Della.' Me and my sister runs over dere to her and wrop ourself round her dress and hold on with all our might. De massa come after us and Miss Mary say, 'What you mean sellin' my slaves?' He say us slaves his and she say, do he want to have to prove what he say. Den she start in and raise so much sand he have to call mammy down off de block and take us back home.

"I heared everybody say a war goin' on and my uncle and cousin run 'way to de head bureau, where de Yankees at. My mammy say it at Milligan, Texas. Time dey ready for freedom in Louisiana, dey refugees us to Texas, in de wagons. Us travel all day and half de night and sleep on de ground. It ain't take us so long to git to Calvert, out dere in de bottom of Texas, and dey puts us on de Barton plantation. We's diggin' potatoes dere when de Yankees come up with two big wagons and make us come out of de fields and free us. Dere wasn't no cel'bration 'bout it. Massa say us can stay couple days till us 'cide what to do.

"Well, den somethin' funny happen dere. De slaves all drinks out an old well. Dey'd drink water in de mornin' and dey'd have de cramps awful bad 'bout dinner time and in de evenin' dey's dead. Dey dies like flies, so fast dey couldn't make de coffins for dem. Dey jes' sew dem up in sacks and bury dem dat way. Some de slaves say massa put de poison in de well. I don't know what kill dem but it sho' look funny.

"Mammy and me goes to Calvert and hires out, but 'fore long us come to Galveston and pappy go back to Louisiana. If he ain't dead he still live dere in St. Mary's Parish. I never seen him no more.

"I marries 'bout 1886, and stays right here in Galveston. I seen Wright Cuney lots of times but I ain't never knowed him to talk to. I 'member when dey say he be governor some day, but dey ain't gwine have no cullud man governor. Course, he did git to congress."

Rosa Washington

Rosa Washington is 90 years old and lives in her own little adobe house at 3911 Manzana St., El Paso, Texas. She was born a slave of the Watson family, on a large plantation seven miles from St. Joe, Louisiana. Her parents came from Georgia. After the Civil War she left her former owners, but later returned and was with them until they died. She came to

Texas in 1921, and her three children provide for her. Her son, Le Roy, has been in the U.S. Emigration service in El Paso for 27 years.

"My name's Rosa Washington and my husban' was Joe Washington. He's been dead a long time. I was bo'n on a big plantation, white man's name Bill Watson, wife Ann Watson, seven miles from St. Joe. Mama had four chillen and I had seven. Marster had a fine house and plenty of slaves. I dunno how many.

"'Fore we was free we was in the fiel' workin' and they come out and got us. Everybody threw up their hands and started to run. The Yanks busted open a sugar hogshead and give everybody all they wanted. Dey threw all de milk away and dey carried our marster away by force and tuk him to jail in Vicksburg. Our missus wept. When the Yankees got us, dey tuk us about three miles from whar we live, put us in a fine house, give us plenty to eat until war's ended. Me and my chillen and my father and mother were together there.

"We had a good cabin on the plantation, made out-a planks, ole rip-rap plunder. Dey treated us good. I worked in water garden, worked in fiel's when 10 years old. Hoe'd my row every day. Dey didn' whop me, though. My mistress wouldn' let 'em. Marsa and missus good to me. I not tell lie on 'em. Tell truf. Truf shines.

"I seed niggers put in stocks, put 'em in stocks head in fust. Tear their clothes off backs, whop till sores come, den dey pour coal oil and turpentine in sores. I see dat with my own eyes. My dad druv the carriage, carried 'em 'round all time. My mother worked in the fiel' like I do. Work every day. Dey give us everything to eat. Marster and missus, too, give plenty, but if ole cow died with cholera, they give to us niggers. I got good shoes once a year. When marster went to New Orleans, mama had to tie my feet up in rags. I had to work with the rest of 'em. Got up at 4 o'clock. We he'ped on other plantations when dey'd git behind. Go he'p 'em out.

"I waited on overseers table, Joe Crusa. He was mean. He stuck a fork in my head. Ole Aunt Clarissie cooked for us. She cook in cabin for us, had big fireplace. She cook for all niggers on the place. She was mean to me, never married. She had two rooms, all she do was cook, tell lies on me to white overseer. That woman told a lie on me 'cause said I lef' a fork dirty. He look at it, says, 'Who rubbed dis fork?' Woman says, 'Rosa,' and he stuck the fork in my head. Missus turn him off nex' day.

"We had co'nbread, no sugar, plenty okra and coffee; plenty milk, 'cause they had 17 cows. They give us clabber and peaches. Every day overseer blow horn in yard to wake us up, a bugle at four o'clock Sundays. We take cotton outta fiel' and put it up on scaffold to dry iffen it rain. Overseer sit in dry, big overcoat on; we work in mud and rain. One mornin' they carried us to stockhouse to whip us. My missus and marster never let 'em whip me, but no white folks he'p me to read and write. He'p me to do nothin' but work.

"White folks had church. I couldn' go. I hadda mind the white chillen every Sunday. Cullud people had to go way back in woods to have church. Never let white folks see 'em.

Had to slip and hide to have our church, run like deer if foun' out. Marster never know a bit more'n this chair whar we was gwine. He couldn' ask us on Sunday, it be against the law. Iffen niggers run away, dogs 'ud catch 'em.

"Dey had doctor right dere. Kep' us well. Kep' us well so's we could work. Brother-in-law to marster.

"When the niggers was married, dey put a broom down and dey jump over the broom, same time missus and marster'd marry 'em. He'd marry 'em and she as witness. Sometimes celebrate. She'd cook 'em some cake, give 'em a fine dress. We'd take meat and skillets down to the bar on Sundays. Had fish frys. Wouldn' take no fussy chillen to the bar. We chillen would have fish fry whar dey couldn't watch us.

"Had to go to gin at four o'clock in evenin'. Couldn' play week-days, had to go in cabin and be still. Never got to play much till Yankees come and got us, but we had a big ball and dance in yard Christmas. Had candy, dey give us dresses and socks and a good feast for Christmas. Give us things for 4th of July. Dey give us dat day. No, dey wouldn' whip us dat day. We had a big quiltin' Christmas day. We'd piece de quilts outta scraps. Some couldn' quilt. Dey'd dance in de yard all day.

"We niggers got wool clothes in winter, good clothes woven on de place. Marster had black sheep and white sheep. He bought our summer clothes in New Orleans—linsey, calicy, plaid, some white ones. Dey'd give us color what we like.

Rosa Washington

"Sure, I seed ghosts. Dey come with no head, come outta de fiel' one night so late, 'bout eight, nine o'clock. I was scared, yes, suh, I sure was scared, but my mammy say, 'Dey ain' goin' to hurt you, baby.' Dey scare me. My mammy give me beads for my neck, china-berry beads to keep me well. They's pretty. I never had no other kind.

"We never git no money befo' freedom. I stay away from Marster and missus de first year, den go back. Dey give us 50¢ a day after war. Had to pay for rations. Better since war, though. No whippin's goin' on like they did 'fore.

"I'se a full Baptist—been ever since '67. I'se happy. Sometimes I gits too happy. I don' move till de spirit move me. I goes to church when I'se able. But I'se gittin' too old to go now—I'se just waitin' to go home."

Sam Jones Washington

Sam Jones Washington, 88, was born a slave of Sam Young, who owned a ranch along the Colorado River, in Wharton Co., Texas. Sam was trained to be a cowhand, and worked for his master until 1868, receiving wages after he was freed. He farmed until 1905, then moved to Fort Worth and worked in the packing plants until 1931. He lives at 3520 Columbus Ave., Fort Worth, and is supported by an $11.00 per month old age pension, supplemented by what Sam raises in his garden and makes out of a few hogs.

"How old I is? I's 16 year when surrender come. I knows dat, 'cause of massa's statement. All us niggers gits de statement when surrender come. I's seed plenty slave days.

"Massa Young run de small farm 'long de Colorado River and him don't own many slaves. Dere my mammy and her six chillen, and Majoria and her four chillens. My pappy am not on de place. I don't know my pappy. Him am what dey calls de travelin' nigger. Dey have him come for service and when dey gits what dey wants, he go back to he massa. De womens on Massa Young place not married.

"Massa raise jes' a little cotton, dat two womens and de chillen could tend to, and some veg'tables and sich. Us have lots of good food. Us sleep in de sleepin' room, nex' to massa's house, but I sleeps in massa's room.

"One night massa say, 'Don't tie my hoss to de stake tonight.' But I's sleepy and gits de nodfies and draps off to sleep. Mammy shake me and say, 'Did you stake de hoss?' Massa sees dat hoss in de mornin' and say, 'You done stake dat hoss and I told you not to.' He gives me couple licks and I larns to do what I's told. He never whip nobody, not de hard whippin' like other niggers gits. He am de good massa.

"I fust runs errands and den massa larn me to ride, soon's I could sit de hoss. Den I stays out with de cattle mos' de time and I's tickled. I sho' likes to ride and rope dem cattle and massa allus fix me up with good clothes and good hoss and good saddle. I stays dere till long after surrender.

"Us have stampedes from de cattle. Dat am cust'mary with dem critters. Dat mean ride de hoss to turn de cattle. Us ride to side de leader and crowd him and force him to turn, and keep forcin' him, and by and by dem critters am runnin' in de circle. Dat keep dem from scatterment. Dat sho' dangerous ridin'. If de hoss throw you off dem cattle stamp you to death. Gabriel sho' blow he horn for you den!

"I sho' 'joys dat business, 'cause we'uns have de good time. Us go to town and have fun. One time I comes near gittin' in trouble, but it ain't my fault. I's in town and massa, too, and a white man come to me and him show de drink. 'Who you 'long to, nigger?' he say. 'I's Massa Young's nigger,' I says, polite-like. 'You looks like de smart nigger and I's de notion smack you one,' he say. 'You better not smack me any,' I says. You unnerstand, dat de way massa raise me. I don't unnerstand some cruel white mens gits de arg'ment, jus' for de chance to shoot de nigger. Massa am standin' near by and him come up and say, 'If you touches dat nigger, I'll put de bullet through you.' Dat man see massa have no foolishment in he words and gits gwine. But if massa am not dere, Gabriel blow he horn for dis nigger's Jubilee, right den, yes, sar.

Sam Jones Washington

"I comes near gittin' cotched by de patterrollers once. I's jus' 12 den and 'nother nigger and me, us want some cane stalk. It good to eat raw, you knows. Jus' peel de bark off and chew dat inside. Well, we'uns in de man's cane patch, breakin' dem stalks and dey makes de poppin' noise. A patterroller come by and hear dat poppin', and holler, 'Who's dere in de cane patch?' Us didn't answer him, no, sar. I 'cides right quick dat I don't like cane and I comes 'way from dat patch. I outsmarts and outruns dat patterroller. I keeps to de cane fields and de woods and I runs dis way and dat way. I twists 'round so he couldn't follow my tracks. Like de snake's track, you can't tell if it am gwine north or comin' back. Lawd a'mighty! How fast I runs. I stays 'head of my shadow. I tells you, I's a-gwine!

"De war? White man, we'uns didn't know dere am de war. We seed some sojers at de start, but dat all. One day massa say to me, 'After dis, you gits $15.00 de month wages. I works for him three more years and den he sold out. Den I goes farmin' till 1905. I works in de packin' plants here in Fort Worth den, till I's wore out, 'bout six year ago. Now I raises de hawgs, not very many, and does what work I can git. Dat pension from de State sho' holps me. With dat and de hawgs and de little garden I gits by, and so I lives.

"Was I ever marry? Man, man, three time. Fust time, 'bout 1869 and we'uns gits de seperment in 1871. Dat woman sho' deal me mis'ry! She am de troublin' woman. Den 'bout 1873 I marries 'gain and she die 'fore long. Den in 1905 I marries 'gain and she's dead, too. I never has de chillen. I's jus' 'lone and old now, and stay here till my time comes. I 'spect it quite a spell yit, 'cause I's got lots of substance left, yes, sar."

William Watkins

William Watkins, born 1850, to Julia and Hudson Watkins. All were slaves on the Watkins plantation where William was born, on the edge of Charlotte County, Virginia. William is tall, heavy set, and does not look his age. He lives with William Branch, who came from an adjoining county in Virginia. Both men served in the same campaigns in the United States Army.

"My name is William Watkins. De name comes frum de name of Terbaccer Watkins, who owned de Watkins Terbaccer Plantation. He got a factory in Richmond and de plantation in Charlotte County in Virginia, 'bout 50 mile east of Richmond. Marse Watkins got a big frame house and 400 acres and 100 acres is terbaccer. Yassuh, dey's other crops—barley, wheat, oats, and den dey's stock—hogs, cows, hosses and mules.

"We lives in log cabins wid plank floors and we made de beds ourself. Dey feeds us good and we gits milk and bread and lotsa pork. Marse Watkins got lotsa hawgs.

"Yassuh, we's got a church. De slaves built it in de woods. We never got no wages but sometimes he give us four bits or six bits. What we do wid it? We buys candy. Sometimes we run de rabbits or goes fishing. De Marster gives us lil' patches of groun'. He's good but de overseer's rough. He whips all de slaves.

"Dey's a patrol what watches for slaves dat runs away, but we don't have no patrol on our plantation. We has dances Sat'day nights. Sundays we didn't wuk much.

"Dey's ghosts dere—we seed 'em. Dey's w'ite people wid a sheet on 'em to scare de slaves offen de plantation. We wears charms to keep us well. Dere's asafoetida in a bag and we wear's it roun' de neck. It cure most ev'ryting. When we gits real sick, dey sends medicine frum de big house.

"Ev'ry year de slave traders comes and de Marster sells some slaves down river to New Orleans. Who dey sell? Jes' no count slaves. Dey walks all de way. De traders dey rides in ox-carts. We never wuk much Sundays, only to milk de cows. Jes' dat. Yessuh, I was married on de plantation. De preacher say de words and we's married.

"Den de war come and de Yankees come down thick as leaves. Dey burns de big house and de slave houses and ev'ryting. Dey turns us loose. We ain't got no home nor nuthin' to eat, 'cause dey tells us we's free.

"We's gotta leave de plantation. De Marster's gone, de crops is gone, de stock's gone. We goes to anudder place and works on shares. De first time we sees de Ku Klux is right after de war. Dey whips de slaves what leaves de plantations, dey don' wan' dem to be free.

"Bout 1870 I goes to Ohio and enlists in de army at Jefferson Barracks and right off dey sends us to Texas to fight Indians. I goes to San Antonio and dey puts me on guard at de Alamo to fight off de Indians. Den I goes to Fort Davis. I'm in de cullud Indian Scouts, Co. K, and dey's a banker name of Miller in de Chihuahua jail. One night de kuhnel takes us from Fort Davis, and we marches all night wid guns and 150 rounds of ammunition in belts, and rations for 30 days. We marches all night long twel we gits to Del Norte, Texas(Presidio) and we crosses de river and takes Mr. Miller out of jail.

William Watkins

"While we's at Fort Davis a wagon train comes through de canyon and de Apaches rolls big rocks down on de white people and kills 26 of dem. Dey scalps all dey kills and we go out and fit de Apaches. De lieutenant is killed in de fight. Yassuh, we fit Apaches all de time and when we goes to Fort Concho dey gives us a fit all 'long de road. Den we fitten de Cheyennes and dey is wust of all. Dey's great big Indians 'bout seven feet tall and at de battle of de Wichita in de Indian Territory a Cheyenne shoots an arrer through my wrist. (He exhibited the scar. Same battle described in interview with Wm. Branch.)

"Den after my wound heals we's sent to Fort Clark and de sergeant, Jeff Walker, got it in for me. Kuhnel Andrews is at Fort Davis and Jeff Walker trumps up some charges dat I'se mistrusted, so dey gives me a dishonnuble discharge 'cause of dat Jeff Walker. I ain't had no court martial nor no trial and I cain't git no pension 'count of de dishonnuble discharge.

"And now I'se strong and well but I cain't git no wuk 'cause I'se so ole. And 'cause Jeff Walker didn't like me, I gits a dishonnuble discharge."

Dianah Watson

Dianah Watson, 102, was born a slave of Tom Williams, at New Orleans. In 1870, Dianah went to Jefferson, Texas. She now lives with a married daughter in the Macedonia Community, five miles northwest of Marshall, Tex.

"My name am Dianah Watson and I used to keep my age, but I done got sick and can't 'member it now. I can't say 'zactly how old I is but I's a past-growed woman when the war broke out, and my old missy's daughter done told me once out the book I's borned in 1835.

"I's borned and bred 'bout a half mile from New Orleans. My mammy was s*arah Hall and she's borned in Galveston, and my papa was Bill Williams. My old missy done take me from my mammy when I's a small baby and raised me to a full-growed woman. I slep' in the same room with my young missy and had a good time in slavery, didn't suffer for nothin' and never was cut and slashed like some. Me and Miss Laura come right up together and I's her own nigger slave.

"Massa Williams treated his black folks with 'spect. They was in the field from 'fore day till dark, but they was took good care of and fed and plenty clothes. Old Master Tom done the bossin' hisself and when he's dyin' he calls all his five boys to his bed and say, 'Boys, when I's gone, I don*t want no cuttin' and slashin' my niggers. They's got feelin' same as us.'

"But the oldes' boy, William, got the debbil in him and hires a overseer, and he rid in the fields with a quirt and rope and chair on his saddle. When he done take a notion to whip a nigger, he'd make some the men tie that nigger to the chair and beat him somethin' scand'lous. He got mad at my mother's sister, Aunt Susie Ann, and beat her till the blood run off her on the ground. She fall at his feets like she passed out and he put up the whip and she trips him and gits the whip and whips him till he couldn't stand up. Then some the niggers threw him off a cliff and broke his neck. His folks gits the sheriff but master's boys orders him off the place with a gun. There warn't no more overseers on the place after that.

"If niggers of these days done see what I seed in slavery time they'd pray and thank they Gawd every day. My master's place sot right 'cross the big road from a place they cut and slashed they niggers. You'd hear that white man's black folks bellerin' like cows. I's stood many a time on our front gallery and seed them cut and slash the blood off them niggers. I seed old women half-bent from beatin's goin' to the field. They overseer had a wooden paddle with nails in it. I used to say to missy, 'Why they cuttin' and slashin' them black folks that-a-way?' Missy say, 'Dianah, that there white man got the debbil in him.'

"I seed them sell my mama. I ask my old missy why and she say, 'To go to her husband.'

371

"When the war broke out I's a full-growed woman. New Orleans was full of sojers and they wouldn't let us go to town. Me and young Mr. Tom used to git on the roof and watch them. The cannons was roarin' like thunder and smoke thick and black as clouds. I got scart when they sot the niggers free, at the niggers shoutin'. I didn't know what 'twas for. Old Miss say to me, 'They been in slavery but you don't know what slavery is, Dianah.'

"Two years after that my old miss carries me to Galveston to my mammy. She tell her to take good care of me and we lived there three years and moved to Jefferson. Our things come by boat but we come in wagons. I married John Smith purty soon after that but he died 'fore long. Then I married Noah Watson and now he's dead. I done raise six chillen but only one am livin' now and that's my younges' gal and I lives with her here.

"I tells the young race iffen they come up like me they wouldn't act so smart. They needs somebody to take the smartness outten them. But my gal am good to me. I gits a pension and pays it to her to take care of me. I been here a hundred years and more and I won't stay much longer, and I don't want to be no 'spense to nobody."

Emma Watson

Emma Watson, born in 1852 or 1853, in Ellis Co., Texas, was one of the slaves of the Carl Forrester family. Emma worked in the fields most of her life, but is now too old to work, and is cared for by her daughter. They live at 318 Allen St., Dallas, Texas.

"I axed my old missus when I's borned and she rec'lect I'm eight or nine year old when de freedom war starts. She say she don't make recall de 'xact time, but I takes May for a birthin' time. They's a time when some sich was writ in de Bible, but it got burnt up 'fore I's ageable. I knows where I'm borned, though, and it am on Capt. Forrester's farm in Ellis County. His mother, Miss Susan, raises me like she am my mammy. I calls her Sis Sue. She was old miss and Miss Lee was young miss.

"My paw, I don't know nothin' 'bout. My sister Anna and me, us have de same paw, but my mammy's sold out of Miss'sippi 'way from my paw 'fore my birthin'. My maw kept de name of Lucindy Lane, but Martha and Jennie, my other sisters, had diff'rent paws.

"I's gone through so much of hard times all my life, but when I's de li'l gal I didn't have much to do 'cept tend my Aunt Matilda's babies and wash they clothes. The rest the time I jes' plays round. Miss Lee have a china doll with a wreath of roses round it head. We takes turns playin' with it. I had a rag doll, and it jes' a bundle of rags with strings tied round it to give it a shape. Us make playhouses. Capt. Forrester goes away and I heared he gone to some war, but, law me, I didn't know 'bout war den.

I's jus' glad to play and eat anythin' I can git. When I git a tin can of clabber and some bread, that's what I wanted. They didn't buy no dishes for nigger young'uns to break up. Us et bacon and beef and salt pork and cornbread with us fingers. Mussel shells is what we dipped 'stead of spoons. I did love de souse, too.

"When I had de chills, Sis Sue, dat Old Miss, come out to de quarters and give me sweet milk boiled with pepper. I got shut of dem chills 'cause I didn't like dat pepper tea, but I like it better'n quinine or sage tea. I didn't like to be sick noways, 'cause dey jus' two bedsteads, one for my mammy and my step-paw, and one for us gals.

"They allus promise me they'll larn me to read and write, but never did git to dat. Aunt Matilda did most de spinnin' and weavin' and sewin'. I used to wear a shimmy and a dress in de week and a clean one for Sunday. In winter sometimes us have a li'l sacque and homemake calfskin shoes but mostly us have to stay inside iffen de weather ain't mod'rate.

"De only frolics I 'member was candy pullin's on Christmas. Dat all us niggers knowed 'bout Christmas.

"One day Miss Tilda git de buggy whip to whip my mammy. It's noontime, and dey had blowed de horn for de field niggers to come eat. Maw grabs de whip and says, 'Miss Tilda, you ain't gwine do dat.' Miss Tilda didn't say nothin' for a day or two, den she say, 'Lucindy, you git your young'uns and leave dis place.' So us goes walkin' down de road till us come to some folk's house and dey takes us in. Us dere 'bout a month when mammy git sick. Dem folks sends word to de Forresters dere niggers am sick and Sis Sue hitch up de hoss and come over. She brung food for us every day, and say, 'Now, Lucindy, when you git able you bring your young'uns on home and 'have yourself.' My mammy dies when I's 'bout ten year old.

Emma Watson

"After Capt. Forrester come back home dey tell us to watch out for de Feds. Sis Sue say dey kill nigger young'uns. One day I's comin' through de fields and see three men in blue coats on big bay hosses. I ran, but dey passes me by big as you please. I seed plenty after dat, 'cause dey come and asks for corn and Sis Sue allus say us don't have 'nough for de hosses. But dat night de corn allus leave de cribs. Dem Feds was sho' thievin' folks.

"I stays with de Forresters till I's 22 year old, and dey give me food and clothes, but never no money. Sis Sue used to say, 'Come here, you li'l old free nigger.' It make me so mad. But den I marries and have de swiss white dress and us walk 'cross de fields to de preachers. Dat every bit of fixin' us have.

"Den us raise crops on de half-shares and sot up housekeepin' with a bedstead, some quilts and a li'l old stove. I has four young'uns and every one of dem had schoolin' and larnin'."

James West

James West, 83, was born a slave to Mr. William West, near Ripley, in Tippah Co., Mississippi. This was close to the battle fought near Corinth and James witnessed some exciting events. In 1885 James came to Texas and now lives with a friend at 1114 Hardy St., Fort Worth, Texas.

"Yes, suh, I 'members de slavery days and de War, 'cause I's born in 1854, on de plantation of Massa William West, in Mississip'. It weren't a big plantation, jus' 'bout 100 acres, and Massa West owned my mammy and four other slaves, Buck, Sam, Rufus and Mary. I don't know nothin' 'bout my pappy, 'cause I ain't never seed him, and my mammy never told me nothin' of him.

"All us cullud folks lived in cabins and they has two rooms. De bunks is built to de wall and has straw ticks and we has floors and real windows.

"Sam and Buck and Rufus am field workers and plants cotton and sich and looks after de stock. Sometimes de work is heavy and sometimes not. When it am finish, de massa lets 'em go fishin' or visitin' or rest. We goes to church when we wants and we has parties with Sam and Rufus to play de music, de fiddle and de banjo. How I wishes I could be back dere for jus' one year and have it like befo'. Jus' one year befo' I die!

"We has a good massa in every way. Him gives all we can eat. Folks don't eat like we used to, 'cause we had home-cured hams, and when you put it in your mouth, it was a treat for your taster. As for de clothes, massa say, 'De 'terial here and if yous don't supply yourselves, its yous fault.'

"Dere never anyone what gits whippin's on massa's place, 'cept dis nigger, but dey only spankin's. You see, dere was allus a bit of devilment in me. But de massa so good, we all tries to please him and we has no whippin's.

"De massa gives me a he goat and de shoemaker makes me de harness and cart for dat goat and when I gits him trained good, I has a job gittin' de chips for kindlin' and de wood and I totes de water. One day I takes Billy, de goat, 'cross de road for wood and it downhill from de woodpile so I jus' rides de load. Billy was gwine jus' as nice as yous kin like, but him says BAAH, and starts to run like a skeert bull. I thinks what kin be wrong with dat fool goat, when somethin' hits me back of de neck like a coal of fire, and de cart hits a rock and off I goes. To says I's skeert am not tellin' de truf, and I starts hollerin'. It was de bee stung me and when I gits to de house I looks Billy over and, sho' 'nough, on his hip was de bee sting. Dat bee sting sho' put de life in Billy.

"'bout de War time, de plantation was near whar dey fights a battle two days and I seed lots of soldiers. Before dat, de soldiers begins to come to massa's house and water de hosses and eat de lunch. Dey never did raid his place like other places 'round dere, but I hides when dey comes, 'cause I skeert of dem. I quavers and gits skeert when I sees 'em.

375

"We is jus' settin' down to breakfast one mornin' and we hears a big boomin'. When dat start, dis nigger don't eat his breakfast. I starts for some place to hide. I runs to one place, den I hears de boom, den I runs to another place. I finally crawls under de shed and dere I stays. Dey couldn't git me out and dere I stays for dat day and night and 'til noon de nex' day. I has no water or food. Lots of folks from Ripley what massa knows was kilt in dat battle.

"Buck and I goes to de battleground after de fightin' quits and dere was heaps of dead hosses but dey had dug de trench and buried de dead soldiers.

James West

"I don' know about de Klux, but we use to sing a song 'bout de patter rollers, like dis,

'Run nigger run, patter roller kotch you,

Run nigger run, 'cause it almos' day,

Dat nigger run, dat nigger flew,

Dat nigger los' his Sunday shoe.'

"I stays with de massa after freedom 'til I's 21 year old and den I leaves and works for diff'runt folks. I marries in Tennessee when I's 22 and we has one chile, but my wife takes him when he's five and leaves, and I never seen or heard of 'em since. I comes to Texas 'bout 52 year ago.

"I has 'joyed talkin' 'bout dem old days, 'cause talk am all I kin do since my legs have de misery so bad."

Adeline White

Adeline White, 90 odd years old, was born at Opelousas, Louisiana, a slave of Dr. Bridget. She lives with her daughter, Lorena, in Beaumont, Texas.

"I's born at Opelousas and my massa and missis was Dr. Bridget and his wife. They was mean and they beat us and put the hounds after us. They beat the little ones and the big ones and when massa ain't beatin' his wife is. It am continual. My pappy call Thomas Naville and my mammy 'Melia Naville. They was born in Virginia. I had four brothers and two sisters, all dead now.

"Like I says, old massa sho' whip us and when he whip he put us 'cross a barrel or chain us and stake us out with a rope. We didn't have much to eat and not much clothes. They weave us clothes on the loom and make the dress like a sack slip over the head.

"Our cabin wasn't so bad, made of logs with dirt 'tween the logs. The chimney make out of sticks and dirt and some windows with a wooden shutter and no glass in 'em. Massa give 'em lumber and paint to make things for the house and they have homemake bed and table and benches to sit on.

"Massa have the hoss power cotton gin and a hoss power sugar cane mill, too. Us work hard all day in the gin and the sugar cane mill and doesn't have no parties nor fun. Sometimes in the evenin' us git together and talk or sing low, so the white folks won't hear.

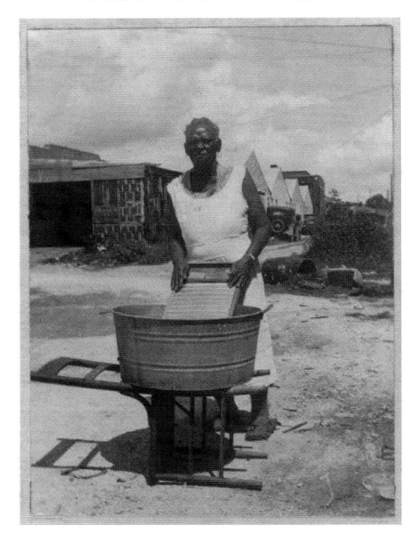

Adeline White

"I 'member going through the woods one time and seein' somethin' black come up 'fore me. It must a been a ghost. I got a boy call' Henry what live in Welch and he kin see ghosties all the time. He jus' look back over he lef' shoulder and see plenty of 'em. He say they has a warm heat what make him sweat.

"Old massa didn't go to the war and his boys was too little. We jus' heared about the war and that it was goin' to free us. In the night us would creep out way in the woods and have the prayer meetin', prayin' for freedom to come quick. We has to be careful for if massa find out he whip all of us, sho'. We stays nearly all night and sleeps and prays and sleeps and prays. At las' we hears freedom is on us and massa say we are all free to go, but if we stay he pay us some. Most of us goes, for that massa am sho' mean and if we doesn't have to stay we wouldn't, not with that massa.

"We scatters and I been marry twice. The first man was Eli Evans in Jennings, in Louisiana and us have six chillen. The second man he James White but I has no more chillen. Now I lives with my gal what called Lorena and she make me happy. She sho' good to her old mammy, what ain't much good no more."

Sylvester Sostan Wickliffe

Sylvester Sostan Wickliffe, of Ames, Texas, was born in St. Mary's Parish, Louisiana, in 1854. A free-born Negro, Wickliffe tells an interesting story about his life and that of his uncle, Romaine Vidrine, who was a slave-holder. Wickliffe has a nicely furnished home in Beaumont, and two of his children have been to college.

"I's what dey call a free-born nigger. Its a long story how dat come about, but I can tell you.

"Three Frenchmen come to Louisiana from France. In three generations dey mix with Indians and Negroes. Dey high-born Frenchmen and 'cumulate plenty property. Before dey die dey make 'greement 'mongst demselves. When one die de property go to de other two; de last one livin' git all three plantations and all dat's on dem. It so happen dat old man Vidrine's daddy live longes', so he git it all. But he so good he divide up and my daddy gits forty acres good land. My daddy's greatgrandpapa was one dem first three Frenchmen.

"My daddy was Michael and mama was Lucy and dey a whole passel chillen, Frances, Mary, Clotilde, Astasia and Tom, Samuel, Gilbert and Edward. My daddy was part Indian and I had some half-brothers and sisters what wore blanket and talk Indian talk. Dey used to come see daddy and set round and talk half de night and I never understan' a word dey sayin'.

"Mama didn't have no Indian blood in her, but she born in Louisiana and a right purty, brown-skin woman, probably some French or Spanish in her.

"My uncle, Romaine Vidrine, de son of old man Vidrine, he have de bigges' property. He was a slave-holder. Dey was a number niggers in Louisiana what owned slaves. Romaine, he have 'bout thirty-eight. Dey was a big dif'ence make 'tween slave niggers and owner niggers. Dey so much dif'ence as 'tween white folks and cullud folks. My uncle wouldn't 'low slave niggers to eat at de same table with him or with any of us free-born niggers.

"Folks come down from de noth sometimes and mistook de slave for de owner or de owner for de slave. My uncle was sech a purty, bright man, he must of been a quadroon. He had long burnsides and a long tail coat all de time. He was very dignified. He was good to all he slaves, but when he say work, he mean work. He ain't never 'low none de slaves be familiar with him.

"De old Romaine house was a old*fashioned house make out of cypress. Dat everlastin'. It come to a peak on top and dere was one big room what run de whole length in de back and dat de sleepin' room for all de li'l chillen. De growed-up folks have sleepin' rooms, too. Dey have a cook shack outside. It a sep'rate house.

"Us live in a purty good house not very far from de big house. Dey have what dey calls a private school. It was kep' by my uncle. Only de free-born niggers went to it. De older ones educated in French and de young ones in French and 'merican, too. After de war dey hire a white man named William Devoe to be teacher. He educate de chillen to de third gen'ration. He come to Texas with me and die 'bout five years ago.

"When a couple want to git marry on de old Romaine place, uncle sent for de priest from St. Martin. Dey wasn't no priest round Franklin or what dey call New Iberia later. When I's most a growed boy de priest come baptise 'bout forty of us. He use de water* out uncle's cistern for de ceremony. When us goin' down de road to de baptisin' dey's a squirrel run 'cross de road and us chillen all broke and run to cotch it. Law, dat jus' 'bout scare my old godmother to death. She took so much pain dat us all nice and clean and 'fraid us git dirty. Her name was Nana Ramon Boutet and she live here in Ames settlement for many year. Us laugh many time 'bout dat squirrel.

"Dey used to call us de free Mulattoes from 'cross de bayou. De nearest town was Pattersonville and it five mile away. Now dey calls de settlement Vidrinville for old man Romaine Vidrine. De plantation suppor' a grist mill and a raw sugar mill. Dey make de sugar dark, big grain, 'cause dey ain't no 'finery in dem days. Dey put de sugar in big five hunerd pound hogshead and take it by boat down de Teche to New Orleans and sell it. Dey use de money to buy coffee and cotton. Us didn't raise cotton. I never see no cotton till I's a big boy and come to Fort LaFayette.

"De grist mill was built 'way from de house. Dey have a long lever what stand out de side and hitch hosses with a rawhide belt to make de mill turn. Us folks all raise rice. Not like now, Lawdy, no. Dey jes' plant rice in rows like corn and cultivate it like any other crop. Dey wasn't no irrigation ditch. After de rice harves' dey put it in a mortar make out a cypress log or block and knock de roughness off de rice with de pestle.

"Every fall us go huntin' deer round Chicimachi Lake. Dey calls it Grand Lake now, but de reg'lar Indian name am Chicimachi. Dere was a tribe of Indians by dat name. Dey wasn't copper skin, but more yaller like.

"When war commence it purty hard on folks. Us see soldiers comin' 'cross de bayou in blue suits. Dey raid de sugar mill and take de livestock and foodstuff on de Pumphrey place. Dey have a awful battle five mile away. Dat at Camp Boesland, on de Teche. Dat a awful battle! My brother go dere next day and see soldiers standin' up dead 'gainst trees with dey bay'nets still sot.

"De Confed'rates come and took all de slaves to build de fort at Alexandria. When dey come to de Romaine place dey see niggers, and ain't know which free and which slaves. Dey line my daddy up with deothers, but a white man from town say, 'Dat a good, old man. He part Indian and he free. He a good citizen. He ain't s'pose do work like dat.' So dey didn't take him.

"De Yankees damage de Romaine property 'siderable. Dey take a whole year crop of sugar and corn and hosses. Afterwards dey pass a law and de gov'ment 'low money for dat. It was 'bout twenty year before dey git de' money, but dey git it. Romaine and he heirs git $30,000 for dem damages.

"After war over, old man Romaine tell he slaves dey free now. But he say, 'You is most born right here and iffen you is bright you stay right here.' Dey all did stay. But dey ain't never git to jine with de free-born. Dey still make a dif'ence.

"After freedom I 'cide to larn a trade. I 'prentice myself to de blacksmith trade for clothes and board. I larn all I can in three year and quit and open a shop on Bayou Tortue, 'tween St. Martin and Lafayette. I charge $2.00 for to shoe a hoss all de way round. Den I beat plows, build two-wheel buggy and hack. I make sweepstocks and Garrett and Cottman plow. Dat after de time of de wood mould boards. I make mine with metal.

"I come to Texas in 1890, to Liberty, and been right round dere and Ame for forty-seven year. I start me a gin and blacksmith shop when I first come. I marry in Houston to Epheme Pradia, 'nother free-born nigger, and I still marry to her after forty-seven year. Dat a good long hitch. We have seven chillen, all livin'. One gal went to de Catholic church school in Galveston. One boy go to Pradeau University in New Orleans. Dey two blacksmith, one farmer, one good auto mechanic and de three gals keeps house.

"I 'member lots of songs us sing in French but I can't give 'merican for dem. I know de song, *LaLoup Garou*. I try to translate one song for you:

"Master of de house
Give me meat without salt;
When de stranger come,
He give me roast chicken."

Daphne Williams

Daphne Williams was born in Tallahassee, Florida, a slave to Mrs. Nancy Herring. Daphne does not know her exact age, but must be close to or over 100. She claims to have witnessed the fall of the stars in 1833. She lives in Beaumont, Texas.

"It won't be long 'fore I's sleeping the long sleep. I expect I's about the mos' agreeables person in the county, 'cause I's so old. I's born in Tallahassee, in Florida, but I don' know when. The Herrings used to own me and I took their name. Missus' name was Nancy

Herring and the marster was still alive when I's born, but he die when I's a baby. I guess I's about 10 or 12 year old when us come to Texas.

"Dat place where I's born was sho' a place! They have a three-story house with a porch at the front and another at the back. They was posties what stand from one porch floor to the nex' and brace it up. I used to live in the big house, 'cause I's nuss for the white chillen. I didn' stay round with cullud folks a-tall.

"The missus was a widow woman ever since I 'member her. She have two boy and three gal, and that sho' was a lovely house. They have they ownself painted in pictures on the wall, jus' as big as they is. They have them in big frames like gold. And they have big mirrors from the floor to the ceilin'. You could see you ownself walk in them.

"My mother was named Millie and my daddy named Daniel. I don' know how many niggers missus have on the plantation. I was never 'lowed to play with the cullud chillen, but I have two brothers named Abram and Handy and I seed them sometimes. I took care of the white chillen and took 'em to church. Iffen baby git to cryin' I walked round with him, but you better be careful not to let the briar scratch him or he git a scar on him and then they gwinter put a scar on you.

"They give me pretty clothes to wear and make me keep clean and expectable. I wore homespun and gingham dresses, jus' cut straight down. They didn' have no sewin' 'chine. They have a woman to cut out and sew and she do that all day long.

"My white folks have mighty nice company. My missus up on the top. They have nice, fine, intelligen' dishes and table cloth.

"They give us holiday on Christmas and sometimes a whole week. They treat the white chillen and black chillen all good and give 'em whippin' iffen they needs it. When there's disturbance, missus holler, 'You all chillen, come in here to me,' and whip us all, then she know she whip the right one.

"I seed the stars fall. God give me a good eyesight. The sun was shinin' and it was plain daylight and the stars fall jus' like hail, only they never fall all the way to the groun'. They fall so far and then they stop and go out. They stay up in the element all the time. Missus sent for the niggers to come up to the house and pray. All that time the stars was a-comin' through the element. All the darkies, little and big, was a-prayin' on their knees, 'cause they thing the jedgment sho' come then.

"Before us move from Florida us git mos' us goods for clothes from North and South Carolina. The war commence in North Caroline to the good of my recollection. That was six month or a year after us lef' Florida. They was a-tryin' to smuggle it down then. When the missus 'cided come to Texas she sent the niggers on ahead and they done make two crops 'fore us git there. The place was five mile from Woodville. We come to Texas in a boat what's big as a house. When the boat git there I was so 'cited when I seed all the pretty trees. I never mever used to trees, 'cause from where us come was jus' prairie land far's you kin see. No tree round Tallahassee and no hill.

"My mother was cook and when she like to die one time they starts breakin' me in to do the cookin'. Then when she die I was cook and been doing that two, three year when freedom come.

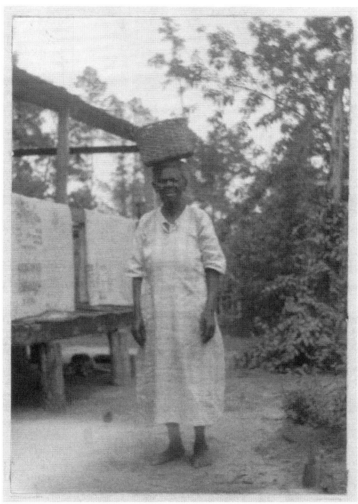

Daphne Williams

"When they tol' us freedom come us thought they was foolin'. My uncle say we's free and to go and look out for number one. They let us stay awhile, but they 'lowanced us. Iffen us spen' the 'lowance us jus' had to go rustle up something to eat or do without. My daddy was a widow man by then and he stay, 'cause he say he want to see further into the subjec'.

"One time I gwineter see my father and had my baby in my arms, 'cause I done married. I was gwine through the wilderness and I heared something squall like a woman cry. I 'gin walk faster. The squall come again. Something say to me, 'You better run.' The hair commence stand on my head and I walk pretty peart. That squall come again and I run fastes' I knows how. I have that poor little baby carried any way.

When I get to the fence I jump over and sot down. The chillen come running and say, 'Yonder Daphne.' They help me into the house but I's so scart I couldn' tell 'em till near bedtime and then I say I hear squall like woman cryin'. Mister Goolsbee say, 'Daphne, make soun' like you hear,' and I makes a squall, and he say, 'That a panther and iffen he kotched you that would have been the end of you and that baby of yourn what you was totin'.' So 'bout four o' clock in that mornin' he gits 'bout fourteen neighbors and the dawgs and they hunts that rascal and runs him in 'bout 8 or 10 o'clock. A span of mules couldn' pull that rascal, I don' 'lieve. He have the biggest tushes I ever seed with these two eyes. They put him in a pot and bile him and make soap out of the grease. That panther didn' git me or my baby but they got him and made soap out of him."

Horatio W. Williams

Horatio W. Williams, known as "Rash" to his friends, is 83 years old. He was a slave of Woodruff Norseworthy, in Pine Bluff, Arkansas. Horatio has lived in Jasper, Texas, for many years.

"I was born in slavery in Pine Bluff in de state of Arkansas, on July 2, 1854, and dey tells me dat make me 'bout 84 years old. Woodruff Norseworthy was my owner and boss all de time I a slave. I marry in 1875 and I lost my wife two year ago, and when a man looses a good woman he loses somethin'. Us had 13 chillen, but only two of dem alive now.

"My boss man was mean to he niggers and I 'member crawlin' down through de woods and listenin' one time when he beat a nigger. Every time he hit him he pray. Boss have 15 slaves and I recollect one time he gwine beat my mother. She run to de kitchen and jump behin' de door and cover herself up in de big pile of dirty clothes. Dey never think to look for her there and she stay there all day. But de next day dey cotch her and whip her.

"Dem what runs away, dey gits bloodhounds after 'em. Dey clumb de tree when dey heered dem hounds comin' but de massa make dem git down and dey shoot dem, iffen dey didn't. When dey gits down de dogs jumps all over dem and would tear dem to pieces, but de massa beats dem off.

"Once de boss has company and one our niggers sleeps on de porch outside de company's room, and in de night he slip in dat room and thiefed de fine, white shirt out de suitcase and wears it round de next mornin'.

"Course he couldn't read and he ain't know de [HW: white] man have he name on dat shirt. When de boss find it out he takes dat nigger down in de bottom and I crawls through de bresh and watches. Dey tie he foots together over de limb and let he head hang down and beat him till de blood run down on de roots of dat tree. When dey takes him down he back look like raw meat and he nearly die.

"Sometime when de nigger won't mind dey puts de chain to one foot and a ball on it 'bout big as a nigger's head, and he have to drag it down with him whe ever he go.

"My white folks moved to Bastrop in Louisiana and den to Texas and brung me with them. When us work in de field us have de cook what put us food on big trays and carry it to de field, den we stop and eat it under shade of a tree, if dey any. Dey give us bread and meat and syrup for dinner and us has bacon long as it lasts.

"When I's free I rents land and crops 'round, after I gits marry. Befo' dat, I was here, dere and yonder, for my board and clothes and four bits de day. I give all my chillen de eddication, leastwise dey all kin read and write and dat's what I cain't do.

"I 'longs to de Meth'dist church and I don't unndestan' some dese other churches very well. Seems strange to me dat at dis late time dey's tryin' find new ways of gittin' to Heaven."

Lou Williams

Lou Williams, said to be the oldest citizen of San Angelo, Texas, was born in southern Maryland in 1829. She and her family were slaves of Abram and Kitty Williams, of that section, and Lou served as nursemaid to her master's children from the age of eight until after the Civil War. She then went to Louisiana where she worked as a cook for several years before coming to San Angelo. She is very active for her 108 years and is a familiar figure about town, with her crutch.

"I's have de bes' white folks in Maryland. I's born in a three-room frame house and I had one of them statements (birth certificates). When I five years old my old missy she say, 'Dat gal, she sho' am gwine be dependable and I makes nursemaid out of her.' When I eight years old she trusts me with dem white chillen. I loves to fish so well I'd take de li'l chillen to de creek and take off my underskirt and spread it out on de bank and put de chillen on it while I sho' cotch de fish. Massa, he start lookin' for me and when he gits to de creek, he say, 'Dar's de li'l devil.' He know dem chillen safe, so he jus' laugh.

"In de fall massa puts us nigger chillen on de bale of cotton and takes us to town and gives us money to buy candy and dolls with. We allus had good food and lots of fish and rabbits and possums, but when my missy see dem possums carryin' de baby possums round she fall out with possum and she say, 'No more possum bein' cooked 'round here.'

"When I jes' a li'l gal I seed de stars fall and when everything got dark like and dem bright stars begin to fall we all start runnin' and hollerin' to our missy and she say, 'Chillen, don't git under my coat, git on your knees and start prayin', and when we begins to pray de Lawd he sends a shower of rain and puts out dem stars or de whole world would a been burned up.

"When massa take us to town he say he want us to see how de mean slave owners raffles off de fathers and de husban's and de mothers and de wives and de chillen. He takes us 'round to de big platform and a white man git up dere with de slave and start hollerin' for bids, and de slave stands dere jes' pitiful like, and when somebody buy de slave all de folks starts yellin' and a cryin'. Dem sho' was bad times. Our massa wouldn't do his niggers dat way and we loved him for it, too.

"We had big gardens and lots of vegetables to eat, 'cause massa had 'bout eight hundred slaves and 'bout a thousand acres in he plantation. In summer time we wore jes' straight cotton slips and no shoes till Sunday, den we puts on shoes and white dresses and ties a ribbon 'round our waists, and we didn't look like de same chillen.

"Dere a big arbor for de whites to go to church and we goes, too. When we starts down de road to church, our mama, she start sayin' things to make us be quiet. We pass de graveyard and she say, 'See dat spirit runnin' 'long here with us?' When we gits dere we hardly moves. We could jine, if we wants to.

"My mama, she Black Creek Indian and none of dem white folks wants her. When massa buys my daddy and us chillen we had done been sold 'way from her and we cry and she cry, and den she follow us to our plantation and cry and beg our massa let her stay. He say, 'She ain't no good but put her in de house and let her do some patchin' and mendin'.' Mama, she cry and say, 'Thank God, Thank God! I's git to be with my husban' and li'l chillen.' She make de good spinner and weaver and old missy, she say she couldn't do without her, 'cause she spin cotton cloth for summer and woolen cloth for winter.

"Niggers didn't have much weddin's, but when massa find dem takin' up he tells everybody to dress in white and de two what was takin' up together has to march up and down till de big supper comes off. Dey was man and wife den, but me, I's diff'rent. I's had a 'spectable weddin', 'cause missy, she say I's her nursemaid. De preacher, he reads, and I's all dressed in white clothes and sech a supper we never had befo'.

"All de slaves wasn't so lucky as we was, though. We lives close to de meanest owner in de country. Our massa wouldn't keep no overseer, 'cause he say his niggers wasn't dogs, but dis other man he keeps overseers to beat de niggers and he has de big leather bullwhip with lead in de end, and he beats some slaves to death. We heared dem holler and holler till dey couldn't holler no mo! Den dey jes' sorta grunt every lick till dey die. We finds big streams of blood where he has whopped dem and when it rained de whole top of de ground jes' looks like a river of blood dere. Sometime he bury he niggers and sometime de law come out and make him bury dem. He put dem in chains and stockades and sometimes he would buck and gag dem.

Lou Williams

"We seed he niggers goin' by our plantation with de oven on de heads 'round three o'clock in de mornin' on de way to de fields. Dese ovens made of wood and tin over de tin cup dat fit de slaves' heads. Each nigger have he bread and some old hairy bone meat a-cookin' with fire coals in dese ovens. Dey made not to burn de head and when dey gits to de fields dey sets dem down to finish cookin' while dey works till breakfast time. De mamas what expectin' babies was whopped to make dem work faster and when babies was sick dey has to put dem in de basket on top dere heads and take dem to de cotton patch, and put dem under de cotton stalks and try to 'tend to dem. Lawd, Lawd, dem was awful times, and I sho' is glad I has good white folks.

Lou Williams' House

"Some dat man's niggers allus runnin' 'way and dey sets de nigger dogs on dem and catch dem mos' times. Den dey treat 'em so bad dey wouldn't never want to run away no more.

"We allus gits Saturday evenin' off to wash our clothes and sometime we has dances Saturday night. I has two brothers, Jim and William and William git kilt in de war. My two sisters named Relia and Laura. We has corn shuckin's and big suppers and on Christmas our massa buys us de present, most times shoes, 'cause we didn't have any shoes.

"When de white folks dies or gits married everybody sho' carries on big. When we sick dey gives us snakeroot tea and cana and sage tea and if we's bad sick, dey gits de doctor. Missy, she make hog hoof tea, jes' bile de hoofs in good whiskey for de cold. Den she put camphor ball and asafoetida 'round our necks to keep off diseases.

"When de war ends we sees a white man comin' down de road on a hoss and de road full of niggers followin' him, singin' and shoutin' and prayin'. I stays with massa till he die, then I marries and has one chile and one grandchile, and I lives with her."

Millie Williams

Millie Williams, 86, lives at 1612 E. Fourth St., Fort Worth, Texas. She was born a slave to Joe Benford, in Tennessee, was sold to Bill Dunn, who brought her to Texas and traded her to Tommy Ellis for some land. She has lived in Fort Worth since the 1870's.

"I don't know when I was born, 'cause I was taken from my folks when I was a baby, but massa told me I was born in de spring of de year, in 1851. I know I been in dis world a long time, but I has have good white folks. I was born on Massa Benford's place in Tennessee and my mama's name was Martha Birdon. She say my pappy's name Milton Wade, but I never seed him. And I didn't know my mama a long time, 'cause she's sold away from Massa Benford's place, and I was sold with her, den he took me back, and I never seed my mama no mo'.

"After I was sold back to Massa Benford, he puts me in de nigger yard. Dat whar de massa kep' slaves what he traded. It was jus' a bunch of shacks throwed together and dirty was no name for it, it was worse than a pig pen. De man what watch over us in dat nigger yard was de meanest man what ever lived. He'd take a club and beat de daylight out of us, 'cause de club wouldn't leave scars like de bullwhip, and didn't bring de price down when we is sold.

"One day Massa Benford takes us to town and puts us on dat auction block and a man name Bill Dunn bought me. I was 'bout seven years old. Talkin' 'bout somethin' awful, you should have been dere. De slave owners was shoutin' and sellin' chillen to one man and de mama and pappy to 'nother. De slaves cries and takes on somethin' awful. If a woman had lots of chillen she was sold for mo', 'cause it a sign she a good breeder.

"Right after I was sold to Massa Dunn, dere was a big up-risin' in Tennessee and it was 'bout de Union, but I don't know what it was all about, but dey wanted Massa Dunn to take some kind of a oath, and he wouldn't do it and he had to leave Tennessee. He said dey would take de slaves 'way from him, so he brought me and Sallie Armstrong to Texas. Dere he trades us to Tommy Ellis for some land and dat Massa Ellis, he de best white man what ever lived. He was so good to us we was better off dan when we's free.

"Massa Ellis' plantation was one of de bigges', and he owned land as far as we could see. Dere was 'bout 50 slaves and we lived in a row of log cabins long side de big house. In winter we sleeps inside but in summer we sleeps in de yard, and de same 'bout eatin'. Sometimes massa fed good and den 'gain he didn't, but dat 'cause of de War. We has cornbread and milk and all de coffee you would drink. On Sundays we fills de pot half full of meat and shell peas on top de meat.

"I 'member de time we steals one of massa's big chickens and its in de pot in de fireplace when we seed missy comin'. I grabs dat chicken and pot and puts it under de bed and puts de bedclothes top dat pot. Missy, she come in and say, 'I sho' do smell somethin' good.' I say, 'Whar, Missy Ellis?' She don't find nothin' so she leaves. When she's gone I takes dat chicken and we eats it in a hurry.

"De overseer woke 'em up 'bout four in de mornin', but I works in de house. De field workers gits off Thursdays and Saturday evenin's and Sunday. De reason dey gits off

Thursday is dat de massa has some kind of thought we shouldn't work dat day. Maybe it was 'ligion, I don't know.

"We has parties and sings
'Massa sleeps in de feather bed,
Nigger sleeps on de floor;
When we'uns gits to Heaven,
Dey'll be no slaves no mo'.'
"Den we has de song 'bout dis:
'Rabbit in de briar patch,
Squirrel in de tree,
Wish I could go huntin',
But I ain't free.
'Rooster's in de henhouse,
Hen's in de patch,
Love to go shootin',
But I ain't free.'

"When de nigger leaves de plantation without no pass, and de padder rollers kotched him, dey gives him 39 licks with de bullwhip. When we's in de fields and sees de padder roller ride by, we starts murmerin' out loud, 'Patter de pat, patter de pat.' One after 'nother took it up and purty soon everybody murmerin'. We allus do dat to let everybody know de padder roller 'round. Den we sing songs 'bout 'em, too.

Millie Williams

"When War start dere a army camp jus' below de plantation, and 'bout a thousand soldiers. We hears 'em shout, 'Halt, march, halt, march,' all day long. Dey sung

'Lincoln's not satisfied,
He wants to fight 'gain,
All he got to do,
Is hustle up his men.'

"I stays with Massa Ellis after we's freed. Dere sho' was a mighty purty sight when de slaves knows dey's free. Dey hug one 'nother and almos' tear dere clothes off. Some cryin' for de husban', and some cryin' for de chillen.

"When I was 'bout 20 I lef' massa's home and moves to Dallas, whar I marries my first man. His name was Bill Jackson. He lef' me and goes back to Dallas and I hear he die, so I marry Will Williams and he dies. Now I been here since de Lawd know when."

Rose Williams

Rose Williams is over 90. She was owned by William Black, a trader whose plantation lay in Bell County, Texas. Rose and her parents were sold in 1860 to Hall Hawkins, of Bell County. Rose was forced to mate with a slave named Rufus when she was about sixteen, and had two children by him, one born after Rose was freed. She forced Rufus to leave her and never married. For the last ten years Rose has been blind. She lives at 1126 Hampton St., Fort Worth, Texas.

"What I say am de facts. If I's one day old, I's way over 90, and I's born in Bell County, right here in Texas, and am owned by Massa William Black. He owns mammy and pappy, too. Massa Black has a big plantation but he has more niggers dan he need for work on dat place, 'cause he am a nigger trader. He trade and buy and sell all de time.

"Massa Black am awful cruel and he whip de cullud folks and works 'em hard and feed dem poorly. We'uns have for rations de cornmeal and milk and 'lasses and some beans and peas and meat once a week. We'uns have to work in de field every day from daylight till dark and on Sunday we'uns do us washin'. Church? Shucks, we'uns don't know what dat mean.

"I has de correct mem'randum of when de war start. Massa Black sold we'uns right den. Mammy and pappy powerful glad to git sold, and dey and I is put on de block with 'bout ten other niggers. When we'uns gits to de tradin' block, dere lots of white folks dere what came to look us over. One man shows de intres' in pappy. Him named Hawkins. He talk to pappy and pappy talk to him and say, 'Dem my woman and chiles. Please buy all of us and have mercy on we'uns.' Massa Hawkins say, 'Dat gal am a likely lookin' nigger, she am portly and strong, but three am more dan I wants, I guesses.'

"De sale start and 'fore long pappy am put on de block. Massa Hawkins wins de bid for pappy and when mammy am put on de block, he wins de bid for her. Den dere am three or four other niggers sold befo' my time comes. Den massa Black calls me to de block and de auction man say, 'What am I offer for dis portly, strong young wench. She's never been 'bused and will make de good breeder.'

"I wants to hear Massa Hawkins bid, but him say nothin'. Two other men am biddin' 'gainst each other and I sho' has de worryment. Dere am tears comin' down my cheeks 'cause I's bein' sold to some man dat would make sep'ration from my mammy. One man bids $500 and de auction man ask, 'Do I hear more? She am gwine at $500.00.' Den someone say, $525.00 and de auction man say, 'She am sold for $525.00 to Massa Hawkins.' Am I glad and 'cited! Why, I's quiverin' all over.

"Massa Hawkins takes we'uns to his place and it am a nice plantation. Lots better am dat place dan Massa Black's. Dere is 'bout 50 niggers what is growed and lots of chillen. De first thing massa do when we'uns gits home am give we'uns rations and a cabin. You mus' believe dis nigger when I says dem rations a feast for us. Dere plenty meat and tea and coffee and white flour. I's never tasted white flour and coffee and mammy fix some biscuits and coffee. Well, de biscuits was yum, yum, yum to me, but de coffee I doesn't like.

"De quarters am purty good. Dere am twelve cabins all made from logs and a table and some benches and bunks for sleepin' and a fireplace for cookin' and de heat. Dere am no floor, jus' de ground.

"Massa Hawkins am good to he niggers and not force 'em work too hard. Dere am as much diff'ence 'tween him and old Massa Black in de way of treatment as 'twixt de Lawd and de devil. Massa Hawkins 'lows he niggers have reason'ble parties and go fishin', but we'uns am never tooken to church and has no books for larnin'. Dare am no edumcation for de niggers.

"Dere am one thing Massa Hawkins does to me what I can't shunt from my mind. I knows he don't do it for meanness, but I allus holds it 'gainst him. What he done am force me to live with dat nigger, Rufus, 'gainst my wants.

"After I been at he place 'bout a year, de massa come to me and say, 'You gwine live with Rufus in dat cabin over yonder. Go fix it for livin'.' I's 'bout sixteen year old and has no larnin', and I's jus' igno'mus chile. I's thought dat him mean for me to tend de cabin for Rufus and some other niggers. Well, dat am start de pestigation for me.

"I's took charge of de cabin after work am done and fixes supper. Now, I don't like dat Rufus, 'cause he a bully. He am big and 'cause he so, he think everybody do what him say. We'uns has supper, den I goes here and dere talkin', till I's ready for sleep and den I gits in de bunk. After I's in, dat nigger come and crawl in de bunk with me 'fore I knows it. I says, 'What you means, you fool nigger?' He say fer me to hush de mouth. 'Dis am my bunk, too,' he say.

"You's teched in de head. Git out,' I's told him, and I puts de feet 'gainst him and give him a shove and out he go on de floor 'fore he know what I's doin'. Dat nigger jump up and he mad. He look like de wild bear. He starts for de bunk and I jumps quick for de poker. It am 'bout three foot long and when he comes at me I lets him have it over de head. Did dat nigger stop in he tracks? I's say he did. He looks at me steady for a minute and you's could tell he thinkin' hard. Den he go and set on de bench and say, 'Jus wait. You thinks it am smart, but you's am foolish in de head. Dey's gwine larn you somethin'.

"'Hush yous big mouth and stay 'way from dis nigger, dat all I wants,' I say, and jus' sets and hold dat poker in de hand. He jus' sets, lookin' like de bull. Dere we'uns sets and sets for 'bout an hour and den he go out and I bars de door.

"De nex' day I goes to de missy and tells her what Rufus wants and missy say dat am de massa's wishes. She say, 'Yous am de portly gal and Rufus em de portly man. De massa wants you-uns for to bring forth portly chillen.

"I's thinkin' 'bout what de missy say, but say to myse'f, 'I's not gwine live with dat Rufus.' Dat night when him come in de cabin, I grabs de poker and sits on de bench and says, 'Git 'way from me, nigger, 'fore I busts yous brains out and stomp on dem.' He say nothin' and git out.

"De nex' day de massa call me and tell me, 'Woman, I's pay big money for you and I's done dat for de cause I wants yous to raise me chillens. I's put yous to live with Rufus for dat purpose. Now, if you doesn't want whippin' at de stake, yous do what I wants.'

"I thinks 'bout massa buyin' me offen de block and savin' me from bein' sep'rated from my folks and 'bout bein' whipped at de stake. Dere it am. What am I's to do? So I 'cides to do as de massa wish and so I yields.

"When we'uns am given freedom, Massa Hawkins tells us we can stay and work for wages or share crop de land. Some stays and some goes. My folks and me stays. We works de land on shares for three years, den moved to other land near by. I stays with my folks till they dies.

"If my mem'randum am correct, it am 'bout thirty year since I come to Fort Worth. Here I cooks for white folks till I goes blind 'bout ten year ago.

"I never marries, 'cause one 'sperience am 'nough for dis nigger. After what I does for de massa, I's never wants no truck with any man. De Lawd forgive dis cullud woman, but he have to 'scuse me and look for some others for to 'plenish de earth."

Steve Williams

Steve Williams was born a slave of the Bennett family in 1855. They were residents of Goliad County, Texas and owners of only a small bunch of slaves. He and the other slaves were driven away hurriedly after the soldiers had threatened the slave owners for not having turned the slaves loose as soon after emancipation as they should have. Steve worked around his old home for his victuals and clothes a few years, then drifted about the country as a farm hand, finally landing in San Angelo, Texas where he worked for awhile as cook at a barbecue stand. He now lives alone in the back yard of his niece and is hardly able to get in and out of his small cabin on his crutches.

Steve relates the story of his life as follows:

"I wasn't very big when I was a slave. Fact is, we was set free 'fore I was big enough to remember much about how dey does but I's hear my mother tells 'bout dem Louisiana slave holders, dem what had dem drivers. Now dey was sho' rough on dem. My mother's name was Charlotte Williams and my father he was name Bill and dey belong to de Williams dere, you see, and was sold to Mr. Bennett and brought to Goliad. Dats how come I's named Williams and my marster named Bennett. Our little log huts was put up 'round in de back yard and our beds was home-made, jes' kind of plank scaffolds like. Our beddin' wasn't too good, jes' fair cotton beds. Ole marster's folks dey have big feather beds and a nice log house.

"I never seen any money when I was a boy to 'mount to anything and for a long time after dat war I never seen too much.

"We had pretty good to eat such as vegetables from de boss's garden and plenty of all kinds of meats. Some of de colored folks likes 'possum de best but I always likes coon. Jes' bile him, den bake him good and brown and aint no 'possum can come up wid dat.

"We had good homespun clothes and some times we have shoes.

"I never did see none of the slaves sold but I hear my mother tells 'bout how horrible dat was. I didn' learn much readin' and writin' 'cause no body never teach me none.

"We goes to camp meetin' after de war but not much, den dat was de white folks meetin'.

"On Christmas we usually have a shoat and cakes and lots of fiddlin' and dancin'.

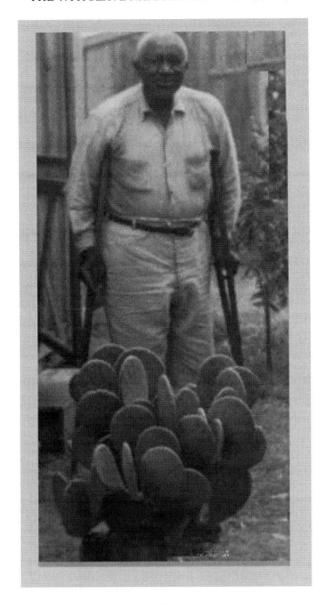

Steve Williams

"Slaves didn' have no weddin's. De boss he jes' puts dem in a cabin and gives dem a wife and dey all calls dat married. Fact is, dey jes' wasn' so much marryin' done 'mong de colored.

"When we hear we was free we hear it from some of de other slaves and we was held longer den some in de north, but one day our boss comes from town and he say to his wife, he say, 'Dem soldiers say iffen we don't git dem niggers 'way from here dey goin' come out here and sweeps us out of de cradle.'

"He sho' got busy den. He comes out and he say, 'You all git, I mean git from here'. So we jes' scatters 'round, here and yonder, not knowin' 'zactly what to do. Some of us works on one farm and some on another for a little co'n or some clothes or food. Finally I works 'round 'til I comes to San Angelo, Texas and I cooks barbecue for a long time 'til I jes' finally breaks down. Now, I don' try to do nothin' but jes' hobble 'round a little on my ole crutches."

Wayman Williams

Wayman Williams does not know his age, but he was a small boy when the slaves were freed. He was born in Mississippi, but the first place he remembers is the Sanama plantation on the Trinity river, in Texas. He now lives on North Falls St., in Mart, Texas.

"I was one of four chillen of Calvin and Julia Williams, of de state of Mississippi, when they was first married, 'fore they come to Texas. But de earlies' 'lection I has, was livin' on a plantation belongin' to a Mr, Sanama. It was on de Trinity river, right down in de bottoms. My folks stayed on dere after freedom and I lived with dem till I was nearly growed. Dere massa give dem supplies and let dem work a piece of land and they give him half de crop.

"I 'member times us go huntin' and kill most anything we want, wild turkeys and wild hawgs and deer. My father used to go out and kill deer and not git out of sight of de house. Livin' was easier den now, for we had all dem things without havin' to buy dem. I 'member de bear hunts. We had great big, brindle dogs for de bears and dey surroun' him and stand him at bay till de men came and kill him.

"A man by name of Burton lived near us, and one day he sent one he boys to town on a little race hoss. On de way home dat boy crossin' de river bottom and a panther git after him, and he race he hoss and outrun dat panther. He Jump off de hoss and run in de house and lock de door. De panther try to git in and de men in de field hear he cries and shoots him. In dose days de men took guns to de fields.

"They cotched wolves and bears in traps but de panther was de most dang'rous animal us have to fight. Us never know when he goin' to strike. One our neighbors go to town after a turkey and on he way home a panther was sittin' in a tree by de road, and he make a lunge at de man and grab de turkey and tear de man's arm. Once my grandpa ridin' 'long one night, crossin' de river, and a panther git after him. He had a fast hoss and outran dat panther, and got to de house, and two our bear dogs kep' it off till he shot it. I knows dese things am true, for they happen jes' like I tell it.

"Our house was close to de boat landin' on de river and my father helped unload supplies from de boats, when he not workin' in de fields. Jedge Beavers own de storehouse what kep' de supplies, and he ship he cotton by boat to de Gulf, mostly to Galveston.

"De 'Federate sojers pass our house and go to Jedge for him to give dem something to eat and he allus did. Sometimes dey was men on hosses and he give dem feed for de hosses.

Once a crowd young fellows comin' home from de war on hosses and dey got supplies, and de Jedge give dem a little toddy for to make dem feel good. Dey feels so good dey gits some ribbon from de store and tie it to de hosses heads and rides off, with dat ribbon jes' a-streamin' from de hosses mane.

"De Jedge enjoy all day. He felt like dey been fightin' for him and dey welcome to what he have. It was de common thing for de sojers to stop at the house and ask for food or to sleep. Sometimes niggers come, what run away to de North 'fore freedom. Dey done got tired of dat cold weather up dere and when freedom come, dey ready to come back home.

"When de slaves sot free, dey have big times, and feel like dey not work at all. But when old massa give dem a place to farm and tell dem iffen dey don't work dey won't eat, dey stays with him and works de crops on halves, mostly. De nigger do de work and massa feed him and give him team and tools, den massa git half de crop.

"De slaves what went up North and come back, tell how dey call 'Contrabands' up dere. Dey didn't know what it mean, but dey come back anyway.

"Some white school teachers from up North come to teach de chillen, but dey didn't talk like folks here and didn't understan' our talk. Dey didn't know what us mean when us say 'titty' for sister, and 'budder' for brother, and 'nanny' for mammy. Jes' for fun us call ourselves big names to de teacher, some be named General Lee and some Stonewall Jackson. We be one name one day and 'nother name next day. Until she git to know us she couldn't tell de diff'rence, 'cause us all look alike to her. Us have good times tellin' her 'bout black magic and de conjure. Us tell her night birds full of magic and dere feathers roast in ashes work spells what kill evil conjure. If a rabbit run 'cross de path, turn your hat round and wear it hind part befo' to keep bad luck away. A buzzard's claw tie round de baby's neck make teethin' easy. De teacher from de North don't know what to think of all dat. But our old missy, who live here all de time, know all 'bout it. She lets us believe our magic and conjure, 'cause she partly believe it, too.

"I lives in dat place till I's a big boy and den works for Mr. John Mergersen and a Mr. Porter. Dey come from Mississippi right after freedom and was jes' like homefolks. So I works for dem till I gits married and starts out for myself.

"I 'member some songs my mammy and old missy larnt me. One go like dis:

"'De top bolls ain' open,
De bottom bolls am rotten.
I can't git my number here,
I has to quit and go 'way.

"'When de sun go down and de moon go up,
Iffen I can't git my number, I can't git my pay.'

"When I was little, my father split de rails out of trees to make fences, and I have an aunt what was de big woman, and she holp. She have a song what go like dis, and when she sing, she come down on a rail, 'biff'.

"'Times are gittin' hard,' (biff)
Money's gittin scarce,' (biff)
Times don't git no better here,' (biff)
I bound to leave dis place.'

"But when de big meetin' goin' on, dis one de songs dey likes to sing:

"'As I went down in de valley to pray,
I met de debbil on my way,
What you reckon he say to me?
You're too young to die,
And too young to pray,
I made him a lie, and kep' on my way.'

"We raised corn and cotton and potatoes and lots of vegetables and fruit. We didn't have no wheat, so we couldn't have flour and it too high to buy. All dem what could buy it, was de landowner.

"When de corn gathered, us pile it in piles and have corn shuckin' at night, cook our supper and all eat together and listen to de stories tell by de old folks. When dey git de piles of corn ready for shuckin', dey lay a rail in de middle and 'vide de piles, and de side what git through first git supper first. De song go like dis:

"'Hits a mighty dry year, when de crab grass fail,
        Oh, row, row, row, who laid dat rail?
        Hit am mighty dark night when de nigger turn pale,
        De big foot nigger what laid dat rail!
        Oh, row, row, row, who laid dat rail?
        Rinktum, ranktum, laid dat rail.
        Show me de nigger what laid dat rail,
        Oh, row, row, row, who laid dat rail?

        "'When de niggers fuss, de white folks fail,
        Oh, row, row, row, who laid dat rail?
        We're gittin' dere now, don't tell no tale,
        Show me de nigger what laid dat rail.
        I'll stick he head in a big tin pail.
        Oh, turn me loose, let me tech dat rail,

Oh, row, row, row, who laid dat rail?

"First us have white preachers and den, after freedom, de niggers starts to git up in meetin' and talk to sinners, and dey call dem 'Exhorters.' De white folks larnt de exhorters to read de Bible and some songs, and de niggers all larn de songs, too. De exhorter git up and read de scripture and it 'bout King Neb'kudneezer, when he have a golden image with silver horns, and all de kings and rulers come and bow down 'fore dat image, 'cepting three. Dem was Shadrach, Meshach, and Abednego. Dey would not bow down, so de old king throw dem in de furnace and dey not burn up, and dey say, 'De Gawd us worship am able to deliver us from de fiery furnace.'

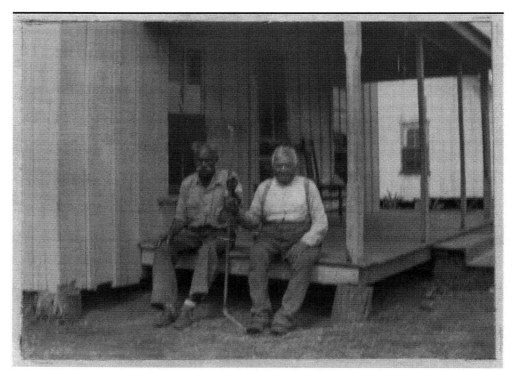

Wayman Williams and Henry Freeman

"Den de exhorter say: 'Now, you no count niggers, what you mean stealin' de white folks chickens and watermillions? Dey ain't safe no longer dan de white man back am turned. Do you think Gawd would save you? No, sir! You be turned into de pillar of salt iffen you don't stop you unrighteous ways, and den where you be? You won't see no dancin' or hear no chickens hollerin'. Come on into de pearly gates and live right. Leave your stealin' and cussin' and dancin' to de debbil, and come to de mourners' bench.

"'Let de sun of salvation shine square on you face,
Fight de battles of de Lawd, fight soon and fight late,
And you'll allus find de latch to de golden gate.
No use for to wait till tomorrow,
De sun mustn't sot on you sorrow,
Sin's sharp as a bamboo briar,

Ask de Lawd for to fotch you up higher.'

"Dem songs was de gateway to enter, de pearly gateway. All de niggers git on de mourners' bench and git saved."

Willie Williams

Willie Williams, 78, was born a slave to Mr. William Maddox, who owned about 90 slaves, including Willie's parents, five brothers and a sister. The plantation was in Vermillion Parish, La., near Sparta. In 1867 Mr. Maddox took Willie, who was still working for him, to Texas. Willie now lives in Fort Worth.

"Dis nigger am 78 years old, and I's born in slavery, down in old Louisiana. Marster William owned me, and he am de father of Marster Ed Maddox what now runs de Maddox Milk and Ice Company here in Fort Worth. I knowed him when him and dis nigger am tiny chiles. I goes and visits with him often and we talks 'bout old times and sich. We laughs 'bout some things and de tears come in de eyes 'bout some things. Him allus give dis nigger de quarter or de half dollar for old times sake.

"Marster William owns sich a big plantation dat it was miles and miles 'round and had 'bout 90 grown nigger slaves. I 'members it well and sho' am glad for to tell yous 'bout it and how dey does. De marster have a two-story house for his family and de place look like a town with all de buildings. Dere was de nigger quarters with 30 cabins and de nursery for de young niggers, de sheds and de smokehouse for de meat. Den dey have de gin and de mill for to grin' de grist, de spinning house and de shoe shop.

"Marster have a nigger what make de shoes out of hides tanned dere off de cattle what am killed for meat. Him makes good shoes, they las' a long time, but they sure is tough on de feets.

"Marster William raises de corn and rice and wheat and barley and vegetables and honey, and lots of cotton. Dey works animals, de mules and de oxen, but I seed de niggers hitched to de plow sometimes. But de marster allus took good care of his niggers and him feeds plenty good victuals. Every Sunday dey measures out de rations, 'cept de vegetables. But if what dey give am not 'nough, we'uns calls for more. De marster wants for we'uns to have plenty.

"All us am given de pass for to go to de church or to de party and dere's a place near de quarters for de dance and sich. Some fool niggers sneaks off without de pass sometimes and gits catched by de patter rollers and gits couple passes from de whup.

"One time de niggers puts one on dem patter rollers. Dere am de dance and some niggers has no pass and de patter rollers am a-comin'. De niggers 'cide to best 'em and one gits de pan of hot ashes and when dem patter rollers comes to de door de ashes am thrown in de face. De niggers all rush out and knocks de rollers down, and de niggers am gone. Dats once de niggers 'prise de rollers.

"On dat plantation dere am sort of hospital fix for to care for de sick. Dey uses herbs and sich and sometimes calls de doctor. De small chillens is kep' dere and de marster sho' am 'ticular 'bout dem. Lots of times he look dem over and say, 'Dat one be worth a t'ousand dollars,' or 'Dat one be a whopper.' You see, 'twas jus' like raisin' young mules.

Willie Williams

"On dat plantation, dere am no weddin' 'lowed for to git married. Dey jus' gits married, but some not 'lowed to git married, 'cause de marster anxious to raise good, big niggers, de kind what am able to do lots of work and sell for a heap of money. Him have 'bout ten wenches him not 'low to git married and dey am big, strong women and de doctor 'xamine dem for de health. Den de marster picks out de big nigger and de doctor 'xamine him, too. Dat nigger do no work but watch dem womens and he am de husban' for dem all. De marster sho' was a-raisin' some fine niggers dat way.

"As for de whippin', dey gives dat punishment. Dey straps de nigger over de barrel but de marster don't 'low for to draw de blood.

"Durin' de War, dere am de shortage of food and one time we is 'bliged eat all de chickens, and 'twarnt hard to do. We hunts de wild hawg and wild turkey and de deer and sich.

"When freedom come, dey tell all us niggers we's free and we can stay or leave and work for wages if we stay. Three year after freedom de marster sells de plantation and comes to Fort Worth and I and five other niggers still with him. I works for him 'til he dies, 'bout 50 year ago."

Lulu Wilson

Lulu Wilson, blind, bedridden Negro, does not know her age, but believes that she is ninety-seven. She was born near the Mammoth Cave, in Kentucky. Lulu owns a little home at 1108 Good Street, Dallas, Texas.

"Course I's born in slavery, ageable as I am. I'm a old time, slavery woman and the way I been through the hackles, I got plenty to say 'bout slavery. Lulu Wilson says she knows they ain't no good in it and they better not bring it back.

"My paw warn't no slave. He was a free man, 'cause his mammy was a full blood Creek Indian. But my maw was born in slavery, down on Wash Hodges' paw's place, and he give her to Wash when he married. That was the only woman slave what he had and one man slave, a young buck. My maw say she took with my paw and I's born, but a long time passed and didn't no more young'uns come, so they say my paw am too old and wore out for breedin' and wants her to take with this here young buck. So the Hodges sot the nigger hounds on my paw and run him away from the place and maw allus say he went to the free state. So she took with my step-paw and they must of pleased the white folks what wanted niggers to breed like livestock, 'cause she birthed nineteen chillen.

"When I's li'l I used to play in that big cave they calls Mammoth and I's so used to that cave it didn't seem like nothin' to me. But I was real li'l then, for soon as they could they put me to spinnin' cloth. I 'members plain, when I was li'l there was talk of war in them parts, and they put me to spinnin' and I heared 'em say it was for sojers. They marched round in a li'l, small drove and practices shootin'.

403

"Now, when I was li'l they was the hardes' times. They'd nearly beat us to death. They taken me from my mammy, out the li'l house built onto they house and I had to sleep in a bed by Missus Hodges. I cried for my maw but I had to work and wash and iron and clean and milk cows when I was most too li'l to do it.

"The Hodges had three chilluns and the olderes' one they was mean to, 'cause she so thickheaded. She couldn't larn nothin' out a book but was kinder and more friendly like than the rest of the lot. Wash Hodges was jes' mean, pore trash and he was a bad actor and a bad manager. He never could make any money and he starved it out'n the niggers. For years all I could git was one li'l slice of sowbelly and a puny, li'l piece of bread and a 'tater. I never had 'nough to stave the hongriness out'n my belly.

"My maw was cookin' in the house and she was a clink, that am the bes' of its kind. She could cuss and she warn't 'fraid. Wash Hodges tried to whop her with a cowhide and she'd knock him down and bloody him up. Then he'd go down to some his neighbor kin and try to git them to come help him whop her. But they'd say, 'I don't want to go up there and let Chloe Ann beat me up." I heared Wash tell his wife they said that.

"When maw was in a tantrum, my step-paw wouldn't partialise with her. But she was a 'ligious woman and 'lieved time was comin' when niggers wouldn't be slaves. She told me to pray for it. She seed a old man what the nigger dogs chased and et the legs near off him. She said she was chased by them bloody hounds and she jus' picked up a club and laid they skull open. She say they hired her out and sold her twice but allus brung her back to Wash Hodges.

"Now, Missus Hodges studied 'bout meanness more'n Wash done. She was mean to anybody she could lay her hands to, but special mean to me. She beat me and used to tie my hands and make me lay flat on the floor and she put snuff in my eyes. I ain't lyin' 'fore Gawd when I say I knows that's why I went blind. I did see white folks sometimes what spoke right friendly and kindly to me.

"I gits to thinkin' now how Wash Hodges sold off maw's chillun. He'd sell 'em and have the folks come for 'em when my maw was in the fields. When she'd come back, she'd raise a ruckus. Then many the time I seed her plop right down to a settin' and cry 'bout it. But she 'lowed they warn't nothin' could be done, 'cause it's the slavery law. She said, 'O, Lawd, let me see the end of it 'fore I die, and I'll quit my cussin' and fightin' and rarin'.' My maw say she's part Indian and that 'countable for her ways.

"One day they truckled us all down in a covered wagon and started out with the fam'ly and my maw and step-paw and five of us chillun. I know I's past twelve year old. We come a long way and passed through a free State. Some places we druv for miles in the woods 'stead of the big road, and when we come to folks they hid us down in the bed of the wagon. We passed through a li'l place and my maw say to look, and I seed a man gwine up some steps, totin' a bucket of water. She say, 'Lulu, that man's your paw.' I ain't never think she's as consid'ble of my step-paw as of my paw, and she give me to think as much. My step-paw never did like me, but he was a fool for his own young'uns, 'cause at the end of the wars when they sot the niggers free, he tramped over half the country, gatherin' up them young'uns they done sold 'way.

"We went to a place called Wadefield, in Texas, and settled for some short passin' of time. They was a Baptist church next our house and they let me go twict. I was fancified with the singin' and preachin'. Then we goes on to Chatfield Point and Wash Hodges built a log house and covered it with weather boarding and built my maw and paw quarters to live in. They turned in to raisin' corn and 'taters and hawgs. I had to work like a dog. I hoed and milked ten cows a day.

"Missus told me I had ought to marry. She said if I'd marry she'd togger me up in a white dress and give me a weddin' supper. She made the dress and Wash Hodges married me out'n the Bible to a nigger 'longin' to a nephew of his'n. I was 'bout thirteen or fourteen. I know it warn't long after that when Missus Hodges got a doctor to me. The doctor told me less'n I had a baby, old as I was and married, I'd start in on spasms. So it warn't long till I had a baby.

"In 'twixt that time, Wash Hodges starts layin' out in the woods and swamps all the time. I heared he was hidin' out from the war and was sposed to go, 'cause he done been a volunteer in the first war and they didn't have no luck in Kentucky.

"One night when we was all asleep, some folks whooped and woke us up. Two sojers come in and they left more outside. They found Wash Hodges and said it was midnight and to git 'em something to eat. They et and some more come in and et. They tied Wash's hands and made me hold a lamp in the door for them to see by. They had some more men in the wagon, with they hands tied. They druv away and in a minute I heared the reports of the guns three or four times. Nex' day I heared they was sojers and done shot some conscripts in the bottoms back of our place.

"Wash Hodges was gone away four years and Missus Hodges was meaner'n the devil all the time. Seems like she jus' hated us worser than ever. She said blobber-mouth niggers done cause a war.

"Well, now, things jus' kind of drifts along for a spell and then Wash Hodges come back and he said, 'Well, now, we done whop the hell out them blue bellies and that'll larn 'em a lesson to leave us alone.'

Lulu Wilson

"Then my step-paw seed some Fed'ral sojers. I seed them, too. They drifted by in droves of fifty and a hundred. My step-paw 'lowed as how the Feds done told him they ain't no more slavery, and he tried to pint it out to Wash Hodges. Wash says that's a new ruling, and it am that growed-up niggers is free, but chillun has to stay with they masters till they's of age.

"My maw was in her cabin with a week old baby and one night twelve Klu Kluxses done come to the place. They come in by ones and she whopped 'em one at a time.

"I don't never recall just like, the passin' of time. I know I had my little boy young'un and he growed up, but right after he was born I left the Hodges and felt like it's a fine, good riddance. My boy died, but he left me a grandson. He growed up and went to 'nother war, and they done somethin' to him and he ain't got but one lung. He ain't peart no more. He's got four chillun and he makes fifty dollars a month. I'm crazy 'bout that boy and he comes to see me, but he can't holp me none in a money way. So I'm right grateful to the president for gittin' my li'l pension. I done study it out in my mind for three years and tell him, Lulu says if he will see they ain't no more slavery, and if they'll pay folks liveable wages, they'll be less stealin' and slummerin' and goin's on. I worked so hard. For more'n fifty years I waited as a nurse on sick folks. I been through the hackles if any mortal soul has, but it seems like the president thinks right kindly of me, and I want him to know Lulu Wilson thinks right kindly of him."

Wash Wilson

Wash Wilson, 94, was born a slave of Tom Wilson, in Louisiana, near the Ouachita Road. Wash and his family were purchased by Bill Anderson, who brought them to Robertson Co., Texas. Wash lives in Eddy, Texas.

"I was 'bout eighteen years old when de Civil war come. Us calls it de Freedom War. I was born in Louisiana, clost to de Ouachita Road, and Marse Tom Wilson owned mammy and us chillen. But Marse Bill Anderson he come from Texas to buy us from Marse Tom. Marse Tom, he 'lowed de gov'ment gwine let dem damn Yankees give de South a whuppin' and dere wasn't gwine be no slaves nowhere. But Marse Bill say we's a likely bunch of chillen and mammy am a grand cook, so guess he take de resk.

"Marse Tom starts to Texas where he had a passel of land. Us was sold on de block to him, 'cause Marse Tom say he gwine git all he done put in us out us, iffen he can 'fore de Yanks take dis country.

"Mammy was named Julia Wilson. Sis Sally was oldest of us chillen, den brudder Harry and me. Marse Bill he had 27,000 acres of land in Robertson County what he git for fightin' Indians and sech. He lived in seven mile of Calvert, Texas, and dat where he brunged us and de supplies and sech. Us traveled in ox carts and hoss back, and de mos' us niggers walked.

"Us was sot free on de road to Texas. Us camp one night and some folks come talk with Marse Bill. De next mornin' he told us, 'Boys, you's free as I is.' Us was only 'bout sixteen mile from where us gwine and Marse Bill say, 'All what want to stay with me can.' Us didn't know nobody and didn't have nothin' and us liked Marse Bill, so all us stayed with him. When we got to his place us did round and 'bout, clearin' new ground and buildin' cabins and houses. Dere was three log houses but us had to build more.

"My pappy name was Bill Wilson. All my folks am dead now, but on de plantation in Louisiana we had a good time. Mammy could cook and spin and weave. Dey raised cotton and sugar cane and corn.

"Dere wasn't many Indians when us come, in our part de country. All I ever saw jes' steal and beg. Dere was plenty wild turkeys and wild hawgs and deer and prairie chickens.

"On Marse Bill's place every quarters had its barn and mule, but Marse and he wife, Miss Deborah, lived in de quality quarters. Round dem was de blacksmith shop and smokehouse and spinnin' house and Marse Bill have a li'l house jus' for he office. De cookhouse was a two-room house side de big house with a covered passage to de dinin' room. De milk house was de back part de cook house.

"In de smokehouse was hams and sides of hawg meat and barrels of syrup and sugar and lard, and bushels of onions, and de 'tater room was allus full. Dey dug a big place and put poles and pieces of cane and lumber cross, like a top, and put dirt and leaves and banked de dirt round de 'tater room. Dey'd leave a place to crawl in, but dey kep' it tight and dem 'taters dey kep' most all winter.

"Dey was hayricks and chicken roosties and big lye hoppers where us put all de fireplace ashes. Come de rain and de water run through dat hopper into de trough under it, and dat make lye water. De women put old meat skins and bones and fat in de big, iron pot in de yard and put in some lye water and bile soap. Den dey cut it when it git cold and put it on de smokehouse shelves to dry. Dat sho' fine soap.

"Mammy worked in de kitchen mostly and spin by candlelight. Dey used a bottle lamp. Dat a rag or piece of big string, stuck in de snuff bottle full of tallow or grease. Later on in de years, dey used coal oil in de bottles. Sometimes dey wrap a rag round and round and put it in a pan of grease, and light dat for de lamp. Dey used pine torches, too.

"De black folks' quarters was log cabins, with stick and dirt chimneys. Dey had dere own garden round each cabin and some chickens, but dere wasn't no cows like in Louisiana. Dere was lots of possums in de bottoms and us go coon and possum huntin'. I likes cornbread and greens, cook with de hawg jowls or strip bacon. Dat's what I's raised on. Us had lots of lye hominy dem days. Marse Bill, he gwine feed everybody good on his place. Den us had ash cake, make of corn meal. Us didn't buy much till long time after de War.

"Us had poles stuck in de corner and tied de third pole cross, to make de bed. Dey called 'Georgia Hosses'. Us filled ticks with corn shucks or crab grass and moss. Dey wasn't no cotton beds for de niggers, 'cause dey wasn't no gins for de long time and de cotton pick from de seed by hand and dat slow work. De white folks had cotton beds and feather beds and wool beds.

"Marse Bill allus had de doctor for us iffen de old woman couldn't git us well. All de seven families Marse Bill done buy in Louisiana stayed round him and he family till dey all dead, white and cullud. I's de onlies' one left.

"Us piled 'bout a hundred or two or maybe three hundred bushels corn outside de shed. Us have corn shuckin' at night and have de big time. De fellow what owned de corn, he give a big supper and have all de whiskey us want. Nobody got drunk, 'cause most everybody carry dey liquor purty well. After shuckin' us have ring plays. For music dey scratch on de skillet lids or beat bones or pick de banjo. Dere be thirty to fifty folks, all cullud, and sometimes dey stay all night, and build de big fire and dance outdoors or in de barn.

"Dere wasn't no music instruments. Us take pieces a sheep's rib or cow's jaw or a piece iron, with a old kettle, or a hollow gourd and some horsehairs to make de drum. Sometimes dey'd git a piece of tree trunk and hollow it out and stretch a goat's or sheep's skin over it for de drum. Dey'd be one to four foot high and a foot up to six foot 'cross. In gen'ral two niggers play with de fingers or sticks on dis drum. Never seed so many in Texas, but dey made some. Dey'd take de buffalo horn and scrape it out to make de flute. Dat sho' be heared a long ways off. Den dey'd take a mule's jawbone and rattle de stick 'cross its teeth. Dey'd take a barrel and stretch a ox's hide 'cross one end and a man sot 'stride de barrel and beat on dat hide with he hands, and he feet, and iffen he git to feelin' de music in he bones, he'd beat on dat barrel with he head. 'Nother man beat one wooden side with sticks. Us 'longed to de church, all right, but dancin' ain't sinful iffen de foots ain't crossed. Us danced at de arbor meetin's but us sho' didn't have us foots crossed!

"When de niggers go round singin' 'Steal Away to Jesus,' dat mean dere gwine be a 'ligious meetin' dat night. Dat de sig'fication of a meetin'. De masters 'fore and after freedom didn't like dem 'ligious meetin's, so us natcherly slips off at night, down in de bottoms or somewheres. Sometimes us sing and pray all night.

"I voted till I's 'bout forty five year old, den I jes' kinder got out de habit.

"I got married in a suit of doeskin jeans, ain't none like dem nowadays. I married Cornelia Horde and she wore a purty blue gingham de white folks buyed and made for her. Us had six chillen, Calvin and Early and Mary and Fred and Frank.

"Iffen you knows someone workin' a conjure trick 'gainst you, jes' take some powdered brick and scrub the steps real good. Dat'll kill any conjure spell, sho'. De bes' watchdog you can get for de hoodoo is a frizzly chicken. Iffen you got one dem on de place, you can rest in peace, 'cause it scratches up every trick lay down 'gainst its owner. Iffen you see dat frizzly chicken scratchin' round de place, it a sho' sign you been conjured. A frizzly chicken come out he shell backwards, and day why he de devil's own.

"De old folks allus told me to make a cross inside my shoe every mornin' 'fore leavin' de house, den ain't no conjurer gwine git he conjure 'gainst you foots. Iffen you wear you under clothes wrong side out, you can't be conjured. 'nother way am to put saltpetre in de soles you shoes. Iffen you wears a li'l piece de 'peace plant' in you pocket or you shoe, dat powerful strong 'gainst conjure. A piece of de Betsy bug's heart with some silver money am good. But iffen you can't git none dose, jes' take a piece newspaper and cut it de size of you shoe sole and sprinkle nine grains red pepper on it. Dere ain't no hoodoo gwine ever harm you den, 'cause he'd have to stop and count every letter on dat newspaper and by dat time, you gwine be 'way from dere.

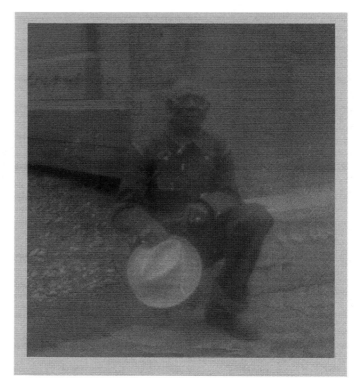

Wash Wilson

"Iffen you want to find de conjure tricks what done been sot for you, jes' kill you a fat chicken and sprinkle some its blood in da conjure doctor's left palm. Den take you forefinger and hit dat blood till it spatter, and it gwine spatter in da direction where dat trick am hid. Den when you find de trick, sprinkle a li'l quicksilver over a piece of paper and put da paper on de fire, and dat trick gwine be laid forever.

"Old folks done told me how to make a conjurer leave town. Make up a hick'ry fire and let it burn down to coals. Den you take up two live coals. One dese gwine be you, and de other gwine be de luck. Take up one dead coal, and dat you enemy. Den you jes' keep 'wake till de rooster crow or midnight. Dat am de end of de day. Now you chunk de live coal what am you to de south, de warm country; den throw de other live coal to de east; den chunk de dead coal, you enemy, to de north, de cold country. Nothin' of de conjurer can't git over fire, and 'fore de week out, dat conjurer be leavin'.

"A old Indian who used to hang round Marse Bill's place say to git de best of a conjurer, git some clay from da mouth a crawfish hole, and some dirt from a red ant's hole. Mix dem and wet dem with whiskey or camphor. Git some angleworms and boil dem and add de worm water to de clay and dirt. Iffen you rubs de conjured pusson with dis, he trouble done go 'way."

Willis Winn

Willis Winn claims to be 116 years old. He was born in Louisiana, a slave of Bob Winn, who Willis says taught him from his youth that his birthday was March 10, 1822. When he was freed Willis and his father moved to Hope, Arkansas, where they lived sixteen years. Willis then moved to Texarkana and from there to Marshall, where he has lived fourteen years. Willis lives alone in a one-room log house in the rear of the Howard Vestal home on the Powder Mill Road, north of Marshall, and is supported by an $11.00 per month old age pension.

"The onliest statement I can make 'bout my age is my old master, Bob Winn, allus told me if anyone ask me how old I is to say I's borned on March the tenth, in 1822. I's knowed my birthday since I's a shirt-tail boy, but can't figure in my head.

"My pappy was Daniel Winn and he come from Alabama, and I 'member him allus sayin' he'd like to go back there and get some chestnuts. Mammy was named Patsy and they was nine of us chillen. The five boys was me and Willie and Hosea and two Georges, and the gals was Car'lina and Dora and Anna and Ada, and all us lived to be growed and have chillen.

"Massa Bob's house faced the quarters where he could hear us holler when he blowed the big horn for us to git up. All the houses was made of logs and we slept on shuck and grass mattresses what was allus full of chinches. I still sleep on a grass mattress, 'cause I can't rest on cotton and feather beds.

"We et yellow bread and greens and black-eyed peas and potlicker and sopped 'lasses. Us and the white folks all cooked in fireplaces. A big iron pot hung out in the yard for to bile greens and hog jowl and sich like. We didn't know nothing 'bout bakin' powder and made our soda from burnt cobs. That's jes' as good soda as this Arm and Hammer you get in the store. We et flour bread Sundays, but you daren't git cotch with flour dough 'cept on that day. Mammy stole lots of it, though. She rolled it up and put it round her head and covered it with her head-rag. Wild game was all over the country, buffalo and bears and panthers and deer and possum and coon. The squirrels 'most run over you in the woods. We et at a long, wooden trough and it was allus clean and full of plenty grub. We used buffalo and fish bones for spoons, and some et with they hands. The grub I liked best was whatever I could git.

Us slaves didn't wear nothing but white lowell cloth. They give us pants for Sunday what had a black stripe down the leg. The chillen wore wool clothes in winter, but the big folks wore the same outfit the year round. They didn't care if you froze.

"I can show you right where I was when the stars fell. Some say they covered the ground like snow, but nary one ever hit the ground. They fell in 'bout twelve feet of the ground. The chillen jumped up and tried to cotch them. I don't 'member how long they fell, but they was shootin' through the air like sky-rockets fer quite a spell.

"Missy Callie had one gal and two boys and Massa Bob had three overseers. He didn't have nigger drivers, but had his pets. We called them pimps, 'cause they was allus tattlin' when we done anything. His place was jes' as far as you could let your eyes see, 'bout 1,800 or 1,900 acres, and he owned more'n 500 niggers.

"I still got the bugle he woke us with at four in the mornin'. When the bugle blowed you'd better go to hollerin', so the overseer could hear you. If he had to call you, it was too bad. The first thing in the mornin' we'd go to the lot and feed, then to the woodpile till breakfast. They put our grub in the trough and give us so long to eat. Massa hollered if we was slow eatin'. 'Swallow that grub now and chaw it tonight. Better be in that field by daybreak.' We worked from see to can't.

"I's seed many a nigger whipped on a 'buck and gag' bench. They buckled 'em down hard and fast on a long bench, gagged they mouth with cotton and when massa got through layin' on that cowhide, the blood was runnin' off on the ground. Next mornin' after he whip you, he'd come to the quarters when you git up and say, 'Boy, how is you feelin'? No matter how sore you is, you'd better jump and kick you heels and show how lively you is.' Massa hated me to he dying day, 'cause I told missy 'bout him whippin' a gal scandously in the field, 'cause she want to go to the house to her sick baby. Missy Callie didn't whip us, but she'd twist our nose and ears nearly off. Them fingers felt like a pair of pinchers. She stropped on her guns and rode a big bay horse to the field.

"Massa had a gin and I hauled cotton to Port Caddo, on Caddo Lake. I druv eight mules and hauled eight bales of cotton. Massa followed me with two mules and two bales of cotton. I usually had a good start of him. The patterrollers has cotched me and unhitched my mules and druv 'em off, leavin' me in the middle of the road. They'd start back home, but when they overtook massa they stopped, 'cause he druv the lead mules. He fetched 'em back and say, 'Willis, what happen?' He sho' cussed them patterrollers and said he'll git even yet.

"They was sellin' slaves all the time, puttin' 'em on the block and sellin' 'em, 'cordin' to how much work they could do in a day and how strong they was. I's seed lots of 'em in chains like cows and mules. If a owner have more'n he needed, he hit the road with 'em and sold 'em off to 'joinin' farms. None of 'em ever run off. They couldn't git away. I's seed too many try it. If the patterrollers didn't cotch you, some white folks would put you up and call your massa. They had a 'greement to be on the watch fer runaway niggers. When the massa git you back home and git through with you, you'd sho' stay home.

"In slavery time the niggers wasn't 'lowed to look at a book. I larned to read and write after surrender in the jail at Hot Springs, in Arkansas.

"They give us cake at Christmas and eggnog and 'silly-bug'. Eggnog is made from whites of eggs and 'silly-bug' from yallers. You have to churn the whiskey and yallers to make 'silly-bug'.

"Corn shuckin's was the things them days. I liked to see 'em come. They cooked up guineas and ducks and chickens and sometimes roast a pig. Massa kept twenty, thirty barrels whiskey round over the place all the time, with tin cups hangin' on the barrels. You could drink when you want to, but sho' better not git drunk. Massa have to watch he corners when cornshuckin' am over, or us niggers grab him and walk him round in the air on their hands.

"When some of the white folks died every nigger on the place had to go to the grave and walk round and drap in some dirt on him. They buried the niggers anyway. Dig a ditch and cover 'em up. I can show you right now down in Louisiana where I was raised, forty acres with nothin' but niggers buried on 'em.

"I 'member lots 'bout the war but can't tell you all, 'cause every war have its secrets. That war had four salutes, and you'd better give the right one when you meet the captain. I's heared the niggers sing, 'Gonna hang Jeff Davis to a sour apple tree.' My pappy fought in the last battle, at Mansfield, and so did Massa Bob.

"When the 'Federates come in sight of Mansfield they was carryin' a red flag, and kept it raised till surrender. When the Yanks come in sight they raised a white flag and wanted the 'Federates to surrender, but they wouldn't answer. It wasn't long till the whole world round there smelt like powder. Guns nowadays jus' goes 'pop-pop', but them guns sounded like thunder.

"After surrender, massa freed the men and missy freed the women, but he didn't let us loose when he ought. They wasn't no places 'vided with niggers as I heared 'bout. Niggers in Louisiana say Queen Elizabeth sent a boatload of gold to America to give the free men, but we never seed any of it. Massa give us each a barrel meal, a barrel flour, a side of meat and ten gallons 'lasses and tell us we can work for who we pleases. Daddy bought two cows and a horse and eight hawgs and a goat from massa on credit and we moved and made three crops.

"The Yanks stayed round Louisiana a long time after surrender. They come to white folks houses what hadn't freed they slaves and busted they meal and flour barrels and burn they meat and say, 'If we have to face you 'gain, we'll sweep you from the cradle up.'

"I's been cotched by them Ku Kluxers. They didn't hurt me, but have lots of fun makin' me cut capers. They pulls my clothes off once and make me run 'bout four hunerd yards and stand on my head in the middle the road.

"They is plenty niggers in Louisiana that is still slaves. A spell back I made a trip to where I was raised, to see my old missy 'fore she died, and there was niggers in twelve or fourteen miles of that place that they didn't know they is free. They is plenty niggers round here what is same as slaves, and has worked for white folks twenty and twenty-five years and ain't drawed a five cent piece, jus' old clothes and somethin' to eat. That's the way we was in slavery.

"Bout four years after surrender pappy say he heared folks say gold was covering the ground at Hope, Arkansas, so we pulled up and moved there. We found lots of money where they'd been a big camp, but no gold. We lived there sixteen years, then I came to Texarkana and worked twelve years for G.W. George Fawcett's sawmill. I never married till I was old, in Little Washington, Arkansas, and lived with my wife thirty-six years 'fore she died. We raised eighteen chillen to be growed and nary one of 'em was ever arrested.

Willis Winn

"I was allus wild and played for dances, but my wife was 'ligious and after I married I quieted down. When I jined the church, I burned my fiddle up. I allus made a livin' from public road work since I left Texarkana, till I got no count for work. The only time I voted was in Hope, and I voted the 'publican ticket and all my folks got mad.

"If it wasn't for the good white folks, I'd starved to death. 'Fore I come here to the Vestals, I was livin' in a shack on the T. & P. tracks and I couldn't pay no rent. I was sick and the woman made me git out. Master Vestal found me down by the tracks, eatin' red clay. I'd lived for three days on six tomatoes. I et two a day: Master Vestal went home and his wife cooked a big pot of stew, with meat and potatoes, and fetched it to me. Then they built a house down behind their back yard and I's lived with 'em ever since.

"I allus say the cullud race started off wrong when they was freed and is still wrong today. They had a shot to be well off, but they can't keep money. You give one a bank of money and he'll be busted tomorrow. I tells young niggers every day they ought to come down where they'll have some sense. I serves the Lord at home and don't meddle with 'em."

Rube Witt

Rube Witt, 87, was a slave of Jess Witt of Harrison County, Texas. He enlisted in the Confederate Army at Alexandria, La., and was sent to Mansfield, but his regiment arrived after the victory of the North. He worked for his master for a year after the war, then moved to Marshall and worked for Edmund Key, Sr., pioneer banker and civic leader. Rube cooked for eighteen years at the old Capitol Hotel in Marshall, and took up preaching as a side line. He and his wife live at 707 E. Crockett St., in Marshall. They receive a $15.00 pension.

"I was born on the Jess Witt place, right here in Harrison County, on the tenth day of August, in 1850, and allus lived in and round Marshall. My father and mother, Daniel and Jane, was bred and born in Texas, and belonged to the Witts. I had five brothers, named Charlie and Joe and George and Bill and Jim, and six sisters, named Mary and Susan and Betsy and Anna and Effie and Lucinda. They all lived to be growed but I'm the onliest chile still livin'.

"Master Witt had a big place, I don't recall how many acres. He didn't have so many slaves. Slavery was a tight fight. We lived in li'l cabins and slept on rough plank beds and et bacon and peas and pa'ched corn. We didn't hardly know what flour bread was. Master give us one outfit of clothes to a time and sometimes shoes. We worked all day in the fields, come in and fed the stock and did the chores and et what li'l grub it took to do us and went to bed. You'd better not go nowhere without a pass, 'cause them patterrollers was rolling round every bush.

"My missus was named Kate and had two chillen. The Witts had a good set of niggers and didn't have to whip much. Sometimes he give us a light brushin' for piddlin' round at work. I seed plenty niggers whipped on ole man Ruff Perry and Pratt Hughes places, though. They was death on 'em. Lawyer Marshall used to whip his niggers goin' and comin' every day that come round.

"I 'members white folks sayin' war was startin' 'bout keepin' slaves and then I seed 'em mendin' the harness and wagons to go and fight. I was the houseboy for the Witts durin' the war and 'bout time it was over I enlisted at Alexandria as a soldier and they sent me to Mansfield. The Yanks had done won the victory when our reg'ment got there. They turned us loose to git home the best we could. I come back to the Witts and master calls up all the slaves and says we was free, but if we stayed and worked for him we'd have plenty to eat and wear, and if we left, it'd be root, hawg or die. Most of 'em left but I stayed a year. You'd ought to seed 'em pullin' off them croaker-sack clothes when master says we's free.

"I come to Marshall with my mother and the whole state was under United States law. The 8th Regiment of Illinois was at Marshall for two years after the war, and no man, black, white or red or what is you, darsn't git cotched after dark without a pass. When they'd stop you, if you couldn't give the U.S. sign, 'Grant's Friend,' they'd shoot the devil out of you. You didn't pass 'less you knowed the sign.

"The Confederates had a big gun powder mill on Mill's Creek, two and a half miles north of Marshall and it stayed operatin' two or three years. But Gen. Atichon and Capt. Bishop and Lt. Rives and a bunch of Yanks tried to capture it and the Confederates blowed it up.

"When I was 'bout sixteen my mother hires me out to a Mr. Acorns, who was refugeed from Georgia to Marshall. Ole man Acorns was a mile of hell anywhere you met him and he nearly beat me to death and I run away. His son and him and 'nother man starts after me and I has to light a shuck. We sho' had some race down that hill over where the new water tower is in Sunny South, but they didn't cotch me. The white folks round here didn't 'lieve us niggers was free then.

Rube Witt

"Then I goes to work for Mr. Edmond Key, Sr., and stays with him till I'm growed. I used to help chase rabbits where the court house is now. I recalls the Buzzard Roost Hotel and some stores was on that square then.

"I cooks for the old Capitol Hotel eighteen years, then I quit and tries railroadin', but it didn't take long to decide to go back to the cook apron. I allus made a livin' from cookin' and preachin', and I've preached forty-five years. The only times I voted was for high sheriff once and for President Garfield and President Grant.

"I marries in 1915 and my wife is still with me. I'm too stove up with rhumatis' now to work and her and me gits $15.00 a month from the government."

Ruben Woods

Ruben Woods, hale and strong despite his 84 years, was born a slave of the John Woods family in Taladiga County, Alabama. He served as houseboy in their home until he was 21, then came to Tyler, Texas, with one of his master's children. He now lives in El Paso, Texas.

"I'se de oldest of seven chillen. My father was John Woods, mother Laura Woods. She was a cook for de marster's family on de plantation. We lived in a log house, logs was hewed in de woods. De marster's house was plastered inside. He had 1,000 acres plantation and 96 slaves. He took good care of 'em. Onct a week dey would come and dey allowanced 'em out pervisions. Not fine stuff; no, dey didn' gib 'em nothin' like dat ham and such. Dey would gib you enough flour for biscuit for Sunday mornin' and dey gib potatoes. I tell you how dey done dat; ev'ry family, he had a basket and when dey blow de ho'n in de evenin' ev'ry chile dat was big enough come and he know his basket and take it home.

"De quarters was all in rows. You had to have a pass frum de massa to go from one place to anudder or the pateroller would ketch you and whop you. Overseers whopped 'em, too.

"You worked frum time you could see 'till dark. You couldn' git outta dat, no suh, time you coul' see de stuff in de fiel', you was out workin.'

"Ole man Woods was a powerful good man. He wouldn' raise cotton for sale, only jus' enough for de women to make clothes. He raised hogs and cattle. I 'member Ben Averit; he had a big plantation over on de island. Took boatloads of slaves and work 'em hard. We'd hear de boats go over, clop-clop.

"We'd take two yoke of oxen with co'n and wheat to de mill, stay all day, den bring it back to give ev'rybody. I go to mill lots of times and allus drive oxen. In hot weather, dey run off to de creek. What you talkin' erbout, when it gits hot and dey smell dat water, dey travel!

"I 'member stagecoach. Had erbout six or eight hosses to 'em. Driver'd blow bugle for stops jus' like trains. Dey didn' have much trains dem days.

"When de war comes, we had soldiers. I se'ed 'em drillin' and marchin'. I se'ed dem hep-hep-hep! Yes, ma'am, when de Yanks come we was a runnin' and a squattin' like partridges a hidin'. Dem guns was a firin' and shootin' dem cannon, spoilin' fiel's and killin' hawgs. Wasn't no fun. Drums a beatin'. It was excitable, yes, ma'am. We had to run and hide. We all run up to whut dey call a cave and down in dat cave we had eats. All come what could git in dere. De soldiers try to roun' 'em up, but not dem niggers. All run from one place to anudder.

"I learned to read and write after freedom. Dey not allow you no book larnin'. Obey your marster and missus, dat's all.

419

"I 'member jist as well as dat I'se sittin' here, when freedom come. Marster had 'em all come near de gate and he say, 'You all is free as I am now.' He hollered and cried. It tickled me to see him cry. And den he say, 'But now iffen you want to, all kin stay and finish up de crop. I'll feed you.' Some, dey go to de neighbors. Dey didn' know whut to do. Dey hadn' been taught to do for demselves. But dey couldn' whop 'em no more. I stayed 'till I was 21.

Ruben Woods

"No, ma'am, I never coul' sing, but I 'member one song. It went dis way:

'1821—Jesus work is jus' begun;
1822—Jesus brought de sinner through;
1823—Jesus sot de prisoner free;
1824—Jesus preached 'mong de poor;
1825—Jesus brought de dead to life;

1826—Jesus had all things fixed;
1827—Jesus rose and went to Heben;
1828—Jesus made de plain way straight;
1829—Jesus turned de blood to wine.'

"We played hide-a-hoop. And hide-a-switch. We do dis; you'se huntin' switch and gittin' hot, gittin' col', dey take after you, dey have a base to go to. Den if dey ketch dem dey whop 'em.

"We played 'Anthony Over,' wid thread balls. We throw dat ball over de house. If dey don' ketch it, dey's out. Dat's de way dey had de sport."

Willis Woodson

Willis Woodson does not know his age, but looks very aged. He was born in Whiterock, but he does not know its location, except that it was somewhere east of the Mississippi River. Willis now lives in Tyler, Texas.

"I'm borned at a place called Whiterock, but don't rightly 'member no other name, but it was a long, long way from here, though. I was the prop'ty of Marse Richards, but he sold me and my maw and a lot of darkies to Marse Ike Isom. Maw said Marse Ike done pay $500 for me, cheap 'cause I's purty little and couldn't do much work.

"Marse Isom moved to Texas and everybody holped load de wagons, and we starts real early in a cold mornin'. De old womens and little chillens rode in de wagons, but de men walked. We traveled real slow, though, and it wasn't no worse'n plowin' all day. One Marse Isom's sons rid behind on a big, white hoss, and seed none of the darkies runned off. At night we fixes a supper and goes to bed and all de niggers is chained together and slept on straw beds. The white men tooked turns guardin' dem with guns.

"We gits to de new farm, long ways from where we lives befo', and starts clearin' land. When we gits settled, Old Miss picks me to be nuss to her chillen. Maw didn't work in de field. She say she done been hurt when she got a whippin' when she ain't growed, and her back ain't good no more. Old Miss say, 'Eva, you come in de kitchen and make some chittlin's, and iffen you cooks good, you can work in my kitchen.' Maw, she make dem chitlin's and dey's damn good, so she gits to cook den.

"Marse and Old Miss lives in de big house, with boards outside, 'steadin' logs. It have big rooms, lots of dem, and a big fireplace all 'cross de side one room. Me and 'nother boy has to bring in logs to build de fire, him totin' one end and me totin' one end. I stays in de house, so I gits good clothes and shoes, too. Some dem niggers didn't have hardly no clothes, though,

"De mostest fun I ever got was when Marse Isom 'lows me to be footman. He gits me a uniform, most like a sojer's, 'ceptin' mine am red with black stripes down de pants. I 'member it jist like yesterday, de first time I puts it on. Marse give a cel'bration at he house and de doorman am sick, so I has to be it. He give me dat suit and say to hurry put it on. Den he make me come to de front door and let him in over and over, so as to git de hang of it. He told me to take his hat and cane and put dem up, and to say, 'Thank you,' and 'Dis way, please,' and not to say no more to nobody, and I didn't. After dat night I opens de door lots of times, but mostest I wears dat suit when I takes de white folks to church, while dey listens to preachin' and I holds de hosses.

Willis Woodson

"I never did see no niggers whipped, but I done see dat whip hangin' in de barn. It a big, long thing, lots bigger'n a horsewhip, and I know it must have been used, 'cause it all wore out at one end.

"All de fun we has am huntin' and fishin'. We can go any night if we gits a permit from Marse Isom. Sometimes at night, he lets all de big niggers git together 'hind de cabins and make a big bonfire. Den we sings all de songs we knows, till nine o'clock, den Marse rings de bell, to cut out all de noise.

"Jus' befo' dat war am over, some soldiers marches through de farm and kilt all de cows and stock and burns de barn, Marse beg dem not to burn he house, so dey didn't. Some dem niggers quits when dey freed, without no supper, but not dis nigger! I stays sev'ral years, den gits a job snakin' logs in a sawmill. Den I marries and has seven chillen and I stays with first one, den 'nother. I holps dem all I can. I been patchin' up some fishin' tackle today."

James G. Woorling

James G. Woorling, of Fort Worth, Texas, tells the story of Uncle Dave, one of the slaves that belonged to Mr. Woorling's father, who owned a large plantation near Point, in Rains County, Texas. The story relates how Uncle Dave provided for his family after they were freed, and is valuable as an example of how many ex-slaves managed to secure a foothold in a world for which slavery had not prepared them.

"During pre-war days my father owned a plantation near Point, in Rains County, as well as a large number of slaves, including one Uncle Dave. After the Negroes were emancipated, my father placed a large number of them on tracts of land within the plantation and furnished them with a mule team, a few sheep, some chickens, and the implements needed to cultivate the land. The Negroes were privileged to occupy the land for seven years and to keep whatever they made during that time. After the expiration of the seven years they were to pay in money or percentage of crops for the use of the land. This plan was followed by a number of plantation owners.

"Uncle Dave was an exceptional Negro. He was a natural mechanic, but could do carpenter work, blacksmithing, shoemaking and many other things equally well. He was a good manager, frugal and industrious, and it is doubtful if he paid out $50.00 in a year's time for food, clothing and other necessities during the seven years that he lived on the seventy-five acres on our plantation.

"He never bought a horsecollar, but made them himself, shaping them to prevent galling and packing them with corn husks. He made the hames from oak timber and made the metal accessories.

"The shoes for Dave's family he made from hides of animals slaughtered for the meat supply. About the only farm implements he bought were those that required high grade steel.

"Aunt Julia, his wife, did her part. She was adept at cooking and preserving, and knew how to cure meat. Salt and spices were purchased, but they raised barley and roasted it, to use in the place of tea or coffee. They raised sugar and ribbon cane and made their own sugar and molasses. Aunt Julia told father that eggs were traded for any articles of food that could not be obtained from the farm.

"Following the Civil War the production of cloth by power driven machines enabled manufacturers to sell cloth at a price that did not warrant continuance of the hand method. But that did not interest Dave and Julia. They had a spinning wheel and a loom made by

Uncle Dave himself, and they made all the cloth needed by the family, dying it with the bark of blackoak, cherry or other trees.

"When the seven year period ended, my father thought that Uncle Dave would stay on the land. He had cleared it, built a house and barn and other structures, which all belonged to my father under the agreement. But Uncle Dave was not interested in renting the land. He had saved enough money to buy a thousand acres between the towns of Point and Emory. He built a house and barn and moved his family.

"Uncle Dave came home one day from a trip to town with a load of cotton. He had a ten gallon keg, which he painted black. He cut a slit in the side of the keg and made a plug for the hole and told Julia the keg was to hold his surplus cash.

"Uncle Dave hid the keg and during the next twenty years refused to tell his wife, children or anyone else where it was. It is obvious that all the money he received for his crops, except a small sum, was surplus. Julia often asked Uncle Dave to tell her where the keg was, and told my father that Uncle Dave had not been well and she feared the possibility of his dying without disclosing the secret. Not long after, Uncle Dave was found dead one morning. Money was needed for funeral expenses, but the keg could not be found and Julia had to borrow the required amount.

"The family searched first in the more likely locations, then made a minute search of the whole place, but the keg was never found. On Uncle Dave's farm a fortune is cached. The keg must have long ago disintegrated, but the gold and silver money, the savings of twenty years, remain in their hiding place."

Caroline Wright

Caroline Wright, about 90 years old, was born near Baton Rouge, Louisiana. Dr. Warren Wortham owned her parents and their 14 children. Caroline was 12 when they were freed. Her father, Robert Vaughn, moved to Texas, [HW: with master, p.2, para. 4 & 5] where he prospered and bought more than 300 acres of Tehuacana bottom land in McLennan County. Caroline and her husband now live at 59 Grant St., Waco, in a little house they bought after their family was grown.

"I was bo'ned in Louisiana on Jones Creek, by Baton Rouge, 'bout 90 years ago. I disremember the year. My pappy was Bob Vaughn and my mammy was Rose Ann. Dey was bo'ned by Baton Rouge. I had six sisters, Betsy Ann, Lydia, Nancy, Paga and Louisan; and three brothers, Horace, Robert and Tom. We was all owned by Dr. Warren Wortham and his wife, Annie. Mr. Bob, de doctor's brother, had us in charge, and he hired us out to Hays White, who owned a sugar plantation on de Mississippi River by Baton Rouge. Us all stayed at his place two year. Dere was sugar cane, co'n, peas and tomatoes raised on de farm. We lived in a log cabin made of pine logs and our beds was made outta pine timber with co'n shucks tacked on de bed, and our kivers was feather beds.

"In Clinton, in Louisiana, we was all put on de block and valued. I was six year old and I was valued at $1,500. But our family wasn' sold to anyone. I was given to Miss Muriel, Dr. Wortham's daughter. Me and my sisters was made house slaves and my mammy and pappy and brothers was made fiel' slaves.

"Our marster, Dr. Wortham, sho' was a fine doctor. He never whip us. De young missus learned us our A B C's 'cause dere was no school for de slaves. Dere wasn' no church on de plantation, but us all went 'casionally to a big log cabin and camp shed. Sometime a white would preach and sometime a cullud preacher.

"I only 'member one slave who ran away. He was so worthless, he came back when he got ready. He wasn' punished, 'cause he wasn' mean, just lazy. I never saw no jail for slaves and never saw any whipped. We allus had from Friday noon to Monday mornin' off.

"On Christmas, the white folks allus give us presents and plenty to eat, and us allus had a big dance five or six time a year. Dr. Wortham lived in a great big log house made from cedar logs.

"One day, I seen a lot of men and I asked de missus what dey was doin'. She tol' me dey come to fit in de war. De war got so bad dat Mr. Bob tol' us we was all gwine to Texas. Us all started out on Christmas Day of de firs' year of Lincoln's war. We went in ox wagons and us had mules to ride.

"On de trip to Texas, one evenin' a big storm come up and Mr. Bob, he asked a man to let us use a big, empty house. Dey put me by de door to sleep 'cause I was de lightes' sleeper. Some time in de night, I woked up and dere stood de bigges' haint I ever saw. He was ten feet high and had on a big beaver coat. I hollers to my pappy, 'Pappy, wake up, dere's a haint.' Nex' mornin' we got up and dey was nothin' outta place. No, ma'am, we didn' cotch de haint, a haint jus' can't be cotched.

"Nex' mornin' we started agin on our journey, and some time in March we reach Texas. They took us all 'cross de Brazos on a ferryboat, jus' 'bout where de 'spension bridge is now.

"De doctor took us all on de farm on de other side of where Bosque is now. On de farm us raised all kinds vegetables and grain and sugar cane to make sorghum, but no cotton. We all lived in one and two room log cabins, made out of cedar posts. Us didn' make any money for ourselves, but us had plenty of hog meat, beef, butter, milk, cornbread and vegetables to eat, lots mo' dan us have dese days. Us did all de cookin' in de fireplaces. Us sho' did have plenty of possum, and rabbit, and us cotched lots of fish outta de Bosque River.

"De women slaves, eleven of us, had our own gardens and us spun all our own clothes. In de summer us all wore cotton stripe and in de winter, linsey dresses. On Sunday us had lawn dresses and us sho' did come out looking choicesome.

"Dr. Wortham had Si for an overseer. It was a big farm and had forty or fifty slaves to work it. Us got up 'bout four in de mornin' and ate breakfas' 'bout nine o'clock. All de slaves had to work from sun to sun, and when us was sick, de marster treated us.

"When I was 'bout 16, I married William Wright. He was bo'n a slave near Rapid Pass, Kentucky. When he was eight year old, his family's owner died, and he went to the daughter, Mrs. Richard Mason, on Black River, in Louisiana, as "heir property." He was raised dere, but when he's freed he comes to Texas and works for Ganey Mason, seven mile east of Waco. He's 105 year old now and you cain't ha'dly unnerstan' what he's talkin' 'bout. We was married on the 23d day of December, in 1869. Will and me sho' did have a fine weddin'. De women cooked for three days and we danced and ate. My weddin' dress was elegant. It was white lawn with blue ribbons. Will and me had 12 chillen and raised 9, and us has 14 grandchildren.

"Will and me has been married 'bout 75 year and is still married. It's disrespectful how de young folks treats marriage nowadays.

"Ten year after our chillen's growed, we swaps what land we has for dis little house, but we had to pay some money, too. Will was more'n 90 years old and I was eighty some years old, but we got this house and we is happy. We can sit under that big china-berry tree in de fron' yard and look at de big trees over dere on Waco Creek, and one of our sons lives with us."

Sallie Wroe

Sallie Wroe, 81, was born a slave on Mike Burdette's plantation near Austin. Her parents were field workers. In 1874 Sallie married John Wroe and they raised eleven children. Sallie owns a small farm on the outskirts of Austin. One of her daughters lives with her.

"Befo' I's married, I's Sallie Burdette. De white folks tell me I's born eighty-one years ago. I reckon I's dat old. I know I's born on Massa Mike Burdette's cotton plantation at Burdette Prairie, right close to Austin, and mammy's name was Het Burdette. She chopped and picked cotton and been dead long time. John Burdette was my pappy and he was jes' a reg'lar fieldman, too. Pappy been dead, mercy, so long!

"Massa Burdette had a overseer and he sho' rough. I think his name must be Debbil, he so rough. My sister, Mollie, was weaver at de loom, and iffen she didn't git out 'nough for de day she am tied up in sittin' form and whipped hard. She had stripes all over de shoulders.

"Dere was a whole row of log cabins close to de big house and de roofs was made of clapboards. It didn't rain in none. De only openin' was de door, no windows. Dere was mud and stick chimnies and a dirt floor. It wasn't no better dan a corncrib but purty warm in winter, 'cause de holes chinked with mud.

"Massa Burdette 'low us nigger chillen come to de big house at night and his chillen larn us to read. Dey had blue-back spellers, but I didn't cotch on much and can't read or write now.

"Pappy a purty good man, 'siderin' he a slave man. One day pappy and Uncle Paul and Uncle Andy and Uncle Joe was takin' bales of cotton on ox wagons down to de Rio Grande. Each man was drivin' a ox wagon down to Brownsville, where dey was to wait to meet Massa Burdette. But pappy and de others left de wagons 'long de river bank and rolled a bale of cotton in de river and all four of dem gits on dat bale and rows with sticks 'cross over into Mexico. Dis was durin' de war. Pappy come back to us after freedom and say he done git 'long fine with Mexico. He larnt to talk jes' like dem.

Sallie Wroe

427

"Me and mammy stays on at Massa Burdette's place de whole time pappy am gone. It was on June 19 we was made free and Massa Burdette say iffen we stays on his place and gather de crops, he give each of us a free eggnog. We ain't never got no eggnog befo' so it sound purty good and we stays and gathers de crops. But dat eggnog made me sick.

"My cousin Mitchell come and got us and brung us to Chapel Hill. He done rent him a farm dere and looks out for us till pappy comes back. He brung some money back from Mexico and taken us all to Brenham and buyed us some clothes. Den he moved us up to Austin and done any work he could git. I stayed home till 1874 and den married John Wroe, and he rented land and farmed and died in 1927.

"We raises eleven chillen and dey all good and 'haved. All my grandchillen calls me 'Big Mama,' but I's so li'l now dey ought to call me 'Li'l Mama.' I owns dis li'l farm. John saved 'nough money to buy it befo' he died. I gits a li'l pension and my daughter works and when she's workin' my grandchil' takes care of me."

Fannie Yarbrough

Fannie Yarbrough, blind and bedridden, was born a slave of the McKinney family, near Egypt, Kaufman Co., Texas. She was about six when the Civil War started. At that time her job was to herd sheep. After "freedom" she, her mother and sister, stayed with the McKinney's for a time. Fannie married Green Yarbrough in Hunt Co., Texas and they now live in a little cabin at 843 Plum St., Abilene, Texas.

"Ole Marster had a world of sheeps. Every day we take dem sheeps and watch 'em. The wolves was mean. We'd git to playin', all us little niggers, and forgit them sheeps and nex' thing you know an old wolf would have himse'f a sheep.

"Sometimes we'd keep playin' so late it was dark 'fore we knowed it and we'd start runnin' them sheeps home. Ol' Marster would be at de big gate to let us in. He says, 'Now, chillen, you didn' git back with all the sheep.' We'd say, 'Ol' wolf got 'em.' But he knowed ol' wolf didn' get all de ones missin' and he'd say, 'You're storyin'.' Then purty soon some of the little stray ones come home. Then he knowed we'd run the sheep home and he'd say, 'I 'spose I'll have to whip you,' but he never did. Those were sweet times! Ol' Marster was so good, and he give us more to eat than you ever saw. Hog meat every day and sweet 'tatoes so big we'd have to cut 'em with an ax.

"After we et our supper, we had to spin a broach of thread every night 'fore we went to bed. I larned all 'bout spinnin' and weavin' when I was little and by time I's 10 I'd make pretty striped cloth.

"How we played and played! On Sundays we'd strike out for the big woods and we'd gather our dresses full of hickory nuts, walnuts and berries and a sour apple called 'maypop.' We'd kill snakes and dance and sing that ol' song 'bout, 'Hurrah! Mister Bluecoat, Toodle-O.' 'O, Dat Lady's Beatin' You.' It meant his pardner was beatin' him dancin.'

"I was jes' lyin' here dreamin' 'bout how we use to go to the woods every spring and dig the maypop roots, then bring 'em home and wash 'em good and dry 'em—but, mind you, not in the sun—then all us chillen would sit 'round and poun' dem roots, tied up in little bags of coarse cloth, till it was powder. Then we'd take a little flour and jes' enough water to make it stick, and we'd make pills to take when we got sick. And work you? Lawd a'mighty! When we took dat stuff we had to keep tendin' to de dress tail!

"We went over to Flat Rock to church and de singin' was gran.' All day long we'd be at preachin' and singin'. Singin' dat good ol' spiritual song 'bout, 'You shan't be Slaves no More, since Christ have made you free.' I lay here yes'day and heared all them foolish songs and jubilee songs that comes over the radio, and den some of them ol' time spirituals come and it jes' made me feel like I was in ol' times.

"I went back every year to see my ol' marster, as long as he lived. Now it won' be long till I sees him agin, some day."

Litt Young

Litt Young was born in 1850, in Vicksburg, Miss., a slave of Martha Gibbs, on whose property the old battleground at Vicksburg was located. Litt was freed in 1865, in Vicksburg, and was refugeed by his owner to Harrison Co., Texas. He was freed again on June 19, 1866, and found work as a sawmill hand, a tie cutter and a woodcutter during the construction of the Texas & Pacific Railroad from Marshall to Texarkana. The remainder of his life, with the exception of five years on a farm, has been spent as a section hand. Litt lives alone on the Powder Mill Road, two and a half miles north of Marshall, and is supported by a $12.00 monthly pension from the government.

"I's born in 1850 in Vicksburg, and belonged to Missy Martha Gibbs. Her place was on Warner Bayou and the old battlefield was right there in her field. She had two husbands, one named Hockley and he died of yellow fever. Then she marries a Dr. Gibbs, what was a Yankee, but she didn't know it till after the war.

"Massa Hockley bought my daddy from a nigger trader up north somewheres, but my mammy allus belonged to the Gibbs family. I had a sister and two brothers, but the Gibbs sold them to the Simmons and I never seed 'em any more.

"Old Missy Gibbs had so many niggers she had to have lots of quarters. They was good houses, weatherboarded with cypress and had brick chimneys. We'd pull green grass and bury it awhile, then bile it to make mattresses. That made it black like in auto seats. Missy was a big, rich Irishwoman and not scared of no man. She lived in a big, fine house, and buckled on two guns and come out to the place most every morning. She out-cussed a man when things didn't go right. A yellow man driv her down in a two-horse avalanche. She had a white man for overseer what live in a good house close to the quarters. It was whitewashed and had glass windows. She built a nice church with glass windows and a brass cupola for the blacks and a yellow man preached to us. She had him preach how we was to obey our master and missy if we want to go to Heaven, but when she wasn't there, he come out with straight preachin' from the Bible.

"Good gracious, what we had to eat. They give us plenty, turnip greens and hog-jowl and peas and cornbread and milk by the barrels. Old women what was too old to work in the field done the cookin' and tended the babies. They cooked the cornbread in a oven and browned it like cake. When they pulled it out, all the chillen was standin' round, smackin' they lips. Every Christmas us got a set white lowell clothes and a pair brogan shoes and they done us the whole year, or us go naked.

"When that big bell rung at four o'clock you'd better get up, 'cause the overseer was standin' there with a whippin' strap if you was late. My daddy got a sleepin' most every morning for oversleeping. Them mules was standin' in the field at daylight, waitin' to see how to plow a straight furrow. If a nigger was a 500 pound cotton picker and didn't weigh up that much at night, that was not gitting his task and he got a whipping. The last weighin' was done by lightin' a candle to see the scales.

"Us have small dances Saturday nights and ring plays and banjo and fiddle playin' and knockin' bones. There was fiddles make from gourds and banjoes from sheep hides. I 'member one song, 'Coffee grows on white oak trees, River flows with brandy-o.' That song was started in Vicksburg by the Yankee soldiers when they left to go home, 'cause they so glad war was over.

"Missy have a big, steam sawmill there on Warner Bayou, where the steamboats come up for lumber. It was right there where the bayou empties in the Mississippi. I 'member seen' one man sold there at the sawmill. He hit his massa in the head with a singletree and kilt him and they's fixin' to hang him, but a man promised to buy him if he'd promise to be good. He give $500 for him.

"Dr. Gibbs was a powerful man in Vicksburg. He was the 'casion of them Yanks takin' 'vantage of Vicksburg like they done. 'Fore the war he'd say to missy, 'Darling, you oughtn't whip them poor, black folks so hard. They is gwine be free like us some day.' Missy say, 'Shut up. Sometimes I 'lieve you is a Yankee, anyway.'

"Some folks say Dr. Gibbs was workin' for the North all the time 'fore the war, and when he doctored for them durin' the war, they say they knowed it. The 'Federates have a big camp there at Vicksburg and cut a big ditch out at the edge of town. Some say Gen. Grant was knowin' all how it was fixed, and that Dr. Gibbs let him know.

"The Yankees stole the march on the 'Federates and waited till they come out the ditch and mowed 'em down. The 'Federates didn't have no chance, 'cause they didn't have no cannon, jus' cap and ball rifles. The main fight started 'bout four in the morning and held on till 'bout ten. Dead soldiers was layin' thick on the ground by then. After the fight, the Yanks cut the buttons off the coats of them that was kilt.

"I seed the Yankee gunboats when they come to Vicksburg. All us niggers went down to the river to see 'em. They told us to git plumb away, 'cause they didn't know which way they was gwine to shoot. Gen. Grant come to Vicksburg and he blowed a horn and them cannons began to shoot and jus' kept shootin'. When the Yankees come to Vicksburg, a big, red flag was flyin' over the town. Five or six hours after them cannons started shootin' they pulled it down and histed a big, white one. We saw it from the quarters.

Litt Young

"After surrender the Yanks arrested my old missy and brought her out to the farm and locked her up in the black folks church. She had a guard day and night. They fed her hardtack and water for three days 'fore they turned her a-loose. Then she freed all her niggers. 'Bout that time Massa Gibbs run out of corn to feed he stock and he took my daddy and a bunch of niggers and left to buy a boatload of corn. Missy seized a bunch us niggers and starts to Texas. She had Irishmen guards, with rifles, to keep us from runnin' 'way. She left with ten six-mule teams and one ox cook wagon. Them what was able walked all the way from Vicksburg to Texas. We camped at night and they tied the men to trees. We couldn't git away with them Irishmen havin' rifles. Black folks nat'rally scart of guns, anyway. Missy finally locates 'bout three miles from Marshall and we made her first crop and on June 19th, the next year after 'mancipation, she sot us free.

"Dr. Gibbs followed her to Texas. He said the Yanks captured his niggers and took his load of corn as they was comin' down the Tennessee River, where it jines the Mississippi. Me and mammy stayed in Texas, and never did see daddy 'gain. When us freed the last time us come to Marshall and I works in a grist mill and shingle mill. I cut ties for 15¢ apiece. I cut wood for the first engines and they paid me $1.25 a cord. I got where I cut three cords a day. I helped clear all the land where Texarkana is now. When the railroads quit using wood, I worked as section hand for $1.25 a day. I farmed five years and never made a cent and went back to the railroad.

"I marries in Marshall so long ago I done forgot. I raises six gals and has three sets grandchillen. They's all livin' 'cept one. Since my wife died and I's too ailing to work, I's been kept by the pension.

"They had provost law in Marshall when us come to Texas. I allus voted when they let us. These young niggers ain't like what us was. Penitentiaries was made for the white folks, but the young niggers is keepin' 'em full."

Louis Young

Louis Young, 88, was born a slave of Hampton Atkinson, on a small farm in Phillips County, Arkansas. When Louis was twelve, his master sold him and his mother to Tom Young, who took them to Robinson Co., Texas. Louis now lives at 5523 Bonnell St., Fort Worth, Tex.

"Mammy done put my age in de Bible and I'm eighty-eight years old now. I'm born in 1849. But I can git round. Course, I can't work now, but, shucks, I done my share of work already. I works from time I'm eight years old till I'm eighty past, and I'd be workin' yit if de rheumatis' misery didn't git me in de arms and legs. It make me stiff, so I can't walk good.

"Yes, suh, I starts to work when eight on dat plantation where I'm born. Dat in Arkansaw, and Massa Hampton own me and my mammy and eight other niggers. My pappy am somewhere, but I don't know where or nothin' 'bout him.

"Us all work from light to dark and Sunday, too. I don't know what Sunday am till us come to Texas, and dances and good things, I don't know nothin' 'bout dem till us come to Texas. Massa Hampton, he am long on de work and short on de rations, what he measure out for de week. Seven pounds meat and one peck meal and one quart 'lasses, and no more for de week. If us run out, us am out, dat's all.

"One day us gits sold to Massa Tom Young. He feels mammy's muscles and looks on her for marks of de whip. Massa Young say he give $700, but Massa Hampton say no, he want $1,000. He say, 'Yous takin' dem to Texas, where dey sho' to be slaves, 'spite de war.'

"Finally Massa Young gives $900 for us and off us go to Texas. Dat in 1861, de fall de year, and it am three teams mules and three teams oxen hitch to wagons full of farm things and rations and sich. Us on de road more'n three weeks, maybe a month, befo' us git to Robinson County.

"When us git dere, de work am buildin' de cabins and house and den clear de land, and by Spring, us ready to put in de crops, de corn and cotton. Massa Young am good and give us plenty to eat. He has 'bout twenty slaves and us works reason'ble, and has good time 'pared with befo'. On Saturday night it am dancin' and music and singin', and us never heared of sich befo'.

"One day Massa Young call us to de house and tell us he don't own us no more, and say us can stay and he pay us some money, if us wants. He ask mammy to stay and cook and she does, but I'm strongheaded and runs off to Calvert and goes to work for Massa Brown, and dere I stays till I'm growed. He paid me $10.00 de month and den $15.00.

"When I's twenty-five I marries Addie Easter and us have no chillen and she dies ten years after. Den I drifts 'round, workin' here and yonder and in 1890 I marries dat woman settin' right dere. Den I rents de farm and if de crops am good, de prices am bad, and if de prices am good, de crops am bad. So it go and us lives, and not too good, at dat. I quits in 1925 and comes to Fort Worth and piddles at odd jobs till my rheumatis' git so bad five years ago.

"I done forgit to tell you 'bout de Klux. Dem debbils causes lots of trouble. Dey done de dirty work at night, come and took folks out and whip dem.

Louis Young

"Some cullud folks am whip so hard dey in bed sev'ral weeks and I knowed some hanged by dey thumbs. Maybe some dem cullud folks gits out dere places, but mostest dem I knows gits whip for nothin'. It jus' de orneriness dem Klux. It so bad de cullud folks 'fraid to sleep in dey house or have parties or nothin' after dark. Dey starts for de woods or ditches and sleeps dere. It git so dey can't work for not sleepin', from fear of dem Klux. Den de white folks takes a hand and sojers am brung and dey puts de stop to dem debbils.

"'Bout de livin' now, us jus' can't make it. Us lives on what de pension am and dat $30.00 de month, and it mighty close us has to live to git by on sich. I thinks of Massa Young, and us live better den dan now.

"I never votes, 'cause I can't read and dat make troublement for me to vote. How I gwine make de ticket for dis and dat? For dem what can read, dey can vote."

Teshan Young

Teshan Young, 86, was born a slave to Buckner Scott, who owned a plantation in Harrison County, Texas, and had over one hundred slaves. Teshan married Moses Young in 1867 and lived near her old home until 1915, when she moved to Fort Worth. She lives in a negro settlement on the outskirts of Stop Six, a suburb of Fort Worth.

"I'se 86 years ole. Bo'n in Harrison County, Texas. Marster Scott owned me and my parents, one brudder and three sisters. Marster never sold any of we'uns, so dere was no separation of de family long's we lived on de Marster's place. He had awful big plantation, 'bout seven miles long.

"On dat plantation de Marster have everything. Hims have de gin and de mill for to grind de meal and feed, de big blacksmith shop and dere was a house whar dey spins de yarn and makes de cloth, de shoes and sich. He have 'bout 30 quarters for de cullud folks back of him's house, and dere am a house for de nursery, wid a big yard dat have swings and sich for de cullud chillens.

"Each cullud family have de cabin for themself. De cabins have bunks for sleeping', fireplace for to cook, bench for to set on—but dat's all de furniture. Marster Scott feeds all us niggers good. We'uns have beans, peas, milk, vegetables, 'lasses and plenty of meat. De marster have hawgs on top of hawgs on dat place, for to make de meat.

"We'uns have all de clothes dat we'uns need for to keep warm. De marster says, 'De nigger mus' have plenty of food and keep wan for to work good. How many hours we'uns work? Dat depen's on de time of de year it am. When its time for de hoein' or de pickin' of de cotton, dey work late. 'Twarn't sich long hours udder times. But de marster makes de cullud folks work and whips 'em when dey don'. I'se 'member one slave dat gits whipped so bad hims never gits up, hims died. We'uns chillens would go roun' whar hims was and look at 'im. De Marster lets we'uns do dat.

"Yes, suh, dey whupped pow'ful hard sometimes. My mammy gits whupped one time 'cause she come from de fiel' for to nuss her baby, and once for de cause she don' keep up her row in de fiel'. My pappy gits shoot in de shoulder by de overseer, 'cause hims runs from de whuppin.' 'Twas dis way, de overseer says, 'Come here, I'se gwine whup you for not workin' like I says.' Dere was a fence dere and my pappy runs for dat and am crawlin' over it when de overseer shoots.

"I'se 'bout 10 year ole when de war starts. It makes no diff'rence, dat I'se 'members, 'cept de Marster jines de army. I'se tend to all de cullud chillen while dey mammies workin' in de fiel'. De Marster am sho' particular 'bout dem chillen. He feeds 'em well, mush, milk, bread, 'lasses, vegetables and sich. De food am put in de long bowl, like de trough. De chillen have wooden spoons and we'uns line dem 'long de bowl. Den de fun starts. I'se have de long switch and keeps walkin' back and forth to make dem debils behave. De Marster comes in sometimes and hims laugh at dem, dey so funny.

"After I'se gits married, I'se has 13 chillen of my own. I'se never calls de doctor for my chillen. I'se goes in de woods and gits de plants and de herbs. For de stomach misery I'se uses de red petals, boils dat and takes de juice. For de cold I'se takes de Kalemas Root, boils dat and takes de juice.

Teshan Young

"When de chores am done on Sunday or Christmas, we'uns can have de music, dance and singin'. We'uns have some good ole times. De songs am de ole timers, sich as Swannee River, Ole Black Joe and dere am de fiddles and banjos dat dey play. We'uns sho' cel'brate on Christmas. De women all cooks cakes and cookies and sich. De men saves all de bladders from de hawgs dey kill, blows 'em full of air and lets 'em dry. De young'uns puts dem on sticks and holds 'em over a fire in de yard. Dat makes 'em bust and dey goes 'bang' jus' like a gun. Dat was de fireworks.

"Marster comes back from de war widout gettin' hurt. At de time freedom comes, some cullud folks stays on and works for money. 'Twas de fust money dey ever had, and dey don' know what to do wid it and what its worth. Some of dem are still on dat lan'! Dey rents or have bought. My brudder lives dere, jus' a few yards from de ole quarters. My pappy worked for ole Marster till he died. I'se stays wid him till I marries.

"I'se married in a cullud church and I'se have a pretty pink dress and hat. My husban' have hims own farm, part of de ole plantation. We finally buys it from de Marster. In 1902 my husban' dies and I'se stays dere till 1915. Den I'se comes to Fort Worth. I'se still missin' some but I'se gettin' de pension of nine dollars a month. Dat sho' helps out."

Transcriber's Note

Original spelling has been maintained; e.g. "stob—a short straight piece of wood, such as a stake" (American Heritage Dictionary).—The Works Progress Administration was renamed during 1939 as the Work Projects Administration (WPA).

PREPARED FOR PUBLICATION
BY
HISTORIC PUBLISHING
SAN ANTONIO, TEXAS
©2017
All Rights Reserved

Slavery Books & African American History Courses & Resources
https://africanamericanhistorybooks.blogspot.com

Printed in Great Britain
by Amazon